WE'LL ALWAYS HAVE THE MOVIES

WE'LL ALWAYS HAVE THE MOVIES

AMERICAN CINEMA DURING WORLD WAR II

ROBERT L. MCLAUGHLIN
SALLY E. PARRY

THE UNIVERSITY PRESS OF KENTUCKY

Publication of this volume was made possible in part by a grant
from the National Endowment for the Humanities.

Library of Congress Cataloging-in-Publication Data

McLaughlin, Robert L., 1957-
  We'll always have the movies : American cinema during World War II / Robert L.
McLaughlin and Sally E. Parry.
     p. cm.
  Includes bibliographical references and index.
  ISBN-13: 978-0-8131-2386-0 (hardcover : alk. paper)
  ISBN-10: 0-8131-2386-8 (hardcover : alk. paper) 1. World War, 1939-1945—Motion
pictures and the war. 2. World War, 1939-1945—United States. I. Title: We will always
have the movies. II. Parry, Sally E. III. Title.
  D743.23.M45 2006
  791.430973'09044—dc22   2005028880

CONTENTS

PREFACE

WE CAME TO THIS PROJECT from different directions. One of us was researching film references in Thomas Pynchon's 1973 novel about the V-2 rocket, *Gravity's Rainbow*. The other was comparing the presentation of army nurses in the Cherry Ames series of novels for adolescents and in contemporaneous films. Our interests met on the topic of Hollywood movies about World War II made during the war era, and with each new film we found and watched, our joint enthusiasm grew. In the process of writing this book, we watched more than 600 films—all in some way about the war and all made between 1937 and 1946—and since completing it, we've found and watched a few more.

When we tell people about our fascination with these films, we frequently hear the deflating response, "Aren't they just propaganda films?" implying that they must be simple and straightforward and offer little to think about. This grates on us, because the best of these films are amazing artistic accomplishments, sophisticated and effective filmmaking, and even the worst offer an opportunity to peer into a complex sociohistorical moment and to better understand how the United States perceived itself as the world was undergoing the great transformative crisis of the twentieth century. As we argue in this book, taken together, these films can be understood simultaneously as products of their culture and as tools that helped shape that culture.

It's for this reason that, despite our interlocutors' amazement that we don't consider *Sands of Iwo Jima* or *Twelve O'Clock High* or even *Saving Private Ryan*, we limit our discussion to films made during the war era. Almost as soon as the war was over, films about the war were coming out of a different American culture and thus started to serve different cultural purposes, purposes that we find much less engaging.

In what follows, we hope to demonstrate how Hollywood's World War II films functioned aesthetically and culturally, to make a case for how they worked together to create a way of understanding the war that still influences how we think about World War II, and, most important, to communicate our enthusiasm for these films and inspire our readers to seek them out and enjoy them.

We would like to acknowledge a number of people who in one way or another contributed to the completion of this project. Many of our colleagues at Illinois State University provided advice, information, and encouragement. We thank Ron Fortune; Charles Harris; Tim Hunt, chair of the Department of English; Jim Kalmbach; William Linneman; Gary Olson, dean of the College of Arts and Sciences; Rodger Tarr; Roberta Seelinger Trites; the late Ray Lewis White; and especially M. Paul Holsinger, who, as World War II area chair for the Popular Culture Association–American Culture Association annual meeting, gave us the opportunity to try out many of these ideas in a professional setting.

Others, from inside and outside academia, also provided us with support, research assistance, and access to movies. We are grateful to Don Daudelin; Ralph Dengler, SJ; Ralph Donald; Ralph and Shirley Dukes; Robert Fyne; Michael Horn; Sarah McHone-Chase; Elizabeth McLaughlin; Thomas McLaughlin; Bruce Parrish; Roberta Parry; Thomas Parry; the students in the fall 1999 Senior Academy at Illinois State University, who responded to many of our ideas; a number of collectors who were kind enough to share copies of their films with us; and the indispensable Turner Classic Movies.

We thank all the people at the University Press of Kentucky for their support, especially Ken Cherry, now retired, who offered enthusiastic encouragement for this project in its early stages, and Leila Salisbury, John Hussey, Nichole Lainhart, and Linda Lotz, who offered invaluable guidance in the home stretch.

We also want to acknowledge the many underappreciated artists, some still living, many sadly passed away, who made these films. Among the actors for whom we developed a special affection are Walter Abel, Philip Ahn, Edward Arnold, William Bendix, Joan Bennett, Ward Bond, Eddie Bracken, Felix Bressart, Helmut Dantine, Harry Davenport, Laraine Day, William Demarest, Philip Dorn, James Gleason, Alan Hale, Marsha Hunt, Walter Huston, Allyn Joslyn, Martin Kosleck, Joan Leslie, John Litel, Richard Loo, Keye Luke, Aline MacMahon, Marjorie Main, Thomas Mitchell, Frank Morgan, J. Carrol Naish, Lloyd Nolan, Margaret O'Brien, Warner Oland, Claude Rains, Sig Ruman, S. Z. Sakall, George Sanders, Ann Sheridan, Akim Tamiroff, Sidney Toler, Henry Travers, Conrad Veidt, Bobby Watson, Ian Wolfe, and Victor Sen Yung.

Finally, we dedicate this book to the memory of our parents, who in various ways—military service, defense work, Red Cross volunteerism—served the war effort and so were our earliest windows onto that time. Their encouragement, support, and love made everything we've accomplished possible: Ensign Leonard McLaughlin, U.S. Navy; Rosemary McLaughlin; First Lieutenant Idwal Parry, U.S. Army Air Forces; and Carolyn Parry.

INTRODUCTION

History is not always a matter of record—facts in dry books
and smashing sensational headlines.
> —Opening narration, *Destination Unknown*

Oh, you mean propaganda. Aw, that's for Japs and crooked
politicians.
> —Lucky Matthews (Lloyd Nolan) in *Manila Calling*

BY MIDWAY THROUGH THE 1942 wartime classic *Casablanca*, relationships among the characters have reached a state of crisis. American expatriate and Moroccan gin-joint owner Rick Blaine, having drunkenly insulted his former lover, Ilsa Lund, the night before, has been rebuffed in his attempts to apologize. Rick becomes bitter and, as his waiters note, drinks too much. Ilsa and her husband, the Czech resistance leader Victor Laszlo, in a morning meeting with the French prefect of police, Captain Renault, and the Gestapo's liaison to Casablanca, Major Strasser, have been informed that the authorities won't allow Laszlo to leave Casablanca. Laszlo and Ilsa turn to the black market but have no success in obtaining the exit visas that would get them to Lisbon and then to the United States. One visa might be obtained for Ilsa, but Laszlo can't convince her to go without him.

That evening, they all gather at Rick's Café Américain (after all, everybody comes to Rick's), where things only get worse. Yvonne, the young French woman Rick rejected the night before, comes into the bar on the

1

arm of a German officer. Sacha, the Russian bartender, disapproves, and a French soldier insults Yvonne, precipitating a fight with the German. Rick steps in, separating the combatants and telling them, "Lay off politics or get out." Shortly thereafter, Laszlo meets with Rick in his office to offer to buy the genuine, unchallengeable exit visas Rick is rumored to have, exit visas stolen by the thief Ugarte but not found on him when he was arrested at Rick's. Rick admits that he has the visas but refuses to sell them at any price. When Laszlo asks why, Rick responds, "Ask your wife."

But at this moment of anger, bitterness, confusion, division, and separation, something magical happens. Rick and Laszlo are interrupted by the sounds of Major Strasser leading the other Germans in "Watch on the Rhine," a military anthem. The two men watch from the top of the stairs, Rick seething with impotent anger. But Laszlo takes action. He strides downstairs to Rick's orchestra and orders them to play the "Marseillaise." The musicians look to Rick, who uncertainly nods his approval. With Laszlo standing tall and shining in his white suit, stiffly marking time with his clenched fist, the orchestra plays. He and Rick's Spanish guitarist and vocalist lead the singing, and the patrons join in—even Yvonne, with tears in her eyes. Ilsa gazes at Laszlo with love and admiration. Their singing is soon so loud that the overpowered Germans give up, to the disgust of Major Strasser. At the song's conclusion, cheers and shouts of "vive la France!" ring in the saloon, and customers and employees crowd around Laszlo seeking to shake his hand or clap him on the back.

This scene is successful not just because of its high, triumphal emotions, not just because of its important role in the sequence of plot events, but because in its words and images it implicitly plays out several other stories, fundamental narratives about World War II. These narratives, which are enacted within the larger, more specific narrative of *Casablanca*, are intended to explain the war to American moviegoers: why it was being fought; how it should be fought; how it concerned Americans.

Most obviously, the "Marseillaise" scene and the scenes leading up to it act out a narrative of pulling together. Rick's Café Américain is practically a United Nations, offering temporary shelter to representatives of many countries at war with or occupied by Germany: the many French, of course; Laszlo, the Czech; Sacha, the Russian; Berger, the Norwegian; Jan and Annina Brandel, the young couple from Bulgaria. The absence of a major British character emphasizes that these individuals all represent countries that were (when the film was released) at least in part occupied by Nazi Germany. Other characters—the Spanish guitarist and the Ital-

Casablanca: Resistance leader Victor Laszlo (Paul Henreid) leads the orchestra and patrons of Rick's Café Américain in the "Marseillaise."

ians, Ugarte and Ferrari—represent countries suffering from fascist rule. That the selfishness of these characters and the bickering among them are overcome by their singing of the "Marseillaise," and that their many conflicts are overshadowed by just one conflict—the one with the Germans—suggest a narrative of nations coming together and rising above their many differences and rivalries to succeed in defeating a common enemy.

That they will succeed is also implied in this scene. The Germans are presented not only as bad but also as defeatable. Major Strasser is a petty little man, in love with his own power. He enjoys bossing around his subordinates, but, as seen in his conversations with Captain Renault, he is suspicious of their loyalty. He likes to give orders, but, as evidenced by his continually changing plans for dealing with Laszlo, he can't lead. The other Germans, Strasser's staff officers, are overweight and stupid. In the "Marseillaise" scene the Germans are shown in one alcove of the saloon, apparently shunned by the rest of the patrons, one of them pounding crudely on Sam's piano. While the camera offers us expansive shots of Laszlo and the others singing, their numbers swelling to the size of a soccer crowd, the Germans are presented in tight shots, emphasizing both their separation from the others and their comparatively small number. The Germans are basically bullies, powerful because they have managed to make everyone else afraid of them. The scene suggests that they can be defeated as any bully can be: by good people joining together. The French national anthem here represents not just a love of France but also patriotism in general and the love of freedom. These ideals are the binding elements that bring ordinary people together to overcome the bullies.

The way the bullies can be beaten is also suggested: leadership. Victor Laszlo represents the subsuming of self to cause. He is single-minded in his dedication. He is unafraid, unselfish, and untiring. He is passionately devoted to his cause but also soft-spoken, courteous, and considerate of others. His civilized manner contrasts markedly with the Germans' behavior. In the "Marseillaise" scene we see how these qualities put him in a position to bring all the others together into a force that can overcome the enemy. Whereas Rick despises the Germans but feels he can do nothing about them, and whereas Captain Renault goes along with the Germans out of personal and political expediency, Laszlo acts: he has the courage to challenge the Germans publicly. In so doing, he provides an opportunity for the great mass of less courageous, oppressed people to express their true feelings and to realize how numerous and strong they are; he also strips away, at least temporarily, the Germans' veneer of power to show them for the bullies they are. This, perhaps, is the most important quality of a leader: to make his people think of themselves as better, braver, stronger than they really are. Interestingly, *Casablanca* doesn't ask us all to be Laszlos; Ilsa's adoring gaze suggests that he is a man beyond most others. But the film does tell us what to look for in a leader and assures us that with the right kind of leadership, we can overcome the fear within us and the external forces that threaten us.

We recognize Laszlo as being superior to us, but we find it easy to identify with Rick, the representative American. In fact, Rick practically becomes a symbol for the American nation and its people. Like America, which had fought a war to end all wars, Rick has been idealistically involved in foreign conflicts—running guns to the Ethiopians, fighting against the fascists in Spain—and like isolationist America, he has withdrawn into himself, no longer willing, as he repeatedly points out, to stick his neck out for anyone. Indeed, in his meeting with Laszlo, his bitterness about the past and his unwillingness to try to solve the world's problems motivate his refusal to sell the exit visas. Shortly before this meeting, however, Rick is presented in a way that undercuts this isolationist position: In a scene that anticipates Rick's meeting with Laszlo, Annina Brandel, the Bulgarian refugee, asks Rick for his advice and help. He rudely dismisses her, but then, in spite of himself, he steps in and, at his own loss (he's right when he tells Laszlo he's not much of a businessman), makes sure that her husband wins enough money at the roulette table to buy the exit visas they need. In addition to foreshadowing the end of the film, when Rick finally gives the exit visas to Laszlo and Ilsa, this sequence offers a narrative about why America should fight in the war. Though they may be right to think that they can't solve the world's problems, Americans are fundamentally too good-hearted to stand by and see injustice done. Having been underdogs themselves, Americans will side with the oppressed against the bullies.

In a few minutes of film, then, *Casablanca*, besides entertaining its audience, has communicated several basic narratives that provide a means of understanding the war. The Germans are bullies who are terrorizing and oppressing much of Europe. They can be defeated by the Allied nations overcoming their own petty differences and joining together. This joining together can be achieved by following true leaders. America, which as a nation loves justice, freedom, and fair play, must shake off its selfish isolationism to provide the leadership the rest of the world needs to defeat these bullies. At the same time, however, the film offers a curious lacuna, an absence that, once noticed, draws more and more attention to itself: Where's Sam, Rick's black pianist and sidekick? Every other character associated with Rick's Café is in this scene. Sam's orchestra is playing the "Marseillaise." His piano is being played by the German accompanying "Watch on the Rhine." But Sam himself is nowhere to be seen. His absence is necessary because his presence would suggest another narrative, one of segregation and exclusion that would undercut this celebratory coming together. In this particular sequence and the narratives it implies, Sam doesn't fit in.

Within hours after terrorists had hijacked commercial airliners and turned them into missiles on September 11, 2001, press reports were comparing the attacks to Pearl Harbor and referring to the site of the former World Trade Center as Ground Zero. These references were cues pointing toward events that marked the beginning and the end of the United States' participation in World War II. By *cues* we mean that these terms, when invoked, imply stories—in the case of *Pearl Harbor*, a story about an unprovoked and treacherous attack on an unprepared America; in the case of *Ground Zero*, a story about unimaginable and apocalyptic destruction—stories that most U.S. listeners and readers recognize, understand, and believe. These cues provide us with a way of connecting newly experienced and not-yet-processed events and information with stories we already know; the cues thus allow us to make sense of the new and not yet understood in terms of familiar stories that have helped us understand the past—in this case, events connected with World War II.[1] Other specific cues and their implied stories drawn from our nation's experience of World War II include *Hitler* (to damningly characterize a brutal tyrant), *Munich* (to argue against any kind of appeasement in foreign affairs), and *Holocaust* (to add moral weight to any large-scale executions based on ethnic, racial, or national identity).

Considering that the events of World War II played out well over half a century ago and that many of us—indeed, most of us—weren't even alive as they were transpiring, it seems amazing that these cues and their implied narratives still have the power to influence our ways of knowing the world. Their staying power may be a sign of the national unity that characterized the World War II era in America and the epistemological homogeneity or shared worldview about the war that arose from it. As we will see in chapter 7, however, this homogeneity probably never existed to the extent we now think it did and may itself be a myth produced by narratives generated during the war. The persistence of the cues, the stories, the myths of World War II is a sign of the astounding success with which the pop-cultural media—everything from news reports to advertising to radio to songs to comic books to movies (especially movies)—articulated and disseminated narratives that would explain the war: why we were fighting it, why our enemies had to be defeated, why our allies deserved our support, how each American could contribute to the eventual victory. The transmission of these narratives to World War II–era Americans through a collaboration of the nation's pop-cultural media was so successful that they became inseparable from the way we still understand the war and were condensed into the kind of shorthand cues mentioned earlier.

Of these various pop-cultural media, Hollywood films played the most important role in promulgating mythmaking narratives about the war, for two main reasons. First, as we will see in chapter 2, because of their status as fiction, films were able to offer completed narratives about the war, whereas, because of their in medias res nature, news reports about the war could not. Reading newspapers and watching newsreels from the war years, we're struck by how infrequently readers and viewers were given a complete narrative. Because of the combination of military censorship, missing information, the general uncertainty about chaotic and protean situations, and editors' sense of what would best serve the war effort, news reports overflowed with incidents but not narratives. Narratives link incidents in a causally based sequence wherein one incident leads to another, which leads to another, and so on, in a developing plotline that eventually reaches some kind of resolution. News reports during the war were necessarily either very big picture (e.g., Patton's Third Army smashes across France) or very up close and personal (e.g., Ernie Pyle's sketches of GI experiences), with little in between to connect them. (Despite advances in technology, the reporting of our own era's war against Iraq, with around-the-clock headlines and embedded reporters, suffers from the same problem.[2]) Hollywood films, because they weren't obliged to stick to facts and because of the conventions of their narrative-based genre, were able to offer complete narratives and thus fulfill a need for viewers that the news could not.

The second reason for films' dominant role in transmitting mythmaking narratives about the war is their greater popularity—popularity to the point of ubiquity—compared with other fictionalizing media, radio, theater, comic strips, and comic books, as popular as these genres were. In the early forties Hollywood produced between 400 and 500 films every year, and 90 million Americans went to the movies every week.[3] A confluence of economic trends contributed to Hollywood's success. During the Depression years, when most Americans had little disposable income, a night at the movies was a cheap and easy form of entertainment. After the United States entered the war, the economy boomed and spending money was more plentiful, but there was little to spend it on. Consumer goods, such as cars and household appliances, were in short supply because their manufacturers were making products for the war; vacations were difficult because gas was rationed, rubber tires were hard to come by, and the railroads gave priority to military personnel. The movies were one of the few easily accessible forms of entertainment for the newly prosperous home front to spend its money on. Because of this, the movies came to play an important role in many people's lives. One such moviegoer reminisces,

> People of my generation lived, breathed, and ate movies. We would see our favorites ten, twelve, fifteen times or more. We would rush to our

neighborhood theaters twice a week, whenever the program changed. We saw the A feature and the B feature; cartoons, news, shorts, coming attractions, and sometimes a piece of china or crystal were [sic] added as going offers. All for ten cents and later twenty-five cents. We would go "downtown" with our adult relatives and stand in long lines when a popular new film opened. Then, as teenagers, we were permitted to take the streetcar or busses with our friends and see a film when the door opened at 11:00 or 12:00 noon; bring a sack lunch with us and stay in the theater until 5:00 or 6:00 P.M. In other words, every local movie house was part of our experience; the center of our lives.[4]

Similarly, Arthur M. Schlesinger Jr. recalls how the movies influenced viewers' sense of self: "We went to the movies for entertainment, of course, but almost as much for instruction in techniques of self-presentation. The movies supplied our models and shaped our dreams. Young men sauntered insolently down the street like James Cagney, wisecracked like William Powell, cursed (expletives deleted by censors) like Humphrey Bogart and wooed like Clark Gable. Young women sighed like Garbo and laughed like Carole Lombard and kidded like Myrna Loy and looked (or tried to look) like Hedy Lamarr." Schlesinger sums up, "Film provides a common dream life, a common fund of reference and fantasy, for a society riven by economic disparities and ethnic discriminations."[5] Movies at this time, then, were far more than a means of escape: they were the focus of their audience's fantasies, the generator of their desires, a source of their ideas.

Looking back at Hollywood films made during the war years from our perspective in the early twenty-first century, we might easily condescend to them, dismiss them as propaganda that was more or less successful in rousing their audiences' emotions for the Allies and against their enemies. Indeed, Robert Fyne has written an entire book, *The Hollywood Propaganda of World War II*, that rates World War II films according to their value as propaganda in this sense. This kind of approach is valuable but goes only so far; it tends both to underestimate the complexity of these films and to grasp only a limited notion of propaganda. There's no denying that the Hollywood films of World War II functioned as propaganda, but *propaganda* is a difficult word; it carries pejorative connotations (propaganda is what the *other* side does), and it has come to be associated with visceral reactions divorced from reason. For Fyne, propaganda addresses "the emotions of the audience, rather than the intellect."[6]

Because of these connotations, we won't be using the word *propaganda* often. However, to understand exactly how World War II films functioned, we return to the way the word was understood by mass-communication specialists in the years leading up to the war; we return, particularly, to an influential book called *Propaganda*, written in 1928 by public-relations pioneer Edward L. Bernays. Bernays argues that emotions that are disconnected from ideas are worthless: "The haphazard staging of emotional events without regard to their value as part of the whole campaign, is a waste of effort." He asserts that propaganda is aimed at getting large numbers of people to think more or less the same thing: "The mechanism by which ideas are disseminated on a large scale is propaganda, in the broad sense of an organized effort to spread a particular belief or doctrine."[7] As his biographer explains, "Bernays's tactics differed, but his philosophy in each case was the same. Hired to sell a product or service, he instead sold whole new ways of behaving, which appeared obscure but over time reaped huge rewards for his clients and redefined the very texture of American life. Some analysts have referred to his methods as strategic or lateral thinking—mapping out a solution based on his client's standing in the wider economy and society rather than on narrow, vertical considerations like how they were faring against other bacon makers or booksellers."[8]

One of Bernays's groundbreaking public-relations campaigns was for the American Tobacco Company, maker of Lucky Strikes cigarettes. His goal was to increase the number of cigarettes sold to women. In what he called a process of "crystallizing public opinion," Bernays capitalized on two ideas current in the culture at large. The first was women's desire to be thin. He enlisted fashion photographers, doctors, and even renowned dancing teacher Arthur Murray to provide testimonials to the effect that sweets and desserts added fat, while cigarettes, as a substitute for dessert, suppressed the appetite. He encouraged restaurants to add cigarettes to their dessert menus and women's magazines to include them in their meal plans. He suggested that kitchens have a built-in place for cigarettes, like those for flour and sugar. He helped some Ziegfeld Girls form the Ziegfeld Contour, Curve, and Charm Club, whose members forswore sweets in favor of cigarettes. The second cultural idea that Bernays sought to make a connection with was feminism. He cast the idea of women smoking, especially women smoking in public, as a symbol of their freedom from artificial and outdated social restraints. To this end, he not only elicited testimony from psychoanalysts (he was Sigmund Freud's nephew) but also planned a classic publicity stunt, the Torches of Freedom. On Easter Sunday 1929 he arranged for several attractive young women to light up cigarettes on

Fifth Avenue at New York's Easter Parade. The stunt was featured in stories and photographs in newspapers across the country and sparked debate about women smoking. As Bernays summed up his method, "emphasis by repetition gains acceptance for an idea, particularly if the repetition comes from different sources."[9]

That Bernays's public-relations theories could be applied to the broader arena of influencing how the great mass of people think about their world was clear to some of his contemporaries, Walter Lippmann for one:

> Leaders, Lippmann said, couldn't be expected to have a rational dialogue with their constituents about essential ideals like justice, or law and order. That would be too unwieldy, would take too long, and wouldn't ensure the desired outcome. Instead, they should find just the right word or image to capture the popular imagination, the way they had in rallying the nation to war [World War I]. The ideal medium through which to exercise such symbols, he added, was the cinema, where Hollywood could make clear in an instant who were the good guys and who the bad, which ideas were worthy of loyalty and which should inspire anger.[10]

In actual practice, of course, controlling what the public thinks is not so deterministic; the rhetoric above suggests something akin to brainwashing. Nevertheless, as Bernays theorized and Lippmann anticipated, during World War II Hollywood movies played the central role in a pop-culture-wide "emphasis by repetition." There are three points to develop from this. The first concerns the Hollywood film's ability—through words and images—to translate the abstract into something specifically knowable via narrative. Many contemporary thinkers—Michel Foucault, Jean-François Lyotard, and Hayden White among them—have discussed the interconnections of narrative and knowledge.[11] That is, in order to know ourselves, our experience, or our culture, we cast it or have it cast for us in the form of a story: beginning and end, protagonists and antagonists, conflict developed over a series of cause-and-effect related events to some kind of resolution. Narrative structure is basic to our ways of knowing. The classic Hollywood film, because of its widespread dissemination and because its fundamental narrative structure overlaps so perfectly with the structure of human epistemology, was ideally placed in the 1940s to interact with and influence the American moviegoing public's understanding of the world. As we hope to show, it's not going too far to say that films helped make that understanding possible.

The second point is the practice of drawing on things the audience already believes. As we saw, in his cigarette campaign Bernays used as his starting point ideas that most Americans were likely to accept as true (thin women are more attractive than fat women) or ideas that most Americans would be aware of as current topics in the culture at large (women's rights), even if they didn't accept them. Invoking such commonly known ideas prepares an audience to accept a new, connected idea. We will see in chapter 3 that, whatever Americans believed about the Japanese before Pearl Harbor, after that surprise attack, they believed them to be treacherous; Hollywood films were able to use that belief as a foundation on which to build their characterization of the Japanese as an enemy.

The third point is repetition. That is, no single film (or, for that matter, no single speech, news report, or song), no matter how powerful or popular, can by itself conjure a way of thinking about the world. Rather, it is in the aggregate, through repetition and accumulation of narratives, character types, conflicts, and their resolution, that movies and other pop-cultural media create the possibilities for ways to think. Repeated often enough, narratives are shorthanded into the kinds of cues discussed earlier. Eventually, filmmakers could merely provide a cue, and viewers would fill in the implied narrative. Thus, in our discussion of Hollywood World War II films, although we analyze some films in more detail than others, the goal is to show that many films repeated the same ideas using the same kinds of narrative and filmic techniques and together offered basic narratives by which the war could be known. It is in this sense of propaganda that we are interested: how Hollywood films provided their viewers with ways to think about the war.

Two examples—one from a famous speech made soon after the beginning of the war in Europe and the other from a film documentary overtly designed to explain the war—can help us see how rhetorical cues with their implied narratives and the generic conventions of film can work together to create the means for thinking about the war. On June 18, 1940, after the debacle and triumph of Dunkirk, as the French government sued for peace and Hitler and Mussolini met to mull over terms for the French surrender, Winston Churchill addressed the House of Commons and the British nation in a speech that would be known as "Their Finest Hour." In it, he briefly considers the mistakes that led to the fall of France; expresses his confidence in the superiority of the British army, air force, and navy over their German counterparts; acknowledges the military support of the British dominions and the economic support of the United

States; and asserts that Britain's position, threatened with invasion, is far from desperate and is in fact advantageous. He concludes in the famous final paragraph:

> What General Weygand called the Battle of France is over. I expect that the Battle of Britain is about to begin. Upon this battle depends the survival of Christian civilization. Upon it depends our own British life, and the long continuity of our institutions and our Empire. The whole fury and might of the enemy must very soon be turned on us. Hitler knows that he will have to break us in this Island or lose the war. If we can stand up to him, all Europe may be free and the life of the world may move forward into broad, sunlit uplands. But if we fail, then the whole world, including the United States, including all that we have known and cared for, will sink into the abyss of a new Dark Age made more sinister, and perhaps more protracted, by the lights of perverted science. Let us therefore brace ourselves to our duties, and so bear ourselves that, if the British Empire and its Commonwealth last for a thousand years, men will still say, "This was their finest hour."[12]

This paragraph moves beyond the immediate situation and masterfully provides a way for the British people and the rest of the world to think about the war. Using the elements of narrative, Churchill defines the war in a series of conflicts that cast the British as the protagonists and the Germans as the antagonists and suggests the means for a successful resolution of these conflicts. On the most basic level the good guys–bad guys dichotomy is established with three general, value-laden images. Light, as in "sunlit," is associated with the British, while dark, as in "Dark Age," is associated with the Germans. Similarly, high, as in "uplands," is connected to the British, and low, as in "abyss," is connected with the Germans. Also, "uplands" suggests nature, while the Germans, who practice "perverted science," are unnatural. In each case—light-dark, high-low, natural-unnatural—the first term is culturally preferred and is metaphorically suggestive of goodness and purity, while the second term is suggestive of evil, perhaps even of hell. These general oppositions are augmented as Churchill brings more terms to the conflict, in each case associating the first, culturally preferred term with the British and the second, culturally abrogated term with the Germans: Christianity-paganism, civilization-barbarism, freedom-slavery, historical progress–historical regression, order and rule of law–chaos and lawlessness.

Having cast the war in terms far more morally compelling than one country fighting another, Churchill suggests the narrative sequence by which these conflicts can be successfully resolved. He calls on his listeners for personal sacrifice; he asks them to put aside differences and pull together. He then cements this vision of a narrative with a happy ending by projecting himself into the future, where historians will be able to look back at this war as a completed narrative; he imagines that in this narrative the British people will have been the heroes of this, "their finest hour."

Prelude to War, the first in Frank Capra's Why We Fight series (documentaries made to educate the armed forces), lays out the conflict in terms remarkably similar to Churchill's.[13] Beginning with Vice President Henry Wallace's statement, "This is a fight between a free world and a slave world," and accompanied by two globes—the well-lit one showing the Western Hemisphere; the other, presumably the Eastern Hemisphere, plunged in darkness—the narrator (Walter Huston) defines the differences between these two worlds. Saying, "Let's take the free world first, *our* world," the narrator connects the words of the world's great religious leaders—Moses, Muhammad, Confucius, and Christ—with the desire for freedom. (Interestingly, the background music, a choir softly singing "It Came upon a Midnight Clear," implies a coming together of the world's religions in Christianity.) He says, "All believe that in the sight of God, all men were created equal, and from that there developed a spirit among men and nations which is best expressed in our own declaration of freedom: 'We hold these truths to be self-evident, that all men are created equal.'" He tells us that this ideal of freedom has inspired many of America's and the world's great leaders ("lighthouses lighting up a dark and foggy world") and that men have always struggled, fought, and died for it. He intones passages from the Gettysburg Address and Patrick Henry's "give me liberty or give me death" speech, the words accompanied by a montage: the Liberty Bell, the Tomb of the Unknown Soldier, the Washington Monument, the Supreme Court, the White House, the Capitol, the Statue of Liberty.

"But what of this other world?" the narrator goes on, as the camera moves to the darkened globe. "Here [the camera shows a cartoon image of Japan, dark ink spreading over it] men insisted that progress lay in killing freedom. Here [ink-stained Germany] they were putting out the lighthouses one by one. Here [ditto Italy] the march of history was reversing itself." The narrator explains how each totalitarian regime rose through the subversion of democracy and the suppression of freedom: "Yes, in these lands the people surrendered their liberties and threw away their human dignity," and "Each system was alike in that the constitutional law-making bodies gave up their power." He tells us that each country abolished free speech, the free press, and labor unions. He especially stresses the stifling of religion in Germany. In a striking image, a stained-glass window is smashed by bricks, and through the holes we see a huge poster of Hitler.

Like Churchill, but using words *and* images, Capra skillfully makes his points by associating *our* side with light, Christianity, freedom, and historical progress. *Their* side is associated with their opposites: darkness, the suppression of religion, militarism, the denial of human freedoms, and historical regression. Thus they are not only made Other—different, by definition, from us—but also identified as a threat to those qualities and institutions that define us. The combination of words, sounds, and images creates a narrative understanding of the war for the audience, informing them and motivating them, providing in essence cognitive lenses through which to see the war.

To sum up, then, through the narratives that exist overtly or covertly within their plots, the narratives that lie embedded in their dialogue and speeches, and the narratives that are implied in their images, Hollywood war films offered ways to understand what the war was all about, what America's place in the war was, why America should hate its enemies and support its allies, what each American's role in the war should be, how the war would be resolved, and what the postwar world would be like. Movie-goers might leave the theater with their emotions stirred, but more lasting and thus more important were the narrative elements—the plots, charac-ter types, symbols, and rhetoric—they were supplied with to think and talk about the war. Films combined with other pop-cultural media to cre-ate, promote, and disseminate an epistemology of the war that the Ameri-can public as a whole had to accept if the war was to be fought and won. This is not to say that this epistemology was untrue, but the creation of a societal consensus is a complex process that involves turning truth into a narrative, making what's true a fiction so that it can be grasped and passed on.[14]

Thinking back to our discussion of the "Marseillaise" scene from *Casablanca*, one might ask, if the film was part of an attempt to create a societal consensus, how could the unsettling narrative suggested by Sam's absence be included? From our twenty-first-century vantage point, aren't we simply reading too much into the film, finding a racial issue that really wasn't there? We think not, for two reasons. First, as will become clear later, the fundamental narratives used to explain the war weren't always in sympathy with the long-standing narratives Americans have used to understand themselves and their world. As a result, these films frequently contain, if not contradictions, places of narrative and epistemological tension. Moreover, the narratives used to explain the war sometimes failed to work well with the conventional plots Hollywood was so dependent on—for example, the love story. The resulting narrative confusion can create, as we will see, some interesting interpretive implications. The second reason for the contradictory narrative elements is a more practical one. Auteur theories to the contrary, no Hollywood film of this time was the result of a single artistic vision. Each film was the creation of a veritable army: producers, screenwriters, directors, actors, lawyers, censors, and, after the war began, military and governmental agencies. One might imagine a stew with dozens of chefs, each adding his or her own ingredients; the results might be brilliant or simply awful.

One brilliant stew that was the product of innumerable chefs is *Casablanca*, an ideal illustration of how many voices contributed to a film in the studio system. In her definitive study of the film, *Round Up the Usual Suspects: The Making of "Casablanca"—Bogart, Bergman, and World War II*, Aljean Harmetz traces the torturous process by which *Casablanca* reached the screen, showing that its excellence and its many narratives about the war were "an accumulation of accidents."[15]

Casablanca was based on an unproduced play, *Everybody Comes to Rick's*, by Murray Burnett and Joan Alison. Burnett was moved to write the play after a European honeymoon during which he saw Nazi anti-Semitism firsthand. Returning home, he wanted the rest of the world to share his horror at what was going on in Europe. Alison seems to have been the more experienced theater professional, shaping the characters and events into a workable drama. After the play was purchased by Warner Bros., producer Hal Wallis assigned Wally Kline and Aeneas MacKenzie to write a screenplay, but apparently nothing of their treatment remains in the film. The play and the Kline-MacKenzie treatment were passed on to twin brothers Julius and Philip Epstein, who, despite being called to Washington to work on the Why We Fight series, were with the *Casablanca* project throughout its production. As the Epsteins finished sections of the screenplay, Wallis handed them over to Howard Koch to revise. Thereafter Koch and the Epsteins would trade drafts, critiquing and revising each other's work, all under Wallis's supervising eye. It was during this process that the film acquired both its political focus and its wit. As Harmetz explains,

"Koch rewrote the Epsteins to give the movie more weight and significance, and the Epsteins then rewrote Koch to erase his most ponderous
symbols and to lighten his earnestness."[16] In addition, Wallis assigned two
other writers to work on the script. Lenore Coffee, a veteran Warner Bros.
screenwriter, worked on the film for less than a week. Casey Robinson,
however, did significant work shaping the love-story aspects of the plot,
especially the Paris flashback.

It is interesting to note the mixture of ideologies that these various
writers represented. Burnett intended his play to be an attack on the Nazis'
anti-Semitism, and Warner Bros. was the most forcefully anti-Nazi studio,
criticizing Hitler long before it was fashionable. The Epsteins were solid
FDR, New Deal liberals. Koch, though not a member of the Communist
Party, was sympathetic with most of the party's positions. Robinson was a
conservative.

To complicate matters even more, people beyond the screenwriters
contributed directly and indirectly to what became the final script. When
the writers learned that Humphrey Bogart had been cast as Rick, they
began revising Burnett and Alison's character to fit Bogart's screen persona. Moreover, Harmetz argues that the available evidence indicates that
Rick's tagline, "Here's looking at you, kid," was improvised by Bogart during the filming of the Paris flashback scenes. Another of the film's famous
lines, its last, "Louis, I think this is the beginning of a beautiful friendship," was written by Wallis and recorded by Bogart weeks after filming
was completed. Director Michael Curtiz depended on Bess Meredyth, his
wife and a former screenwriter, for advice whenever he made a movie, and
evidence suggests that she contributed ideas to the *Casablanca* screenplay
as well. And in an example of corporate thinking that was never (thank
heaven) acted on, just before the film was set to open, Warner Bros.' New
York office, inspired by the U.S. landings in North Africa in November
1942, proposed adding a new ending showing Rick and Renault with the
Allied armies liberating Casablanca.

Of course, the stories that a movie tells and the messages it sends
depend on more than the screenplay and the words the actors speak. If we
broaden our attention to those who contribute to how the film looks and
its visual messages, most important is the director. Curtiz was responsible
for many of the film's striking visual moments: neither Ilsa's knocking
over of the champagne glass during her good-bye to Rick in Paris nor Carl
the waiter's hilarious response after being jostled by the local pickpocket
was in the screenplay. Curtiz also turned at least one scripted moment into

a visual one: he filmed Rick and Ilsa driving through Paris and the French countryside without the dialogue that had been written, letting the pictures tell the story. Beyond this, though, is the composition of every scene and the story those pictures tell. Others contributed to this as well. As producer, Wallis responded to the screenplay and the daily rushes, making suggestions about how the film should sound and look. Another producer, David O. Selznick, had loaned Ingrid Bergman to Warner Bros. for *Casablanca*, so he offered suggestions about everything from her lines to how she was photographed to her costumes. In fact, Harmetz argues that his voice was vital in convincing Warner Bros. not to add the proposed liberation scene.

Another aspect of how the film's story is told is the music, composed in this case by Max Steiner. Steiner tried to replace "As Time Goes By" with another song of his own, but when this proved impossible because Bergman was unavailable to reshoot key scenes, he made "As Time Goes By" the centerpiece of his score. But knowing that melodies tell stories too, Steiner made use of a mélange of popular songs to support and comment on the action. Harmetz explains: "As conspirators, refugees, Fascists, patriots, and desperate gamblers take the foreground [in Rick's], those songs, subliminally, make the café an outpost of America, an oasis in a foreign land. . . . The carpet of background music includes 'Crazy Rhythm,' 'Baby Face,' 'I'm Just Wild About Harry,' 'Heaven Can Wait,' 'Love for Sale,' 'Avalon,' 'If I Could Be with You One Hour Tonight,' 'You Must Have Been a Beautiful Baby,' and 'It Had to Be You.' Often the songs underscore the dramatic content. When Ilsa enters the café for the first time, the band plays 'Speak to Me of Love.'"[17]

Beyond all the artistic contributions, the legal and distribution branches of the studio made demands that ultimately affected the film. Movie studios had to be aware of how a film would play not only in Peoria but also in Portugal. Until the late 1930s, 40 to 50 percent of industry revenues were generated overseas. Dorothy B. Jones, who was head of the Film Reviewing and Analysis Section of the Hollywood branch of the Office of War Information from 1942 to the beginning of 1945, noted that once the war started, "most film makers failed to realize that the melodramatic blood-and-thunder combat film, with the American hero single-handedly disposing of a score of Nazis, would bring jeers and hisses in a London movie house, or that a musical singing out that the Yanks had done it once and would do it again would cause a riot between American and British soldiers in a theater in Bombay."[18] Thus the head of Warner Bros.' foreign publicity, sensitive to potential foreign profits, insisted that *Casablanca* depict foreigners inoffensively. So three unsavory characters, the pickpocket, the man who kills the couriers, and the owner of the Blue Parrot, were made Italian; the Spanish singer had to be presented with dignity; and references to Islam were removed. Wallis was also advised that for the "Marseillaise" scene, the Germans couldn't sing the "Horst Wessel" song, because the film would violate the German copyright when distributed in neutral countries.

We could go on and on, but the point is clear. The *Casablanca* we all love is the result of collaboration in the broadest sense. Moreover, although *Casablanca* is unique, the process by which it was created was not: similar if not more complicated collaborations defined the creative processes of practically every Hollywood studio film.

The variety of contributory voices within any given studio was joined by still more voices from outside the studio that sought to control what the film could and couldn't say and to insert certain messages into it. The most important of these for our purposes were the Hays Office, which administered Hollywood's industry-created Motion Picture Production Code, and, during the war years, the military and the Office of War Information. The jumbled and potentially conflicting interests of all these voices are described by historians Clayton R. Koppes and Gregory D. Black: "American film makers kept at least three audiences in mind as they made their pictures: a fickle mass audience, the box office, and their own peers, whose approbation they sought. Government propaganda officials represented yet another audience, whose goals potentially were at odds with those of the other audiences."[19]

The Production Code was created by the Motion Picture Producers and Distributors of America (MPPDA) in response to several things: public outrage at a number of Hollywood scandals; various public-interest groups' complaints that films contained too much sex, violence, and immoral behavior; and especially the threat that individual states and communities might enact their own codes for screen content, thus requiring multiple versions of every film. In 1930 the MPPDA agreed to the "self-discipline and regulation" of a production code that would govern the sort of films that could be made and what could be shown in them. The main idea behind the Code was that "No picture shall be produced which will lower the moral standards of those who see it. Hence the sympathy of the audience shall never be thrown to the side of crime, wrong-doing, evil or sin." The MPPDA, under president Will H. Hays, postmaster general during the Harding administration, was required to enforce the Code; it became, in effect, the censor of the industry it was representing. In 1934 Joseph Breen was appointed to head the Production Code Administration, the censorship enforcement arm, although the censorship office was known colloquially as the Hays Office. The Hays Office played an active role in limiting what American movies could show, usually couched in terms of what the public would pay to see. At the 1930 Academy Awards ceremony Hays spoke for fifty minutes on "the connection between morality and business": "Good taste is good business, and to offend good taste is to fortify sales resistance," he told the large crowd.[20]

Adherence to the Code was voluntary, but Breen threatened to withhold the MPPDA seal from any picture that didn't follow its guidelines. Since most exhibitors wouldn't show films without the seal, film studios were forced to comply. The Code urged that "Correct standards of life shall, as far as possible, be presented." More specifically, the presentation of crimes—including graphic depictions of murders, methods of committing crimes, and the drug trade—and the gratuitous use of liquor was to be curtailed. Moreover, because the Code stated that "The sanctity of the institution of marriage and the home shall be upheld," adultery, excessive kissing, and seduction or rape could never be more than suggested, and sexual perversion, white slavery, miscegenation, and sexual hygiene were considered inappropriate subjects. Also considered inappropriate were vulgarity, obscenity, profanity, nudity, indecent exposure, and repellent subjects, such as actual hangings, gruesomeness, branding of people or animals, apparent cruelty to children or animals, the sale of women, and surgical operations.[21]

A second major voice contributing to the making of Hollywood's World War II films was the military. The armed forces needed Hollywood to help disseminate their messages, but they insisted on tight control over those messages. Audience interest in the portrayal of overseas battles, military operations, and American technology was high, of course, but to make such films, the studios needed the cooperation of the military due to "their increased need to use military facilities, equipment and footage in film production." As Paul Fussell notes, "Because no film company could be expected to possess its own tanks, bombers, or warships, the services' had to be used, and the services refused to co-operate without approving the screenplay in advance, insisting on changes to make sure that little remained but the bromides of wholesome behavior and successful courageous action." The result was a quid pro quo in which the military provided equipment, battle footage, and technical advice and the studios presented the branches of the service as they wished to be seen.[22]

The military had sought to harness the power of the film industry and influence its output even before the United States entered the war. In early 1941 the Joint Army and Navy Public Relations Committee proposed a system for "complete censorship of publications, radio, and motion pictures within the U.S.A." Thankfully, President Roosevelt rejected this "wild scheme," and by the summer of 1941 a more congenial relationship was established between the studios and the War Department's Bureau of Public Relations (BPR). This was reflected in a mid-1941 memo from the director of the BPR: "the continuous and equitable contact of this branch with the picture industry assures their confidence and cooperation to a remarkable degree." This cooperative relationship assumed new importance after Pearl Harbor. The BPR knew that a stirring presentation of the armed forces was an excellent recruiting tool and so sometimes suggested ideas and provided technical advisers for films that earned its stamp of approval. For example, the BPR approved both *Little Tokyo, U.S.A.* (1942) and *Air Force* (1943), despite objections from the Office of War Information about inappropriate racial stereotyping. The Marine Corps was particularly helpful when it came to films that presented that branch positively, even allowing Twentieth Century–Fox to use documentary footage for *Guadalcanal Diary* (1943). The marines also provided five technical advisers, a technical director, and a "wealth of information" to *Wake Island* (1942), which depicted a defeat but glorified the Corps.[23]

The military would also discourage or veto films that showed the services or servicemen in a bad light. For example, the navy stalled on giving approval to Warner Bros.' *Action in the North Atlantic* (1943) because the convoy system being dramatized was not faring well in real life. The army refused authorization for *A Walk in the Sun* (1945) because the script had a platoon launching an unlikely World War I–type bayonet charge against a farmhouse. Screenwriter Robert Rossen had to revise the script to show the platoon running out of ammunition for their bazookas, thus justifying the bayonet charge at the end. Sometimes film ideas that presented the armed forces in a less than serious manner were doomed before the production got under way. When the War Department refused to provide assistance to Paramount's proposed *Advance Agent to Africa*, the project was killed. Even after the war ended, the armed forces objected to films that dealt with returning servicemen in a less than positive way, although if the film didn't use military equipment, there was little the military could do to prevent filming. For example, the navy objected to *The Blue Dahlia* (1946) because of its "suggestion that wounded veterans capable of both violence and amnesia were being demobilized and sent forth into the civilian world."[24]

The third major voice influencing Hollywood's films during the war years was the Roosevelt administration's Office of War Information (OWI). Even before Pearl Harbor, the United States had begun strengthening its defenses; thus the movie industry created the Motion Picture Committee Co-operative for National Defense. After the United States entered the war, this committee was reconstituted as the War Activities Committee. Mindful of Hollywood's need to support the war effort, the committee asked for government guidance. In May 1942 Washington set up the Office of the Coordinator of Films in Hollywood. A month later, it was transformed into the Bureau of Motion Pictures (BMP) of the OWI. President Roosevelt appointed Lowell Mellett, former director of the Office of Government Reports, to head the bureau in Washington, with an assistant, Nelson Poynter, in Hollywood.[25] Hollywood studios made many different types of films to support the war, including propaganda shorts, newsreels, documentaries, and educational films, but the type that had the largest audiences and the largest public impact was the traditional dramatic film.

Although the OWI made suggestions and tried to influence the films that were made, technically, its function was only advisory. As one historian stresses, "The motion picture industry had final responsibility for the films produced during the war." The OWI had six aims for the industry to consider when making movies about the war: "(1) The Issues of the War: what we are fighting for, the American way of life; (2) The Nature of the Enemy: his ideology, his objectives, his methods; (3) The United Nations: our allies in arms; (4) The Production Front: supplying the materials for victory; (5) The Home Front: civilian responsibility; (6) The Fighting Forces: our armed services, our allies and our associates." These ideas were articulated in the *Government Information Manual for the Motion Picture Industry*, which came out in the summer of 1942. The OWI asked each studio to consider seven questions as they were making their films:

    1. Will this picture help win the war?

    2. What war information problem does it seek to clarify, dramatize or interpret?

    3. If it is an "escape" picture, will it harm the war effort by creating a false picture of America, her allies, or the world we live in?

4. Does it merely use the war as the basis for a profitable picture, contributing nothing of real significance to the war effort and possibly lessening the effect of other pictures of more importance?

5. Does it contribute something new to our understanding of the world conflict and the various forces involved, or has the subject already been adequately covered?

6. When the picture reaches its maximum circulation on the screen, will it reflect conditions as they are and fill a need current at that time, or will it be out-dated?

7. Does the picture tell the truth or will the young people of today have reason to say they were misled by propaganda?

Ideally, the manual advocated inserting a "constructive 'war message'" whenever possible:

> At every opportunity, naturally and inconspicuously, show people making small sacrifices for victory—making them voluntarily, cheerfully and because of the people's own sense of responsibility, not because of any laws. For example, show people bringing their own sugar when invited out to dinner, carrying their own parcels when shopping, travelling on planes or trains with light luggage, uncomplainingly giving up seats for servicemen or others travelling on war priorities; show persons accepting dimout restrictions, tire and gas rationing cheerfully, show well-dressed persons, obviously car owners riding in crowded buses and streetcars.[26]

Although all films made during the war were subject to the government's Board of Censorship to ensure that filmmakers weren't releasing military secrets, only about a third of the movies made between 1942 and 1944 were actually concerned with war-related issues.[27] And although the OWI entreated the studios to show scripts and films to the Domestic Branch of the BMP, some cooperated more than others, and at times only grudgingly; the studios were reluctant to go through yet another level of bureaucracy. Although the studios generally wanted to support the war effort, they also wanted to make audience-pleasing pictures and thus didn't want to burden films with OWI-generated discussions of fascism, the Four Freedoms, and the goals of the Allies, turning them into nothing but propaganda—and dull propaganda at that. Some films that the studios allowed the OWI to greatly influence, such as *Pittsburgh* (1942) and *An American Romance* (1944), ended up being aesthetically poor movies and thus poor vehicles for the government's messages. One way around the BMP review, as we have seen, was to get the blessing of the army or navy; then the OWI would have to grant approval, even if it was strongly opposed to the film. Usually, films that showed one of the branches of the military in a positive light (and thus increased enlistments) were approved by the War Department. Bolder studios could simply refuse to cooperate. Paramount was notorious for resisting the BMP. When Preston Sturges refused to submit a rough cut of *The Miracle of Morgan's Creek* (1944), the BMP's Hollywood representative sent an indignant letter to Washington headquarters: "THIS IS THE ONLY STUDIO WHICH HAS EVER REFUSED SPECIFICALLY REQUEST OF THIS NATURE. IT IS ONLY STUDIO NOT FULLY COOPERATING AND IS NOT COOPERATING ONE IOTA."[28]

Eventually the OWI inadvertently gained a greater degree of control over the filmmaking process. In 1943 congressional Republicans, concerned that there were too many liberals in the OWI, tried to end its domestic operations. In a House compromise with the Senate, the funding of the Domestic Branch of the OWI was preserved, but its budget was cut by 73 percent. Most of the BMP's film reviewers moved to the Overseas Branch, headed by Ulric Bell, who convinced the Office of Censorship to refuse export licenses to those films not approved by the OWI. Because lack of access to the overseas market would drastically reduce a film's profits, this new arrangement effectively strengthened the OWI's influence over the movie community until the end of the war.[29]

This overview of the many voices—voices inside the studio, voices in the Hollywood community, voices in the military, and voices in the government—that contributed to the making of a motion picture during the war years raises the question of intention. In other words, when we claim that a particular film is making use of a narrative to provide a way of knowing some aspect of the war, are we saying that someone—director, screenwriter, studio head, OWI—made a conscious choice to construct the film in that way and intended for its viewers to get that message? Well, yes and no. There were certainly instances, and we've already noted some examples, when conscious choices were made—whether about having sympathy for our British allies or not wasting rubber. However, in many cases, a film's presentation of the war arose out of other considerations or no conscious consideration at all. Filmmakers were a part of the wartime zeitgeist they were helping to create and were presumably influenced by it. As Hollywood movies generated ways of knowing the war, these ways of knowing were replicated and reproduced, probably unconsciously, by other filmmakers. In any case, what the studios and filmmakers intended their movies to do is less important to us than the films themselves, how their audiences saw them, and what happened to those audiences who saw film after film, week after week, for the three and a half years the United States was at war.

In what follows, we examine the effects of Hollywood's World War II films and how they gave viewers ways to know the war. Chapter 1 discusses the films Hollywood made in the years after the war began but before U.S. entry into the war. The studios performed a balancing act between the anti-Nazi, pro-intervention positions of many Hollywood executives and artists and the public's and many politicians' more isolationist stance. With a few exceptions, prewar films treated their ideas about the war in Europe carefully, but they prepared viewers to think about Nazi Germany as a threat to America and about America's potential role in the war. Chapter 2 examines the many films based on actual events in the Pacific theater after Pearl Harbor and how they link those events into a coherent narrative. They also work together to make the Pacific an extension of the U.S. West Coast and thus something for Americans to fight and die for. Chapter 3 looks at the ways movies constructed the Germans, Italians, and Japanese as our enemies. Filmmakers tended to draw on existing film types that audiences were already familiar with and adapt them for the contemporary situation. Chapter 4 shows how movies presented our British, Soviet, and Chinese allies as nations to be valued for their uniqueness but also—and somewhat contradictorily—for their similarity to the United States. Chapter 5 looks at films about countries under Nazi occupation. Here there is little concern with valuing a particular nationality; rather, they provide the opportunity for Americans to imagine how they would behave under occupation. Chapter 6 analyzes the presentation of American men and women in wartime films; in many ways, this presentation revised traditional film constructions of masculinity and femininity because wartime needs forced a major reworking of male and female types. Chapter 7 looks at films about the U.S. home front, particularly those that broke rank and presented a version of American life at odds with the official depiction promulgated by most films. Chapter 8 discusses films made just after the end of the war. Some of these movies address the anxiety about the type of country postwar America was becoming; some demonstrate the power that Hollywood's World War II films had as a group to influence the way the war would be understood historically.

This influence is the result of the power these films had to take the confusing and chaotic elements of wartime and make them knowable by turning them into narrative, and it is the result of the power of narrative, through repetition and widespread dissemination, to naturalize its fictionalization of the war into a mythic history that transcends and obscures what really happened. In short, this book explores the process by which actual events become film history and by which film history becomes myth.

1

BEFORE PEARL HARBOR

The truth is, fascism isn't as pretty as it looked.
—Alex Hazen (Robert Young) in *The Searching Wind*

RETROSPECTIVELY, THE UNITED STATES' ROLE in World War II seems inevitable. In the late thirties, however, as Japanese aggression in China and Germany's expansionist claims both grew, and after September 1939, when the war in Europe began, things in the United States weren't so clear. American society's feelings about the war were confused and contradictory; there was a general feeling of sympathy for the victims of fascist aggression, but at the same time, most people were determined that the United States shouldn't become involved in these foreign wars. This determination, however, was not necessarily pacifistic, since many people supported a strong defense for the Western Hemisphere. Hollywood was similarly conflicted. The majority of the studio executives and artists were antifascist, and many of them were in favor of U.S. involvement in the war; at the same time, they were concerned about making films that were too far out of step with the opinions of the American moviegoing public, and they also had their lucrative foreign markets to consider. To understand the films made during this time, then, we have to consider them in the context of their historical moment, not from the post–Pearl Harbor perspective of the inevitability of U.S. involvement. Looking at a variety of films made between 1937 and 1941, we can see reflected the various contradictory social currents of the time, but also an unmistakable drift toward criticism of Nazi Germany and, to a lesser extent, Japan; sympathy

26

for Great Britain after the war in Europe began; a celebration of the American military buildup; and, eventually, in some films, indirect and sometimes overt calls for American intervention.

Evidence from the time clearly shows that as China and Europe plunged deeper into war, much of the American public was firmly against U.S. involvement in a new foreign war. Even after the Nazi attack on Poland in September 1939, only 2.5 percent of those interviewed in a Roper poll "expressed a willingness to enter the war at once on the side of England, France, and Poland." As late as June 1940, the American public "remained in great part bound by the continentalist, anti-European, and pacifist ideas which had prevailed for two decades." Some of the reasons for isolationism dated back to the end of World War I. The memory of the carnage was still fresh, as was anger over allies defaulting on American loans. Other reasons included an appreciation, in some quarters, of the fascist methods of creating order, antipathy for Britain, and, of course, fears about the economy. Although President Roosevelt used great ingenuity to find ways to send aid to Britain, even he recognized the American public's rejection of intervention and in his 1940 reelection campaign famously proclaimed, "I have said this before, but I shall say it again, and again, and again. Your boys are not going to be sent into any foreign wars." By the fall of 1941, a few weeks before Pearl Harbor, a Roper poll showed that nearly three-quarters of the public supported "Roosevelt's policy of 'all aid short of war' to nations fighting the Axis"; sympathy for Britain was growing, but not to the point that Americans were willing to go to war.[1]

This general support for nonintervention was more specifically represented by a number of noisy organizations, the best known of which was the America First Committee. Founded in September 1940, it drew most of its support from midwestern businessmen and political leaders. National chairman Gen. Robert E. Wood (head of Sears, Roebuck) and such celebrity members as Charles Lindbergh, Alice Roosevelt Longworth, and Lillian Gish didn't care whether Britain was defeated, as long as the United States stayed out of the war. Far from being pacifist, though, the committee encouraged a strong defense. Its four guiding principles were "(1) the United States must build an invulnerable defense for America; (2) no foreign powers can successfully attack *prepared* America; (3) American democracy can be preserved only by staying out of war in Europe; (4) 'aid short of war' weakens national defense at home and threatens to involve Americans in war abroad."[2] Other prominent isolationist organizations included the Keep America Out of War Congress, the National Council for the Prevention of War, and the Women's International League for Peace and Freedom.

Of course, there were equally vocal organizations created to support the already embattled Allies. In May 1940 the Committee to Defend America by Aiding the Allies was formed, with newspaper editor William Allen White as national chairman. This committee sided with President Roosevelt, arguing that the Axis powers must be defeated and supporting any aid short of intervention to Great Britain and the other Allies. They helped publicize the need to support the Lend-Lease Act, but there was later internal dissension about whether to support America's entry into the war. This led to White's resignation in January 1941, the loss of momentum of the committee's activities, and eventually less access to the White House. Some members went on to form a new organization in April 1941, Fight for Freedom, Inc. The main purpose of this group was clear: they believed that it was necessary for the United States to enter the war as a full belligerent.

The Hollywood community was ahead of general public opinion in its support for the victims of fascist aggression, organizing antifascist groups as early as the mid-1930s. The Motion Picture Artists Committee arranged for a boycott of Japanese goods and raised money to ship medical supplies and food to the wounded and homeless in China and Spain. In 1936 the Hollywood Anti-Nazi League was created "to combat Nazi influence and Nazi propaganda," and the Motion Picture Democratic Committee brought together supporters of President Roosevelt. In 1940 the House Committee to Investigate Un-American Activities, also known as the Dies Committee after its chair, Martin Dies of Texas, accused the Hollywood Anti-Nazi League and the Motion Picture Democratic Committee of Communist leanings. (The Dies Committee had investigated the entertainment industry before; its hearings on the Federal Theater Project in 1938 had caused the project's funding to be withdrawn by Congress.) Although these allegations of Communist control were eventually discredited, the focus on communism caused both organizations to lose their most powerful supporters and to fold. Nevertheless, there seemed to be more vocal antifascists in Hollywood, especially actors and directors, than there were elsewhere. As Leo Rosten noted at the time, "The fact that the movies are an international commodity drove politics home to Hollywood with a hard, unyielding impact. The paroxysms of power politics flung the impending chaos of the world into Hollywood's lap. . . . The political advertency of Hollywood preceded the political awakening of America."[3]

Because of the Hollywood community's outspoken and, in many respects, out-of-step antifascism (what would later be called "premature antifascism"), Senator Gerald P. Nye of North Dakota, a leading spokesman for America First, charged that the movie industry was encouraging intervention in its films. As early as 1934 he had encouraged federal inspection of movies. On August 1, 1941, he and Bennett Champ Clark, senator from Missouri, astutely assessed motion pictures and radio as "the most potent instruments of communication of ideas" and urged a Senate subcommittee to investigate whether motion pictures were designed "to influence public sentiment in the direction of participation by the United States in the present European war." In a radio address given in St. Louis that day, Nye claimed that the motion picture companies had "become the most gigantic engines of Propaganda in existence to rouse the war fever in America and plunge this Nation to her destruction." He then listed the men he considered the dominant forces of intervention—the heads of the major studios, including Columbia, MGM, RKO, Paramount, Twentieth Century–Fox, United Artists, Goldwyn, and Warner Bros. During the Senate hearings on "Motion Picture Screen and Radio Propaganda" that followed, Nye further explained his concern: "Arriving at the theatre, Mr. and Mrs. America sit, with guard completely down, mind open, ready and eager for entertainment. In that frame of mind they follow through the story which the screen tells. If, somewhere in that story there is planted a narrative, a speech, or a declaration by a favorite actor or actress which seems to pertain to causes which are upsetting the world today, there is planted in the heart and in the mind a feeling, a sympathy, or a distress which is not easily eliminated."[4]

As the hearings proceeded, Nye seemed to be most concerned that Hollywood was supporting the Roosevelt administration and its interventionist stance and that the film industry was controlled by a small group of men, primarily Jewish, who had a major investment in distributing films to the British Commonwealth market. Nye put it bluntly: "Many people seem to assume that our Jewish citizenry would willingly have our country and its sons taken into this foreign war." Charles Lindbergh made a similar argument in a speech at an America First rally on September 11, 1941; he claimed that America's Jews were "agitating for war" through "their large ownership and influence in our motion pictures, our press, our radio, and our government." Indeed, under questioning by Wendell L. Willkie, whose law firm was counsel to Hollywood's interests before the committee, a number of movie executives, including Harry M. Warner of

Warner Bros. and Darryl F. Zanuck of Twentieth Century–Fox, proudly admitted that they were strongly against Hitler and the Nazis. Warner told the committee, "I am ready to give myself and all my personal resources to aid in the defeat of the Nazi menace to the American people." However, the reality of the studios' output doesn't support Nye's and Lindbergh's charges. The Nazi persecution of the Jews is rarely directly mentioned in prewar Hollywood films, and with only a few exceptions, some of which are discussed later in this chapter, the wars in Europe and China were not the main focus of Hollywood's output. In 1941 Rosten noted the problem of the studios' conflicted position: "If Hollywood, for example, produces a picture dealing with the war, it is accused of 'war-mongering': if Hollywood doesn't, it is accused of feeding pap to the public and putting profit above the national welfare."[5]

So, far from being in the forefront of encouraging intervention overseas, Hollywood studios were, especially from our contemporary viewpoint, relatively slow in drawing attention to the conflicts in Europe and Asia. As the world descended into war, the Motion Picture Production Code's specifications about national feelings became important to the Hays Office. The Code stated, "The history, institutions, prominent people and citizenry of all nations shall be represented fairly." Joseph Breen interpreted this to mean that Hollywood shouldn't be taking sides in the European conflict, including the Spanish civil war. He insisted, "the movie industry must not urge American involvement in the war." Even more important than the Production Code, however, was industry economics. Except in unusual cases, if it seemed unlikely that a film would make money, that film probably wouldn't be made, no matter how worthy its political messages, and as we noted in the introduction, the studios were keenly aware of the profits generated in foreign countries and were reluctant to jeopardize them just to make a political point. As early as November 1935 the *Hollywood Reporter* stated, "It is admitted that today, due to the political situation throughout Europe, censorship on pictures touching on topics considered dangerous to those in power is tougher than ever. The picture companies are through with their former stand, 'We'll make it anyway.' They now listen to foreign departments whose business it is to keep in touch with problems confronting the sales department abroad." By the late 1930s the German market for films became less important and the British market more important to a film's profitability, leading to the cynical conclusion that "Hollywood's boldness was inversely proportional to the extent of its German and Italian market." Sensitivity to the Germans became even less important, when, on August 17, 1940, Germany banned American films in countries under its control.[6]

Nevertheless, from the late 1930s on, Hollywood studios produced some films that at least indirectly sympathized with the victims of fascism and criticized to a lesser or greater degree the aggressors. This is most clearly seen in the films that depict the Chinese as victims of Japan. The adventure plot of *Shadows over Shanghai* (1938), involving Japanese agents trying to prevent some Americans from getting a precious amulet to San Francisco, is set against the background of Chinese orphans and refugees and the Japanese bombing of Shanghai. In *Mr. Wong in Chinatown* (1939) the detective solves the murder of a Chinese princess who had come to the United States to raise money for her country's air force. Similarly, in *Ellery Queen's Penthouse Mystery* (1941) an American ventriloquist, carrying donated jewels to be auctioned off for Chinese war relief, is murdered. In *Burma Convoy* (1941) two American brothers prevent the disruption of a convoy of supplies bound for Chinese forces in Chungking. In *They Met in Bombay* (1941) Clark Gable and Rosalind Russell are con artists and jewel thieves in Hong Kong who end up protecting Chinese evacuees from Japanese troops. Gable's character, a Canadian who had been cashiered from the British army, ends up masquerading as a British officer, leading British troops against the Japanese, and being awarded the Victoria Cross. In all these films the Chinese are presented as hopelessly overmatched against the Japanese military machine, and the Japanese are presented as unfairly and cruelly waging war against helpless civilians and children, though in none of these films is this the main focus of the plot.

Similarly, a number of Hollywood films sympathized with the British resistance to the Nazi blitz.[7] As in the Chinese films, they implicitly take the side of the British, though that aspect remains background to a story that usually features an American character at the heart of the action. In *Escape to Glory* (1940) Pat O'Brien, playing an American soldier of fortune who has been fighting fascism, helps defend a British freighter from U-boats when war breaks out. In *Confirm or Deny* (1941) American newspaperman Don Ameche's efforts to get censored war stories out of London is set against the stoicism of the English during the Battle of Britain. In *A Yank in the RAF* (1941) hotshot American pilot Tyrone Power romances Betty Grable but also shoots down Luftwaffe planes during the evacuation from Dunkirk. Similarly, in *International Squadron* (1941) hotshot American pilot Ronald Reagan joins the Royal Air Force (RAF), causes trouble because he can't learn to be a team player, but redeems himself by dying on a suicide mission. The effect of these films was augmented by British-made films that were released in the United States and, predictably, made a plea for sympathy with the British cause by showing the horror of Nazi aggression. These include *Night Train to Munich* (1940); *Women in War* (a joint British-Republic production, 1940); *Freedom Radio* (1941); *Dangerous Moonlight* (a joint British-RKO production, 1941); *Pimpernel Smith* (1941), Leslie Howard's skillful and effective *Scarlet Pimpernel* update; and *The 49th Parallel* (1941), in which a U-boat officer stranded in Canada works his way across the country to the neutral United States, only to be turned away at the border and handed over to Canadian authorities.

Hollywood studios also offered some films that were critical of Nazi Germany. They usually focused on the effects of Nazism on common men and women and their families. *Beasts of Berlin* (1939), whose initial release was banned in New York for being too inflammatory, shows the brutality with which the Nazis respond to a fledgling resistance movement in Germany. In *Escape* (1940) an American man tries to rescue his mother from a German concentration camp. *Four Sons* (1940) shows the effect of Nazism on a Czech-German family living in the Sudetenland: one brother goes to America, one becomes a Nazi, one fights for Czechoslovakia, and one is drafted into the German army; only the one in America survives. In *The Man I Married* (1940), which we discuss in chapter 3, an American woman travels to Germany with her German husband, who becomes swept up in Hitler worship. *Underground* (1941), also discussed in chapter 3, centers on the conflict between two brothers—one a German soldier, the other the leader of a resistance group. All these films show the brutality of the Nazi regime, the loss of personal liberty, and the difficulty of enacting opposition.

Some films combined their critique of German fascism with the fear of fascism at home. As early as 1935 Sinclair Lewis had written about a possible fascist takeover of the U.S. government in *It Can't Happen Here*. Although the novel was bought for a screen treatment and production was started, MGM bowed to pressure from the Hays Office and canceled the project. But in 1937 *Nation Aflame* showed a con man with a talent for demagoguery tapping into working-class anger by blaming "foreigners" for all of America's economic troubles; he founds an organization called the Avenging Angels and uses it as a political base to gain control of an unnamed state. Other films identified the undercutting of freedom of speech and freedom of the press as the first steps toward fascism in the United States. One of the best known of these films is *Mr. Smith Goes to Washington*

(1939), in which freshman senator Jefferson Smith (James Stewart) finds that his political mentor, Senator Paine (Claude Rains), is actually in thrall to a political boss (Edward Arnold) and votes however he is told to help certain businesses prosper. When Smith attempts to bring this corruption to the attention of the public, the newspapers are told not to report his accusations, and the political boss's goons even beat up children who try to distribute newspapers. Only a one-man filibuster by Senator Smith and Paine's tortured confession defeat the political machine.

Nineteen forty-one offered two strong films concerned with the rise of internal fascism. In *Citizen Kane* Orson Welles portrays a powerful newspaperman, similar in many ways to the ultraconservative William Randolph Hearst. Kane wants political power as well as corporate power, but an ill-timed love affair derails his chances as a gubernatorial candidate. Kane is shown manipulating public opinion, and in a "News on the March" newsreel he is shown chatting amiably with Hitler. In *Meet John Doe* Edward Arnold shows up again as a powerful businessman, D. B. Norton, who buys a newspaper to bring down a governor and get access to the public. He also creates the D. B. Norton Motor Corps, a black-jacketed paramilitary group recalling Hitler's storm troopers in both look and violence. Norton uses the idea of an unidentified man—John Doe—who wants to jump off a building to protest corruption in the world to gain the political support of ordinary Americans. As he tells the shocked John Doe (Gary Cooper), "what the American people need is an iron hand." Motioning to the business and labor leaders sitting around him, he states, "we know what's best for America." At the end, members of a John Doe Club, plus a journalist who loves him, convince Doe not to jump but to stay and fight this incipient fascism. Norton's former editor (James Gleason) says, "There you are Norton: the people, try and lick that."

One of the most troubling films about the possibility of American fascism is *Keeper of the Flame*. Based on a novel by I. A. R. Wylie and released in 1942, *Keeper of the Flame* follows the quest of hardened foreign correspondent Steve O'Malley (Spencer Tracy) to document the life of Robert Forrest, an American hero and political figure who has recently died in a car accident. O'Malley, like real-life journalist Dorothy Thompson, has been thrown out of Berlin by the German government; he returns to the United States anxious to write about something good in the world. However, O'Malley learns that what seems to be safe and good may not be. America is shown as a country struggling for direction, and as O'Malley's editor tells him in the novel, "We've mislaid our vision. We've been told what happens to people without vision. They perish. But Forrest had it. He might have given it back to us. He was giving it back."[8] Forrest had set up a national organization, the Forward America Movement, to guide Americans. However, as his widow Christine (Katharine Hepburn) tells O'Malley, this organization was merely a front for Forrest and a group of fifth columnists to create fascist rule under the guise of "true Americanism." His plans included marshaling a group of veterans who would function as storm troopers and turning groups against one another in order to create a need for martial law—rural against urban, management against labor, Christians against Jews, Protestants against Catholics, whites against blacks. Christine tells O'Malley, "I saw the face of fascism in my own home . . . of course they didn't call it fascism. They painted it red, white, and blue and called it Americanism." When Christine realized that Forrest "no longer believed in God, but only in himself," she acted, though passively, not warning him about a bridge that had been washed out and thereby causing his death. She says, "I had to destroy the man to save the image," but she is merely concealing what Americans need to be on guard against. Christine is shot by her husband's secretary (Richard Whorf), and after her death, O'Malley changes his assignment and writes a biography of Christine Forrest, a real American hero because she destroyed the seeds of homegrown fascism.

In contrast to Hollywood's cautious treatment of the political climate abroad and its subtle warnings about the possibility of fascism in the United States, the studios' films about the American military and the defense buildup were ostentatiously celebratory. After the introduction of the draft in September 1940, there were, not surprisingly, a number of draft comedies. All released in 1941, these films tend to follow the same general pattern: comic actors are drafted or enlist (usually reluctantly), are screwups in boot camp, are often attracted to the daughter of their sergeant or commanding officer, redeem themselves and often get the girl by becoming the hero of the climactic war games. Probably the best of these (which isn't much of an endorsement) is *Caught in the Draft*, with Bob Hope as a cowardly actor who joins up to impress Dorothy Lamour. Abbott and Costello enlist in the army in *Buck Privates*, and in *Keep 'Em Flying* they become mechanics for the army air forces. In *Great Guns* Laurel and Hardy enlist in the army to look after their wealthy employer, who has been drafted. In *Tanks a Million* William Tracy plays a draftee with a photographic memory. In *You're in the Army Now* failed vacuum-cleaner salesmen Jimmy Durante and Phil Silvers enlist and cause pandemonium on their base. The effect of these films is to humanize the army—to make being drafted seem less threatening—and also to define the citizen army as a place where quirky individuals, like the various comics in these films, can succeed. In addition, these films send a message—in retrospect, an overconfident message—about America's military preparedness.

Military preparedness is also the point of what we call technology films, films that set their plots against an explanation of some kind of military armament or special operations. In *20,000 Men a Year* (1939) Randolph Scott initiates a program wherein flight training will become part of college curricula, with the goal of turning out 20,000 pilots per year (hence the title). The film's opening asserts that these pilots are being trained for peace, not war, but the urgency of the training and the number of pilots needed imply otherwise. *Flight Command* (1940) focuses on a melodramatic love triangle, but it also shows how a squadron of navy fliers works. *Dive Bomber* (1941) is about the development of the titular aircraft. *Parachute Battalion* (1941) combines elements of the draft comedy with a story about the training of airborne troops. Technology films continued to be made during the war: for example, *Bombardier* (1943), about high-altitude bombing with the Norden bombsight; *Destination Tokyo* (1943), about submarines; and *They Were Expendable* (1945), about PT boats.

Another indication of the overconfidence in American military technology is the large number of espionage films made from the late 1930s through 1941. In these films agents of unnamed foreign countries or traitorous Americans in their employ try to steal the secrets of American technology, often having to do with airplanes, but the spies are usually foiled. As early as 1937, in *Crack-Up*, Peter Lorre plays the ringleader of a network of foreign spies trying to get hold of a revolutionary new plane. In *Charlie Chan at the Olympics* (1937) the famous Chinese detective helps to recover a remote-control device for planes while visiting the Berlin Olympics. Nineteen thirty-eight saw *Smashing the Spy Ring*, in which FBI man Ralph Bellamy infiltrates a gang smuggling military technology out of the country. Nineteen thirty-nine produced *Exile Express*, about the formula for a vegetation-destroying chemical; *Navy Secrets*, about two naval intelligence agents trying to recover the plans for a range finder; *Nick Carter, Master Detective*, in which Walter Pidgeon stops espionage in an airplane factory; *The Lone Wolf Spy Hunt*, in which Warren William's title character foils an attempt to steal the plans for an antiaircraft gun; *Panama Patrol*, about cryptographer Leon Ames breaking up a plot sponsored by an unnamed Asian country to sabotage the Panama Canal; *Television Spy*, in which foreign agents recognize the military potential of new TV technology; and *They Made Her a Spy*, in which federal agent Sally Eilers infiltrates a Washington-based spy ring. Nineteen forty saw *Calling Philo Vance*, a remake of *The Kennel Murder Case* (1933), in which the inventor of a new bomber is murdered by foreign agents—the spies here are both central European and Asian; *Charlie Chan in Panama*, about another attempt to sabotage the Panama Canal; *Murder over New York*, another Charlie Chan mystery in which the detective foils the sabotage of a new bomber; and *Enemy Agent*, about more espionage in an aircraft factory. Nineteen forty-one offered *Adventure in Washington*, about foreign agents trying to get defense secrets from senators; *Flying Wild*, in which the East Side Kids (for something different) prevent spies from stealing secrets from an airplane factory; *Meet Boston Blackie*, in which the criminal-detective breaks up a spy ring that uses flickering neon lights at an amusement park to send messages to an offshore submarine; *Man at Large*, in which pre-*Superman* George Reeves and goofy journalist Marjorie Weaver expose a Nazi spy ring run by a blind mystery writer; and *Mystery Ship*, about the deportation of a boatload of criminals, many of them apparently spies.

This type of film was obviously very popular, at least partly because of its versatility; the basic espionage plot could support action films, mysteries, comedies, and romances. Beneath the plot, however, these films consistently suggest two messages. First, they offer confidence in America's defenses by implying the superiority of American military technology. After all, if American technology weren't superior, why would all these unnamed foreign countries be so eager to steal it? This confidence is augmented by these films always showing military personnel, federal agents, or just average Americans preventing the attempted theft of our secrets. Second, and somewhat contradictorily, they send a message about the extent to which America is threatened from the outside: foreign spies are ubiquitous. As the blind spy Karl Botany (Steven Geray) says in *Man at Large*, "We are everywhere over here, just below the surface of everyday life, invisible and efficient." America may wish to be neutral, but that doesn't mean that other countries will respect that neutrality. But more important than these implied messages is the cautious way these films avoid connecting their espionage to any specific countries. Viewers might connect the spies to Germany or, less frequently, Japan, but as far as the studios are concerned, they are generic bad guys. In a rare case such as *Man at Large*, where the spies are identified as German, their target is not specifically

America but rather convoys to Great Britain; and just to be safe, Twentieth Century–Fox ended the film and preceded the credits with a full-screen disclaimer: "The events depicted in this photoplay are entirely fictional." All in all, it would have been difficult to indict Hollywood studios on the charge of making political propaganda based on the evidence of these films.

One film that broke the pattern of these politically neutered espionage films was Warner Bros.' 1939 *Confessions of a Nazi Spy*. The Warners, the most liberal of the studio owners and the most fervent supporters of FDR and the New Deal, had been looking for an appropriate anti-Nazi vehicle ever since the Jewish head of their German office, Joe Kaufman, had been murdered in Berlin. *Confessions of a Nazi Spy* is a fairly accurate fictionalization of the actual FBI investigation of a German spy network that was gathering information about U.S. East Coast defenses. Four spies were tried and convicted in October 1938, and only a few months passed before the film version was released in April 1939. Like typical espionage films, *Confessions of a Nazi Spy* shows the nefarious means by which foreign agents try to obtain American military secrets, but there are also two important differences. First, the documentary style of the film—a voice-over providing names, dates, and places; the artless cinematic style; the deferral of the credits until the end of the film—reinforces the connection between the film and recent news events. Second, as is obvious from the sensational title, the film identifies the country that is doing the spying and stealing—Nazi Germany. Thus, just as other espionage films use their basic plots as vehicles for comedy, romance, or adventure, the Warners' film uses its spy plot to point out the threat Germany poses to the United States.

This threat is founded in the basic philosophy of fascism, which the narrator (John Deering) describes as the camera shows us a superimposed swastika growing from Germany to cover the entire globe:

> Following faithfully the program of the new bible of Adolf Hitler, *My Battle*, the Nazi Party has created a new fascist society based on a devout worship of the Aryan superman, a new fascist culture infused with the glorification of conquest and war, a fascist system of life where every man, woman, and child must think alike, speak alike, and do alike, a rigidly censored press with all news colored by the ministry of propaganda, a fascist literature shorn of its greatest writers and poets, a new religion ridiculing the brotherhood and equality of man before God, a fascist economy with its watchwords, "Cannons, not butter," a fascist

philosophy with its supreme command: blind obedience to the Führer. For six long centuries men throughout the world had fought their way out of the dark ages of medieval barbarism, but in six short years Hitler's Nazis cast their ominous shadow over the entire earth.

Of course, several of the films we mentioned earlier offer similar explicit or implicit critiques of fascism; what's different here is the film's arguing that Nazi fascism is a direct threat to the United States. The film shows us Nazism at work, not in Germany or in the unfortunate countries Germany has occupied, but in America. The German-American Bund is shown promoting German Americans' loyalty to the Fatherland and discouraging their assimilation into the American culture. Bund-sponsored summer camps are shown brainwashing young boys and girls into a militaristic obedience. The Bund puts into action a pro-German, anti-Semitic propaganda campaign orchestrated by Joseph Goebbels himself (Martin Kosleck). Moreover, the Bund is shown working hand in glove with the spy ring seeking to undermine America's defenses. All these activities are explicitly presented as preparing for Germany's eventual invasion of the United States.

Confessions of a Nazi Spy: Dissenters are silenced during a meeting of the German-American Bund. Note Ward Bond in the center of the disturbance.

In the offices of the FBI, one man (John Hamilton) remarks wonderingly, "You'd think from the number of spies they've been sending over here that we're at war with Germany." In response, agent Edward Renard (Edward G. Robinson) lays out the film's basic argument: "On the contrary, it looks more as if Germany were at war with *us*. Nazi bunds meeting all over the nation, openly training men for street fights, teaching them how to use guns and bayonets, the whole country swamped with Nazi propaganda fresh from Germany. Tie the two together. It looks as if the storm troopers are training to finish off what the propaganda starts. It's a new kind of war, but it's still war."[9]

The Warners made their point, and the film was successful, but it also caused a great deal of protest. Warner Bros. soon decided against making any more "propaganda pictures,"[10] which resulted in something of a mixed message in a later 1939 release, *Espionage Agent*. This film made many of the same points as *Confessions of a Nazi Spy*, but at the same time it tried to emphasize its own neutrality. It begins in 1915 with a montage showing German agents sabotaging American industry. A brief scene follows in which U.S. State Department officials lament that they have no laws with which to effectively fight foreign spies' operations. One man (Addison Richards), sounding like Edward Renard, says, "we are being attacked, not by troops in uniform, but by an internal army of spies, saboteurs, and propagandists." Another montage—war graves blending into harvests blending into yet another war—brings us to the narrative present, where the United States is faced with the same problem because of the new European war. Interestingly, now the spies are not connected to a specific country. They have German names, they are addressed as "Herr," many of them have German accents, and their presence on screen is accompanied by German martial music, but Germany is never named. At the end of the film, when officers from the spies' country appear, they wear SS-style uniforms, but the swastika is noticeably absent. Instead of targeting Germany, the film argues that spies from "both sides" are at work in the United States, and London, Paris, and Berlin are named as interchangeable sources of untrustworthy propaganda. In a radio broadcast an American journalist (George Bancroft) concludes, "let the hatreds of Europe remain in Europe. Keep them out of our country. Remember that America *should* be neutral." Earlier, however, he had advised two foreign service officers, "when you get back to the States, try to convince them that isolation is a political policy and not a brick wall around the nation."

The strategies *Espionage Agent* uses to walk softly around the issues of intervention, neutrality, and simply taking sides are found in many other prewar films. Some films use various techniques of indirection to make their cases about intervention; others stress their own neutrality by equating the two sides in the conflict, that is, implying that there's no difference between them. This approach is especially evident in films about the Spanish civil war. Films such as *Last Train from Madrid* (1937) and *Blockade* (1938) encode the cues for which side is which so deeply that the loyalists' and republicans' ideological associations are lost and so become irrelevant.[11] In *Conspiracy* (1939) a radio operator who discovers that his American merchant ship is carrying material for chemical warfare lands in an unnamed fascist country (judging from the various accents, it could be Germany, Italy, or Spain) and becomes a target for both the government's secret police *and* the underground resistance. *Washington Melodrama* (1941) features a conflict between a philanthropist who wants to send humanitarian aid to Europe and a radio commentator who thinks that such aid supports fascist governments. By the end of the film, however, this serious issue is deflated as the two men simply agree to disagree.

This hedging of bets is perhaps not surprising if we consider Hollywood economics. When *Confessions of a Nazi Spy* was rereleased in 1940, with added footage about the invasion of Norway, Holland, and Belgium, the film flopped with moviegoers. With the Nazi blitzkrieg apparently unstoppable, the Hollywood studios became even more cautious about criticizing and possibly offending Germany. As *Variety* reported, "Belief is strong in some circles that Uncle Sam will crack down on American distribution of any films objectionable to Adolf Hitler should he happen to come out on top in the European conflict."[12]

At the other end of the spectrum from *Confessions of a Nazi Spy* is Paramount's 1941 comedy *World Premiere*, a film that seems to mock the very idea of Hollywood's having any political ax to grind or any influence over world affairs. The film begins with Italy and Germany sending their top espionage agents to America to disrupt the filming and prevent the premiere of Bengal Studio's new film about the situation in Europe, *The Earth's on Fire*. The film is dangerous because, as the Italian agent Scarletti (Luis Alberni) puts it, it "abuses our cause." When the German agent, Franz von Bushmaster (Sig Ruman), is told that this propaganda film shows "our leader" murdering 1,300 friends, he responds, "Nonsense! Our leader has no friends." After establishing the narrative premise that Germany and Italy are threatened by Hollywood films, *World Premiere* takes us to Hollywood to demonstrate how ill founded this premise is. First, what we

see of *The Earth's on Fire* is difficult to take seriously as a political statement. In one scene an actress (Virginia Dale) says to the hero (Ricardo
Cortez) as he's being led away by German soldiers, "For mercy's sakes,
John! Tell them! Civilization's not worth it!" Second, what we see of the
film's artists and producers suggests no possibility of serious aesthetic or
political intent. Rather, they are involved in career advancement, good
publicity, and behind-the-scenes romances; in short, they are completely
self-involved. Moreover, the studio head, Duncan DeGrasse (John
Barrymore), is something of a fascist dictator himself, demanding absolute power, firing anyone who annoys him, betraying friends, bending
laws, and breaking rules to get what he wants. In a key moment DeGrasse
has decided that it would be a great publicity stunt to hire two actors to
portray espionage agents sent to disrupt the film. When von Bushmaster
and Scarletti stumble onto the studio lot, publicity man Joe Bemis (Don
Castle) hires them for the job. He explains to a guard, "They're from central casting," and an offended von Bushmaster replies, "Central casting!
We are from Central powers!" Hollywood is depicted not as being concerned about the world at war but as being completely wrapped up in its
own world; Hollywood not only can't tell the difference between reality
and make-believe, it doesn't care. One can imagine *World Premiere* as the
answer to Senator Nye and others who were concerned about the movie
industry's political agenda.

Clearly, the Hollywood studios had no agreed-on agenda or common set
of film conventions for depicting the pre–Pearl Harbor international situation and America's role in it. The films we've looked at reflect the confused and conflicted state of the American public. In the two years and
three months between the outbreak of the war in Europe and the U.S.
entry into the war, however, Hollywood released several films that, though
avoiding the ostentation and controversy of *Confessions of a Nazi Spy*, helped
establish the basic narratives with which films would present the war and,
more subtly, encourage Americans to think about the war in certain ways.
    One way that the Hollywood studios could address the war in Europe
without seeming to do so overtly was to displace it to another time and
situation. The most obvious method, as we saw briefly in *Espionage Agent*,
was to utilize the previous European conflict, World War I. Before 1939
films about World War I, like much of the fiction of the time, tended to use
the war as a vehicle for antiwar messages. Cynicism about the political and
national motives for the war, disgust at the stupidity of the war's strategy

and tactics, horror at the overwhelming loss of human life, and regret at the loss of human dignity are the themes of such films as *The Big Parade* (1925), *What Price Glory?* (1926), *All Quiet on the Western Front* (1930) and its sequel *The Road Back* (1937), both the 1930 and 1938 *Dawn Patrol*, *Broken Lullaby* (1932), the first film adaptation of Hemingway's *A Farewell to Arms* (1932), and *The Road to Glory* (1936). Even Howard Hughes's fascination with the spectacle of the war's technology (and a barely dressed Jean Harlow) in *Hell's Angels* (1930) couldn't completely conceal the sense that in this war the honorable characters are misguided and the nihilistic characters have sound judgment. Other films not specifically about the war explored its deleterious psychological effects on individuals and the concomitant social effects on the United States; these include *The Lost Squadron* (1932), *They Gave Him a Gun* (1937), *The Man Who Wouldn't Talk* (1940), and, most famously, *The Roaring Twenties* (1939).

But after the war in Europe began in September 1939, World War I was presented very differently in Hollywood films. It was simple to use the previous war of German aggression as a way to comment on the new one. The best example of this, because it's the most blatant, is the 1940 Warner Bros. spy drama *British Intelligence* (based on the play *Three Faces East*, which had previously been filmed in 1926 and 1930). After a brief opening sequence set in the trenches and a hospital, the film moves to London to follow the British intelligence service's attempts to uncover the Germans' master spy, played by Boris Karloff. But more interesting than the plot twists are the occasional moments of editorializing when the film spells out the connections between the Great War and the new conflict and between the earlier German enemy and the Nazis. At one point, while giving an assignment to Helene von Lorbeer (Margaret Lindsay), a German baron (Frederick Vogeding) rants, "No nation, no group of nations, can stop our advance, the advance of German culture. We are destined to conquer the world. If our Kaiser is taken from us, a new leader will arise. I may not live to see it, but someday, someday, Germany will own the world!" Later, in London, another German spy, Henry Thompson (Lester Matthews), tries to convince Helene to throw over her mission and run away with him. She protests that their work is for Germany, and he responds, "'It's for Germany.' I'm sick of that phrase. How many millions of people have been killed in the past for those words? How many millions more must die, just because one man sets himself above the Almighty so that he might boast of 'my country, my people'? It's happened before. It's happening now. It will happen again." At the end of the film, after the

German spies are killed—ironically, by a bomb dropped from a zeppelin—intelligence man James Yates (Leonard Mudie) intones, "We want to help humanity. We fight wars only because we crave peace so ardently, and we pray that each war will be the last. But always in the strange scheme of things, some maniac with a lust for power arises and in one moment destroys the peace and tranquility we've created through the years. [Looking directly into the camera] We *hate* war. We despise it. But when war comes, we must and will fight on and on and . . ." (fades out as "The End" title card fades in). The film not only uses World War I to attack Hitler as the cause of Germany's aggression in the late thirties but also ends with an argument for *our* (the world's civilized, peace-loving people, presumably) responsibility to go to war to stop him.

Two other Warner Bros. films similarly displace the new war in Europe to the Great War, but they make their points more subtly. The focus here is on why U.S. involvement in the war is necessary and how the individual soldier can rise above his faults and selfishness to become a hero to the larger community. The first film is *Sergeant York*, Warner Bros.' prestige film for 1941. In broad outline, *Sergeant York* follows the real story of Alvin C. York, a rural Tennessee man who had sought conscientious-objector status but who, on October 8, 1918, became a hero in the Argonne: with his men surrounded and badly outnumbered, York killed 28 Germans and captured 132 more. Directed by Howard Hawks and released on September 27, 1941, the film became the highest-grossing film of the year and was nominated for eleven Academy Awards, winning Gary Cooper his first Best Actor Oscar. In subsequent years critical opinion about *Sergeant York* has been less positive. Many critics argue that the film's aspirations to realism clash miserably with its use of Hollywood narrative conventions. As Robin Wood sums up his disappointment with the film, "One feels Hawks continually hampered by having to 'stick to the facts'; an intuitive artist, he is ill-equipped to handle big issues explicitly on any but a superficial level." Although there may be some justice in these judgments, we think that *Sergeant York* is interesting *because* of its skillful use of the narrative conventions; it is the treatment of narrative that allows its big issues to be played out and that makes this film biography relevant to its contemporary scene.[13]

The inhabitants of York's Tennessee valley are clearly representative of Americans of 1941, isolated from and belligerently ignorant about what is going on in the rest of the world. This is demonstrated in a key early scene in Preacher Rosier Pile's (Walter Brennan) general store. When Lem

(Howard Da Silva) gets his four-day-old Nashville newspaper and skips past the front page to the local news inside, the camera shows us the ignored headline, "Germans Smash at Verdun," accompanied by a low, ominous treatment of the "Marseillaise." Meanwhile, the various men take interest when a salesman (Frank Orth)—obviously an outsider, based on his snappy attire and cosmopolitan speech—tells Pile, "I'd like to sell you some of these garments before the price goes up on account of the war."

> ZEKE (Clem Bevans):   What war?
> DRUMMER (*surprised*):   Why, the . . . the war in Europe.
> ZEKE: Oh, that war.
> DRUMMER: Yes. Certainly. Looks like the Germans might get into Paris, don't you think?
> ZEKE: Well, we ain't done much thinkin' on it, mister. It ain't in our corner, nohow.

This independent and isolationist attitude is reinforced in the York home. Ma York's (Margaret Wycherly) prayer over the evening meal is "The Lord bless these vittles we done got, and help us to be beholden to nobody." Later, as Alvin rides off to be inducted into the army, his little sister (June Lockhart) asks Ma York, "Ma, what are they a-fightin' for?" Ma York replies, "I don't rightly know, child. I don't rightly know." This confusion about the war's causes and purposes, this sense of isolation and independence, and this hostility toward the idea of foreign entanglements all mirror attitudes in 1941 America toward the new war in Europe. The film establishes this context so as to explore the themes justifying why Americans should care about and eventually fight in Europe.

These themes are developed through the evolution of York from backwoods hell-raiser to pacifist to war hero, an evolution connected to his changing notions of authority. In the first part of the film Alvin has a deep attachment to limited sources of authority, all represented by the oral. As Alvin carouses with two cronies (Ward Bond and Noah Beery Jr.) in a seedy bar on the Tennessee-Kentucky border, he is recalled to home and duty by the voice of his little brother George (Dickie Moore): "Ma wants you, Alvin." Later, when Alvin is trying to earn the money to buy some rich bottomland so he can win a local beauty, Gracie Williams (Joan Leslie), he is persuaded by the authoritative echo of his own voice: when he cries "I cain't do it," the echo responds, "Do it!"; when he says of the money, "I cain't get the rest," the echo replies, "Get the rest!" Submitting to this seeming supernatural voice, Alvin returns to work.

Although devotion to these authorities demonstrates positive qualities in Alvin, the film also reveals their limitations. Alvin discovers that oral authority can be insignificant next to written authority. Having persuaded land dealer Nate Tompkins (Ervile Alderson) to give him a four-day extension on his deadline to buy the bottomland, Alvin wins a beef and turkey shoot, earning the balance of the money. But when he offers it to Tompkins, he learns that the land has just been sold to a rival for Gracie:

TOMPKINS: Your time was rightly up last Tuesday.
ALVIN: Why, you 'lowed I could have more time.
TOMPKINS: But it warn't in writing.
ALVIN: But I was a-takin' your word for it.

Although he has been treated unfairly, he lacks the written authority to support his case. Alvin learns the limitations of oral authorities in a more positive way when he finally gets religion. Earlier, Pastor Pile had told Alvin that faith can come "maybe slow, like the way daylight comes, and maybe in a flash, like a bolt of lightning." The latter is literally true in Alvin's case: knocked off his mule by a bolt of lightning so strong that it bursts his gun—the gun he was planning to use on Tompkins—Alvin rises up a changed man. He enters the nearby church, where he is brought into a larger social institution. His family is there, but dozens of others help lead him up the aisle, encourage him to kneel, and welcome him into their faith. Significantly, when Pastor Pile sees Alvin enter the church, he leads the congregation in "Give Me That Old-Time Religion," where the authority of the family—"It was good for your father"—is augmented by other, biblical authorities: the old-time religion is also good for Paul and Silas and the prophet Daniel and so should be good enough for me. The scene ends with Alvin accepting the authority of God as manifested through the authority of the patriarchs, tradition, and the Bible.

This last is especially interesting because it marks an almost immediate transformation of faith based in the experiential—faith from a bolt of lightning—to faith based in written narrative—the Bible. In a scene in which Alvin is teaching Sunday school, a young boy asks, "Alvin, how do you know that it happened just that-a-way, seeing how you warn't there?" Alvin replies, "The Book says so. And there ain't nothing written in the Book that ain't the truth." This faith in the Bible and the appellation "the

Book," as if it's the only book, suggest that the Bible is being set up as a master narrative, in Jean-François Lyotard's sense of a foundation myth that serves as a basis for knowledge and behavior in a culture. For Alvin, the Bible's knowledge is absolute and unchallengeable. When Pastor Pile tells him that he has to register for the draft, Alvin replies, "I ain't a-goin' to. I ain't a-goin' to war. War is killing, and the Book's agin killing. So war is agin the Book." Alvin rejects the draft board's assertion that the Bible is open to multiple readings and can be "interpreted by [the church's] members as they choose." In boot camp, when Captain Danforth (Harvey Stephens) tries to demonstrate this by challenging him with biblical verses that support fighting, Alvin easily reconciles the seeming contradictions and ends up with a message of peace. Alvin has completely submitted to the authority of this written narrative.

This explains Alvin's confusion when at boot camp Major Buxton (Stanley Ridges), trying to convince York to accept a promotion and lead men in battle, concedes the validity of the biblical master narrative but offers him another book and a second master narrative, a history of the United States. Indicating the history book, he explains,

> That's the story of a whole people's struggle for freedom. From the very beginning until now. For we're still struggling. It's quite a story, York. How we all got together and set up a government whereby all men were pledged to defend the rights of each man and each man to defend the rights of all men. We call it a government of the people, by the people, and for the people. . . .
>
> You're a religious man, York. . . . You want to worship God in your own way. . . . You're a farmer. . . . You want to plow your fields as you see fit and raise your family according to your own lights. And that's your heritage. And mine. Every American's. But the cost of that heritage is high. Sometimes it takes all we have to preserve it. Even our lives. How are you going to answer that, York?

Alvin, in awe of all he's heard, can only respond, "I never knowed it was all written down," once again submissive to written authority. The major gives Alvin a week's furlough to try to reconcile these two narratives. He returns home, with the U.S. history in one hand and the Bible in the other, and meditates. In his mind he hears the voices of Pastor Pile and Major Buxton representing the demands of the two master narratives: "Put your trust in the Book, Alvin"; "But here's another book, York, the history of the United

States"; "Obey your God"; "Defend your country." The conflict is temporarily resolved when the wind blows the Bible open to a page where Alvin
reads, "Render therefore unto Caesar the things which are Caesar's and
unto God the things that are God's." As revelation fills his face, the dawn
light floods the screen and the strains of "Give Me That Old-Time Religion" segue into "My Country 'Tis of Thee." Alvin returns to camp and
accepts the promotion.

Alvin balances but is unable to reconcile the demands of the two master narratives until the moment of his heroic action. In the aftermath he
explains it to now-Colonel Buxton:

BUXTON: That night that you reported back to me at Camp Gordon,
you as much as told me that you were quite prepared to die for
your country but not to kill. What made you decide to change
your mind? . . .

YORK: Well, I'm as much agin killin' as ever, sir. But it was this way,
Colonel. When I started out, I felt just like you said. But when I
hear them machine guns a-goin' and all them fellers a-droppin'
around me, I figured that them guns was killin' hundreds, maybe
thousands, and there weren't nothin' anybody could do but to
stop them guns. And that's what I done.

BUXTON: You mean to tell me that you did it to *save* lives?

YORK: Yes, sir. That was why.

York's reconciliation here has wider applications: it is an answer to the
angry isolationism of Zeke and the men in the general store; it is a justification of America's involvement in the First World War; and it makes a
case for American involvement in the new conflict. The case is based not
on any specifics of the European situation or American foreign policy;
rather, it is based on the ideals of the two master narratives. Like the Tennessee men, Americans might prefer to ignore foreign conflicts. Like York,
Americans might see war as going against fundamental beliefs. But, York's
story argues, Americans have an obligation to defend other people's right
to freedom from those who would take it away. Moreover, in defending
others' right to freedom, Americans are in effect helping to preserve their
own. Finally, in making war on those forces that threaten freedom, Americans are saving lives that would be lost without our support and, in the
long run, saving our own. This last point is emphasized when Alvin returns home to the share of the American Dream he has earned by his

heroic actions: a beautiful wife, his own land, his own home. The demands of God and country are thus met and reconciled in American involvement in the European war; in fact, American involvement is essentially a duty.

A year earlier, Warner Bros. had released *The Fighting 69th*, another film that displaced the new European conflict onto World War I. The film follows the famous New York 69th "Irish" Regiment (which becomes the 165th Infantry of the Rainbow Division) and its military and spiritual leaders, "Wild Bill" Donovan (George Brent) and Father Francis P. Duffy (Pat O'Brien), from boot camp to the battlefields of France. It focuses particularly on Pvt. Jerry Plunkett (James Cagney), a tough kid from Brooklyn who turns coward in the trenches, causing the deaths of several fellow soldiers. Sentenced to death, he finds his courage with the help of Father Duffy, returns to the pinned-down 69th, and becomes a hero by knocking out a machine gun nest and blowing a hole in some barbed wire so the regiment can advance. He also sacrifices himself, falling on a grenade to save his sergeant (Alan Hale). His progress—the cocky, independent, and selfish American who must learn to repress his individuality in the service of teamwork and higher ideals—will become a familiar trope in Hollywood's World War II films, as we will see in subsequent chapters.

The film waits until the end to make the connection between the Great War and the new war in Europe explicit. After American troops, including the surviving members of the 69th, are shown parading triumphantly through Paris, the film flashes into the future, showing the famous statue of Father Duffy near Times Square, thus bringing the film into its viewers' present. Then, as ghostly soldiers of the 69th march in the background, Father Duffy utters one more prayer: "Hear, I beseech You, the prayer of this, America's lost generation. They loved life too, O Lord. It was as sweet to them as to the living of today. They accepted privation, wounds, and death that an ideal might live. Don't let it be forgotten, Father. Amid turmoil and angry passions, when all worthwhile things seem swept away, let the tired eyes of a troubled world rise up and see the shining citadel of which these young lives formed the imperishable stones: America, a citadel of peace, peace forever more." The prayer hedges its bets by describing America as a "citadel of peace," seemingly supporting the anti-interventionist position. But the bulk of the prayer stresses the sacrifices made in World War I to keep American ideals alive and suggests that failure to act now when they are threatened again would be a betrayal of the young men who died two decades earlier. Interestingly, in all three of these World War I films—

British Intelligence, Sergeant York, and *The Fighting 69th*—the cynicism with which the war had been treated in films of the twenties and thirties has been replaced with new claims for its idealism. The new message about America's involvement in the war, a message that is also implicitly about the new war in Europe, is that it was fought by a peace-loving people *because* they love peace.

Three other prewar films—*Foreign Correspondent, Man Hunt,* and *The Great Dictator*—found more direct ways to consider the war in Europe and prepare Americans to think about it and their possible involvement in it. They do this in different ways, but they share one element: they were directed by European émigrés, men who began their careers in Europe and, for various reasons, had come to Hollywood and whose homelands were now under Nazi control or at war with Germany.

This is not to suggest that these émigré directors were necessarily strident anti-Nazis and, therefore, creating art out of political conviction. Although he directed three films with strong messages about the war effort (*Foreign Correspondent* [1940], *Saboteur* [1942], and *Lifeboat* [1944]), there is little evidence that Alfred Hitchcock felt strongly about the war. In discussing these films in his famous interviews with François Truffaut, he rarely mentions the war as a consideration; indeed, he dismisses the secret agreement in *Foreign Correspondent* that might prevent the war as his MacGuffin, "the gimmick." He says, "The only thing that really matters is that in the picture the plans, documents, or secrets must seem to be of vital importance to the characters. To me, the narrator, they're of no importance whatever."[14] The vision that informs *Foreign Correspondent's* subtext of encouraging America's involvement in the war in Europe apparently belonged to producer Walter Wanger, who, inspired by reporter Vincent Sheean's memoirs, had long wanted to make a film about a foreign correspondent in Europe. Having rejected several screenplays, he borrowed Hitchcock from David O. Selznick, the producer who had lured Hitchcock to America, and turned the project over to him.[15]

The film, released by United Artists on August 29, 1940, focuses on Johnny Jones (Joel McCrea), a crime reporter for a New York newspaper who is sent to Europe by his editor (Harry Davenport) to get the real story on whether there will be a war. He discovers that Dr. Van Meer (Albert Basserman), one of only two men who know the secret clause of a peace treaty, has been kidnapped, apparently by the Germans, and a double has been assassinated, so that the world will think he is dead. With the help of Carol Fisher (Laraine Day), daughter of Stephen Fisher (Herbert Marshall), the head of a peace organization, Jones escapes enemy agents and makes his way to London. There, a bodyguard (Edmund Gwenn) hired by Fisher attempts to kill him, and Jones realizes that Fisher is an enemy agent working to ignite the war. With British newsman Scott ffolliott (George Sanders), Jones rescues Van Meer; tracks down Fisher, who is escaping on the Atlantic Clipper; survives the plane being shot down; reconciles with Carol; and gets the story back to his editor—but the war begins anyway, and, under the pen name of Huntley Haverstock, he becomes a famous foreign correspondent.

The problem with this plot summary is that this isn't what one remembers from the film. Instead, one remembers images, powerful visual moments not particularly connected to the sequence of plot events: the assassination of Van Meer's double, with its *Battleship Potemkin* homage and the killer escaping under a crowd of umbrellas; the scene in the windmill, with Jones barely avoiding discovery as he uncovers the Van Meer conspiracy; the bodyguard playing cat and mouse with Jones on the cathedral tower and then falling to his death; the crash and sinking of the Atlantic Clipper, with the survivors clinging to a wing in raging seas. Similarly, the film's interesting messages about the war aren't found in its war-related plot, which, with its emphasis on the MacGuffinesque, serves Hitchcock's desire to craft a thriller, but in its images, its character relations, and its incidental moments. In these, important ideas about the war are presented in terms of heroes and villains.

The ideas about heroes are presented in the transformation of Jones and ffolliott. Johnny Jones begins as the typical American, his name drawn from a musical by George M. Cohan, *Little Johnny Jones*, whose eponymous character sings "I'm a Yankee Doodle Dandy." Unfortunately, he also exhibits the typical American's ignorance of world affairs. When his editor orders him to investigate the crisis in Europe, he responds, "What crisis?" His transformation begins when his editor changes his name to something more European, Huntley Haverstock. Indeed, much of the humor in the first third of the film comes from Jones's attempts to fit in while in Europe—his ridiculous pen name and the running gag of losing his very British bowler hat.

Jones's transformation takes place not on a superficial sartorial level but on emotional and intellectual levels. His guides and companions for this transformation are Carol and ffolliott. By falling in love with Carol, whose father is at the heart of the conspiracy he's investigating,[16] Jones becomes involved in the events; he is no longer able to observe and report on them as a good, objective newspaperman should. Whereas earlier he was willing to print his story even if it meant Van Meer's death, at the end of the film he says, "I came 4,000 miles to get a story, I get shot at like a duck in a shooting gallery, I get pushed off buildings, I get the story, and then I got to shut up," because he doesn't want to hurt Carol by exposing her father. His emotional attachment to Carol marks the loss of both his professional detachment and the geographic distance between America and the crisis on the Continent.

Jones's companion ffolliott functions very oddly but interestingly in the film. On the one hand, he provides an education for Jones; he's a source of information that gets Jones up to speed on the burgeoning war. But on the other hand, as he aids Jones's transformation, he becomes transformed himself. When we first meet him in Amsterdam, just after the Van Meer double has been shot, he seems well spoken, smug, unflappable, smarmily condescending, and vaguely threatening as a rival for Carol. But when he next appears on the scene in London, after the attempt on Jones's life, he's an eager investigative reporter, on Fisher's trail long before Jones was even suspicious and willing to work as Jones's sidekick. Before long, he has become something of a co-hero of the film. He follows Fisher to the hideout where Van Meer is being tortured, brazenly barges in on the interrogation, and, when Van Meer is about to reveal the secret clause, starts a fight, leaps from an upper-story window (in a wonderful trick shot we see his body, presumably a dummy, fall from the window and land on a canopy, which rips open so George Sanders can emerge), and immediately leads a rescue team back up the stairs. These are the kind of action stunts we expect from the lead, not the sidekick. For the rest of the film, Jones and ffolliott share hero duties. This is most clear in the plane-crash scene. Jones and ffolliott are equally responsible for getting Carol and her father safely out of the plane as it sinks, and when Fisher quietly slips out of his life belt and slides off the wing, to avoid the shame of arrest and to alleviate the overcrowding, both Jones and ffolliott dive into the stormy sea in a futile rescue attempt—ffolliott, in fact, returns to the wing after Jones and, in a moment of suspense, is almost lost in a wave.

This odd conflation of the conventional narrative functions of the two characters provides a way for American viewers to think about their connection to the war in Europe. From ffolliott and Carol, Jones gains an intellectual understanding of and emotional involvement in the war. Thanks to Jones, ffolliott has become an action hero. The film suggests a sort of Anglo-American alliance, a bringing together of the best of both nationalities in order to defeat the Germans.[17] The resulting synthesis at the end of the film is a new Huntley Haverstock; he is no longer a comic figure, as headlines from the early days of the war assure us by blaring his byline. The last scene shows this new Huntley Haverstock giving a radio address from London to America. As he begins reading, the air-raid sirens sound, the lights are turned out, and the noise of bombs comes closer and closer. Still, with Carol at his side, he improvises his speech:

> All that noise you hear isn't static—it's death coming to London. Yes, they're coming here now. You can hear the bombs falling on the streets and the homes. Don't tune me out. Hang on a while. This is a big story and you're part of it.
>
> It's too late to do anything here now except stand in the dark and let them come. As if the lights were all out everywhere. Except in America. Keep those lights burning. Cover them with steel. Ring them with guns. Build a canopy of battleships and bombing planes around them. Hello, America. Hang on to your lights. They're the only lights left in the world.

To emphasize the point, the lights fade on Haverstock and Carol until, by the end of the speech, they are in the dark. Part of the speech's power comes from the imagery of light and darkness, recalling Edward, Viscount Grey's remark on the eve of World War I, "The lamps are going out all over Europe; we shall not see them lit again in our lifetime." This allusion suggests another European crisis that America (from its point of view) idealistically had to put right. Here, it works in Huntley Haverstock's implied plea to Americans to undergo the same transformation he has.[18]

The presentation of the villains in the film similarly underscores the need for Americans to become involved in the war. At first glance the villains seem too vaguely presented to be connected with any very specific critique of Nazi Germany. The men who kidnap Van Meer and threaten Jones are never specifically called Germans, although they seem to be speaking German in the windmill scene. The first mention of Germany occurs after war is declared, when a German ship fires on the Atlantic Clipper. Rather, the grim-looking men with sharp features who are working to start the war seem to be operating in a generic tradition of bad guys: they could be Germans; they could be gangsters; in a few years they could be Soviets. Their evil is communicated by the conventions of their presentation, not by any specific critique of their cause or country.

This lack of specificity might be seen as a way to avoid criticizing a country with which the United States was not at war, but we think it works in another way. These villain types are most threatening because of their ubiquity—they're everywhere. One of them infiltrates the press corps to assassinate the Van Meer double. Two of them come to Jones's Amsterdam hotel room disguised as police. When Jones and Carol escape Amsterdam and return to what they assume to be the safety of London, their security is shattered when they find one of the conspirators (Eduardo Cianelli) at the breakfast table with Fisher. Even the bodyguard who should be protecting Jones is a source of danger. One wonders whether Jones can be safe anywhere.

This stripping away of Jones's—and the viewers'—sense of security is balanced and augmented by the presentation of Fisher. In a wonderful performance by Herbert Marshall, this man at the center of a bloody conspiracy is the most human person in the film. Before we learn of his duplicity, he is established as cultured, witty, and polite. But even after we know who he really is, he remains surprisingly sympathetic. His clearly uncomfortable reactions when witnessing the torture of Van Meer contrast with the sadism of the other villains. He obviously dislikes many aspects of his job, and he has a difficult time reconciling his mission with his love for his daughter. When he sends Jones off with his bodyguard to what he thinks is certain death, he returns to find Carol crying. She says, "Nothing must happen to him, Father." In a flash he realizes that she is in love with Jones and knows how she'll be hurt by his death. He turns as if to stop Jones and then realizes that he must let him go, the conflict between loving father and espionage agent written on his face. Later, on the Atlantic Clipper, his confession to Carol and his plea for her understanding make her and the viewer feel sorry for him; he's a man who has made a mistake and regrets the hurt he has caused his family. Who can't sympathize with that? But this sympathy is tempered by Fisher's self-consciousness about his mission. In trying to convince Jones to take on the bodyguard, Fisher speaks of how dangerous the conspirators are; Jones doesn't notice that he's also talking about himself: "These people are criminals more dangerous than your rum-runners and house-breakers. They're fanatics. They combine a mad love of country with an equally mad indifference to life, their own as well as others'. They're cunning, unscrupulous—and inspired." Fisher, who resembles the kind of people we know, who could be someone we admire, turns out to be one of these dangerous fanatics.

That message reminds us of many of the espionage films discussed earlier. The danger connected with the European conflict is not something Americans can dismiss because we are so far away from it. We can be threatened in our country, in our homes, in the places we feel most secure. Enemies can be anywhere around us, even among the people we most admire and count on to protect us. Enemies don't have to look like movie villains; they can be soft-spoken and love their children. In short, the presentation of the villains here works with the transformation of the hero in order to reduce the geographic, intellectual, and emotional distances between Americans and the war in Europe. The film seeks to cultivate both a healthy sense of paranoia and the kind of Anglo-American cooperation needed to defeat a common threat.

Unlike Hitchcock, Fritz Lang was virulently anti-Nazi after he came to Hollywood. As biographer Patrick McGilligan points out, it's unclear to what extent his political passions were sincere and to what extent calculated. Depending on who was telling the story, in Germany, Lang may have been apolitical or he may have cozied up to the Nazis; he may have emigrated because he was being pressured by Goebbels to head the Nazi film industry or because he was denied the job; he may have left in early 1933 or summer 1933. After arriving in Hollywood, Lang grew increasingly left-leaning and outspoken against Nazi Germany.[19] Regardless of whether his views stemmed from public-relations savvy or moral and political principles, he leaped at the chance to replace John Ford as the director of a film version of the 1939 novel *Rogue Male*, by Geoffrey Household.

Man Hunt, released on June 13, 1941, begins with Capt. Alan Thorndike (Walter Pidgeon), renowned British big-game hunter, creeping through the woods, preparing his rifle at the edge of a cliff, setting his sights, and carefully aiming at Hitler, standing on a balcony far below him. He pulls the trigger, but nothing happens; the rifle isn't loaded. Thorndike smiles, salutes the oblivious Hitler, but then has second thoughts. He puts a bullet in the chamber, aims again, but is captured by a soldier before he can fire. Under interrogation by Gestapo officer Quive-Smith (George Sanders), Thorndike explains that he was engaged in a "sporting stalk": bagging animals is no longer a challenge to him, so he decided to see whether he could get close enough to take a shot at the most guarded man alive, but with no intention of killing him. Even after torture, Thorndike refuses Quive-Smith's offer of freedom in exchange for a confession that he had intended to kill the Führer, under orders from the British government. The Germans throw him off a cliff, planning to find his body the next day and report the death as an accident. To their surprise, the next morning

Thorndike is alive and on the run, his fall apparently having been broken when his backpack caught on a tree limb. At this point, he becomes the hunted. He manages to return to England, but Quive-Smith and his agents track him down. With the help of Jerry, a Cockney prostitute (Joan Bennett), he avoids them, and after learning that he's become the center of an international incident, he disappears, heading for Lyme Regis, where he lives in a cave.[20]

Man Hunt asks its viewers to think about the war in Europe in some of the same ways as *Foreign Correspondent* and then goes beyond them. Like *Foreign Correspondent, Man Hunt* presents the villains—in this case, specifically presented as Nazis—as ubiquitous. As he prepares to leave the ship he has stowed away on to get back to England, Thorndike dismisses the cabin boy's (Roddy McDowall) warnings that he be careful, saying, "Stop worrying, my boy. This is England! I'm home again." But he is barely off the ship when he realizes that he is being followed by threatening men; there's no safety at home. Interestingly, the Nazi agents represent a cross section of British society: a wharf rat, a lower-middle-class pub patron, a white-collar executive type, and a representative of the landed aristocracy (Quive-Smith himself). When Jerry tries to escape from these men, she turns to her local bobby, but he too turns out to be a Nazi. Here again, a figure who should offer protection from danger becomes the source of danger.

The paranoia engendered here connects to one of the film's continuing themes: the problem of whom to trust. When Thorndike thanks the cabin boy for saving his life, he boils it down to one act of faith: "You've taken me on trust." His relationship with Jerry begins by him convincing her to take that same leap of faith. Later, he tells her, "From now on, I'll distrust everybody but you." When Quive-Smith tracks him to his cave, blocks the entrance, and demands that he sign a confession, his survival depends on what extent he can trust the Nazi: Has he killed Jerry, as he says? Have the Germans invaded Poland, as he claims? Does he really have his pistol in his holster? "You'll have to take my word as a fellow hunter," Quive-Smith says as he prepares his weapon.

This issue of trust is interwoven with the film's continuing concern with game playing. People can't play games if they can't trust their opponents to follow the rules. This concern is established in the first interrogation scene. In arguing about the nature of a sporting stalk, Thorndike and Quive-Smith establish their different thinking about games and rules, and their attitudes are explicitly connected to their nationalities:

THORNDIKE: The sport is in the chase, not the kill. I don't kill any longer, not even small game. I know what I can do with a rifle. If I can stalk an animal and get within range, the rest is a mathematical certainty, and that's sheer cruelty, and I don't like cruelty. The real fun is matching my wits against the instinct of an animal that isn't going to let me get near enough to shoot.

QUIVE-SMITH: Your conversation fascinates me, Thorndike. But this softness in your nature with regard to the ultimate purpose of firearms betrays the weakness, the decadence, not only of yourself but of your entire race. Yes, you're symbolic of the English race.

THORNDIKE: I'm beginning to think that you're symbolic of yours.

As their conversation continues, Quive-Smith asks Thorndike why, if he didn't intend to kill Hitler, he brought his rifle. Thorndike hesitates, then replies,

THORNDIKE: I've asked myself that. And I think the answer is that . . . that it wouldn't have been sporting. It wouldn't have been playing the game.

QUIVE-SMITH: Nothing betrays the hypocrisy of the English more than their use of that phrase "playing the game." One plays a game to win, Thorndike!

THORNDIKE: Nonsense. I don't expect *you* to understand. Even pulling a trigger on an empty gun was a kind of cheating with myself. It didn't prove anything. I did, you know.

QUIVE-SMITH: Oh, naturally.

THORNDIKE: It had to be a loaded rifle with my finger on the trigger, with only my individual will, my civilized conscience between me and the extermination of your strutting little Caesar.

This long exchange establishes two of the film's interconnected conflicts: playing by the rules versus winning by any means; and civilization versus barbarism. Thus, in Churchillian fashion, as we saw in the introduction, the film associates barbarism, chaos, and anarchy with Nazi Germany and civilization, order, and rules with not just England but all those who value them and who would feel threatened by their loss.

Trapped in his cave, dirty, angry, screaming at Quive-Smith, Thorndike seems far fallen from his position as the representative of civilization. But rather than marking a breakdown of Thorndike's notion of civilization or, as Reynold Humphries suggests, a deconstruction of the opposition between Thorndike and Quive-Smith,[21] this scene marks the final stage in the transformation of Thorndike. In the first interrogation scene he clearly has little respect for Hitler but also has little committed opposition. When Quive-Smith reproves him for calling the Führer a "strutting little Caesar," he replies, "I mean no insult [!], but how do you expect me to describe a man who wants to play God and have everyone else in the world run around and say 'Heil Hitler!'" This is precisely his attitude at this point: he dislikes Hitler but doesn't take him seriously. After his escape from Quive-Smith, however, he learns why Hitler and the Nazis need to be taken seriously. He finds his world turned topsy-turvy because of them. The rules of the game and the social order they represent are suddenly thrown into chaos. Most immediately, Thorndike, the great hunter, becomes the hunted beast. He must learn to think not like the predator but like the prey. Connected to this is the film's play on the word *game*: Thorndike, once concerned with how the game is played, becomes, in Quive-Smith's win-by-any-means world, the game that is the object of the Nazis' hunt. As we have seen, the rules about one being safe at home do not apply; Thorndike is hunted in England as he was in Germany. And in the most confusing inversion of order, Thorndike loses his identity: one of Quive-Smith's men (John Carradine) is traveling with Thorndike's passport, and when Thorndike kills him in a fight in the Underground, he becomes hunted by the police as a suspect in his own apparent murder.

However, this breakdown of rules and order does not cause Thorndike to lose faith in the civilization that order makes possible. We see this in his relationship with Jerry. Although Jerry is clearly in love with him (she is obviously disappointed when Thorndike gallantly sleeps on the couch in her apartment), he is oblivious to the possibility of a sexual relationship between them. He constantly calls her by diminutives, as if she were a child; in fact, he treats her in much the same way he treated the cabin boy. His fury when Quive-Smith tells him of her death is caused not by any romantic love for her but by his sense that her childlike nature has been ruined. He shouts, "She was innocent, innocent!" Thorndike treats Jerry according to the social codes connected with the British class structure. He is certainly polite to her, but he does not think of her as an equal. Jerry and the viewer may hope for a romance between them, but Thorndike doesn't even seem to be aware of the possibility.

Quive-Smith's gloating over Jerry's death ("Do you expect me to lie to you, Thorndike? Do you expect me to tell you it was a sporting stalk?"), rather than breaking down his commitment to rules, order, and civilization, brings home to Thorndike the threat that the Nazis pose to these things he values. Whereas before he intellectually disapproved of Hitler, he now has the knowledge and the emotional urgency to kill him. He raves at Quive-Smith's suggestion that the Führer would have been an innocent victim: "No, he's guilty, guilty against me and against humanity, against every decent, peaceful person in the world. He's guilty of hatred, intolerance, and murder. . . . Yes, yes, I intended to shoot. I didn't know what I was doing. I didn't realize my purpose. I wouldn't face the fact that I could make myself the instrument of all the pitiable, oppressed, suffering people in the world. I wondered why I put that shell in my gun. Now I know. Yes, I intended to kill. I intended to avenge the crimes of this monstrous tyrant. I know it now." This speech marks the transformation of Thorndike into a man who understands why Nazism must be destroyed and who is willing to act on that understanding. Like *Foreign Correspondent, Man Hunt* goes beyond being a film that encourages sympathy for the British as victims of Nazi aggression. It asks its viewers to think of Nazi Germany's enemy as being not a country but a way of life, a way of conceiving an ordered and meaningful existence in the world.

While Alfred Hitchcock may have been fairly indifferent to the war and Fritz Lang ambiguous in his politics, without question, British émigré Charles Chaplin was ferociously anti-Nazi. Biographer Charles J. Maland explains how Chaplin's rather unformed political beliefs—a general sympathy for the little guy subject to abusive power—developed during the late thirties and early forties into the more specific antifascist beliefs that would motivate his making of *The Great Dictator* and the pro-Soviet positions that would eventually lead to his exile from the United States. Maland reports that Chaplin "was influenced by the antifascist atmosphere of the 1936–1939 era" and that he attended meetings of the Hollywood Anti-Fascist League and the Committee to Defend America by Aiding the Allies. This growing political awareness was combined with the desire to make an important statement in what would be his first all-talking picture.[22] Chaplin was in a position to make this statement as explicit as he liked. Unlike Hitchcock and Lang, who had to work within the collaborative confines of the studio system, Chaplin, as part owner of United Artists, was able to produce, direct, write, and star in his own films. The result was *The Great Dictator*, an innovative and in some ways unique attack on Hitler and the Third Reich.

The Great Dictator, released on October 16, 1940, has two only slightly overlapping plots. The first focuses on the pretensions, cruelty, and insecurities of Adenoid Hynkel (Chaplin), der Phooey of Tomania, and his plans to invade neighboring Osterlich. He temporarily suspends his persecution of the nation's Jews as he attempts unsuccessfully to persuade a Jewish banker to finance the invasion. Then he must negotiate with visiting Benzini Napaloni (Jack Oakie), dictator of Bacteria, who is also massing troops on Osterlich's border. After a battle of egos, Napaloni agrees to withdraw his armies, setting the stage for a Tomanian invasion of Osterlich. The second plot focuses on a Jewish barber (also Chaplin), who, suffering from amnesia caused by a World War I injury, leaves the hospital in 1938 with no knowledge of the changes Hynkel's reign has brought to Tomania. He returns to his shop in the ghetto and immediately has a run-in with storm troopers. During the period of relative peace caused by Hynkel's banking negotiations, the barber flourishes and becomes special friends with Hannah (Paulette Goddard), an orphan living with neighbors. But after the financing is refused, storm troopers attack the ghetto, burning the shop and eventually arresting the barber and sending him to a concentration camp. By coincidence, the barber escapes in a stolen uniform on the day Tomania invades Osterlich. Soldiers searching for him come across the informally dressed Hynkel out duck hunting, mistake him for the barber, and drag him off. The barber, meanwhile, is mistaken for Hynkel. Asked to give an address celebrating the victorious invasion, he makes an impassioned plea for the end of fascism.

As with *Foreign Correspondent*, the plot isn't what one remembers about *The Great Dictator*; the plot is an excuse to expose the foibles of the Hitler-like character and to demonstrate the awful effects of fascism on common people. Thus, one remembers Hynkel's gibberish speech, in which Chaplin captures and parodies Hitler's speaking style and physical movements; his ballet with an inflated globe as he dreams of world conquest; Hynkel and Napaloni rising to the ceiling in barber chairs as each tries to one-up the other; and the final speech. More than the plot, the structure and arrangement of the images communicate the film's ideas about Hitler and fascism.

The primary weapon in the film's attack is humor, one source of which is Chaplin's parody of Hitler. The film misses no opportunity to undercut Hynkel and expose him as pretentious, temperamental, vain, stupid, and weak; in short, it presents him as the quintessential bully. In his opening speech to the Sons and Daughters of the Double Cross, Hynkel speaks with apparent angry sincerity, but the speech is in gibberish, with only occasional phrases understandable ("Democracy shtunk!"). Der Phooey's speech is vacuous and blustering, violent but with no intelligible or intelligent content. The persona of the powerful man is undercut by Hynkel's question to aide Garbitsch (Henry Daniell) as soon as they're alone: "How was I?" The blustering hides his insecurity. In his palace, although the voice-over tells us that Hynkel is a man of "ceaseless activity," we see action with no purpose: posing for artists ten seconds at a time, preening in front of mirrors built into his file cabinets, dictating letters he then tears up, indulging in a brief amorous embrace with a secretary before being called away to approve of another invention that doesn't work. In his dance with the globe we see both the enormous ego that seeks to control the world and the childish man who pouts and cries when his balloon bursts. The technique that Chaplin establishes here—bringing the most dangerous man in the world down to earth by making him laughable—was taken up by many other films when the United States finally entered the war: *To Be or Not to Be* (1942), *Hitler—Dead or Alive* (1943), *That Nazty Nuisance*

The Great Dictator: Adenoid Hynkel (Charles Chaplin) engages in a brief amorous moment with a secretary (Florence Wright).

(1943), some Three Stooges shorts, and innumerable Warner Bros. and Disney cartoons.

In the ghetto scenes the humor works in two ways. The first occurs early in the film, when the barber returns home with no knowledge of Hynkel and the persecution of the Jews. This mild-mannered, sane man from a normal world is suddenly dropped into the cruel, insane, nightmare world of Nazi Germany. A storm trooper paints the word *Jew* across the barbershop windows, and the barber, naturally, begins to clean it off. When the storm trooper returns and tells him to stop cleaning, he replies with a laugh, "Don't be silly." The storm trooper chases him, and the barber confidently goes up to another storm trooper, saying, "Are you a policeman? Arrest that man for assault!" Instead, the barber is grabbed. The humor here comes from the barber's sanity exposing the insanity of the world he has entered.

The second technique at work in the ghetto scenes is a curious tension between the comic and the serious. When the barber is fighting with the storm troopers outside his shop, Hannah helps him by leaning out a window and hitting them on the head with a large frying pan. Eventually, she inadvertently hits the barber. Stunned, he staggers up and down the street to the music of a German folk song. This sort of scene is familiar from silent comedies, but unexpectedly, as Claudia Clausius has pointed out, in following the barber up and down the block, the camera reveals the word *Jew* scrawled on every shop and building.[23] The comedy is tempered by the ubiquity of the storm troopers' anti-Semitism. A short while later, after the storm troopers have captured the confused barber, they try to hang him from a lamppost. They put the noose around his neck and raise him off the ground; he squirms, trying to relieve the pressure on his windpipe. But just as the viewer is wondering what kind of comedy shows a lynching, a passing officer, Schultz (Reginald Gardiner), demands to know what is going on. The storm troopers immediately come to attention, letting go of the rope, and after the briefest of pauses, the barber plummets to the sidewalk. Slapstick breaks the tension of the scene. Similarly, whenever the storm troopers enter the ghetto, the Jewish residents react with fear, but the viewer is likely to laugh because of the silly song they sing—"We're the Aryans, the Ary- Ary- Ary- Ary- Aryans!"—making them sound like frat boys. When the storm troopers come searching for the barber and Schultz, who has joined the opposition, Schultz can't hide before gathering all his luggage, including his golf clubs. The golf clubs inject humor into an otherwise desperate situation. This tension between the comic and the serious is present in much of the film, with the result that the comedy serves to parody and make ridiculous the ideology and actions of the Nazis, and the serious moments and undertones keep the film's ideas connected to real things happening in the real world.

The film employs a similar tension between different scenes to help communicate its themes. Although there is little interaction between the Hynkel plot and the ghetto plot, scenes in each seem carefully balanced to reveal important contrasts. The most obvious of these, as Eric L. Flom points out, is Hynkel's ballet with the globe and the scene immediately following it—the barber shaving a customer to the music of Brahms's Hungarian Dance no. 5.[24] The monomaniacal desire to control the world is contrasted with the mundane pleasures of working at one's trade. Later, the scene in which the barber and Hannah watch from the roof while the storm troopers set off a firebomb in the barber's shop is followed by a scene in which the ghetto residents reject Schultz's plan for a suicide bombing of the palace to assassinate Hynkel. The Jews pointedly refuse to use the same methods of violence that are used against them. After the barber's arrest, we see Hannah and her guardians leave Tomania and happily arrive in Osterlich, where they will be safe and free. But this scene is followed by the sequence in which Hynkel and Napaloni compete to see which of them will invade and dominate Osterlich. The film's structure repeatedly condemns Hynkel and the storm troopers by balancing their actions with scenes showing common people taking pleasure in everyday life.

This contrast supports two of the film's other concerns. The first is the unique emphasis on the Nazis' persecution of the Jews. In other Hollywood films, both before and after U.S. entry into the war, the Nazis are shown persecuting people, but rarely are the Jews singled out as the focus of this persecution. Typical is *This Land Is Mine* (1943), a film about the Nazi occupation of a presumably French town, in which one Jewish man is included in the group of intellectuals and resisters who are rounded up and executed. In films contemporaneous with *The Great Dictator*, Nazi persecution of the Jews is handled very delicately. In both *The Mortal Storm* (1940), about the destruction of a Jewish chemist and his family just after Hitler becomes chancellor, and *So Ends Our Night* (1941), about the hardships of Jewish refugees without passports, the word *Jew* is rarely uttered; instead, these characters are euphemistically referred to as *non-Aryan*. Perhaps the studios were being sensitive to Senator Nye's charges that their films were serving a Jewish agenda. *The Great Dictator*, however, offers a startling contrast. Near the end of the gibberish speech, Hynkel begins speaking of "der Juden," snorting, becoming even angrier, and shouting so viciously that one of his microphones bends backward, trying to escape his rhetoric. As the crowd cheers, the translating voice-over mildly explains that der Phooey "has just referred to the Jewish people." Later in the film, in a scene that is especially disturbing from our postwar point of view, Hynkel threatens to wipe out all brunettes, but Garbitsch reminds him to destroy the Jews first, then the brunettes: "We'll kill off the Jews, wipe out the brunettes, then will come forth our dream of a pure Aryan race."

A second thematic concern is the nature of being human. Hynkel and his regime are associated with a near worship of technology at the expense of the human. The critique of technology is established at the beginning of the film, in the World War I prologue. We see the Tomanian army about to introduce its new superweapon, the Big Bertha cannon, which can fire a shell 100 miles; its first target is the Cathedral of Notre Dame in Paris. But this image of technology used in the service of destruction—specifically, the destruction of the spiritual—is immediately augmented by the technology's failure to work properly. The first shell goes a short distance and destroys an outhouse. The second falls even shorter. The barber, being the lowest-ranking soldier there, is ordered to investigate. He approaches the shell cautiously, but it seems to sense him, spinning to point at him wherever he goes; he barely escapes before it explodes. The message seems clear: nations seek to use technology to increase their capacity to destroy, but that technology is far from perfect and threatens to turn on those who use it; more specifically, it threatens not the nation's leaders—the ones who order its creation and use—but its common people.

The film establishes over and over Hynkel's reliance on technology to maintain and extend his power and the failure of that technology. We see the testing of new inventions—a bulletproof suit, whose inventor Hynkel shoots dead, and a parachute in a hat, whose inventor leaps to his death. "Why do you waste my time like this?" Hynkel moans. When Hynkel tries to impress Napaloni with the size and extent of his military, the Bacterian dictator tops him with descriptions of his country's flying-submersible tanks, to which air force commander Herring (Billy Gilbert) responds, "Those are obsolete now." At another point the double-edged dangers of technology are revealed when Herring, without a trace of irony, announces, "We've just discovered the most wonderful, the most marvelous poison gas. It will kill *everybody*!"

Inseparable from this reliance on technology to provide power and control is, as the previous examples imply, the devaluing of human life.

Indeed, Hynkel values human beings precisely to the extent that they can be used as machines. This is seen not only in the shots of his soldiers marching, goose-stepping in rows like a huge, complex machine, but also in Hynkel's office, where one aide's job is to stick out his tongue to lick der Phooey's envelopes and where all the secretaries look and dress the same, as if they were interchangeable parts. It isn't going too far to say that Hynkel despises life: while waiting in a boat for the invasion of Osterlich, he grabs his rifle with glee and savagely hisses "Ducks!" as a flock passes overhead; when Napaloni wonders how Hynkel feeds the goldfish in his clear glass walls, he replies, "You can't. They're all dead!"

All the film's themes are brought together in the final speech, which the barber disguised as Hynkel delivers to a worldwide radio audience. This speech has inspired wide-ranging reactions among viewers, reviewers, and scholars, both then and now.[25] More than three minutes long and delivered by Chaplin directly into the camera, the speech does not tie up the film's narrative—there are many unanswered questions: Will Hynkel get out of the concentration camp? Will the barber and Schultz escape? Will the barber and Hannah be reunited? But it is the film's thematic resolution, its most blatant indictment of fascism. It is prepared for and balanced by Hynkel's early gibberish speech, full of passion and unintelligible, and by a midfilm address to the camera in which Hannah hopefully wonders whether the storm troopers will leave the ghetto dwellers alone. Coming at the end of the film, the barber's speech contains the sense that Hynkel's lacked and makes a case for the kind of world Hannah wished for.

The immediate inspiration for the barber's speech are the comments Garbitsch makes when introducing Hynkel. His comments sum up the film's idea of fascism: "Today, democracy, liberty, and equality are words to fool the people. No nation can progress with such ideas. They stand in the way of action. Therefore we frankly abolish them. In the future each man will serve the interests of the state with absolute obedience. Let him who refuses beware. The rights of citizenship will be taken away from all Jews and other non-Aryans. They are inferior and therefore enemies of the state. It is the duty of all true Aryans to hate and despise them."

The barber's response is the film's response to fascism. He begins with what seems to him to be the obvious—people are naturally made to be happy: "We all want to help one another. Human beings are like that. We want to live by each other's happiness—not by each other's misery. We don't want to hate and despise one another. In this world there is room for everyone. And the good earth is rich and can provide for everyone." This natural state of human relations is perverted by greed and the uses to which greed puts technology: "The way of life can be free and beautiful, but we have lost the way. Greed has poisoned men's souls—has barricaded the world with hate—has goose-stepped us into misery and bloodshed. We have developed speed, but we have shut ourselves in. Machinery that gives abundance has left us in want. Our knowledge has made us cynical; our cleverness, hard and unkind. We think too much and feel too little. More than machinery, we need humanity. More than cleverness, we need kindness and gentleness. Without these qualities, life will be violent and all will be lost." His message to the Tomanian soldiers in front of him and to people everywhere over the radio is to resist the efforts of the dictators who would make them less than human:

> Soldiers! Don't give yourselves to brutes—men who despise you—en-slave you—who regiment your lives—tell you what to do—what to think and what to feel! Who drill you—diet you—treat you like cattle—use you as cannon fodder. Don't give yourselves to these unnatural men—machine men with machine minds and machine hearts! . . . You, the people, have the power. The power to create machines. The power to create happiness! You, the people, have the power to make this life free and beautiful—to make this life a wonderful adventure. Then—in the name of democracy—let us use that power, let us all unite.

The barber says here what the film has been showing us all along: be human; treat others as humans; don't let others treat you as less than hu-man; use technology to enhance life, not destroy it.

Critics have argued over what *The Great Dictator* proposes should be done about Hitler. Maland sees the film as arguing that the oppressed must stand up to the bully, such as when Hannah, after decking storm troopers with her frying pan, says, "We can't fight alone, but we can lick 'em together." Joyce Milton finds a case for neutrality, such as when the ghetto dwellers reject the bomb plot, saying, "Our place is at home look-ing after our own affairs." And in the final speech the barber's address to the soldiers seems to argue for pacifism. This confusion is apparently the point. Julian Smith argues that "the film is devoted to the struggles of the people of the ghetto to find the right response to madness." In fact, the film demonstrates that each of these responses is inadequate for deal-ing with fascism. Rather than answering the question of what to do, the film points out the complexity of the problem and the advantages and disadvantages of the possible answers. In this sense it is more ambiguous and more challenging than the other pre–Pearl Harbor films we have looked at. But it is unambiguous in its depiction of fascism. More than any other prewar Hollywood film, *The Great Dictator* made a persuasive case for the pervasive, threatening evil of fascism.[26]

Taken as a group, then, these prewar films had a cumulative effect in preparing Americans to think about and understand the coming war in certain ways. They prepared Americans to think about their responsibilities with regard to the rest of the world and about how fighting for Europe was really fighting for the United States. They prepared Americans to think about how the events in Europe could be a threat to us at home. They prepared Americans to think about why fascism is an evil that needs to be stamped out. That they succeeded in all this is evidenced by the way these same themes were quickly and easily adapted in Hollywood films made just after U.S. entry into the war.

2

THE WAR IN THE PACIFIC

You know, that's the worst part about war. You meet somebody. You get to know them. Wham! You never see them
again. You see something, but you never know how it ends. It
would be nice to know right now how all this is going to end,
wouldn't it?
      —Bindle Jackson (Paul Fix) in *Back to Bataan*

We like the element of surprise.
      —Yamato (Abner Biberman) in *Betrayal from the East*

HOLLYWOOD, LIKE THE REST OF AMERICA, was surprised by the
Japanese attack on Pearl Harbor. The studios, as we have seen, had been
preparing Americans to think about their potential involvement in the
war in Europe in various ways; the narratives and rhetoric supporting this
involvement had already become film conventions, easily recognized by
audiences and presumably influencing or at least interacting with their
ideas about Hitler, Germany, the European war, and America's part in it all.
Japan, however, was a different story. Even though Japan had been waging
a ruthless war against China since the summer of 1937, and even though
U.S. diplomatic relations with Japan had been strained for some time due
to competing interests in the Pacific, the Hollywood studios had not depicted the Japanese as a potential enemy—cruel invaders of a helpless
China, yes, but not a threat to America. Indeed, the pathos of the Chinese
seems to have been more the point than the cruelty of the Japanese. Two

films, *North of Shanghai* (1939), about newspaper reporters uncovering fifth columnists (strangely, all Anglo-Saxon) in Shanghai, and *International Settlement* (1938), about an American pilot mixed up in an arms-smuggling plot in Shanghai, talk about "fighting in the north" and depict attacks on Chinese cities, some by tanks with the Rising Sun on them, but they never name the Japanese as the attackers. So after December 1941, the studios, like the U.S. armed forces, had a great deal of ground to make up. They had to explain to the moviegoing public why Japan had attacked, why the United States had been unprepared, how it should respond, and, most important, why Japan had to be defeated, even at the cost of American soldiers dying to capture and hold Pacific islands whose names few people could even pronounce.

The first few months of the war in the Pacific were surprising, depressing, and confusing to the American public. The Japanese attacked an ill-prepared American fleet at Pearl Harbor on December 7, 1941, hoping to inflict enough damage so that the United States would be unable to interfere with their plans to seize the Philippines, Burma, Malaya, Thailand, Borneo, the Netherlands East Indies, and a number of islands in the central Pacific. At the time, the American losses were thought to be devastating: eight battleships and ten other ships sunk or damaged; 200 planes destroyed, mostly on the ground; 2,400 people killed and another 1,100 wounded.[1] Shortly after the attack on Pearl Harbor, the Japanese air force attacked Wake Island. The marines there beat back a December 12 invasion attempt but were finally overwhelmed by a reinforced Japanese fleet on December 23. In the early days of the Pacific war the British fared no better than the United States. By the end of December, Japanese forces had captured Hong Kong and were well on their way to capturing Malaya and Singapore, the East Indies (defended by British and Dutch troops), and Burma.

Amid the Japanese offensive, the story that the American public found most compelling—after the shock of Pearl Harbor had passed—was the doomed defense of the Philippines. The Japanese waited ten hours after the attack on Pearl Harbor before attacking the Philippines, time the American forces used poorly. Despite the warning, the initial Japanese air attacks caught and destroyed most of the U.S. air forces on the ground. Without air defense, army positions and facilities and navy ships were open to relentless air attack; the bulk of the navy was ordered to the defense of the Netherlands East Indies. Having established air and naval superiority and having successfully landed some troops on December 10, Japan launched its invasion of the Philippines on December 22 at Linguyen and Lamon

Bay. Earlier in the year, Douglas MacArthur, commander of U.S. and Philippine forces, had rejected a long-standing strategy for responding to an invasion of the Philippines: retreating to the Bataan peninsula, where supplies would be stockpiled, and holding the position until reinforcements could arrive from Hawaii. In an ill-advised move he substituted a plan to stop an invasion on the beaches. Although the combined U.S. and Filipino troops outnumbered the invading Japanese, they were undertrained, undersupplied, and unsupported from the air and sea. As a result, by December 24, MacArthur was forced to order a retreat to the Bataan peninsula, in effect returning to the original strategy, but without a stockpile of supplies.[2] The Allied forces were able to hold on far longer than the Japanese expected, but with Washington deciding against attempting a relief mission, the outcome was inevitable. On March 11, 1942, MacArthur was ordered to Australia to take up a new command. On April 9 Allied forces on Bataan surrendered; on May 6 Corregidor, the island fortress at the mouth of Manila Bay, followed suit. The remaining Allied forces in the Philippines, minus a few Americans and Filipinos who would fight as guerrillas for the duration of the occupation, surrendered by June 9. In the aftermath of the surrender on Bataan came the Bataan Death March: 78,000 U.S. and Filipino servicemen, many wounded, sick, and exhausted, were forced to march from Mariveles to San Fernando, some sixty-five miles; those who fell or couldn't keep up were beaten and killed by Japanese soldiers.

These combined events created the impression among the American people and even in the armed forces that the Japanese were unbeatable. However, a series of key events in 1942 would reverse this impression and the momentum of the Japanese offensive. On April 18, in a morale-boosting retaliation for Pearl Harbor, sixteen B-25 bombers commanded by Col. James Doolittle bombed Tokyo and several other Japanese cities. Between May 3 and May 8, Japanese and U.S. naval forces fought the Battle of the Coral Sea, the first naval engagement in which the opposing ships never sighted or fired on each other; attacks on each side's ships were carried out by planes. Although the results of the battle slightly favored the Japanese, for the first time since the war began, the United States was able to prevent the Japanese from accomplishing a main objective—the capture of Port Moresby in New Guinea. A month later, the Battle of Midway turned the tide of the war in the Pacific. The Japanese fleet, under the command of Adm. Isoroku Yamamoto—architect of the attack on Pearl Harbor—hoped that an attack on Midway Island would draw the American fleet into a battle that it would certainly lose. That would pave the way for an attack on Hawaii and, presumably, a negotiated peace favorable to Japan. But Yamamoto made several mistakes: he split his naval force between Midway and an invasion of the Aleutian Islands, his information about the strength and position of the U.S. forces awaiting him was wrong, and he didn't know that the Americans had broken the Japanese codes and thus knew of his plans. The result was four Japanese aircraft carriers sunk, with the loss of only one American carrier. America's production of ships and planes increased throughout the war years, and Japan was never able to recover from the loss of these carriers, some 300 planes, and thousands of experienced pilots and sailors.[3] After June 7, 1942, the Japanese were fighting a defensive war.

The American offensive began in August 1942. On August 17–18 Lt. Col. Evans Carlson led his Raider Battalion of marines, trained in the style of the Communist Chinese guerrillas, in an attack on Makin Island in the Gilbert Islands. This strike-and-withdraw action caused considerable damage to the Japanese forces there and, more important, provided a diversion for the landing of the marines on Guadalcanal. This bloody Guadalcanal campaign lasted from August 1942 until early February 1943 as the United States and Japan struggled on the island and on the sea. When the Japanese finally withdrew, each side had lost thousands of men and dozens of ships. Historian Gerhard L. Weinberg sums up the results of this first step in the island-hopping that would push the Japanese forces back toward their home:

> The Americans learned here . . . that the Japanese were hard fighters but not invincible. When the odds were reasonable, and the leadership competent, the Allies could hold and defeat the seemingly invincible Imperial army and navy. But obviously only at great cost. It would be a very long and a very tough fight. As for the Japanese, they had seen that their basic strategy of defending the perimeter of their newly won empire was evidently not working the way they had planned. The assumption had been that the Americans would be unwilling to pay the price in blood and treasure to retake islands of which they had never heard, to be returned to allies for whose colonial empires they had only disdain. Here was proof that they would; and, in the face of this, the leaders in Tokyo displayed a bankruptcy of strategic thinking.[4]

Hollywood films combined with other pop-cultural media to create a mind-set that enabled Americans to accept their sons and husbands risking their lives in these foreign places and thus do what was necessary to defeat Japan. Interestingly, once the United States entered the war, far more Hollywood films focused on historical events—actual places, battles, and campaigns—in the Pacific theater than in the European theater. This may be partly explained, as we suggested earlier, by the fact that the studios had already prepared the United States for war in Europe but hadn't touched on the Pacific as a possible place of conflict. But it goes further than that. Historical overviews like the one we narrated here—a series of events linked coherently by principles of cause and effect—are common knowledge today. But in 1942 Americans were smack in the middle of these events and naturally lacked the historical distance to appreciate their structure and sense. Moreover, in 1942 relatively little of this information was known to the general public. As we saw in the introduction, newspapers of the time offered general, big-picture reports of theaters and campaigns and more specific, up-close-and-personal reports on combatants in the field, but not the narrative links that would make a coherent story of it all. To complicate the narrative situation even more, although Americans knew about the attack on Pearl Harbor, the loss of Wake Island, and the fall of the Philippines, they weren't told all the details about these events; in fact, because of secrecy or the potential loss of morale or even military behind-covering, some information about these early defeats remained undisclosed until later in the war or well after it was over. For example, the story of the Bataan Death March, though known to the army and the federal government from reports of escaped prisoners, wasn't made public until January 1944.[5] Even the details of U.S. victories were frequently kept from the American public.

An excellent example of this is the United States' first blow against the Japanese empire: the April 1942 Doolittle raid. The raid was part of President Roosevelt's plan to boost American morale by striking Japan directly. The problem was how to launch bombers toward their targets without bringing America's precious aircraft carriers within range of Japan's air force. The solution was to train pilots flying land-based B-25s to take off from the deck of a carrier. Once airborne, these long-range bombers would be able to fly to Japan, hit their targets, and fly on to safety with the Chinese forces in Chungking. Unfortunately, not everything worked out as planned. The sixteen B-25s had to take off some 400 miles farther away than expected because the carrier *Hornet* and its escort were spotted by Japanese picket boats well within the Japanese defensive perimeter. Thus, instead of attacking at night, Doolittle and his men arrived at their targets around noon. Luckily, a general feeling of disbelief kept Japanese antiair-craft batteries from responding in a timely or efficient way, and the bomb-ers hit targets in Tokyo, Yokohama, Kobe, Osaka, and Nagoya. A more significant problem was that the bombers no longer had enough fuel to reach their Chinese landing fields; in addition, bad weather over the Chinese coast complicated navigation in what would now have to be a night-time landing. With the exception of one plane that diverted from its course and touched down safely in the Soviet Union, Doolittle's B-25s were all lost in crash landings, many behind the Japanese lines in China.

However, little of this was immediately known on the home front. In the United States the news about the raid was at first confusing and incom-plete. Army officials didn't hear from Doolittle immediately after the raid and feared total failure, so they kept silent: After all, how could the loss of sixteen planes and eighty men boost morale? When news of the raid broke, it was from an unlikely source: Radio Tokyo. On the day after the raid, the *New York Times* and other newspapers picked up a Japanese report of the bombing, which claimed that only schools and hospitals had been hit and that nine planes had been shot down. In subsequent days reports from a Swiss news agency and from the Soviet Union confirmed that American planes had bombed several Japanese cities. The U.S. government and the army, however, refused to confirm or deny the reports. Moreover, there was some attempt to shift the blame; one Pentagon spokesman suggested that "such an attack could have been made without direct orders from Washington. Even if plans for a raid on the Japanese capital had been worked out with the assistance or at the instigation of Washington strate-gists, the fact that the raid was undertaken at a specific time would be the concern chiefly of the army and navy officials entrusted with the task of carrying it out."[6] Meanwhile, the U.S. press was hungry for details of the operation. At an April 21 press conference, when pressed for information about where the bombers had come from, President Roosevelt responded, "Shangri-la."

When Doolittle finally got in touch with Washington, and when his men were accounted for as they made their way to Chungking, it became clear that the raid had been successful, and more information was given to the public. However, for several reasons, many of the details of the raid still couldn't be revealed. Secrecy afforded some protection. It was assumed, correctly, that the Japanese would try to wreak revenge on the partici-pants: the raiders who were now Japanese prisoners, the *Hornet* and its crew, and the Chinese who had assisted the raiders. Also, the army didn't want the Japanese to know that fifteen bombers had been lost. Finally, it was hoped that the Japanese, not knowing how the raid had been accomplished, would be expecting and preparing for more American bombers. The army didn't release the details of the raid until a full year after the event; on April 19, 1943, the *New York Times* printed an interview with Doolittle and several of the raiders still serving with him in North Africa in which it was revealed for the first time that the bombers had taken off from an aircraft carrier.[7] The next day the War Department released its official report on the raid.

How could this morale-boosting event serve its purpose if the general public couldn't be told very much about it? How could our defeats be turned into rallying cries if the extent of our losses had to remain secret? The answer, we think, is in Hollywood's focus on the historical events of the early months of the war in the Pacific. By presenting these historical events in fictional form, the studios were, in effect, taking the public record and filling in the gaps, making fully developed narratives out of the newspapers' skeletal outlines. Taken together, these films defined the war in the Pacific and explained why these far-flung places with peculiar names were important to the United States.

These films about the war in the Pacific, then, can be seen as serving two purposes: first, to fill in the narrative gaps in the news reports and turn them into complete, coherent narratives; and second, to invest the places in the Pacific theater with value, making them something that Americans should fight for—making them, in effect, part of America. Because of the need to serve these two purposes, films set in the Pacific more frequently connect themselves, at least peripherally, to actual events than do films set in Europe. Along with other films discussed in detail later in this chapter, the following films give a sense of the ubiquity of this narrative strategy. Both *Submarine Raider* (1942) and the serial *Adventures of Smilin' Jack* (1943) present American military personnel who find out about the impending attack on Pearl Harbor but are unable to get a warning back in time. Many films were inspired by the battle for the Philippines. In *Remember Pearl Harbor!* (1942) three army pals fight fifth columnists just before and after the Japanese attack on the Philippines. In *Manila Calling* (1942) a band of American and Filipino guerrillas defends a plantation-house stronghold while struggling to repair a generator to power their anti-Japanese radio broadcasts. In the climactic broadcast, as Japanese bombs explode around him, Lucky Matthews (Lloyd Nolan) links the

Philippine and American people and their cause and offers this construction of the loss of the islands: "The blood of Americans and Filipinos flowed together on the battlegrounds of Bataan and Corregidor. America can never forget that, and her people have sworn to avenge and change what happened here. . . . Filipinos and Americans, we didn't surrender. We just ran out of soldiers, because the soldiers ran out of blood, but we're still in this fight." At the end of *Somewhere I'll Find You* (1942) reporter Clark Gable (in his last film before entering the army air forces) dictates a story about a small group of U.S. and Philippine forces that defeats a Japanese landing party. He too links the Philippine and American forces: "Brown men and white men fought and died together. When they bled, their blood was the same color." In *Salute to the Marines* (1943) retired marine sergeant Wallace Beery leads a group of American and Filipino civilians to safety and organizes some men to try to hold up the Japanese advance. *Bataan* (1943), which we discuss in chapter 3, focuses on a ragtag group of American military men who sacrifice themselves to defend a ravine crossing on the Bataan peninsula. *Corregidor* (1943), an especially weak film, features a love triangle among civilian doctors and nurses on the titular island fortress. In *Cry "Havoc"* (1943) American army nurses are joined by American, British, and Filipino women who volunteer to care for troops on Bataan; at the end of the film their bunker is overwhelmed, and they are captured.

Other Pacific areas of operation also provided inspiration for Hollywood films. *The Sullivans* (a.k.a. *The Fighting Sullivans;* 1944) is based on the true story of five brothers who died together when their ship was sunk in the fighting off Guadalcanal. *Pride of the Marines* (1945), also based on a true story, features a horrific banzai charge against American lines on Guadalcanal, during which hero John Garfield is blinded. *The Story of Dr. Wassell* (1944) is based on the true story of a doctor on Java who helped several wounded sailors, left behind in the general evacuation, escape the Japanese. *The Fighting Seabees* (1944) is loosely based on actual events in the Pacific; when civilian construction workers were attacked by Japanese troops, the solution was the creation of naval construction battalions— the Seabees of the title. *Objective, Burma!* (1945) follows a squad of American paratroopers caught behind enemy lines; their rescue coincides with a general American offensive that drives the Japanese out of Burma. This film was reportedly booed in London theaters because it downplays the British contribution to the Burma campaign, illustrating our contention that wartime viewers on some level recognized Hollywood films as providing a narrative history of the war.[8]

Even films that were not specifically about actual events and places in the Pacific theater frequently anchored themselves to allusions to historic events. Many of these quickly became familiar, if not clichéd, tropes: references to the date December 6, or shots of a calendar revealing that date; references to, newspaper headlines about, or newsreel footage of the special Japanese envoy going to Washington on a peace mission just before the sneak attack on Pearl Harbor; President Roosevelt's speech to Congress on December 8; the announcement of General MacArthur's evacuation from the Philippines and his "I shall return" promise.

The cumulative effect of these films' focus on the first year of the war in the Pacific is to create a sort of mythic history that stands in for the unavailable real history. In doing this, the films work together, using common or similar themes, character types, and narrative conventions, to define the war in the Pacific as a war against the United States, to make connections between the island and mainland battlefields of the Pacific and the United States, and to project their endings into the future to offer a speculative but victorious outcome of the war's narrative—a narrative that is, for the original moviegoers, still in progress.[9] Air Force, a Warner Bros. release, is a good place to begin because of its ambitious depiction of the key events of the first six months of the war. By linking in a single narrative the separate stories of these early months, Air Force manages to create an overarching sense of the war as a whole and to present specific characters as they grow into the kind of Americans who will be able to win the war.

Directed by Howard Hawks from a screenplay by Dudley Nichols (with assistance from an uncredited William Faulkner) and released on March 20, 1943, Air Force tells the story of a single B-17 Flying Fortress, the Mary Ann, and its crew as they travel from the U.S. mainland to Pearl Harbor, arriving at the height of the Japanese attack,[10] then on to Wake Island, Clark Field in the Philippines, the Battle of the Coral Sea, and an Australian beach. This Cook's tour is interesting for its presentation of the history of these places and events and for the effect they have on the crew.

Significantly, the film begins in San Francisco as the crews of the Mary Ann and several other B-17 prepare for the flight to Hawaii. This allows the film to present mainland America, the America most viewers are familiar with, and then connect it via the animated maps that mark the Mary Ann's journey to the remote places where the actual fighting is taking place. In fact, this entire film is about making the connections—geographic, narrative, familial, emotional—that draw the Pacific battlefields into the world of the American viewer. In San Francisco, just before the *Mary Ann* takes off, crewmen say good-bye to sweethearts, wives, and mothers; the viewers, because we know what they are flying into and recognize the irony of their assurances of a quick return, feel the sorrow of this leave-taking. But this sad farewell is almost immediately countered, once the plane takes off and then throughout the film, by the presentation of the army air forces as a metaphorical family. Navigator Lieutenant Munchauser (Charles Drake) is the son of a World War I aviator who served with the *Mary Ann's* crew chief, Sgt. Robby White (Harry Carey), whose own son is now a pilot stationed at Clark Field in the Philippines. Disgruntled Sgt. Joe Winocki (John Garfield) was washed out of pilot training several years previously by the *Mary Ann's* captain, Mike Quincannon (John Ridgely). Copilot Bill Williams (Gig Young) is dating the sister of crewmate Tommy McMartin (Arthur Kennedy). At each stop on their journey they meet officers they have served under, pilots and crewmen they have served with, friends, and relatives.

The effect of all these connections is twofold. First, it creates the impression of the army air forces as an extended family or close-knit club where everyone knows everyone else; where rivalries, grudges, and black sheep exist but are mitigated by an ever-present foundational love; and where everyone shares a sense of tradition, common ancestors, and a heritage to be bequeathed. Second, these familial connections create an emotional net of sorts, bringing the characters and, more important, the places they visit into the viewers' world. In other words, these connections help the viewers understand these far-off, foreign places as part of America.

This understanding results from a series of emotional moments, each threatening to disrupt the sense of family the film has created and each associated with one of the geographic spots from the early months of the war. At Pearl Harbor Williams and McMartin learn that McMartin's sister, Susan (Faye Emerson), was seriously wounded in the attack. At Wake Island the marines stoically wait for the end they know is coming. They have no concerns for themselves, but they plead with the *Mary Ann's* Corporal Weinberg (George Tobias) to save the dog they have adopted. "Just give him to the marines in Manila," one says, suggesting another extended family, and for the rest of the film the dog serves as an emotional reminder of the marines' sacrifice. At Clark Field the crew learns that White's son

Air Force: The crew of the *Mary Ann* (John Garfield, Harry Carey, George Tobias, and Robert Wood) rescue the marines' dog from Wake Island.

was killed in the initial attack, never even getting his plane off the ground. Later, Quincannon is wounded in the *Mary Ann*'s first combat action and then dies at the base hospital, his crew around him. The cumulative effect of all these emotional moments in which the metaphorical or literal family is threatened or disrupted is to demonstrate the stake Americans have in the Pacific, in effect, extending the U.S. border from California across the Pacific, all the way to the Philippines.

This sense of the disrupted family is augmented by the film's presentation of the Japanese attacks, especially in Hawaii. Interestingly, *Air Force* is one of the few films to represent the attack on Pearl Harbor visually. In an already noted war-film convention, viewers are ominously clued in to the imminence of the attack—here, after the B-17s take off, we are shown an innocuous log entry for December 6. As the B-17s approach Hawaii, they hear Japanese voices and the sound of gunfire over their radios. When they call Hickam Field for instructions, we see a brief shot of the control tower, planes buzzing by and explosions in the background. The planes are ordered to emergency landing fields elsewhere on the islands, and later, when the *Mary Ann* flies back to Hickam, a shot from above shows the damage to the fleet at Pearl Harbor. Quincannon tells the somber crew, it's "something you'll want to remember." The shot recalls an earlier one when Quincannon tells the crew to take a look at San Francisco as they take off; we see the city, complete with Golden Gate Bridge, from above. The juxtaposition again connects the West Coast with Hawaii.

These connections are augmented by the film's repeated insistence that the Japanese attack was aided by Japanese living in Hawaii. While the *Mary Ann* is down at an emergency landing field on Maui, the crew is threatened by local Japanese snipers. At Hickam Field they're told that when the attack began, vegetable trucks driven by Japanese raced through the field smashing the tails off planes. Fighter pilot Tex Rader (James Brown), who was out with Susan McMartin when the attack began, tells McMartin and Williams that his route to the field was blocked by a truck driven by Japanese.[11] We know now that there is no historical evidence of this kind of sabotage, but for the purposes of this film, these stories of treachery and betrayal contrast sharply with the familial loyalty and support that have been established. As enemies, the Japanese threaten to disrupt family connections, and they do so by means that are antithetical to the concept and practice of family.

In addition to geographic, familial, and emotional connections, the film creates narrative connections, linking the different events of the early months of the war by means of the story of the *Mary Ann* and its crew. The improbability of the same plane and crew being involved in all these events is lessened and the sense of coherent narrative is increased by the film's obvious conflation of historical chronology. The *Mary Ann* leaves Hickam Field for the Philippines with a refueling stop at Wake Island on the morning of December 8, yet they arrive at Wake apparently after the December 12 attack by the Japanese and with the final December 23 attack imminent. They arrive at Clark Field in the aftermath of the December 8 attack there, but two days later, Bataan is falling (April 9) and the *Mary Ann* just barely makes it out. Flying away from the Philippines, the crew spots a Japanese fleet heading for Australia, reports it, and leads a devastating attack on it. But the Battle of the Coral Sea, the apparent model for this engagement, didn't occur until the first week of May. By condensing the historical chronology, the film takes scattered events and makes a coherent narrative based in a Japanese-strike and U.S.-response structure.

This narrative coherence is also important in showing how the crew members mature, turning into men who know why and how they must fight the Japanese. In a variation on the extended-family metaphor, the film uses sports references, especially to baseball and football, to help establish the notion of the B-17 crew and the entire army air forces as a team. Individuality has to be suppressed so that every member of the team can perform his job and the team can win. Sergeant White—who is never seen without his Chicago Cubs baseball cap—tells one young crew member to "stay in the box, son, and keep right on pitching"; after restraining Winocki from going after Japanese snipers, White says, "Why, they'd have cut you down before you got to first base." An officer at Hickam Field (Willard Robertson) says of the Japanese, "They took the first round, but there'll be others." Rader tells Williams and McMartin that during the attack Susan was "yelling and rooting like she was at a football game." While repairing an engine, Sergeant White predicts, "We'll have her hitting home runs in ninety minutes flat," and the commander of Wake Island (James Flavin), in something of a mixed metaphor, tells Quincannon, "We'll be in here pitching till they strike us out." In trying to reach the bitter Winocki, Quincannon discounts the rank- and function-based hierarchy of the bomber and stresses its teamlike interdependence: "We all belong to this airplane. Every man has got to rely on every other man to do the right thing at the right time. You played football, Winocki, you know how one man can gum up the whole works. You got to play ball with us and play the game, or I'm going to have to get rid of you." He had suggested the same idea back in San Francisco, when the mother of one of the younger crewmen asks Quincannon to look after her boy. He replies, "In a way he'll be looking after me. That's the way the crew of a bomber functions."

This concept of interdependence is further developed in the running argument between the *Mary Ann*'s officers and Rader, the fighter pilot, over which type of plane is better. Rader sums up his argument by saying, "I don't want to be responsible for eight or ten other guys or depending on them either." In the subsequent action, however, Rader learns the value of being part of a team. In the escape from Bataan Rader becomes the *Mary Ann*'s pilot, and after the success of the attack on the Japanese invasion fleet he says of the plane, "I'll take her for mine." In the film's final scene, projected into the future, Rader is a B-17 pilot.

This theme can also be seen in the stories of the two crew members, Munchauser and Winocki, who were unable to fulfill their dreams of becoming pilots. Munchauser, for vague reasons of ability, failed at pilot training and so became a navigator; though he tries to hide it, his disappointment at not following in his father's footsteps is clear. Winocki washed out of pilot school after a training accident in which the plane he was flying collided with another, causing it to crash and killing the other pilot. Winocki is bitter and feels that he was unfairly denied his chance to be a star; the chip on his shoulder is evident to everyone. But over the course of the *Mary Ann*'s journey, both he and Munchauser have the chance to become heroes by playing their roles on the team. Pressure is put on Munchauser, the navigator, to direct the plane to tiny Wake Island, their refueling point. It is implied that if he can't find the island, the plane will run out of fuel and crash. All the crew members check in with Munchauser, trying to be casual as they ask how it's going, demonstrating their anxiety and their dependence on him. Of course, he gets the *Mary Ann* to Wake and learns that he can be a hero like his father, even if he isn't a pilot. Winocki, who is shaken out of his apathy by the Japanese attack, becomes a hero when he brings the crippled *Mary Ann* in for a crash landing at Clark Field, after its unsuccessful attempt to bomb a Japanese transport. He proves his worth as a pilot, saves the plane, and gives the doctors a chance to save Quincannon. But significantly, despite this moment of success as a pilot, Winocki returns without grumbling to his position as a gunner, and it is in this position that he contributes to the *Mary Ann*'s survival. Learning a lesson from their first action, Winocki comes up with the idea of providing the rebuilt *Mary Ann* with a tail gun. He mans this gun and saves the plane from pursuing Zeros during the attack on the Japanese invasion force. Like Munchauser, he learns that his role on the team is important and offers, in its own way, the chance for heroism.

The *Mary Ann*'s story ends when the plane is ditched on an Australian beach after the Battle of the Coral Sea, but the crew's story apparently goes on. The film provides an epilogue, projected into the future, in which dozens of B-17 pilots, copilots, navigators, and bombardiers—Rader, Williams, Munchauser, and McMartin prominent among them—are briefed on an imminent mission to bomb Japan. After the planes take off, a superimposed message reads, "This story has a conclusion but not an end—for its real end will be the victory for which Americans—on land, on sea and in the air—have fought, are fighting now, and will continue to fight until peace has been won." This is the film's way of completing the narrative connections it has tried to make. The film's focus, necessarily, has been on connecting the places where the Japanese defeated U.S. forces. Even with the presentation of the Battle of the Coral Sea as a U.S. victory, the overall impression is of the United States on the defensive. Thus, the epilogue serves as a way of showing how the narrative logic of what we've seen—

the types of men and what they've learned, the potential in everyone to serve heroically, the B-17 itself and the sophistication of American technology—points toward an inevitable victory, even if the film's characters and audience aren't experiencing it in the present.

Many of the films that focused on the early events of the war with Japan used strategies similar to the ones we've discussed to create a narrative of the war and to connect the viewers in the continental United States to the places, people, and events of the war in the Pacific. In the previously mentioned *Somewhere I'll Find You* Jonny Davis's (Clark Gable) climactic dictation of a story from the Philippines back to his New York newspaper offers the clearest example of projecting the end of the war, the end of the in-progress narrative of the war, into the future as a conclusion to the film:

> Tomorrow morning the headlines will read "Bataan Falls." The headlines will be wrong though, because Bataan has not fallen. It stood for ninety-four days, and it still stands. The greatest delaying action of the war was fought in an area the size of a county. Three hundred thousand Japanese were tied in knots long enough for the U.S.A. to get its Sunday clothes off and go to work. . . . If a handful of Americans and Filipinos can do all that, living off rice and mule meat, fighting with bricks, bats, and bolos, then Bataan still stands. The Battle of Bataan was lost—by Japan.
>
> In case the Japanese don't realize that, I have a message for them from the men dead and living of Bataan: "More to come." It's a newspaper term, and it means the story isn't finished, the punch line hasn't been written yet. Remember that, Tokyo. More to come.

Wake Island, released by Paramount on August 12, 1942, tells the story of the marines' gallant defense of a small island. Like *Air Force*, it creates geographic connections by showing maps marking the lines between the mainland United States, Hawaii, Midway, and Wake and by presenting the men about to leave for Wake saying good-bye to loved ones at Pearl Harbor. It also creates familial connections, as the men arriving on Wake meet men who served with them previously or with their fathers. In an interesting emotional strategy, the film shows the new commander of marines on Wake, Major Canton (Brian Donlevy), being given an inscribed cigarette case by his daughter before he leaves Hawaii. Each time he uses the case, we are reminded of his emotional attachment; he most frequently uses the cigarette case when he's seeking to make a connection of some kind with another person on the island—it becomes a gesture of goodwill and friendship, an attempt to make the human connections fundamental to a community of men fighting to preserve not just their lives but also a way of life they value. When Canton has to tell Lieutenant Cameron (Macdonald Carey) that his wife was killed in the attack on Pearl Harbor, he offers his notion of a substitute family: "You're like me now: a man with a memory. But we're not alone. In this war, in any part of the world, wherever they've dropped a stick of bombs, they've made thousands like us—men without wives, without children, without a single thing they've ever loved or held dear. And for those men there's a job to do: to fight."

Wake Island also makes connections through allusions to historical events. Its written prologue invokes Valley Forge, Custer's Last Stand, and the Lost Battalion of World War I, all presented in popular American history as desperate stands that led to eventual victory. Similarly, when Canton tells his men to hold their fire as he draws the Japanese fleet closer, he quotes the order from the Battle of Bunker Hill: "Don't fire until you can see the whites of their eyes." Here, the Wake defenders are associated with another hopelessly outnumbered fighting force, the colonial army, that nevertheless was able to win. This connective strategy serves both to place the Pacific conflicts in the company of battles fought more directly in defense of the United States and to put the loss of the battle in the context of heroic sacrifices in wars that were eventually won.

Wake Island ends with Canton and construction crew chief Shad McCloskey (Albert Dekker), the last living Americans on the island, firing away at the Japanese from a machine gun nest.[12] The image fades before we can see the inevitable end, but, as in *Air Force*, the film assures us that the real ending is in the future. As the Wake Island scene is replaced by footage of marching marines, superimposed with a U.S. flag, a narrator tells us, "This is not the end. There are other leathernecks, other fighting Americans, 140 million of them, whose blood and sweat and fury will exact a just and terrible vengeance."

Whereas *Air Force* focuses on the way a crew of a Flying Fortress functions, *So Proudly We Hail!* (released by Paramount on June 22, 1943) focuses on a group of army nurses in the early days of the war. Like *Air Force* and *Wake Island*, it makes geographic connections. The nurses, led by Lt. Janet Davidson (Claudette Colbert), ship out from San Francisco just before December 7, 1941. The attack on Pearl Harbor occurs while they are at sea, and their convoy is attacked by Japanese submarines. They arrive at Manila after the initial attacks on the Philippines, join the troops making their stand on Bataan, and are nearly captured during the retreat down the peninsula. They escape to Corregidor and are eventually evacuated just before the island falls. As in the other films, there are familial connections: army officers in the Philippines served with Janet's father; the senior nurse, Captain McGregor (Mary Servoss), is known affectionately as Ma; Janet marries John Summers (George Reeves), an officer she met after his transport was torpedoed and he was picked up by her ship. Here, too, familial relationships are disrupted by the enemy: nurse Olivia D'arcy's (Veronica Lake) fiancé is killed at Pearl Harbor; Ma's son is killed on Bataan; Janet breaks down after John fails to return from an attempt to bring medical supplies back to Corregidor.

Interestingly, though, the film also points an accusing finger at the movie audience back in the United States for breaking a familial relationship by abandoning the Americans in the Philippines. At one point, as we see shots of the nurses caring for soldiers in a jungle hospital, one of the nurses (Mary Treen), narrating in flashback, says, "We called ourselves the battling orphans of Bataan—no father, no mother, no Uncle Sam—as we wondered where the reinforcements were." Later, as the constant bombardment of Corregidor and the dwindling supplies threaten to break the nurses, Janet makes the most explicit articulation of the link between the locations in the Pacific and the U.S. mainland, again accusing the audience of not recognizing the connection: "It's our own fault. . . . Because we believed we were the world, that the United States of America was the whole world. Those outlandish places—Bataan, Corregidor, Mindanao— those aren't American names. No, they're just American graveyards. . . . We've become what they call a delaying action. That's what those 50,000 men over there were. They were merely saving time. I hope to God the people back home aren't losing it for us. Do you remember what the chaplain once told us? It's our present: we're giving them time." This accusation is mitigated at the end of the film when a doctor (John Litel) reads to the comatose Janet a last letter from John, which conjures an image of a future where the connections have been made: "This is not a people's war because civilians also get killed. It's the people's war because they have taken it over now, and they are going to win it and end it with a purpose—to live like men, with dignity and freedom. This is the good I've found. There's a small voice whispering around the earth, and the people are beginning to talk across their boundaries. This voice will grow in volume until it thunders all over the world. . . . It says: this is our war now, and this time it'll be our peace." This speech, combining elements of the barber's final speech in *The Great Dictator* with other films' projections into a victorious future, awakens Janet and relieves the tension the film created in its depiction of the audience's betrayal of American forces in the Philippines.

Two other films, *Back to Bataan* and *They Were Expendable*, take similar approaches but focus exclusively on the Philippines. *Back to Bataan*, released by RKO on May 31, 1945, connects the main events of the fall of the Philippines—MacArthur being ordered to Australia, the surrender of Bataan and the Death March, the surrender of Corregidor—into a narrative but then goes beyond them to show the Filipino resistance to the Japanese occupation and the eventual liberation by U.S. forces. The film also uses an interesting thematic technique to connect the Philippines to the United States. At the beginning of the film, as Bataan is falling, a propaganda broadcast implores Filipinos not to fight America's war. Subsequently, the Philippine insurrection against U.S. colonization is frequently mentioned by American and Filipino characters. The U.S. Army's Colonel Madden (John Wayne) fought in the insurrection against the grandfather of Philippine scout Captain Bonifacio (Anthony Quinn). Considering that this fight for independence was against the United States, it seems potentially divisive for the film to repeatedly invoke it. But instead, the effect is to remind us that the Filipinos, like Americans, have a long history and tradition of fighting for liberty, and this similarity is more important than the fact that for the previous half century the fight was against U.S. colonizers. Moreover, as we saw in *Manila Calling* and *Somewhere I'll Find You*, this similarity is emphasized as conflicts are resolved and differences conflated to the point that Americans and Filipinos are practically interchangeable. The guerrilla band Madden leads is headquartered near Balintawak, the birthplace of Philippine freedom, as we're frequently reminded. Schoolchildren are shown discussing with enthusiasm the things America has given to the Philippines. When a school principal who refuses to haul down the American flag is hanged, we see his body draped by the flag he defended. Bonifacio at one point says to Madden—the all-American John Wayne—"You're a better Filipino than I am." And in preparation for the landings on Leyte, Bonifacio refuses to evacuate civilians to protect them from navy bombardment because it will reveal the locations to the Japanese. He says, "If it'll save American lives and help make the landings safe, our people will not evacuate." The effect of all this is to conflate Philippine and American history and, in effect, nationality.

Back to Bataan, because of its late release date, deals with the projected ending of the war differently from the other films we've discussed.

Back to Bataan was in production as the battle for the liberation of the Philippines was being fought, and it was released several months after the American victory there. Unlike the other films, which were released in 1942 and 1943, when the eventual outcome of the war was still uncertain, this film relates to its subject matter from a position of confident knowledge that the United States has indeed triumphed in that one part of the war and is on its way to total victory. So here the film begins with the recreation of the January 30, 1945, liberation of a prisoner of war (POW) camp at Cabanatuan.[13] As a voice-over assures us that the film is based on "real facts," we are shown actual POWs marching out of their captivity. This in itself isn't unusual; almost every film we discuss in this chapter claims to be based on actual events and records. What's unusual is the end of the film, where footage of the real POWs returns, but in a split-screen effect—the real POWs on the right and the characters from the film on the left. The result is to suggest another conflation, this time of the actual events of the war and the Hollywood history of the war.

Based on W. L. White's best seller, *They Were Expendable* was directed by John Ford and released by MGM on November 23, 1945. This release date seems ill timed, as the Japanese had surrendered more than two months earlier. Even during production, while the war was still being fought, the U.S. victory must have seemed inevitable. So it's striking how similar this film is to a film like *Air Force*, made relatively early on. Like *Air Force*, *They Were Expendable* is a technology film: the former explains the workings of a B-17; the latter the workings of the navy's torpedo boats, more popularly called PT boats. Here again is a narratization of the early events of the war: the attack on Pearl Harbor, the initial attacks on the Philippines, the evacuation of MacArthur (we see PT boats ferry the general from Corregidor to Mindanao), the fall of Bataan. Here again are the familial connections, as the main characters encounter men they went to school with or served with. An aging boat mechanic (Russell Simpson) who is called Dad by everyone has lived in the Philippines since he arrived with American forces during the Spanish-American War—another link to past conflicts; Dad's theme music is "Red River Valley," connecting him to an idea of America's frontier past. Here again, the need for the suppression of self in favor of the team is stressed. PT boat squadron commander Lt. John Brickley (Robert Montgomery) must constantly remind Lt. Rusty Ryan (John Wayne) that accomplishing their common goal is more important than being a star. There's even a return to sports metaphors as the admiral (Charles Trowbridge) has to remind Brickley, "You and I are professionals. If the manager says sacrifice, we lay down a bunt and let somebody else hit the home runs." As Brickley and Ryan are flown out of the Philippines on one of the last planes to leave Bataan—they are needed in the States to train PT boat crews and plan strategy—the film superimposes the dramatic words "We Shall Return," a projection toward a future victory that seems confusing, given that the audience knew that victory had already been achieved.

Why are all these filmic conventions at work in *They Were Expendable*, even though the late production and release date would have made them obsolete or at least unnecessary? Perhaps by this time, through sheer repetition, these devices had gone beyond the conventional to the epistemological. That is, rather than serving a conscious or articulated purpose in the film, they had become embedded in the consciousness of filmmakers and filmgoers alike, a part of the intellectual fabric by which the American mind made sense of and understood the war in the Pacific. This conclusion is supported by the way narrative devices from World War II films continue to crop up in postwar films about the war, even as recently as *Pearl Harbor* (2001), *U-571* (2000), and, despite its claims to realism, *Saving Private Ryan* (1998); divorced from their original purposes, however, these devices seem clichéd and sappy. Even less successful were films about the Korean War and the Vietnam War that tried to apply conventions from World War II films to these later conflicts. We return to this idea in chapter 8.

The films we've looked at so far in this chapter all focused on the early defeats in the Pacific. Many other films dealt with the early victories, from the Doolittle raid to Midway to Makin Island and Guadalcanal, the series of events that turned the tide of war and pointed toward eventual victory. Some of the same implied narratives—the need to overcome differences and pull together, for example—are at work in these films, but many new ones are introduced as the emphasis moves from how the war began to the means by which the United States will win. The most important of these new narratives focus on the ordinary American—as opposed to the larger-than-life heroes of Bataan—and how he can rise to this occasion, a fine-tuning of the pulling-together theme to stress individuality within the team, and an attempt to restore confidence in American leadership.

Earlier in this chapter we discussed the Doolittle raid, America's first strike back at the Japanese. This adventure seems to have occupied a far larger place in the public imagination than one might have expected, given its modest results. As we suggested earlier, the many film treatments of the

Doolittle raid helped to imaginatively fill in the narrative gaps left, for various reasons, in the press accounts of the mission. Beyond this, the narrative of the raid also served as a frame to support a number of other narratives that were important for Americans' understanding of themselves, their leaders, and their technology as being able to defeat the Japanese.

One of the first film accounts of the Doolittle raid was the RKO film *Bombardier*, but it took a long time to reach the screen. The film had been in preproduction before Pearl Harbor, and after the war began, the project was delayed as the screenplay was rewritten and many of the principals were called to military service.[14] It was finally released on May 13, 1943. The film follows a familiar wartime pattern used in *They Were Expendable* and in many of the technology films discussed in chapter 1. That is, a visionary promotes some new military technology, in this case, high-altitude bombing with the Norden bombsight; the visionary comes into conflict with pigheaded elements of the military establishment but finally proves the worth of the technology. In *Bombardier* the worth of high-altitude bombing is proved in a raid on Nagoya, obviously based on the Doolittle raid, but written and produced before many of the details of the raid were made public. The climactic sequence of the film is a stupendous night bombing of Nagoya, footage of which shows up in dozens of other World War II movies. An animated map shows us that the bombers are taking off from an unnamed "Island Base," clearly recalling Roosevelt's Shangri-la, and as the bombers approach Nagoya, the city is blacked out and searchlights slice through the night sky. The bombardiers are briefly stymied when they can't find their targets because the lead plane of Maj. Buck Oliver (Randolph Scott) has been shot down (bombardier Joe Conners [Robert Ryan] responsibly destroying his bombsight). Oliver, the pilot who most strongly opposed high-altitude bombing because it made the bombardiers more important than the pilots, manages to escape his Japanese captors and start a huge fire that illuminates the bombardiers' targets. As he shouts, "C'mon all you bombardiers!" the planes drop their bombs, blowing much of Nagoya and, unfortunately, Major Oliver to bits.

Although this sequence imaginatively fills in the gaps of the Doolittle raid, most of it turned out to be wrong: the Doolittle raiders didn't take off from an island; they didn't hit their target cities at night; and, most ironic from the point of view of the film's purpose, they dropped their bombs not from a high altitude but from 1,500 feet. In fact, the Norden bombsights had been removed from their B-25s.[15] The narrative choices the screenwriter and director made served not history but the more immediate need to explain elements of the war to the American public. By having Buck Oliver recognize the importance of high-altitude bombing and the bombardier, the film, like *Air Force*, incorporates a narrative about the privileging of teamwork (the crew of the bomber—the pilot, the bombardier, and the others—sharing responsibility) over the individual (the hotshot dive-bomber pilot working alone). With the success of the top-secret Norden bombsight, the film incorporates a narrative about the superiority of American know-how and technology; the bombsight signifies the American ingenuity and productivity that will eventually win the war. In the triumphant bombing of Nagoya, courtesy of the bomber crews and the Norden bombsights, the film incorporates a narrative about the accuracy and morality of American bombing techniques. The United States defended its use of high-altitude strategic bombing against charges of indiscriminate terrorism by claiming that the Norden bombsight made bombing so accurate (the bomb-in-the-pickle-barrel-at-20,000-feet theory) that only legitimate military, not civilian, targets were hit.[16] *Bombardier* shows its version of the Doolittle raiders hitting only military targets with ease and accuracy; one bombardier asks his crewmates which factory smokestack he should drop his bombs down.

A second film representation, Warner Bros.' *Destination Tokyo*, released on December 31, 1943, is the story of a submarine and its contribution to the success of the Doolittle raid. The *Copperfin*, commanded by Captain Cassidy (Cary Grant), sails to the Aleutian Islands to pick up an army meteorologist, then across the Pacific to sneak into Tokyo Bay. The sub sends the meteorologist and two others ashore to observe and record weather conditions and then moves close to the city to note the positions of barrage balloons and possible targets. All this information is radioed to the *Hornet* and given to the bomber crews. As the raiders bomb the city, the *Copperfin* sneaks out of the bay under a fleeing Japanese ship. Once in open water, the captain decides to join in the fight and torpedoes an aircraft carrier, but subsequently the sub becomes the target of a depth-charge attack by the carrier's escort. After a long, tense, damaging pounding, the captain finally surfaces and sinks the only remaining Japanese ship. Submarine and crew then return to San Francisco.

Like *Bombardier*, *Destination Tokyo* imaginatively fills in the gaps in the Doolittle raid narrative. Because more information about the raid was available when the film was produced, it is much more accurate: the raiders take off from the *Hornet*—the film even includes actual footage of the B-25s taking off—and it is mentioned that their plan is to land in China.

More significant, however, are the ways the film consciously fictionalizes the raid. Most obviously, there was no submarine in Tokyo Bay sending information to the *Hornet;* in fact, the *Hornet* sailed under radio silence.[17] The film also made some strange changes in the raid's chronology. Shortly after leaving San Francisco, the submarine's crew celebrates Christmas (Christmas 1941?), which seems much too early for the April 1942 raid; the raiders didn't begin training until the end of February. Moreover, the film seems to be set later than the first five months of the war. The captain refers to several previous missions, and the crewmen speak pointedly of the mission "last year." They also discuss the imminent invasion of Europe. One wonders how many missions a submarine crew could get under its belt between December 7, 1941, and April 18, 1942, and how the invasion of Europe could be discussed with certainty so early in the war. More to the point, one wonders why the screenwriters and director chose to disregard a readily available, historically accurate chronology.

One answer is that the Doolittle narrative was being used as a vehicle for two other interconnected narratives. The first is a celebration of the submarine service. There is a great deal of attention given to the technology of submarining: how the ship submerges and rises; how sonar works; how torpedoes are fired; how damage control is accomplished; and, in the best scene, how depth-charge attacks are withstood. The second narrative is less informational and more inspirational; it is about rising to the occasion. When the voyage starts, one new sailor confesses to a veteran that he doesn't know if he will have the nerve to do the things required of him under the pressure of battle. This concern is a paradigm for much of the action and many of the incidents that ensue. The smallest sailor on the sub must disarm a Japanese bomb lodged in the bulkhead, which only he can reach. The ship's pharmacist must perform an emergency appendectomy with the cook's knives as another crewman reads him instructions.[18] The entire crew must perform under the pressure of the pounding depth-charge attack. For this film, the war is about facing pressure, rising above oneself, and meeting the challenge. As the captain says during the attack, "We can't win if we can't take it." This idea is emphasized by means of the link to the Doolittle raid, a real event already associated in the public mind with pressure, heroism, and success.

MGM's *Thirty Seconds over Tokyo,* released on November 15, 1944, was adapted from Ted Lawson's best-selling 1943 memoir, written with journalist Robert Considine. Lieutenant Lawson, one of the Doolittle raiders, wrote about his experiences—volunteering for a secret mission, training at Elgin Field in Florida, the voyage on the *Hornet*, and, of course, the bombing of Tokyo. But the great bulk of the book focuses on his plane's crash landing on a Japanese-held island off the Chinese coast, his crew's escape and arduous journey across China to Chungking—made possible by hundreds of Chinese—and, especially, the horrific injuries he suffered in the crash that resulted in the amputation of his leg. The film version, easily the most historically accurate of the films about the raid, follows the narrative of Lawson's book fairly accurately, but it makes some subtle changes in emphasis. Preparations for the raid and the raid itself receive more emphasis than the postcrash adventures in China, with the result that the film is less Ted Lawson's story and more the story of the raiders as a group. Connected with this, the film fleshes out the supporting characters in a way that allows the plot to support a number of broader narratives about the war.

Several of these narratives are already familiar from the other films we've discussed. As in *Air Force, Wake Island,* and *So Proudly We Hail!* there is the sense of the army air forces as a big, informal family. When the various volunteers arrive at Elgin Field for their top-secret training, there is something of a family reunion atmosphere: they all know one another, their commanding officers, and the other men's wives. They even familiarly refer to the mission's leader as "Jimmy" Doolittle. As in *Air Force,* there is also a coming together across differences. Emphasis is given to the raiders being from various regions of the country, especially Montana and Texas ("Deep in the Heart of Texas" isn't sung a thousand times, but it sure seems like it); these regionalisms, though colorful, are superficial compared to the raiders' commitment to the mission and one another. On the *Hornet* there is a good-natured rivalry between the sailors and the airmen, but when the goal of the mission—to bomb Japan—is announced, the sailors go out of their way to support the fliers, and the fliers gain a new appreciation of the value of the sailors' work. As in *Bombardier,* there is a justification of America's bombing strategy. In briefing sessions aboard the *Hornet,* the military nature of the planned targets is stressed, and in the final briefing, Colonel Doolittle (Spencer Tracy) directly addresses the necessary and moral nature of the bombing: "Now let me repeat something I've said previously: you are to bomb the military targets assigned to you and nothing else. Of course, in an operation of this kind, you cannot avoid killing civilians, because war plants are manned by civilians. If any of you have any moral feelings about this necessary killing, if you feel that you might think of yourself afterward as a murderer, I want you to drop out." Of course, no one does, because all the fliers accept—as the viewer is encouraged to—the common sense of Doolittle's argument: the bombing is moral because the greatest care has been taken to ensure that the targets are all legitimate military targets; if deaths result, they are "necessary" deaths within the scheme of America's moral action.

Another type of narrative that became increasingly common as the war's end neared (discussed in chapter 8) is the serviceman's anxiety over being accepted by his family and fitting back into society. As in the book, Lawson in the film (Van Johnson) fears that his wife, Ellen (Phyllis Thaxter), won't accept him with a missing leg and scars on his face. He tells everyone who might be in contact with her not to mention his injuries, and when he returns to the States, he delays contacting her; his plan is to wait until he's fitted with a prosthetic leg and has plastic surgery to cover his scars. Doolittle steps in, calls Ellen, and arranges for her to come visit Ted. Of course, when she sees him in his hospital room, he and the viewer realize how foolish his fears were. Moreover, when Lawson wonders what kind of future he might have with only one leg and suggests that he might go back to school after being mustered out, Doolittle snaps, "What are you talking about? Do you think we'd let a man of your experience get away from us?" Lawson ends the film loved and useful, despite his injuries.

Doolittle's role in resolving Lawson's personal story happily connects with yet another narrative supported by *Thirty Seconds over Tokyo:* faith in the military leadership. In the aftermath of the surprise attack on Pearl Harbor and the many early defeats in the Pacific, and in light of the Allies' Europe-first commitment, which put the war against Japan on the back burner, it's not surprising that anxiety about the competency and effectiveness of America's military leadership might arise. The story of the Doolittle raid as presented in *Thirty Seconds* addresses that anxiety in at least two ways. First, it takes us behind the scenes and demonstrates the necessarily secret ways in which the military is determined to strike back at Japan to turn the war around. Having Doolittle and the other officers continually remind the pilots and crews not to say a word to anyone about what they're doing (not that they know much—they don't learn the point of their training until they're well on their way to Japan) helps the viewer see that there are plans in the works that the public can't know about; the public must accept being kept in the dark and have faith that the military is leading the country to victory.

The second way the film addresses anxiety over our military leadership is in its characterization of James Doolittle. Presenting a real person as a major film character was unusual during the war years. Other fact-based films tended to fictionalize the commanding officers, even when the actual figure behind the character was obvious; for example, in *Gung Ho!* (1943) Col. Evans Carlson becomes Colonel Thorwald. The only other significant biographical presentation we can find is in *God Is My Co-Pilot* (1945), where the Flying Tigers' Gen. Claire Chennault is a character. Doolittle's association with the raid probably makes his presence in the film inescapable, but beyond that, the heroism of the raid, much of which was associated with its leader, allows the Doolittle character to stand in for a larger idea of a wartime leader. In other words, the Doolittle character represents all the qualities one would want in a leader. He is calm and confident in his plan. He is well prepared and insists that his men be too. He works his men very hard, but in doing so, he is enabling them to rise above themselves. His training is rigorous—in the Elgin Field scenes he seems humorless and all business—but he makes it clear that this is not just for the sake of the mission but also for the men's own good. He does everything he asks his men to do: his plane is the first to take off from the *Hornet*. And, as we see in the final scene with Lawson, he cares about his men and takes care of them paternalistically. The picture of leadership presented here augments the implied plea for faith in the military's plans and assures us that the servicemen and the country are in good hands.

Interestingly, in addition to supporting myriad narratives about the war, *Thirty Seconds over Tokyo* marks something of an apotheosis of the process by which filmic narratizations of historic events acquire a "reality" that substitutes for the actual events. Many of the reviews of *Thirty Seconds* commented on its "documentary" quality,[19] implying that it is a comparatively direct presentation of reality. For anyone viewing it today, however, the cinematic techniques, the technical limitations, and the now clichéd narrative conventions are obvious; seeing it as anything but a Hollywood film is impossible. This demonstrates how the narratives about the war and their conventions had been naturalized to the point that, for 1940s audiences, they *were* reality. This may mark the greatest success of these films: that by imaginatively filling in the narrative gaps of the historic Doolittle raid, by using it as a frame to support many other necessary narratives about the war, these films, working together with other films and other pop-cultural representations of the war, created for their viewers a reality—the real war and the real history of the war.

Like the Doolittle raid films, *Wing and a Prayer*, about the Battle of Midway, creates narrative coherence of the early months of the war, but it also makes the process of creating that narrative coherence its subject. Released by Twentieth Century–Fox on July 24, 1944, and subtitled *The Story of Carrier X*, the film follows a single, unnamed aircraft carrier around the Pacific in April and May 1942; the carrier serves as a decoy, convincing the Japanese that the Pacific Fleet is scattered and afraid to fight, buying time and luring the Japanese into a disastrous encounter at Midway.

The film immediately establishes a conflict between appearances and the truth behind appearances. We see a montage of newspaper headlines, editorials, and cartoons lamenting the sequence of military disasters in the three months since Pearl Harbor and asking: Where is our navy? Why doesn't it fight? The impression is of chaos on the part of the U.S. military as it offers a bumbling, sporadic, and inadequate response to Japanese attacks. We next see a Pentagon briefing room where an admiral (Cedric Hardwicke) answers these questions by laying out the navy strategy of using carrier X to roam the Pacific, allowing it to be sighted by the enemy at specific locations on specific dates but refusing to engage them. The plan is to lull the enemy into an overconfident attack on Midway as a step in their ultimate goal of seizing Hawaii. This strategy, of course, must remain secret; it can't be explained in the daily newspapers. Thus the editorials rail and the public stews over the appearance of inaction, while behind the scenes a plan is being put into operation.

This opening sequence sets up the tension that operates through much of the film. Like the general public, the crew and fliers of carrier X can't be told about the plan in which they are participating. They must simply follow orders, and their orders are not to engage the enemy, even if attacked. The film focuses on the fliers of Torpedo Plane Squadron 5, recently assigned to carrier X. Arriving eager to fight, they move from confusion to frustration to anger as they find themselves running from the enemy and suffering losses they aren't allowed to avenge. The viewer is put in the position of sympathizing with the fliers' feelings while at the same time being aware of the big-picture plans that dictate their orders. The viewer, in effect, occupies the position of the admiral and the other top officers: they know the plan and the reasons behind the orders, but they also sympathize with the men's emotions. The emotional release of the film comes not after the Battle of Midway but on the morning of the battle, when it is announced that the plan has worked and the men can finally fight. The overall effect, as in *Thirty Seconds over Tokyo*, is to persuade the viewer that despite appearances, despite the fragmented and incoherent story of the war presented in the news, there is a behind-the-scenes design at work.

Many of the film's elements contribute to making the case for the almost religious leap of faith suggested here. Some of these elements invoke two media of illusion that the audience is presumably familiar with: movies and radio. One of Squadron 5's pilots is a film star, Hallam Scott (William Eythe), a man who keeps his Academy Award near him the way a child might keep a teddy bear for security. At one point, when the other pilots want to know what it's like to kiss Betty Grable and other leading ladies, Scott establishes the romantic atmosphere leading up to the kiss, then says, "Well then the hairdresser yelled out, 'Don't hold her so close, you're mussing up her hairdo.' The director screamed, 'Hey, take your arm from around her neck, you're tilting her collar.' The cameraman said, 'You can't kiss her square on the lips like that, I can't see her nose.' So I just kissed her way off center and smacked the air!" What appears real in a film is actually a carefully crafted illusion. Later, when the sailors break into the sacks of fan mail for Scott that somehow keep getting forwarded to the carrier from Twentieth Century–Fox, the humor comes from the fans not being able to distinguish between the images projected on the screen and the reality behind them. The suggestion here is that sophisticated moviegoers ought to know that what is seen in films is the product of behind-the-scenes, off-screen work. Radio is introduced in a curious moment when, after the successful attack on the Japanese carriers at Midway, the torpedo planes are pursued by Zeros. Their communications are heard all over carrier X, not unlike a radio broadcast.[20] We join the crew as listeners and must use our imagination to picture what's happening based on overlapping dialogue and sound effects. Viewers are asked, in effect, to apply the narrative-making techniques they use when listening to the radio to the war itself; the war can be made sense of through narratives if one is willing to help fill in the gaps.

This shipwide broadcast is important in another way. The sudden pulling away from the visual presentation of the battle to the broadcast of it suggests that in some sense the experience of war is unrepresentable. Earlier in the film, when the novice fliers crowd around an experienced and decorated pilot (Kevin O'Shea), asking him about combat and what dueling with Zeros is really like, he is confused and unable to answer; he finally demurs, saying, "I'm sorry, fellows, I'm writing my memoirs for the *Saturday Evening Post*. You can read them after the war for a dime." This idea that the war is unrepresentable is interestingly self-referential, foregrounding the illusory nature of the film we're watching, and augments the film's contention that a leap of faith is necessary. The war, as presented in film or in the news media, will never be completely, coherently present to us; we must nevertheless be assured that there is some sense to our country's participation in it.

Whereas *Thirty Seconds over Tokyo* and *Wing and a Prayer* encourage faith in the plan behind the war news and in our military leadership, other films about the burgeoning offensive in the Pacific focus on ordinary fighting men. As in *Air Force*, these men must put aside their egos to function as a team, but even as team members, they maintain their individuality. *Gung Ho!* was released by Universal on December 20, 1943, and is, as its subtitle claims, *The Story of Carlson's Makin Island Raiders.* In retrospect, the Makin Island raid seems an odd choice for celebration in a film treatment. It was a minor action that succeeded in wiping out the Japanese on the island but failed to divert Japanese attention from the landings on Guadalcanal. In the long term it even proved harmful, since it encouraged the Japanese to fortify their Gilbert Island defenses, resulting in the bloody campaign for Tarawa in 1943. Furthermore, from a post-1949 perspective, the film's positive attitude toward the Communist Chinese guerrillas seems surprising. Beyond that, however, *Gung Ho!* can be seen as trying to reconcile the contradictions between a democratic tradition of valuing individuality and the suppression of individuality necessary for the teamwork required in the armed forces.

Gung Ho! employs many of the elements we have seen in other films focusing on the history of the war in the Pacific. An animated map connects mainland San Diego with Pearl Harbor and, eventually, Makin Island. We even see real footage of the burning battleships at Pearl Harbor, and we're assured by the subtitle and by text at the beginning of the film that we're watching the true story of the Second Marine Raider Battalion, even though Col. Evans Carlson has become the fictional Colonel Thorwald (Randolph Scott). Like the other films, too, *Gung Ho!* encourages teamwork, but a distinctly American teamwork. In his speech to the volunteers, Thorwald talks not only about the combat tactics he learned from the Chinese guerrillas but also about their philosophy of gung ho, working together harmoniously. He tells his men:

> You are to receive a course of training unique in the history of the Marine Corps. If you justify the effort to be spent on you, you may be able to point the way in which this tremendously difficult war in the Pacific can

be won. Briefly, it can be won by teamwork, by trained men fighting together with the precision of a machine. But it's more than that. It must be a harmonious machine. Now, you start with the fundamentals. And at the bottom of everything is self-discipline. You must start by casting out all prejudices—racial, religious, every other kind.

I want you to feel free to ask questions, even embarrassing ones. Come to me with suggestions. We're going to be more than officers and men in this. We're going to be comrades. What I eat, you will eat. Where I sleep, you will sleep. I will take you into my confidence whenever it's possible before going into battle. We'll have a meeting in which I'll explain our plans and objectives so that each of you can make a more intelligent contribution to the result. Afterward, we'll have another meeting to criticize the way in which the operation was conducted. We'll fight and endure and win together.

This philosophy, which sounds less like a military structure than a laidback corporate culture, suggests that the Raider Battalion is a microcosm of American society as a whole. As the narrator (an uncredited Chet Huntley) intones, "Some of us are going to die for democracy and freedom and equality. But right here in the Second Raider Battalion, we're going to live it while we can."

Contributing to the democracy of the Raider Battalion, and presumably to American society at large, is the fact that the harmonious team is made up of unique individuals. This is underscored in the scenes where potential volunteers give their reasons for wanting to be a part of this unit. No two reasons are the same, and they frequently reveal the unarticulated motivations of the men, as the officers engage in amateur psychologizing. Tedrow (Rod Cameron) is feuding with the members of a rival Kentucky family over who will kill more Japanese. Harbison (Alan Curtis) is a minister who wants the most dangerous assignment so that he'll be with the men who need him the most. Montana (Harold Landon) has been dismissed as a "no good kid" all his life. Pig Iron Matthews (Robert Mitchum) is a boxer who learned that fighting solved his problems and earned him respect. Richter (Noah Beery Jr.) and O'Ryan (David Bruce) are rival stepbrothers. One man's brother was killed at Pearl Harbor. Another's sister was captured by the Japanese in Manila. One last man says simply, "I just don't like Japs."

This emphasis on the differences among individuals is set against a picture of the enemy as regimented drones. Thorwald tells his men, "The

Japanese are crafty, tenacious, tough, but they have a weakness. It lies in their inability to adapt themselves to unusual situations." This notion is confirmed by what some U.S. forces were actually learning about the Japanese from their banzai attacks on Guadalcanal. When a marine officer asked a prisoner "why they had mindlessly repeated their attacks instead of probing for a weaker sector of the line, the enemy soldier protested that the assault had been so meticulously planned that there could be no question of deviating from the strict orders of General Hyakutake."[21] The raiders win their battle on Makin Island by taking advantage of their individuality—their ability to think for themselves, to be innovative, to be spontaneous, to be surprising. One marine strips off his uniform and dashes across a field of enemy fire like a track star. Two men turn a bulldozer into an impromptu tank. Thorwald tricks the Japanese air force into bombing its own men by painting an American flag on the roof of a building on the island. The lesson seems clear: the individuality fostered by the American democratic system is the strength that will allow us to defeat the regimented, conformist, closed-minded enemy. Individuality is to be prized, even in the context of the teamwork demanded by the armed forces.

Much more significant than the raid on Makin Island, the campaign for Guadalcanal was the subject of *Guadalcanal Diary*, adapted from the best-selling book by war correspondent Richard Tregaskis and released by Twentieth Century–Fox on October 27, 1943. In its early stages the film follows Tregaskis's book fairly closely, but soon after the marines take Henderson Field, the book and actual events are lost amid the coming-of-age adventures of one platoon. Yet this coming-of-age process is important to the film's thematic purposes. As in *Destination Tokyo* and *Gung Ho!* we see a group of young men learning to become the kind of soldiers needed to win the war: they move from insecurity to confidence and learn a lesson about the dangers of overconfidence. As in *Air Force* and *Wing and a Prayer*, the men learn that the Japanese can be defeated, and as in *Gung Ho!* they learn that their individuality can help them win.

The battle for Guadalcanal, probably even more than Midway, signaled the turning point in the war for most Americans. After Guadalcanal, the army and navy would be pushing the Japanese backward. It would take time, but America would win the war. In this context we can see two of *Guadalcanal Diary*'s concerns at work. First, despite the historic fact that in the early months of the campaign the marines' main goal was defensive, to defend the lines around Henderson Field from repeated, suicidal enemy attacks, the film concentrates on the marines advancing— taking territory away from the Japanese and eventually driving them into the sea. This is connected to the idea that Guadalcanal marked the beginning of the U.S. offensive in the Pacific. The second concern seems to be the danger of overconfidence. On the troop ships before the landings, the marines are quietly insecure, concerned about what lies ahead. But shortly after they hit the beaches, encountering little enemy resistance, many of them become cocky. The film then presents a series of incidents in which overconfidence is punished; this is part of the process by which the marines, and presumably the audience, learn an appropriate attitude toward the enemy, the U.S. offensive in the Pacific, and our eventual victory. Strolling along Henderson Field, one marine scoffs, "I bet there ain't a Jap within ten miles of here," and then is immediately killed by a sniper's bullet. Taking the word of a prisoner that a group of Japanese soldiers, starving and without weapons, will surrender without a fight, a small patrol of marines falls into a trap from which only one escapes alive. Pvt. Johnny Anderson (Richard Jaeckel) is seriously wounded when he tries to take a sword for a souvenir from a seemingly dead Japanese officer. Private Soose (Anthony Quinn) shouts, "Hey Jap, you forgot something," and kills a fleeing soldier by throwing his own knife into his back. Sauntering up to the body, laughing over his joke, he is killed by a sniper. The need to overcome this overconfidence is emphasized by both the narrator and the officers. When reinforcements come ashore, the narrator (Reed Hadley) intones, "Kids full of big talk, itching for a fight: just like us a few months ago." Colonel Grayson (Minor Watson) tells a newly arrived officer about the lesson his troops have learned (and echoes the lesson of *Gung Ho!*): "At least we've learned not to underestimate them, Colonel. We know now they won't surrender, and we've got to bring them to their knees. . . . We out shoot them, we out fight them, and we usually out guess them, because our men have learned to act as individuals. Of course, it's taken a little while to get rid of our cockiness, but I think we're ready now." As we're shown the troops moving into position for the ultimate battle, the narrator tells us, "Gone now is the loud surface toughness of last summer. In its place is the cool, quiet fortitude that comes only with battle experience." As the marines push the Japanese into the sea, the audience understands that in this offensive phase of the war, Americans need to be confident but not overconfident; victory will come, but only in time, after much hard work and much blood. Further, the audience sees the difference between the mindless drones produced by the fascist Japanese military and the individuals working as a team in the U.S. military.

These films depicting the historical events of the early war in the Pacific, then, functioned in several important ways. First, they filled in the narrative gaps left by newspaper accounts of the events, in effect creating a complete story. Second, they used these stories to justify America's efforts in the Pacific. Third, they used these stories to draw a picture of the kind of servicemen America would need if it expected to fight and win the war. In the next chapter we explore how Hollywood films depicted and defined our enemies—the Germans, Italians, and Japanese—in order to explain how they were different from Americans and why they had to be defeated.

3

OUR ENEMIES

Now look here, Fräulein, it isn't very pleasant to have to beat
a pretty girl like yourself, but I have a duty to perform.
        —Gestapo colonel Heller (Martin Kosleck)
                in *Underground*

Well, I don't hate Japs—yet. It's a funny thing. I don't *like* 'em,
but I don't *hate* 'em.
        —Lt. Bob Gray (Robert Mitchum) in
                Thirty Seconds over Tokyo

POPULAR MEDIA HAVE ALWAYS BEEN an important cultural vehicle
for transmitting ideas to people about who they are and, just as important,
who they aren't. As Edward Said and others have shown, a society's sense
of national identity is based to a great extent on the way it contrasts itself
to other societies that are different, foreign, strange, and often threatening—in short, its enemies. Hollywood films, because they were seen by
huge numbers of people over the whole country, were the most efficient
and powerful means of communicating ideas about American national
identity and America's enemies in the 1940s. We discuss how Hollywood
films promoted certain ideas about Americans' identities in chapter 6. Here
we explore how Hollywood films made just before and after Pearl Harbor
constructed the Germans, Italians, and Japanese as enemies. We've already touched on (see chapters 1 and 2) some of the ways Hollywood
films prepared Americans to think about the Germans and the Japanese.

100

We now examine more specifically the narrative and cinematic techniques films used to construct ways to know our enemies.

One frequently heard truism is that Hollywood films crudely and obviously present the enemy as Other to the point of denying their humanity. The late newspaper columnist Mike Royko expressed this view in an interview with Studs Terkel: "And all those movies. I took a vacation in Florida recently and every time I looked up at a palm tree, I expected a Jap sniper up there. In these movies, every tree had a little Nip sittin' up there. . . . Our guys were the good guys and the other side was evil. That was years before anybody made a movie in which they showed any compassion, any understanding at all for the others—that they were human beings."[1] A variation of this truism is that only late in the war do films start making a distinction between Nazis and "good" Germans. Like most truisms, however, these are only partly true. Certainly, the great majority of films dealing with the war in the Pacific construct the Japanese as Other, though more complex presentations of Japanese characters occasionally crop up. But we found that throughout the war, distinctions were made about different kinds of Germans. And the Italians were never presented as a threatening enemy at all. In short, the movies' construction of the enemy was more complex—and more interesting—than today's viewers assume. Employing already familiar movie conventions, the films succeeded in defining our enemies in such a way that Americans could understand why they must be fought and defeated; yet at the same time, to varying degrees, Hollywood films made connections between Americans and their enemies, both to heighten the contrast with the enemy and to prepare for rebuilding relationships after the war.

We saw in chapter 1 that in the prewar films *Foreign Correspondent* and *Man Hunt*, many of the Germans (though they weren't specified as Germans in the former) were presented as stock spy or gangster movie figures: thuggish, inarticulate, threatening, mindlessly obeying orders. Audiences knew that they were evil simply from the way they were costumed, lit, and photographed; viewers recognized the type and so knew how they were supposed to respond. The first thing to note, then, about the presentation of the German enemy during World War II is that filmmakers already had an arsenal of German types that they had been using at least since World War I and that were available for updating for this new war. We argued in chapter 1 that World War I films made in 1940 and 1941 displaced the contemporary war in Europe onto the earlier war, but something of a reverse process was happening as well: films about the contemporary war employed character types perfected in films about the previous war. Think, for example, of Baron von Kranz, played by Lucien Prival, in *Hell's Angels* (1930): he is a Prussian aristocrat, formal, stiff, humorless—except when faced with the opportunity for cruelty—and a natural and enthusiastic fighter. Think, too, of Captain von Rauffenstein, played by Erich von Stroheim in *Grand Illusion* (1937; U.S. release 1938): also aristocratic, stiff, and formal, but cultured and intellectual as well— qualities that, regretfully, he must repress so that he can do his duty. That each of these character types was easily transferred to the Nazis can be seen by the number of times these two actors played such roles in World War II films—Prival in *Confessions of a Nazi Spy* (1939), *Beasts of Berlin* (1939), *The Mortal Storm* (1940), *The Great Dictator* (1940), *Submarine Base* (1943), and *Assignment in Brittany* (1943), and von Stroheim in *So Ends Our Night* (1941), *The North Star* (1943), and *Five Graves to Cairo* (as General Rommel, 1943). Further, the Prival-type character can be seen in the many evil Nazis played by Martin Kosleck and other actors in scores of films; the von Stroheim type can be seen in intellectual Nazis played by Conrad Veidt, Otto Preminger, George Sanders, Laird Cregar, Sydney Greenstreet, and others. The Hollywood presentation of the Nazis thus began with depictions of Germans that were already familiar to audiences and operated within accepted stereotypes.

This adoption of available German types was combined with techniques that contrasted the Germans to the Allies. In the introduction we saw how Winston Churchill persuasively conjured up the binary oppositions between the British and the Germans in order to define the Germans and the war for his listeners, and we saw the way Frank Capra adapted those binary oppositions in his Why We Fight series. Other films participated in the same rhetoric—associating culturally preferred qualities with the Allies and culturally abrogated qualities with the Germans—to make their case about the Germans as enemy.

A good example from early in the war is MGM's *Mrs. Miniver*, directed by William Wyler and released on May 13, 1942. In a key scene Mrs. Miniver (Greer Garson) discovers a wounded German pilot (Helmut Dantine) whose plane was shot down during a recent bombardment of London and environs. The only German character to appear in the film, he becomes the personification of all the otherwise anonymous destruction that Germany is inflicting on England. His sudden, startling appearance in the Minivers' well-kept garden and ordered suburban home is representative of the larger threat of a German invasion. Just before Mrs.

Miniver discovers the pilot in her garden, she has been chatting with Mr. Ballard (Henry Travers), out early to fish. He quotes from the Bible and tells Mrs. Miniver that the community's annual flower show, held at the local aristocratic manor, will go on despite the war. This dialogue telegraphs to us the qualities the film wants to associate with the British: Christianity, tradition, civilization, culture. The German, in contrast, is associated with the opposite qualities. Whereas the fleeing Mrs. Miniver keeps to her garden path, he smashes through bushes and plants to catch her. He speaks broken English in a guttural accent. While eating he spills milk down his uniform and shoves meat and bread into his mouth. Whereas Mrs. Miniver tries to show compassion and can't even bring herself to hold a pistol on him, he returns hate and threatened violence. He boasts, "Rotterdam we destroy in two hours," and to Mrs. Miniver's protest that 30,000 innocent people, including women and children, were killed, he rejoins, "Not innocent. They were against us." Contrasted to Mrs. Miniver and the British in general, he is barbaric, destructive, barely human; he

Mrs. Miniver: Mrs. Miniver (Greer Garson) gets the better of a downed German pilot (Helmut Dantine).

shows no respect for compassion, culture, or the rules of war. Most frighteningly, he is presented as the typical German. He tells Mrs. Miniver, "I am finish. But others come. Like me. Thousands. Many thousands."

The opposition here is created via a contrast between an upstanding Englishwoman and a supposedly typical German. Films depicting life in Nazi Germany create their arguments for the Germans as enemy through a more complex series of oppositions. These oppositions—in such films as *The Hitler Gang, The Man I Married, The Mortal Storm, Underground, So Ends Our Night, Hitler's Children, The Seventh Cross,* and *None Shall Escape*—work in different ways, but they share the technique of using conflicts within German society or between Germans and other nationalities as a means of defining Nazis as enemy, frequently finding ways to introduce an explicit or implicit American point of view with which the audience can identify. The result is a fairly consistent picture of the Germans as enemies, but with a suggestion that the evil in Germany flows from the top down, corrupting those who, in different circumstances, would be fine people and creating enclaves of resistance inhabited by the "good" Germans, who are like us.

The evil at the top of the hierarchy of German society is most concisely articulated in *The Hitler Gang,* a weird pseudodocumentary released by Paramount on May 7, 1944. The screenplay sought to present Hitler's rise to power, and the film's preface promises authenticity, "insofar as decency will permit." But more effective in creating the aura of reality is the strategy (as in *Confessions of a Nazi Spy*) of postponing the credits until the end: at the beginning we get only the title; no actors, writers, director, or producers are mentioned. As the title suggests, the film doesn't invest all the evil of Nazism in Hitler (Bobby Watson). The men around him— Goebbels (Martin Kosleck), Himmler (Luis Van Rooten), and Göring (Alexander Pope)—contribute to the film's construction of Nazism. The Nazi leaders are presented as unstable and perverse: a doctor finds Corp. Adolf Hitler insane at the end of World War I; the film implies a homoerotic relationship between Hitler and Rudolf Hess (Victor Varconi) and, more overtly, an incestuous relationship between Hitler and his niece Geli (Poldy Dur); Göring is a morphine addict. The Nazi leadership is egotistical and temperamental: Hitler must be coddled like an opera star; at the least resistance he pouts and says he can't go on. The Nazi leadership is untrustworthy and hypocritical: until he has power, Hitler toadies to the powerful, telling them whatever they want to hear; his henchmen delight in betraying others and even plot against one another and Hitler. The Nazi

The Hitler Gang: Adolf Hitler (Bobby Watson), Rudolf Hess (Victor Varconi), Heinrich Himmler (Luis Van Rooten), Joseph Goebbels (Martin Kosleck), and Hermann Göring (Alexander Pope) consider how best to conquer the world.

leadership is cowardly: they are always the first to flee fights and are experts at getting others to fight their battles for them. The Nazi leadership's only ideology is power for power's sake: they have no commitment to any issue or idea beyond its use in gaining power.

In one scene, set in 1920, the German Workers Party, precursor to the Nazi Party, looks for a scapegoat to energize its platform, illustrating many of these ideas. After several suggestions for attackable minorities are made and rejected, Himmler modestly proposes the Jews. Hitler is inspired and launches into an oration:

> HITLER: The Jews are the cause of all our troubles. The Jews started the war! The Jews were the cause of our defeat!
>
> STRASSER (Fritz Kortner):   Let us at least be logical. They cannot be responsible for both the war and the peace.
>
> HITLER: I cannot work under these conditions. I cannot work with

people who don't believe in me. I resign. I resign! . . . I have nothing to do with logic. Logic is the business of little minds, the so-called intellectuals who sit and talk and do nothing. I want action. I accept anything that leads to action.

STRASSER: I want action as much as you do, but let us pick on something that's nearer to the truth.

ROSENBERG (Tonio Selwart):   The truth? What is the truth? It's something you've heard so often that you accept it as the truth.

HITLER: Then I shall *make* it the truth! And I shall repeat it again and again, in different ways, but the meaning will always be the same! The Jew is responsible for all our trouble. The Jew is responsible for all our trouble!

Here we see Hitler as madman and as prima donna. We also see the cynicism and hypocrisy of the party's realpolitik and the ruthlessness that permits any act if it will obtain power. These qualities in one way or another are found in most depictions of Nazi leadership—at any level of the hierarchy—in Hollywood films. Conrad Veidt's Major Strasser in *Casablanca*, Erich von Stroheim's Dr. Von Harden in *The North Star*, Laird Cregar's Herr Funk in *Joan of Paris* (1942), Otto Preminger's Major Diessen in *The Pied Piper* (1942), and Sydney Greenstreet's Colonel Robinson in *Background to Danger* (1943)—along with the various Nazi characters in the films discussed later—are ready examples of characters on the lower end of the party and military hierarchy who act in much the same manner as the leaders at the top.

The Man I Married, a Twentieth Century–Fox second feature released on July 16, 1940, shows the corrupt power at the top of the Nazi hierarchy trickling down through the entire German society. As American journalist Delane (Lloyd Nolan) says of average Germans' willing participation in Nazism, "They catch it from Schickie," his pet name for Hitler. Only a few Germans recognize the evil of his power, and they are overwhelmed by it. The film sets up an opposition between Germany under national socialism and a young American woman visitor who gets an education she didn't expect. Carol (Joan Bennett), a single mother and writer for a glossy magazine, meets a charming German immigrant, Eric Hoffman (Francis Lederer), in New York and marries him in July 1938. For their honeymoon, they travel to Germany so that Carol can meet Eric's father and Eric can tie up some unfinished business before he moves permanently to the United States. Carol, like the naïfs in *Foreign Correspondent* and *Man Hunt*, is largely unaware of what's going on in Germany and dismisses much of what she reads as journalistic sensationalism. As she becomes increasingly concerned about what she sees happening in Germany—the military buildup, the persecution of the Czechs, the restriction of individual liberties—Eric becomes swept up in Nazism to the point that he no longer wishes to return to New York. He plans to divorce Carol and send her back to the States but keep her son Ricky (Johnny Russell) to raise as a German. Carol manages to get Ricky safely back to New York with the help of Delane and Eric's father (Otto Kruger), who threatens to reveal to the authorities that Eric's mother was a Jew.

Carol enters Germany with an open mind, willing to be fair and to discount what she perceives as propaganda, but her education about Nazism is marked by several instances in which she and her German hosts respond differently to the same event. Upon arriving at the train station in Berlin, Johnny imitates his hero, the Lone Ranger, and yahoos while shooting his cap pistol. While Carol is charmed by his innocence, the German civilians cower and take cover, and the soldiers point their rifles, ready to fire. At a military parade the German spectators enthuse over the Wehrmacht paratroopers, but Carol remarks that it "looks like something you see at the circus." Carol's joke about Hitler—she calls him Schickie, which she picked up from Delane—shocks Eric and later serves as grounds for divorce. Conversely, when Delane and Carol see Gestapo officers forcing Czechs to clean garbage off the street, Carol is horrified, while the German passersby laugh. These incidents are summed up by Delane when he says, "We can still laugh at ourselves. These poor boys over here lost their sense of humor, if they ever had any. And any nation that doesn't know how to laugh is dangerous." The issue of humor here marks the difference between the American point of view and the German: the two societies are operating from completely different assumptions—about right and wrong, about how nationality is defined, about how patriotism is enacted, about how power is employed. For Carol, the absurdity that leads to laughter turns into an absurdity that causes terror as she realizes that hardly anyone in Germany recognizes what she sees to be absurd.

Mrs. Miniver presents a fairly straightforward enemy, one who embodies everything we fear and nothing we respect; *The Hitler Gang* presents a more layered picture of the enemy, but an enemy that is nevertheless despicable; *The Man I Married* presents German society as a through-the-looking-glass world where American values have been lost. More often, however, films focusing on Germany show a conflicted society in which many enthusiastically throw themselves into the workings of national socialism; others go along reluctantly, through weakness, fear, or ignorance; and still others resist. These films construct an idea of the enemy, but they also define the enemy more sharply, demonstrate the enemy's use of power, and make connections between those who would oppose the Nazis and the American viewing audience.

One of the best prewar film critiques of Nazi Germany uses oppositions within German society to help define America's distinctiveness from its potential enemy. *The Mortal Storm*, the screen adaptation of Phyllis Bottome's novel, was released on June 11, 1940. Opening on January 30, 1933, the day Hitler was named chancellor, the film tells the story of how ascendant Nazism affects the family of a Jewish chemistry professor and their small Bavarian town. The always cautious MGM began the film with a voice-over suggesting that the film was promoting peace, not intervention, but reviews at the time argued that its anti-Nazi themes had been made outdated by real-world events. Howard Barnes in the *New York Herald Tribune* wrote, "There have been a dozen plays, in my recollection, which pointed out the terror that swept Germany when Hitler was appointed Chancellor. None of them was very convincing for the simple reason that they presupposed that there was a strong liberal sentiment in Germany which opposed the Third Reich. At this late date, this thesis may be pleasant to contemplate, but it certainly doesn't stand up factually or dramatically."[2]

This approach to the film—seeing it as a story about the defeat of German liberalism by Nazism—seems to miss the point. The film can more profitably be seen as defining Germany under Hitler by contrasting the Nazis with liberal German characters who are, in effect, stand-ins for Americans. This contrast is established very early in the film as Professor Roth (Frank Morgan) is surprised on his birthday—January 30, 1933—by a celebratory gathering of family, colleagues, and students in his chemistry classroom. Presentations are made by two students: Fritz Marberg (Robert Young) and Martin Breitner (James Stewart). Fritz walks, stands, and bows stiffly; his speech is clipped and his presentation formal. In contrast, Martin seems as American as, well, Jimmy Stewart; he shuffles, he fidgets, he searches his pockets for notes he can't find, he stutters, he speaks in a nasally twang, and after being introduced in Latin as "candidatus medicinae vetrinarae," he explains, "in plain language, horse doctor."[3] Before any ideological conflicts have been introduced, the film, through casting and direction, has made a distinction between "German" characters and "American" characters. Indeed, though not as blatantly as in Stewart's case, the other actors playing German characters with whom we are meant to sympathize—Morgan as Professor Roth, Margaret Sullavan as his daughter Freya, Irene Rich as his wife—speak in their normal American voices, making no attempt to suggest a foreign accent.

The ideological differences are introduced that evening at the professor's birthday party. The small gathering—the family plus Fritz and Martin—is interrupted by the radio announcement of Hitler's being named chancellor. At this point the warmth and unity that had characterized the film break down as Fritz and the professor's two stepsons, Otto von Rohn (Robert Stack) and Erich von Rohn (William T. Orr), are revealed to be Nazi Party members. They immediately begin spouting a doctrine of totalitarianism, intolerance, and submission to the state. To a demurring Martin, Fritz says, "Now, there'll be one party and only one." Otto adds, "A man's got to take a stand. If he's not for us, he's against us, and against Germany." Freya objects, "You're getting very intolerant, all of you," to which Otto responds, "We *should* be intolerant! Of anyone who opposes the will of our leader." Soon after, Fritz, Otto, and Erich are called to a party meeting; the local leader also wants Martin to attend, but Martin says, "Tell him peasants have no politics. They keep cows." Fritz answers, "If they want to keep their cows, they'd better have the *right* politics." When Professor Roth laughingly laments that Hitler has broken up the birthday party, his youngest son, Rudi (Gene Reynolds), explains what he's learned in school: "You oughtn't to mind. . . . The individual must be sacrificed to the welfare of the state."

Martin and Professor Roth try to oppose Fritz, Otto, and Erich's party philosophy with a position of pluralism. When Fritz contemptuously accuses Martin of being a pacifist, he responds with a line that will recur as a credo of liberalism throughout the film: "I think peace is better than war. A man's right to think as he believes is as good for him as food and drink." The professor tries to patch up the vehement argument that follows by urging everyone to put Martin's philosophy into practice: "Can't we discuss these matters without quarreling? After all, every hen thinks she's laid the best egg. May we not believe as we choose and allow others to do the same?" Later, after Nazism has transformed the small university town, the family is again disrupted as Otto and Erich choose to leave their home because of Freya's continued friendship with Martin. Professor Roth tries to reason with them: "You ask me to force your sister to give up a life-long friend, a young man we've always liked and respected. No, I couldn't do that. You and your brother have chosen your way, and we've respected your decision. We're entitled to the same tolerance." Needless to say, the brothers are not persuaded.

This intolerance for a diversity of opinion is connected to a closed-mindedness toward any idea that diverges from Nazi dogma. Professor Roth becomes the subject of a student boycott because he refuses to say in his chemistry class that Aryan and non-Aryan blood are different. Although he is in favor of pluralism when it comes to ideology, in science there is only truth and falsehood. Shortly afterward, he looks out his classroom window and sees the university's students burning books because they assert facts that Hitler refuses to recognize. The professor is eventually arrested and sent to a concentration camp because of his refusal to recant his work. He tells his wife, after she has managed a single visit, not to have false hope for his future: "You see, even if they let me out, I should still fight for scientific truth." As it turns out, he's correct: the family soon receives notice of his death.

These disruptions of family and personal relationships—beginning with the interruption of the professor's birthday party and continuing with the off-screen guard who continually interrupts the final conversation between the professor and his wife—reach their thematic climax when Fritz is ordered to lead a patrol to capture Freya and Martin before they can escape into Switzerland. He asks to be relieved of this duty, saying to the local party leader (Rudolph Anders), "I once looked upon these two people as my closest friends. . . . I realize that this duty must be carried out, but I beg of you to understand a human weakness." The leader responds, "You have sworn allegiance to the Third Reich. In the service of your country, there are no human relationships." The extent of Fritz's transformation is underscored here by the lighting, which creates a shadow under his nose reminiscent of Hitler's mustache.

Connected to the Nazi state's intolerance and the continual disruption of human relationships is the distrust of individuality. When a local Nazi commander (Dan Dailey) enters a pub, all the patrons are expected to stand and sing Nazi anthems. The camera lingers over the conformity of the scene, the pub patrons all standing in precise rows, their arms held forward in a salute at precisely the same angle. When a middle-aged teacher (Thomas Ross) tries to eat his dinner without standing and without drawing attention to himself, he is singled out for abuse. He defends himself by saying, "Surely, a man is free to sing or not as he pleases." The Nazis, of course, refuse to respect his individualism. Throughout the film the Nazi characters repeatedly justify their actions by saying, "I have no choice." This is contrasted to the idea of the independent individual, marked by the refrain we hear from Martin and his mother (Maria Ouspenskaya): "I can take care of myself."

In the climactic scene, in which Martin and Freya dash to the Swiss border as Fritz's patrol pursues and finally shoots Freya dead, the film suggests that Hitler and Nazism have transformed Germany into a sort of hell. Martin and Freya's flight suggests Orpheus's attempt to bring Eurydice out of the underworld. Martin even says at one point as they struggle up a mountain, "Every time I look back, you seem to be smaller." The final lesson seems to be that any country that embraces totalitarianism, intolerance of dissenting opinions, loss of individuality, and the demeaning of human relationships is indeed hell.

Another element of Nazism, the desire for national purity, is critiqued in a film released about six months after *The Mortal Storm*. *So Ends Our Night* also uses clearly defined oppositions to make its points. Adapted from the Erich Maria Remarque novel *Flotsam*, *So Ends Our Night* was released by United Artists on January 27, 1941. Set between 1937 and 1939, the film tells the story of several refugees, people without a nation or a home because they have been evicted from Nazi Germany owing to their non-Aryan background. These refugees are essentially nonpeople because they have no passports to give them identities or to allow them to reside anywhere legally. This point is made early in the film by Brenner (Erich von Stroheim), a Gestapo agent, as he tries to persuade Josef Steiner (Fredric March) to betray his friends in the German underground in exchange for a passport: "Just compare our situations. Yours is hopeless. You're a man without a country or a legal right to live, a living ghost. My situation on the other hand is a secure and comfortable one. And all that stands between us is this [the passport]." The Orwellian absurdity of this thinking is remarked by Ludwig Kern (Glenn Ford), whose expulsion from France is halted when he receives official papers allowing him to stay. He says to an uncomprehending border guard, "Through this piece of paper, I've become a respectable person, a free man who can do what he likes, haven't I? . . . Don't you find that strange? . . . Well, yesterday I was the same man I am today, and yesterday everything was prohibited, illegal." The guard replies, "I find it quite in order. You have the right to live— in writing, stamped and signed."

The absurdity of this opposition—between those with and without passports—is used to critique the bureaucratic notion of nation, identity, and home that supports the Nazi effort to create a pure, exclusionary nation and, incidentally, to critique those nations that refuse to help the refugees created by Nazism. The film also sets up an opposition between this bureaucratic notion and an informal, ad hoc idea. As refugees Steiner and Kern slog from country to country—Austria, Czechoslovakia, Switzerland, France—they encounter the same people over and over again until something of a family is formed—a family that helps to replace the lost nation and provide a stable identity. One man (Leonid Kinskey), for example, is known by his fondness for roast chicken, another (Alexander Granach) by his appetite for eggs. This nonbureaucratic idea of nation is made most clear at the end of the film, when Kern and his lover, Ruth Holland (Margaret Sullavan), speculate on where they might live. Kern says, "The first thing we'll do, we'll get married. Understand? Married. We may not have a home anywhere for a while, but we'll be together." Ruth responds, "That's home, darling." As in *The Mortal Storm*, a home based on personal relationships is preferred to one defined by a totalitarian state.

Another prewar film, *Underground*, uses conflicts within Germany to create oppositions by which the Nazis can be understood. A June 18, 1941, Warner Bros. release, *Underground* tells the story of two German brothers; one is a soldier, just returned to Berlin after losing his arm at the front, and the other is a leader of the underground resistance, broadcasting anti-Nazi messages over an illegal radio. Early in the film, the latter brother, Eric Franken (Philip Dorn), makes a broadcast that sets up the film's defining oppositions. He tells his listeners, "Tonight we come to you again in spite of the Gestapo with the news of the real conditions inside of Germany. And we take courage in knowing that thousands of you are willing to risk your lives in order to hear the only words of truth spoken in our unhappy and desecrated country today. And yet how else can you know the truth? You are forbidden to listen to any foreign news broadcasts. You are not allowed to read any newspaper or publication except those owned by the government or censored by Dr. Goebbels himself." He encourages wives and mothers to write to their husbands and sons at the front about the real shortages at home, defying Hitler's orders that they lie. He wonders why Rudolf Hess defected: "He went to England because that is the only place in Europe where the Gestapo can't stop him from talking and can't keep him from telling the truth." He twice reminds his listeners that Hitler has broken his promises to the country and the world. The pattern established here and then repeated throughout the film is clear: the Nazi government is associated with lies; the underground opposition to the government is associated with the truth.

Connected to this main opposition between lies and truth is another opposition, this one between appearance and reality. As Eric argues in his broadcast, the success of the Nazi state is an illusion based on lies. The members of the underground can see through these illusions and find the truth behind them as easily as they can see through the document a torture victim is forced to sign saying that she wasn't hurt or mistreated. The Nazis, in contrast, rarely see through the illusions the underground conjures up: a tow truck hides the underground's illegal radio; the underground's meeting place is guarded by an apparently blind lookout; Gestapo colonel Heller (Martin Kosleck) never suspects that Fräulein Gessner (Mona Maris), his secretary, is a mole for the underground; Fräulein Gessner successfully spreads demoralizing rumors throughout Gestapo headquarters. These deceptions are so successful because the Nazis, living in a world based on lies, are ill equipped to negotiate the slippery differences between appearance and reality.

These themes come together in the story of Eric's brother, Kurt (Jeffrey Lynn). He plays the role of naïf (like Carol in *The Man I Married* or Johnny Jones in *Foreign Correspondent*), an innocent whom the film sets about educating. Kurt, returned from the front, takes what he sees and hears at face value. He unknowingly begins moving among the fringes of the underground when he falls in love with Sylvia Helmuth (Kaaren Verne), one of Eric's colleagues. When Sylvia is arrested, he is convinced of her innocence and concerned for her safety. He asks Eric, "They wouldn't hurt her, not a girl, would they?" Eric responds, "Why not?" Later, after he sees firsthand evidence of her involvement with the underground, instead of turning her in, he tries to rescue her, inadvertently betraying his brother instead. At the Gestapo headquarters afterward, he laments that he didn't know his brother was in the underground; Fräulein Gessner says to him, "It's just possible there are many more things you don't know, Herr Franken." She shows him his brother and father (also arrested) being tortured. His eyes at last opened, Kurt articulates his opposition to the Nazis: "I'm sick of them, their lies and their beatings." Fräulein Gessner shows him how he can put this opposition into action: "Help us. Help the underground. Help us show to the people the truth." In being initiated into the job of spreading the truth, however, Kurt is also introduced into the world of appearances: to prove his loyalty, he must let Heller and Eric believe that he knowingly turned in his own brother. He learns to appear to be a loyal

German on the surface so that he can, in reality, oppose the Nazis, taking Eric's place as the underground's broadcaster.

Unlike *The Mortal Storm*, which used its "good" Germans as stand-ins for Americans, *Underground* suggests a genuine division in German society. The Nazis are evil, but there are right-thinking, freedom-loving Germans who are doing what they can to oppose Hitler. More interesting, the film also shows us the Germans in between. There are naive patriots, like Kurt, who believe that their country is right because they haven't thought very much about it and so don't see through the lies. There are also those like the Frankens' maid, Ella (Lisa Golm), who believe the lies because they're afraid not to. Testifying against Herr Franken, she tells Kurt, "Please Herr Kurt, you don't realize what they do to you nowadays. They make you so afraid, you don't know what's right and what's wrong." The structure of lies that is the Nazi state is supported by fear: make people afraid, and they will believe whatever you tell them to.

A similar distinction between the Nazis in power and the general populace they contaminate and corrupt is made in *Hitler's Children*, a January 6, 1943, RKO release. A Romeo-and-Juliet–like love story between a young Gestapo officer, Karl Brunner (Tim Holt), and a young American girl of German extraction, Anna Muller (Bonita Granville), is at the center of the film, but more interesting is its exploration of the transmission and enforcement of Nazi ideology.

Hitler's Children focuses on the idea of reproduction in two senses. First is biological reproduction. We see women in 1938 Berlin being encouraged to have children for the welfare of the state. One woman is reassured that once she has her fifth child, the state will forgive her family's debts. At a women's labor camp, the prisoners are supposed to let themselves be impregnated by visiting young men without worrying about marriage. This is euphemistically called sharing "the experience that makes them worthy of the Führer." This service to the state is repeatedly compared to men serving in the armed forces. As one pregnant woman (Carla Boehm) explains, "I shall have a child for the state and for the Führer. Isn't that much nobler than having a child just for a home and a husband. . . . Do you know what I'm hoping? I hope I shall have much pain when my baby is born. I want to feel that I'm going through a real ordeal for our Führer." Connected to this procreative encouragement, as in *So Ends Our Night*, is a concern for national purity. We see women who are deemed unfit to reproduce being sterilized in a kind of clinical assembly line. A Gestapo officer (Otto Kruger) explains, "We are building a new Germany, a strong Germany. There is no room for the sick and the weak and the unstable. . . . Of course, although the majority of our cases are the weak and the unstable, our doctors operate for a number of other reasons. . . . They range from eliminating hereditary color blindness to dangerous political thinking." Once again, we see the Nazis interfering in personal human relationships.

The second sense of reproduction is ideological reproduction, the transmission of Nazi ideology to young people. The Nazi state is committed to brainwashing children in its dogma. We see this over and over: the lessons at the Horst Wessel school at the beginning of the film, the games of the Hitler Youth, the informal catechisms that party members rehearse to children on the street, the discipline of the labor camp. It's no coincidence that the vocabulary here suggests a religion; the film presents Nazism as a secular religion, complete with rites and ceremonies (as in the carefully choreographed whipping scene) and reverent obeisance to the state.[4] This transference of religious authority from the church to the state, according to Franz Erhart (Lloyd Corrigan), speaks to the German character: "You Americans will never understand us. Maybe it is the will to obey that is in us Germans. How easy to march in step once you have started."

The film ends by suggesting that there are some Germans who have enough humanity and desire for freedom to resist the state's attempts to pervert human relations and religious authority. Karl is one of them, as he uses his show trial to speak out for freedom and love. There are also some Germans who have just enough courage to overcome the state-generated fear and find small ways to express their resistance. The film's last scene shows timid Franz Erhart disconnecting the wires of a loudspeaker blasting martial music as a voice-over tells us, "if he isn't as much a hero as he ought to be, he isn't as much a coward as he used to be either." Interestingly, both Karl and Franz are inspired to take their stands through art—for Karl, the poetry of Goethe; for Franz, the music of Beethoven. Art remains a medium for the expression of what's best and most valued in human beings, even under dictators.

This idea of the humanity at the heart of the average German is also the heavy-handed theme of MGM's *The Seventh Cross*, released on July 24, 1944, and based on the novel by Anna Seghers. Set in 1936, the film follows George Heisler (Spencer Tracy), one of seven escapees from a concentration camp, as he tries to avoid capture and find a way out of the country. The narration by Wallau (Ray Collins), another escapee, keeps a parallel focus on Heisler's moral journey. Wallau argues that the Nazi state maintains its power by dehumanizing the populace. Wallau is concerned that Heisler, once a rebel, has become dehumanized through the loss of faith in other people. As he hides and eventually escapes from Germany, we see Heisler regain his faith in the inherent goodness of people. The focus here is not on the wielders of power—the camp commandant and the Gestapo officers appear infrequently. Rather, the focus is on the average German. We see several characters who, through fear or ideological commitment, refuse to help Heisler or even threaten him. But we also see a large number of people who do help him. Some who don't know him help out of charitable impulses; members of the underground help because of their dedication to the movement; friends from before his arrest help out of loyalty. By the end of the film, as he's about to leave Germany for Holland, he explains what he's learned: "I know that no matter how cruelly the world strikes at the souls of men, there is a God-given decency in them that will come out if it gets half a chance. And that's the hope for the human race." Like *Underground* and *Hitler's Children, The Seventh Cross* encourages viewers to see that there are different types of Germans, many of whom are good, decent people, even if their goodness and decency have been beaten down by those in power.

All these narratives about our German enemies can be seen at work in an interesting way in *None Shall Escape*. This film was released by Columbia on January 28, 1944, more than four months before D-day and more than a year before the end of the war, yet it is remarkably prescient, anticipating not only the Nuremberg trials but also the accused war criminals' line of defense. It is set in the future, after the Allies have defeated Germany, at a war crimes trial convened by the United Nations (representatives from around the world are present). The accused is Wilhelm Grimm, Reichscommissioner for western Poland (Alexander Knox). Most of the film is presented in flashbacks as witnesses give their testimony. We see Grimm as a civilian, returning to the Polish village of Litzbark after World War I to take up his post as schoolmaster. His fiancée, Marja (Marsha Hunt), postpones their wedding because she's concerned by the abuse he heaps on the Poles. Returning from a sojourn in Warsaw, she discovers that Grimm has raped one of his students, who then killed herself. There is not enough evidence to convict him, so he borrows money from the local priest and rabbi and leaves the village. Grimm's brother Karl (Erik Rolf) testifies to his return to Munich, where he joins and rises in the ranks of the Nazi Party. When Karl prepares to move his family to Vienna, Grimm has him arrested and takes his son Willie under his care. Marja testifies to Grimm's return to Litzbark as Reichscommissioner in 1939, with a grown Willie (Richard Crane) as his aide, and to the terror he institutes.

There are many familiar elements here. As a stand-in for the Nazi Party leadership, Grimm is irrationally convinced of his superiority to everyone; he is egotistical but cowardly, as we see when he runs away or betrays someone close to him every time he faces a crisis. He is also presented as sharing the self-serving hypocrisy of the Nazi leadership: in jail for his part in the Beer Hall Putsch, he eats caviar from a silver service, and while demanding that Litzbark produce impossible quotas of food to feed the Wehrmacht, he eats gourmet meals and drinks imported coffee and brandy.

The film also makes a distinction between Nazis and other, presumably decent Germans. On the one hand, the film stresses that Grimm is typical, not an unusually cruel Nazi. At the end of her testimony, Marja says that after Grimm left Litzbark, "Those of us who felt that such cruelty, such complete lack of human decency, was peculiar to him alone learned otherwise in the years that followed. Those who came after him may have varied their forms of torture and brutality, but they were the same. They were all Wilhelm Grimms. They were Nazis." On the other hand, we see that not all Germans are Nazis. Karl stands up as a decent man appalled by what he sees happening to his country. And, as in *Hitler's Children*, Willie learns to see beyond the Nazi ideology and find his own humanity through his love for a young woman, Janina (Dorothy Morris), Marja's daughter. When Janina dies, shot by another officer presumably while resisting being raped, Willie rejects Nazism and finally acknowledges the disruption of his family that Grimm has engineered. Following the procession carrying Janina's body into the church, he tells his uncle, "I want to pray. I want to pray to my father to ask him to forgive me. I want to let him know that now I understand what he did. I want to be forgiven for having deserted him and my mother. For having been a traitor." Grimm then completes the destruction of the family by shooting and killing his nephew.

More graphically than in *So Ends Our Night*, the film shows the Nazis' process of creating Others, enemies who threaten the purity of the German nation. Grimm has no respect for the Poles while he's a teacher in Litzbark. After the German invasion, they are objects to be used in the service of the German army. Men aged sixteen to sixty are sent to labor camps. Young women, including Janina, are rounded up and imprisoned in a brothel, euphemistically called the Officers' Club. One officer (Kurt

Kreuger) sums up this process of objectification: "These aren't people, they're dogs. But good dogs. You can train them." More surprising, considering the film's release date, is the presentation of the persecution of Litzbark's Jews. The synagogue is emptied of its contents, which are burned, and it is turned into a stable. The rabbi and other Jews are shown wearing yellow Star of David armbands. Finally, the Jews are taken en masse to a railroad siding and herded into cattle cars, where they are to wait to be attached to a longer train full of Warsaw Jews. When Rabbi Levin (Richard Hale) urges them to resist, they are gunned down at Grimm's orders. Willie explains to Janina, "They weren't people. They were Jews."

Running through *None Shall Escape* is a conflict reminiscent of *The Mortal Storm:* lack of free choice versus individual human agency. The conflict is especially interesting here because the film systematically attacks the "I was only following orders" defense used by so many actual war criminals at Nuremberg. Father Warecki (Henry Travers) begins his testimony by explicitly challenging this defense: "The trial of these criminals marks a milestone in human history. It is being argued today that we, having defeated the Nazis, should show tolerance and mercy. That these men are the victims of circumstance and of history, and that they enjoyed no freedom to act in accordance of the dictates of their own consciences. I'd like to relate an incident which occurred many years ago to prove that the accused acted of his own volition and that he had freedom of choice and of will." This idea that people have the freedom to make their own choices and create their own destinies is repeated throughout the film. When young Grimm, acquitted of rape charges but humiliated, comes to Father Warecki and Rabbi Levin for money so that he can go back to Germany, the priest tells him, "Today you stand before two roads. Upon one humanity walks in brotherly love and human understanding. On the other run wild the forces of destruction. You started on the wrong road, Grimm, but it's not too late to turn back." This same fork-in-the-road idea is expressed to young Willie by his father, explaining why the family is moving to Austria: "There comes a time in a man's life when he has to make some great decision, and when that time comes for you, I want you to be ready for it." Later, when Father Warecki, Rabbi Levin, and Marja protest the expulsion of Litzbark's Jews, Grimm responds, "I merely carry out orders." Rabbi Levin's speech to his people responds to this abrogation of agency: "We have submitted too long. If we want equality and justice, we must take our place alongside all other oppressed peoples, regardless of race or religion. Their fight is ours, ours is theirs. We haven't much time left. By our actions we will be remembered. This is our last free choice, our moment in history. I say to you, let us choose to fight. Here! Now!" The beginning of Willie's transformation, his discovery of his own humanity, comes when Marja taunts him after he discovers a wanted man hiding in her basement. She says to him, "You obey orders because you haven't the courage to disobey. You don't dare. . . . Your uncle doesn't dare disobey even though he knows he's wrong. Rabbi Levin made a choice as a free man. But you're afraid. Your father dared." When she tells him to take the man away, Willie responds, "Don't tell me what to do! Nobody can make me do anything I don't want to do! I make my own decisions." Then, surprisingly, he leaves without the fugitive. This claiming of free choice introduces a contradiction into Willie's thinking that eventually leads to his rejection of Nazism and his uncle.

This film, more than any other, takes the distinctions between German and Other, Nazi and "good" German, and reduces them to the level of individual agency. Promoting, submitting to, or resisting Nazism is a matter of individual choice, a choice for which the individual can be held accountable in the projected future, after the war. After years of presenting the horrors Nazis inflict on others, Hollywood presents in *None Shall Escape* its most explicit promise that a reckoning will be made.

Compared to the Germans and Japanese, the Italians were only infrequently depicted in Hollywood films just before and during the war. Shull and Wilt suggest that this may have been because "the Italians were never considered a serious threat."[5] One might also speculate that the studios were reluctant to alienate the large number of Italian American moviegoers. But as with the portrayal of the Nazis, filmmakers drew on long-established stage and film conventions—most of them comic—to depict Italians as an enemy. These conventions may partly account for the condescending way Italy-as-enemy was shown in these films. Think, for example, of Jack Oakie's portrayal of the Mussolini parody Benzini Napaloni in *The Great Dictator*: blustering, with rustic manners, broken English, and mispronounced words. Or think of Luis Alberni's espionage agent Signor Scarletti in *World Premiere*: officious, inept, and cowardly. These characterizations come out of the same tradition as Chico Marx's stage and film persona. Even in more serious films, Italian characters provide comic relief, such as the talkative and irrelevant Italian liaison to the Vichy French in *Casablanca*. The only Hollywood war films actually set in Italy come late in the war, well after the Italian surrender. *A Walk in the Sun*, made during the war but not released until December 1945, is set in Italy, but its focus is the psychology of a platoon's men in battle; the setting could be anywhere. *A Bell for Adano* (1945) offers the most sophisticated presentation of the Italian people, but not as an enemy. Rather, they are victims of the war, and the American occupation forces must help them return to normalcy.

The most interesting presentation of an Italian as enemy occurs in *Sahara*, a September 29, 1943, Columbia release. In the film, which takes place in June 1942, an American tank crew, commanded by Sgt. Joe Gunn (Humphrey Bogart) and attached to the British army, is lost in a general retreat. After picking up a diverse collection of stranded allies—including British, French, South African, and even a British Sudanese—they make their way to a well, which they defend against a German motorized unit in an apparently suicidal delaying action. On the way to the well, they pick up two prisoners. The Sudanese, Tambul (Rex Ingram), has an Italian prisoner, Giuseppe (J. Carrol Naish), and the tank crew shoots down a German plane and captures its pilot (Kurt Kreuger). This situation allows the film to contrast the two prisoners and to explore the differences between them as enemies.

When the tank crew picks up Tambul and Giuseppe, Sergeant Gunn orders that the prisoner be given a package of rations and left behind to make his own way out of the desert. He reasons that the large group won't have enough water over the long journey to share with an enemy. Ominously, vultures circle above, already anticipating the Italian's death. Giuseppe begs to be taken along, and in the process, he turns himself from an enemy, an Other, into an individual. He offers to show Gunn a photograph of his wife and child and tells the group that he can speak English—he studied it in school and practices by reading letters from his wife's uncle's cousin, who lives in America. He says, "He work now in Pittsburgh, U.S.A., in the steel factory. Maybe he make the steel for this tank in Pittsburgh, U.S.A." Gunn resists this attempt at connection-making and individualization, refusing to look at the picture and trying to keep the man objectified: "I'm not taking on a load of spaghetti." He finally relents when he sees Giuseppe stumbling helplessly and pathetically in the trail of the tank's treads.

After the tank reaches the well, where Gunn and the men hope to make a stand, Giuseppe gradually becomes less a prisoner and more a member of the group. Having been a mechanic in civilian life, he offers to help Gunn work on the tank, and the offer is gratefully accepted. A little later, when the French member of the group, Jean "Frenchy" Leroux (Louis Mercier), fantasizes about the cheese made in his hometown and describes how one eats it ("a little cheese, a little bread, then you wash your throat with wine"), Giuseppe hesitantly suggests adding a little onion to the sequence, and Frenchy obliges; Giuseppe is allowed to participate in the fantasy and, in effect, is welcomed into the group. While working on the tank, Gunn asks Giuseppe about life under Mussolini; his response reveals both an interesting self-conscious awareness of how fascist ideology is reproduced in its subjects and a recognition of the necessity of submitting to it. He says of Mussolini, "He tells me he knows best. Everywhere he writes his mottoes, on the walls, on the street, so we got them in the brain, and we must believe these mottoes. . . . Obey. Believe. Work." When Gunn suggests that Mussolini thinks he's God, Giuseppe explains, "Yes, he thinks, but I think maybe Hitler is God, and Mussolini is just his prophet." But he ends this commentary with a weary acceptance: "For some people is alright to laugh at Il Duce, but when you got a wife and a baby, is no good to laugh." In films about the transmission of Nazi ideology to the populace, we saw some characters who embraced Nazism, some who accepted it out of fear, and some who recognized the processes by which it was being propagated and in large or small ways resisted it. Giuseppe, representing Italians, seems to do all three at once, suggesting a fundamental difference between Germans and Italians: Italians may embrace Mussolini's fascism, but they embrace it with a self-conscious fatalism because there seems to be no alternative.

One of the mistakes the film's characters make is not to recognize the differences between their two prisoners, the German and the Italian. When they capture the German pilot, there's no debate about whether to take him along or leave him in the desert to die, even though he has attacked them and fatally wounded one of them. The unspoken logic seems to be that they should treat him just as they've treated the Italian. As they go along, however, whereas Giuseppe becomes individualized, makes connections to the allies, offers to help, and becomes part of the group, the German hides his knowledge of English, insists on his superiority to the allies (especially Tambul), works constantly to undermine the group, and remains more a type than an individual. When the German and Giuseppe are imprisoned together, he tries to force the Italian to help him escape and betray the allies. Giuseppe responds with the clearest statement not only of the differences between Germany and Italy but also of the antagonism:

Italians are not like Germans. Only the party wears the uniform and not the soul. Mussolini is not so clever like Hitler. He can dress his Italians up only to *look* like thieves, cheats, murderers. He cannot like Hitler make them feel like that. He cannot like Hitler scrape from their conscience the knowledge right is right and wrong is wrong, or dig holes in their heads to plant his own ten commandments: steal from thy neighbor, cheat thy neighbor, kill thy neighbor. . . .

Are my eyes blind that I must fall to my knees to worship a maniac who has made of my country a concentration camp? Who has made of my people slaves? Must I kiss the hand that beats me? Lick the boot that kicks me? No! I rather spend my whole life living in this dusty hole than escape to fight again for things I do not believe, against people I do not hate. As for your Hitler, it's because of men like him that God—my God—created hell.

The German then stabs Giuseppe, but he manages to report the Nazi's escape before he dies.

A prewar film, *Sundown* (1941), presents a similar Italian character and puts him to similar uses. This United Artists film focuses on colonial officials in British East Africa trying to prevent a native uprising inspired by and supported with guns from an unspecified foreign power, presumably Germany. When Major Coombes (George Sanders) arrives from Nairobi at the outpost of Manieka, he is shocked to see an unconfined Italian prisoner, Captain Pallini (Joseph Calleia). District Commissioner Crawford (Bruce Cabot) explains, "We hardly regard Pallini as a prisoner." Nor does Pallini regard himself that way: "I am not a prisoner of war. I give myself up—and that is different." Indeed, even the priggish Coombes comes to see that the man is no threat and is more valuable in the kitchen preparing meals than in the lockup. Though not to be taken seriously as an enemy, Pallini is in many ways more savvy about Africa than the British, and in a key scene he explains to them the danger of the potential uprising and, at the same time, reveals (as Giuseppe did) the Italians' underlying dissatisfaction with fascism, Italian or German style. Like Giuseppe, Pallini is given a prewar civilian vocation; he had been a teacher of political history in Milan but was sent to Africa because, he says, "I teach too much." His theory is that the German plan of conquest depends on Africa as a land bridge to the rest of the world: "Here in Africa is your key of everything. If you lose Africa, you lose the war, you lose the world." He adds, "I know I look like a coward because I give myself up and do not fight you.

But where there is power there can only be one master. And I know what that means to my people too. To all people." Like Giuseppe, Pallini is murdered by a German but manages to leave a message to help the British before he dies.

These films suggest that the Italians are less like an enemy than a friendly country occupied by hostile German forces. Fundamental flaws in the Italian character—a pathetic temerity, a willingness to bend with the prevailing wind—have led to the Mussolini regime and its partnership with Nazi Germany. The Italians are not so much a threat to us as they are a victimized people who need to be rescued.

The December 22, 1941, issue of *Time* offered a sidebar titled "How to Tell Your Friends from the Japs," with helpful hints for distinguishing Chinese from Japanese, including the following: "Chinese, not as hairy as Japanese, seldom grow an impressive mustache," and "the Chinese expression is likely to be more placid, kindly, open; the Japanese more positive, dogmatic, arrogant." The fact that *Time* published this sidebar suggests a widespread confusion over the difference between the Japanese and other Asian nationalities, a confusion that offered a challenge to Hollywood as well.

The Japanese, in one sense, were easier to construct as Other than the Germans and Italians. They looked different from the average American of European extraction, and they did not share a cultural and religious heritage with most Americans. However, this Othering process also presented some problems. Prior to World War II, American popular culture made use of Asian stereotypes and stock characters, just as it had German and Italian stock figures, but there were few specifically *Japanese* stereotypes. Compare the title characters of two popular 1930s mystery series, Charlie Chan and Mr. Moto. Chan, the Chinese detective, as played by Warner Oland and Sidney Toler, and Moto, the Japanese detective, as played by Peter Lorre, are very much alike: polite to the point of obsequiousness, modest and self-effacing but concealing great intellect and a host of skills.[6] The probably inadvertent conflation of Japanese and Chinese is made explicit in *Doomed to Die* (1940), a film in the Mr. Wong series, starring Boris Karloff as a Chinese detective. At one point, annoying female reporter Bobbie Logan (Marjorie Reynolds) suggests that a murdered Chinese smuggler must have committed suicide: "Well, Wong, an Oriental would, wouldn't he? You know, commit hara kiri, or whatever you call it." The humor here comes not from Bobbie's ascribing a Japanese practice to a Chinese man but because the man had been stabbed in the back. The general Asian stereotype, manifested in all three film detectives, was used in Hollywood depictions of the Japanese—with the characteristic of deceptive appearances turned from an admirable to a negative quality—but filmmakers needed to find a way to construct a film image of the Japanese that would be distinct from other Asians—Filipinos, Burmese, and Koreans, whose lands were occupied by the Japanese, and especially our Chinese allies.

The picture of the Japanese that developed in Hollywood films early in the war seems to have evolved out of four main sources. The first is the stereotype of obsequious modesty discussed earlier. Filmmakers simply twisted this slightly to suggest a false modesty hiding aggression, a deceitful appearance masking evil. The second source is the news reports that had been coming out of China for several years. These reports of Japanese brutality against a helpless civilian population had excited sympathy but little outrage among most Americans before Pearl Harbor, but afterward they offered a ready supply of images to characterize the Japanese fighting man. Susan D. Moeller demonstrates how, after Pearl Harbor, the U.S. press quickly and easily demonized the Japanese as untrustworthy, brutal, and subhuman.[7] The third source is a construction of the attack on Pearl Harbor that was being promoted as early as December 8 in President Roosevelt's speech to Congress requesting a declaration of war. The president characterized the attack as a betrayal and the Japanese as a treacherous people. After announcing the attack by Japan, he said,

> The United States was at peace with that Nation and, at the solicitation of Japan, was still in conversation with its Government and its Emperor looking toward the maintenance of peace in the Pacific. Indeed, one hour after Japanese air squadrons had commenced bombing in the American Island of Oahu, the Japanese Ambassador to the United States and his colleague delivered to our Secretary of State a formal reply to a recent American message. And while this reply stated that it seemed useless to continue the existing diplomatic negotiations, it contained no threat or hint of war or of armed attack.
>
> It will be recorded that the distance of Hawaii from Japan makes it obvious that the attack was deliberately planned many days or even weeks ago. During the intervening time the Japanese Government has deliberately sought to deceive the United States by false statements and expressions of hope for continued peace. . . .

But always will our whole Nation remember the character of the onslaught against us.[8]

This construction of the Japanese as untrustworthy and as operating outside the rules of war worked with the stereotype of deceitful appearances and the news reports of brutality in China to create an idea of the Japanese that would be at work in one way or another in every film about the war in the Pacific.

As we noted in chapter 2, the war against Japan caught the Hollywood studios by surprise. Filmmakers needed a ready set of narrative conventions and character types on which to draw when creating their stories about the Japanese. We think that consciously or unconsciously they drew on a fourth source, conventions and techniques that had been used to depict another group that had been considered an enemy in American popular culture practically from the founding of the colonies—the American Indian. If this seems far-fetched, consider that the connection between the Asian and Indian characters had been made in American popular culture 100 years before Pearl Harbor. In *The Deerslayer* (1841) James Fenimore Cooper uses the following simile to describe a Native American in the process of bargaining with a white man: "The effect on this rude being of the forest was an exclamation of surprise; then such a smile of courtesy and wave of the hand succeeded as would have done credit to Asiatic diplomacy."[9] Indeed, one can look to Cooper's novels, especially the Leatherstocking series, for a clear articulation of how American popular culture constructed the idea of the Indian. The Indian was more intimately connected with nature than the white man was, which made him both comfortable in uncivilized areas where whites felt lost, frightened, and threatened and closer to an animal than a human being. The Indian's nature and social system encouraged brutal atrocities, including scalping and torture, against enemies. The Indian believed that his tribe was superior to all other tribes and to the white man. The Indian lived by an eccentric and hard-to-understand system of honor but, at the same time, was treacherous and not to be trusted. These characteristics reigned in the popular presentation of Indians well into the 1960s, most prominently in Hollywood Westerns. World War II–era audiences were already familiar with the presentation of these characteristics and knew what to think of them; it was fairly easy to transfer them to a new enemy. A telling example is *Manila Calling* (1942), which adapts Gen. Philip Henry Sheridan's famous remark, "The only good Indians I ever saw were dead," to the

Japanese. On being informed that a crashed Japanese pilot is dead, Lucky Matthews (Lloyd Nolan) says, "Well, that's one good Jap." In *China Sky* (1945) Chinese guerrilla leader Chen-Ta (Anthony Quinn) recasts this same remark: "We have learned that among the East Ocean dwarfs the good are of two kinds—the dead and the unborn." This film even ends like a Western, with a wild shootout in a Chinese town between its defenders and Japanese paratroopers, complete with men on rooftops dramatically falling to the street and Chen-Ta's cavalry riding in to save the day.

We can see many of these characteristics being applied to the Japanese in *Bataan*, a May 28, 1943, MGM release. Like several of the Pacific-theater films we discussed in chapter 2, *Bataan* is set amid actual historical events: the retreat down the Bataan peninsula and the fall of the Philippines. A thirteen-man patrol is assigned to keep the Japanese from crossing a ravine for as long as possible; there is little chance that they will receive orders to withdraw. The film assures us that although they are "getting killed holding onto some place you never heard of," their delaying action is invaluable to the United States. We're told, "The men who died here may have done more than we'll ever know to save this whole world." But beyond these tropes for justifying the war in the Pacific, the film spends much of its time defining the Japanese as enemies. The idea is established in the first exchange of dialogue. Corp. Jake Feingold (Thomas Mitchell), helping to cover a stream of retreating civilians and wounded soldiers, takes careful aim at something high in a tree and shoots. His sergeant, Bill Dane (Robert Taylor), tells him that it was a monkey. Feingold responds, "Well, I missed him anyway. I'd hate to hit him by mistake for a Jap." Later, after a sniper kills the commanding officer, Dane warns the remaining men, "You better know right now those no-tailed baboons out there are . . . number-one skillful. They climb trees better than monkeys, got all the best trees marked on their maps. They can live and fight for a month on what wouldn't last one of you guys two days." These are just two of many instances when the characters refer to the Japanese as animals; they are most often called monkeys but are also called fleas, possums, and rats. Moreover, in the film's climactic scene, as Dane, the last surviving member of the patrol, prepares for the enemy's final assault, we see the Japanese soldiers slithering through the ground mist like snakes.

These references create an idea of the Japanese as less than human, but they also suggest that the Japanese are somehow more at home in a natural environment, such as the tropical jungle setting, than the Americans are. The patrol chooses a grove as its headquarters because it provides "some natural advantages. Being up on that shelf ought to give us some protection. That cliff at the back ought to help us a lot." But ominously, the grove's water supply is undrinkable—too many germs. Nature thus presents a threat as well as safety. The film develops this idea further as the Japanese threat becomes synonymous with the jungle setting. We don't see the Japanese soldiers until about two-thirds of the way into the film, and only once in close-up. Instead, for most of the film, the threat is invisible: snipers' bullets come without warning from somewhere among the trees; men who wander too far from the safety of the camp are found dead; when the Japanese finally mount an all-out charge on the patrol, they disguise themselves as bushes and trees, so it appears that the jungle itself is attacking. In contrast, the Americans are clearly out of their environment in the jungle. One man, Matowski (Barry Nelson)—a city boy from Pittsburgh who can't wait to get back there—is ordered to duplicate the Japanese trick of climbing a tree to observe the enemy, but he is immediately shot.

This association between the Japanese and the threatening natural setting, as opposed to an urban, presumably civilized setting, connects with the film's presentation of Japanese duplicity. The Americans complain that the Japanese refuse to come out into the open and fight fairly. Instead, they snipe at the patrol, picking off the careless and the weak. When they do attack in a frontal charge, the five remaining Americans drive them back, killing dozens of them. But even in this battle, Japanese treachery comes into play. One Japanese soldier motions as if to surrender, and when his American attacker hesitates he nearly kills him. After the battle, a Japanese soldier pretending to be dead manages to kill two of the three remaining Americans. Throughout, the Japanese are cunning, cruel, and not to be trusted.

The duplicity and treachery of the Japanese are stressed in almost every film about the war in the Pacific. Filmmakers make this point through the repeated use of four basic tropes. The first, of course, is the sneak attack on Pearl Harbor, rarely depicted but referred to continually. The second comes from President Roosevelt's address to Congress: the fact that the Japanese ambassador and a special envoy from Tokyo were still involved in negotiations with the secretary of state when the attack on Pearl Harbor was launched. The special envoy even appears in *Wake Island*, where he is feted during a stopover on his way to Washington. The third is the presentation of Japanese officers who were educated in the

United States and then returned to Japan to use their knowledge against America. This suggests both a betrayal and the comforting notion that the Japanese couldn't compete with us were it not for the knowledge they acquired in the West. The fourth is the reminder of the relief provided by the United States after the devastating earthquake in 1923. This presents the Japanese as having repaid American compassion and kindness with violence.

The construction of the Japanese as untrustworthy is best seen in one of the most vitriolic anti-Japanese films of the war years, *Little Tokyo, U.S.A.* A Twentieth Century–Fox B picture, *Little Tokyo, U.S.A.* was released on July 8, 1942, only seven months after Pearl Harbor. As a result, it participates in the West Coast anti-Japanese hysteria of the war's early months. Set in the days just before and just after Pearl Harbor, its plot follows a Los Angeles police detective, Michael Steele (Preston Foster), as he investigates a Japanese spy ring working to prepare for the invasion of the mainland United States. Although the film reminds us several times—at the insistence of the Office of War Information, according to Shull and Wilt[10]—that many Japanese Americans are loyal, the film's blatant message is that they are not. In the opening scene, as the head of the Los Angeles spy ring, Takimura (Harold Huber), receives his orders from his superiors in Tokyo, he explains, "I was born in the United States and consequently enjoy the privileges of citizenship, but, as you know, I am pledged to the service of the son of heaven, our emperor." His leader answers, "That is the case with many of our countrymen." Even when the film avers that many Japanese are loyal Americans, it undercuts itself, suggesting instead that they may not be. At one point Steele's captain (J. Farrell MacDonald) tries to convince him that he's imagining a conspiracy: "The Japanese are harmless, peaceful, industrious citizens. They're loyal, too, most of them. Of course, there may be some rats in the bunch, but that's nothing to get excited about. I was reading only this morning that 93 percent of the vegetable crop of California is in the control of the Japanese." Steele responds, "Yeah, I know. They've got farms right next to all the airplane factories and the dams and the oil storage concentrations. . . . Those farmers are subsidized by the Japanese Specie Bank, straight from Tokyo. Why?" Later, after Pearl Harbor, we see footage of "dangerous aliens" being rounded up, but the Japanese Americans shown putting up "We Are Loyal U.S. Citizens" signs in their shops are all characters that we know are involved in the spy ring.

At the end of the film, after Steele has broken up the spy ring, we see a newspaper headline that reads, "All Japs to Be Evacuated," followed by actual footage of Japanese American citizens, with their belongings, being marched away from their homes and bused to the Santa Anita racetrack. (Interestingly, this is one of the few films of the time that acknowledges the evacuation and internment of Japanese American citizens.) Another newspaper headline reads, "Last Japs Leave L.A. Area Today: Military Area Cleared of Possible Saboteurs." In the final scene, the film's ultimate judgment on the detention and the loyalty of Japanese Americans is made known through the character of Steele's girlfriend, Maris Hanover (Brenda Joyce), a radio reporter. Surrounded by docile Japanese, apparently in the process of being evacuated, and with "My County 'Tis of Thee" playing in the background, she reports,

> And so in the interests of national safety, all Japanese, whether citizens or not, are being evacuated from strategic military zones on the Pacific coast. Unfortunately, in time of war the loyal must suffer inconvenience with the disloyal. . . .
>
> America's attitude toward this wholesale evacuation can best be summed up, I believe, by the last four lines of a poem by Robert Nathan entitled "Watch America":

> > God, who gave our fathers freedom,
> > God, who made our fathers brave,
> > What they built with love and anguish,
> > Let our children watch and save.

> Be vigilant, America.

The film argues that although some Japanese may be loyal, they are so few in number that it is safer to assume that no Japanese can be trusted. We risk our own security by regarding them with anything but suspicion.

The paranoia about Japanese treachery exhibited in *Little Tokyo, U.S.A.* is perhaps understandable in the confusing months after the first Japanese attacks in the Pacific. Yet the theme of Japanese Americans and Japanese nationals living in U.S. territory being disloyal and potential saboteurs recurs in films throughout the war. In John Ford and Gregg Toland's documentary *December 7th* (released in an edited version in 1943; the complete version wasn't made available until 1991), a complacent, prewar Uncle Sam (Walter Huston) is warned by Mr. C (Harry Davenport) about the

Japanese living in Hawaii; their number, their embrace of Japanese culture, and their resistance to assimilation are suspicious, he implies. As in *Little Tokyo, U.S.A.*, there is some acknowledgment that most Japanese living in U.S. territories are loyal, but the overall impression left with the viewer is that they are not to be trusted. In the Three Stooges short *The Yoke's on Me* (1944) the boys, while working on a farm to grow food for the war effort, are threatened by three Japanese who have escaped from an internment camp—another rare reference to the internment of the Japanese. Interestingly, the escapees are presented as violently dangerous, as if they were criminals escaped from prison; they are even dressed in striped prison-style clothing. As late as 1945, *Betrayal from the East* presented American con man Lee Tracy being recruited by a huge prewar, West Coast Japanese spy ring to steal the defense plans for the Panama Canal. Again, the spies are shown as having insinuated themselves into all aspects of American life to gain information useful to the Japanese war machine and to implement sabotage efforts once the war begins. Even the postwar *Samurai* (1945) continues to make the case for Japanese American treachery. Here a California couple adopts a Japanese boy after the 1923 earthquake. Though they try to raise him as an American, he comes under the influence of the Bushido philosophy. As an adult (Paul Fung), he becomes the leader of a spy ring preparing for the invasion of California. Over and over again these films make the point that the Japanese, no matter how polite, helpful, or assimilated they may appear, harbor an unwavering loyalty to Japan that will cause them to lie, steal, betray, and kill.

Yet Japanese treachery is presented in the context of an arcane and eccentric system of honor that outsiders, especially Americans, can't understand. This is best seen in another Doolittle raid film, *The Purple Heart*, released by Twentieth Century–Fox on February 23, 1944. The story is based on the Doolittle raiders who were captured by the Japanese. Here, they are put on trial in a Tokyo civil court for murdering civilians during the April 18, 1942, bombing of Japanese cities. The evidence is clearly trumped up; the real purpose of the trial is to discover the base from which the raiders launched their attack. The fliers withstand torture and a final offer of their lives in exchange for the information. The film ends with them marching off to their executions.

But much of the film is also about the Japanese idea of honor. In the wake of the Doolittle raid, the honor of the military has been marred by the attack on the cities, especially Tokyo, the emperor's home. The honor of the navy is threatened by the accusation that the attack was launched from aircraft carriers inside the Japanese defense perimeter. The honor of chief investigator and prosecutor General Mitsubi (Richard Loo) is staked on his claim that the raid was launched from an aircraft carrier. The importance of honor is emphasized in the exaggeratedly polite rhetoric with which Mitsubi and his navy antagonist, Admiral Yamagichi (Keye Chang), argue their points; neither wants to seem to be impugning the honor of the other. In objecting to the general's theory, Yamagichi says, "General Mitsubi, your brilliance in matters of military investigation is famous throughout the empire. I therefore rebuke myself for calling to your attention certain matters which you must already have investigated most exhaustively." Later, the general vows, "If it is proved that I am in error, I shall feel that I have falsely accused the Imperial Navy of negligence, and I shall apologize with my life."

But the civility with which the idea of honor is expressed masks the brutality and treachery—seen in the torture and psychological manipulation the Japanese use to try to get the fliers to confess—that are fundamental to the system. This corruption at the heart of the Japanese system, a corruption that is masked by beautiful things, is revealed at several points in the film. The trial is conducted with a strict sense of ritual and ceremony and with repeated references to the guiding authority of law and the emperor, yet the presiding judge and the court clerk coarsely shout their remarks like petty tyrants. Moreover, the so-called rule of law allows clearly false evidence to be introduced and effectively prevents it from being challenged. The absurdity of the illusion of Japanese civility is perhaps best punctured when the fliers are taken to their cell—a small space for seven of them, with no chairs or cots—and they are ordered to remove their shoes before entering.

The scene that best represents the inaccessibly foreign nature of Japanese honor—in concept and practice—occurs when the trial is interrupted by the news that Corregidor has fallen. The judges leap about like delighted children and run from the room to join the celebration in the streets, and the military officers present begin a samurai sword dance, a strange combination of dance and fighting. The film, classically realistic up to this point, becomes almost expressionistic here. Strangely angled close-ups of the officers pulling out their swords and preparing to do battle alternate with close-ups of the Americans' faces showing fear (are they going to kill us?) and astonishment (what on earth are they doing?). The lighting then casts weird, elongated shadows of the swordplay behind and over the Americans. The film style here forces the audience to share the fliers' disbelief

The Purple Heart: General Mitsubi (Richard Loo) menaces captured Doolittle raiders (including Dana Andrews and Sam Levene). Note the shadows of the samurai sword dance.

and incomprehension. One is left with the impression that we will never be able to understand these people.

The vast majority of Hollywood World War II films about the Japanese explicitly or implicitly reach this same conclusion: as a people and as a culture, the Japanese are so completely foreign, so Other, that Americans cannot understand them, only fight them. *Behind the Rising Sun* is an exception—in fact, it's unique in our viewing—in that it makes distinctions among different types of Japanese, some of whom are admirable, much as the films *The Mortal Storm, Underground, Hitler's Children*, and *The Seventh Cross* make distinctions among Germans. The film, based on a book of the same name by James R. Young, a nonfiction account of the author's time in prewar Japan, was released by RKO on July 21, 1943. It is narrated by Reo Seki (J. Carrol Naish), a newspaper editor turned propaganda minister who is writing a letter to his son Taro (Tom Neal), recently killed in action, to explain how their country and each of them have changed and, especially, how Taro turned from a decent human being into a monster.

The film employs many of the same elements we've seen in other

Behind the Rising Sun: "Japan is the very center of the universe." Reo Seki (J. Carrol Naish) explains Japan's plans for world conquest to his son Taro (Tom Neal).

films about the Japanese as enemy. It shows the Japanese as brutal; indeed, this film is particularly horrific, with its scenes of Japanese atrocities in China, including the bayoneting of babies, and the torture of American residents of Tokyo after Pearl Harbor. It shows the Japanese sense of superiority to the rest of the world, when, at one point, Seki explains to his son Japan's plan for world domination: "Japan is the very center of the universe." We see an example of the Japanese code of honor, which Americans don't understand, in the duel by proxy between Taro and an American engineer, O'Hara (Don Douglas). Representing O'Hara is Lefty (Robert Ryan), the American manager of a local baseball team, who expects a boxing match; representing Taro is a wrestler and judo expert (Mike Mazurki) who is expected to fight to the death. We also see the beneficial influence of America on the Japanese. Both Seki and Taro were educated in the United States; as the film goes to flashback, Taro is just returning to Japan after graduating from Cornell. Tama (Margo), Taro's fiancée, is fascinated with America, remembering the help provided by the Red Cross after the 1923 earthquake.

Combined with these familiar elements, however, are a number of other themes, more often seen in the film treatment of Nazi Germany. We see, at least briefly, something of the rise of militarism in Japan, as the army silences or assassinates the liberal elements of society. Early in the film, an army officer (Philip Ahn) murders Takahashi (Fred Essler), the "last liberal" in Japan, because he is a "foreigner"; like the Nazis, the Japanese militarists can tolerate no dissent from their views and so make those who would disagree Other, foreigners, to purify society. This desire for a pure society becomes evident in the methods of repression that develop during the film, from subtle to blatant, and in the always disguised but always present thought-control police. It is also evident in the way the American influence, which is seemingly everywhere in Tokyo, is twisted to serve Japanese militaristic needs. Between two games of a doubleheader— American baseball—the ballplayers and military band march around the stadium. In disgust, Lefty paraphrases the announcer's words: "Baseball isn't just baseball anymore. They mustn't come here to enjoy it just as a sport. They must come here to enjoy it as a military exercise." The romantic atmosphere of an American-style nightclub is shattered when military officers, reacting to the news of the Marco Polo Bridge incident, which provided an excuse for Japan's invasion of China, begin a samurai sword dance. After Pearl Harbor, the American influence is erased altogether. The engineer O'Hara is arrested as a spy for having plans of important Japanese buildings in his office—buildings he designed and built.

This manipulation and eventual erasure of things American mirrors the transformation of Taro. Taro returns from his college experience in the United States with American slang, American habits, and American ideas. Though he presumably hasn't been away from Japan for very many years, he has forgotten many Japanese customs, such as how to greet his father and removing his shoes when he enters his father's home. Rather than follow the path his father has prepared for him, he wants to work for the American O'Hara and marry Tama, despite her inferior social level. The film demonstrates how a decent, reasonably liberal young man like Taro can be transformed into a closed-minded, militaristic nationalist by a dehumanizing, totalitarian social environment. After Taro resists Seki's explanation of Japan's destiny of world domination and his father's plans for his participation in it, Seki echoes the phrase we hear from so many defenders of Nazism in films about Germany: "There is nothing to talk over. You will see, my son. You have no choice." Soon after, Taro is drafted into the army as an engineer and is sent to China. He begins by defending some of the Chinese civilians from mistreatment by the Japanese soldiers, but after a while he tries to just ignore the atrocities and ends by participating in them. He returns to Tokyo hard and cold, a militarist and a nationalist. He requests a transfer from the engineers to the air force so that he can be more actively engaged in the fighting. Seeing his son's transformation, Seki becomes disenchanted with Japan's ambitions. He explains to O'Hara:

> I have made a great mistake. There will be war with America. There is nothing I can do to stop it. . . . I can see now things I never could see before. We are not fit to rule the world. We have come of age too quickly. . . . Would I be so concerned if I thought Japan would lose? If that were so, there would be nothing to fear. No, it is because she will win that I am afraid, afraid for the whole civilized world. . . . You have seen what Japan has done to my son, haven't you? Yes, I know, I was responsible too. I used to say let's line up race against race, color against color. But I hadn't counted on this. I tell you, O'Hara, we're playing with the kind of fire no man in his right mind should ever touch. It destroys the victor as well as the vanquished. Today, my son is nothing more than a savage. Already he has asked for more active duty in the air corps. He wants to kill now for the sheer joy of killing.

In short, Taro has become the kind of Japanese we see in the jungles of *Bataan*, the spy ring of *Little Tokyo, U.S.A.*, and the torture chambers of *The Purple Heart*.

But interestingly, not all the Japanese characters are like Taro. His father obviously regrets his role in the militarist government. He uses his influence to help O'Hara and the other arrested Americans escape the country, and, in atonement for helping to destroy his son and for the mad acts of his country, he commits seppuku. But more important is Tama, who is fascinated with America from the beginning and is willing to question Japanese traditions. Because of this, she is arrested with the Americans after Pearl Harbor, and Seki also arranges for her passage out of the country. She refuses to leave, however, explaining, "All my life I wanted to go to America, but that must wait now. My place is here. . . . I know there isn't very much I can do alone. But someday, perhaps, we will be delivered by those who are free, and it will be important that there are some of us here who understand the world outside, and a few outside who understand Japan—the Japan that is yet to be born." The implication is that when the

United States wins the war, there will be some "good" Japanese ready to work with us to rebuild the country. In an interesting reversal, Hollywood, which has been committed to Othering the Japanese in order to define them as our enemy, projects a postwar world where the peace will be built with Japanese who want to be like us.

The claim that some Japanese can be like us is rare in Hollywood films, however. Whereas the construction of the Germans as enemies is, as a whole, done with some distinctions among the good and the bad, overall, the Japanese as a people are presented as practically inhuman. This can be seen in a B picture from RKO released only days after the Japanese surrender, *First Yank into Tokyo*. It concerns an American officer (Tom Neal) who undergoes irreversible plastic surgery to look Japanese so that he can infiltrate a prison camp and bring out a scientist needed to work on the atomic bomb. He also manages to save his girlfriend, a nurse, but as they are about to board a rescue boat, he decides to stay behind, sacrificing himself to save the others, because he can't imagine living the rest of his life looking Japanese. He explains, "Abby and I could never be happy. I'm saddled with this [indicating his Japanese features]. Every time she looked at me, I'd remind her of the other Japs on Bataan and Corregidor. We couldn't find any happiness together." The film presents the assertion that it's better to be dead than to look Japanese.

Hollywood films, then, employed a complex process involving preexisting pop-cultural representations, recent events, and ideological comparisons and contrasts to construct an idea of the countries we were at war with to help the American public understand why they had to be defeated. In the next two chapters we will see that filmmakers used a similar process to engage a more complicated problem: helping Americans understand why they had to fight for our allies.

4

OUR FIGHTING ALLIES

They marched into Poland, haven't they? That means war if
   you ask me. And if war comes, it's good-bye roses.
Don't talk silly. You might as well say "Good-bye England."
   There'll always be roses.
   —Mr. Huggins (Forrester Harvey) and
   Mr. Ballard (Henry Travers) in Mrs. Miniver

If I didn't know I'd met you in Moscow, you might be an
American girl.
   —John Meredith (Robert Taylor) to
   Nadya Stepanova (Susan Peters) in Song of Russia

He went there to teach Christianity to the Chinese. He always
said he stayed because the Chinese made such a good
Christian out of him.
   —Ruth Kirke (Deanna Durbin), speaking of her
   missionary father, in The Amazing Mrs. Holliday

IN THE LAST CHAPTER we examined the various strategies filmmakers
used to define as Other the nations with which the United States was at
war. In this chapter we examine the similar but more complex process by
which our main fighting allies—Britain, the Soviet Union, and China—
were constructed through film. In the next chapter we examine the somewhat different way European countries occupied by Germany were
presented.

137

During the war, the U.S. mainland was never attacked or seriously threatened. This left Americans with the question of how U.S. interests were served by our participation in the war. Why should American soldiers be dying in what seemed to be other countries' fights? We saw in chapter 1 that before Pearl Harbor most Americans were swayed by this anti-interventionist logic, and we saw in chapter 2 that Hollywood films joined in the effort to help Americans understand how far-flung places in the Pacific could be seen as being part of America. However, this particular strategy wasn't appropriate for most of America's other allies. In these cases, similar to the presentation of a shared American and Philippine history and culture in *Back to Bataan* (1945), filmmakers tried simultaneously to make these allies distinct, so that viewers could understand why they should be valued as nations and nationalities, *and* to make them appear to be like Americans. This case for similarity had two purposes. First, by making the allies seem like Americans, the films helped justify why we were fighting for them. Second, it allowed American viewers— safe in the Roxy, thousands of miles from the fighting and the dying—to participate vicariously in the experience of the war, to imagine themselves resisting the invasion of their homeland or suffering the occupation of foreign armies, to see themselves, like the film versions of their allies, as brave, resolute, pure, indomitably free.

It is probably easiest to see this double purpose at work in films about the ally with which America had the most in common to begin with: Great Britain. Hollywood released a host of films designed to elicit sympathy for the British, usually by depicting British pluck—the grace under pressure, good humor, and stiff upper lip with which the British people faced German aggression, especially the Blitz. In chapter 1 we mentioned some of the pre–Pearl Harbor films that depicted the British character this way, and films continued to do this after the United States entered the war. *Passport to Destiny* (1944), about a scrubwoman who works her way to Berlin to try to kill Hitler (believing that she has a charm that will protect her from harm), shows working-class Londoners casually accepting the nightly bombing and making the deprivations of war part of their routine. *Tonight and Every Night* (1945) tells the story of a London music hall that establishes a record for never canceling a performance during the war, despite the bombs and the deaths of cast members' lovers and cast members themselves. *Sherlock Holmes and the Voice of Terror* (1942) and *Sherlock Holmes and the Secret Weapon* (1942) transplant the Victorian detective

(Basil Rathbone) to World War II London, where in the former he tracks down saboteurs and prevents an invasion of England and in the latter he breaks up a spy ring while protecting the plans for a new bombsight. *Return of the Vampire* (1943) shows the English coping with the Blitz and the ravages of Bela Lugosi's vampire, unearthed by a German bomb.

Some films, following the narrative pattern established in *Foreign Correspondent* and other films examined in chapter 1, show the British and Americans teaming up to defeat the Nazis. *Desperate Journey* (1942) follows the crew of a downed British bomber as they make their way across much of Europe, avoiding capture and returning to England; the crew includes an American volunteer. In *Above Suspicion* (1943) an American couple honeymooning in Germany takes on a dangerous espionage mission for the British foreign office. *Sherlock Holmes in Washington* (1943) brings the famous detective to the United States to solve a case involving missing microfilm. All these films promote Anglo-American cooperation, and although they introduce some conflict between their British and American characters (sometimes only for humor, as in *Sherlock Holmes in Washington*), they assume a common cultural and historical background and a common cause. Other films address these issues in a more complex way, highlighting what is to be treasured about the British and also pointing out that the less appealing aspects of Britain (at least less appealing from an American point of view) are transforming into something new and recognizably American.

Mrs. Miniver (1942), as we noted in chapter 3, makes use of the same kind of oppositions established in Churchill's "Their Finest Hour" speech to define the Germans as enemy. Concomitantly, it draws on these same oppositions to illustrate the positive qualities of the English as a people. We have already seen how the English are associated with order and the rule of law when Mrs. Miniver (Greer Garson) is contrasted with the German flier. The film also shows us how the British, through the Miniver family, are associated with civilization. For example, when the Minivers must move into their bomb shelter, they take much of their civilized life with them: it is cozily decorated with lamps and chairs from the house; the children are read their bedtime story; Mr. Miniver (Walter Pidgeon) enjoys his pipe, coffee, and biscuits, while Mrs. Miniver does her knitting; the two share passages from *Alice in Wonderland*, a treasure of Britain's literary heritage; and they self-consciously pursue conversation about everyday life until the bombs are too close to ignore. Similarly, the townspeople of Belham refuse to cancel their annual flower show and arts festival, symbolic of their artistic and cultural legacy, held annually at Beldon Hall, symbolic of a historic legacy going back to the Crusades. Predictably, the irreverent Germans interrupt the festival with their biggest bombing raid yet; whenever the film establishes a British virtue, it is almost immediately threatened with German bombs.

The British are also associated with Christianity. Two key scenes take place in the Belham church. In the first, the Sunday service is interrupted by the announcement of the declaration of war. In the second, the final scene of the film, the church has been badly damaged by bombing, but as the congregation sings "Onward, Christian Soldiers," the camera tilts up, and through a hole in the roof we see the Royal Air Force (RAF), presumably the Christian soldiers of the song. When war is declared, the vicar (Henry Wilcoxon) ends his service with these words, tying together England, Christianity, and the country's cultural and historical heritage:

> I will say simply this: that the prayer for peace still lives in our hearts, coupled now with the prayer for our beloved country.
>
> We in this village have not failed in the past. Our forefathers for a thousand years have fought for the freedom that we now enjoy and that we must now defend again. With God's help, and their example, we cannot and shall not fail.

When he mentions the community's forefathers, the camera shows us Lady Beldon (Dame May Whitty), the local aristocrat, with the sepulchre of a crusader, presumably one of her ancestors, in the background.

Like many of the films we mentioned earlier and as the scene in the bomb shelter suggests, *Mrs. Miniver* depicts British stoicism under the German attack. At the beginning of the film, the Minivers are presented as pampered and a bit self-indulgent. They have a beautiful home on the Thames, a boat, two servants, and a son at Oxford, and they have each bought something—Mr. Miniver a car and Mrs. Miniver a hat—they really can't afford. But after the war begins, so do the sacrifices: the servants go to do war work, their son joins the RAF, the boat is shot up at Dunkirk, the house is bombed. But each loss is accepted with wry humor and a stiff upper lip. More tragically, Carol (Teresa Wright), their daughter-in-law, is shot during an air raid and dies on the living room floor when no ambulance is available. But here, too, the sadness is accepted without bitterness or recrimination. Interestingly, as if to stress the characters' stoicism, the film avoids the predictable emotion-wrenching scenes that might have been used. Carol dies in an understated moment while Mrs. Miniver is out of the room, and her husband Vin (Richard Ney) has already been told by the time he gets home, so we do not see his reaction. The film's most efficient presentation of the characteristic British pluck occurs in a pub: the camera is tightly focused on a radio, over which we hear a Lord Haw-Haw type broadcasting German propaganda and describing England's desperate situation; the camera pulls back to show us the room full of Englishmen laughing at the broadcast.

Thus are the British defined as a nationality, but the film simultaneously works against the idea of the cultural and historical legacy it has been praising. Early in the film, when Vin, the Minivers' oldest son, comes home from Oxford, he is full of talk about the things he's been learning, including a critique of the British class system. He argues that England is still in essence a feudal society. Of the local aristocrat, he says, "Lady Beldon's the living proof of the survival of the feudal system today. You can't escape from the pernicious Beldon influence. It contaminates the entire fabric of village society." The film, however, encourages us not to take Vin's arguments very seriously, mostly through Mr. Miniver's reactions to his son's speeches. More important, though, is the conflict over the Miniver rose, grown by Mr. Ballard, the stationmaster (Henry Travers). Mr. Ballard has decided to enter his rose against Lady Beldon's in the annual rose competition, starting an uproar in the community between those who see this as a breach of social etiquette and those who find it a refreshing democratic gesture. Lady Beldon begins the film as a symbol of class position and privilege, seemingly justifying Vin's critique as she goes about huffing and puffing against the middle and lower classes. When the war starts, she insists, "We can take care of ourselves. We've been doing it for the last 800 years. We don't take orders, we give 'em. The worst thing about the war is the chance it gives dreadful little persons to make themselves important." As time goes on, however, the class boundaries begin to break down. First, Lady Beldon allows her granddaughter to marry Vin. Then, she overturns the flower-show judges' ruling and gives the first prize in the rose competition, which she has always won, to Mr. Ballard. The camera lingers on her face, showing her reaction to the cheers of the townspeople when she announces herself as the second-place winner, and she realizes that it is better to be loved than feared. Soon after, when the air-raid sirens sound, she invites all the assembled into her cellar. This collapsing of a once-rigid class system suggests a democratizing of England, which makes it seem more like the popular idea of America—a classless society.

This democratization is emphasized in the vicar's final sermon. Whereas earlier he had invoked the community's historical legacy to define its participation in the war, here the vicar articulates, with Churchillian rhetoric, an idea of democratic stoicism. He points out that the dead from the latest bombing raid include Carol, Mr. Ballard, small children, and old people and asks,

> Why should *they* be sacrificed? I shall tell you why. Because this is not only a war of soldiers in uniform. It is a war of the people. Of *all* the people. And it must be fought not only on the battlefield but in the cities and in the villages, in the factories and on the farms, in the home and in the heart of every man, woman, and child who loves freedom.
>
> Well, we have buried our dead. But we shall not forget them. Instead, they will inspire us with an unbreakable determination to free ourselves and those who come after us from the tyranny and terror that threaten to strike us down.
>
> This is the *people's* war. It is *our* war. *We* are the fighters. *Fight it then.* Fight it with all that is in us. And may God defend the right.

Released by Twentieth Century–Fox on May 14, 1942, the day after *Mrs. Miniver's* release, *This above All* explores the democratization process even more explicitly. The film opens as the announcement of France's surrender is broadcast from the radio of the Cathaway mansion's library. The assembled family exudes the privilege of class, and for some of them—especially Aunt Iris (Gladys Cooper) and Uncle Wilfrid (Melville Cooper)[1]—this privilege has effected a sort of social, intellectual, and moral inertia, a stuffy fog that surrounds them and prevents them from recognizing the changes going on in English society and the threat posed by Germany. When they put on blinders to the imminent invasion and plead that no one get excited, Roger (Philip Merivale), a doctor who has been treating the wounded from the evacuation at Dunkirk, replies, "Do you know what our enemies say every night in their prayers? They say, 'Please, God, keep the English from getting excited for one more year, and we shall never need Your help again.'" At dinner, the arguing continues as Roger makes the case for equality across classes, and Iris responds, somewhat nonsensically, "I'm not against equality. I'm perfectly prepared to be equal with anybody, providing they don't start being equal with me."

These exchanges prepare for the arrival of Roger's daughter Prudence (Joan Fontaine), who has just enlisted in the Women's Auxiliary Air Force

(WAAF) as a private. Iris and Wilfrid are shocked not that she joined but that she didn't apply for a commission. In their view, she is abrogating the privilege and responsibility afforded her by her family's background and associating unacceptably with lower-class women. Wilfrid says, "For generations, the Cathaways have been leaders, Prudence, not followers. In joining this woman's army, you are throwing aside certain, shall I say, traditions which have always entitled the Cathaways to lead." When Iris suggests that contemporary young women like to be different simply to challenge tradition, Prudence erupts:

> When you and Uncle Wilfrid talk, I seem to hear words oozing from the holes of a moth-eaten sofa. . . . I'm in 1940 and you're in 1880. You and people like you are a worse danger to us than Hitler is. Yes, I mean it. One day we may look back and thank Hitler for some of the things he's done to wake us up, but we'll never look back and thank you.
>
> You believe that forty million people exist in England to make you comfortable. You hate this war because you knock your shins in a blackout. You grumble about it because it deprives you of your favorite German bath salts. And what's more you fear it, because the common men who are doing the fighting may suddenly begin to doubt the importance of risking their lives to keep the Uncle Wilfrids and Aunt Irises an immortal part of England.

This last prediction comes true when Prudence meets Clive Briggs (Tyrone Power), a hero of the Dunkirk evacuation who has deserted the army because of his realization that he is fighting for the privileges of the wealthy, while his class continues to suffer. The two argue over this, talking about a man (actually Clive) who has deserted. Clive says, "Do you know what England means to this man? It means poverty, hunger, begging for work, no matter how cruel and humiliating. And if our armies did win this war, what share will this man have in the England that he's helped to save? They'll give him nothing. It'll return to the men who have owned and disgraced it, so they can go on disgracing it until the next war comes." Prudence responds with a flowery speech in which she weaves an idea of England out of its history, its cultural legacy, and its rustic beauty. She says, "Whatever this man is, blood and bone, mind and heart and spirit, England made him. Every part of him. . . . When he says the word *England*, it must be for him as it is for me, like music that's rich beyond the power of music." By the end of the film, Clive, primarily through his love for Prudence, has been convinced that she's right. He says, "Someday we're going to fight for what I believe in, but first we've got to fight for what you believe in. You were right: we've got to win this war." As in *Mrs. Miniver*, the promise here is that the legacy of class privilege is breaking down and that the war itself is helping to erect a new, more genuinely democratic social structure.

Another set of films continues this presentation of the democratization of England, while also arguing for Britain and America's shared cultural and historical legacy and the benefits of an Anglo-American alliance. An example of this is *Forever and a Day*, a film produced under unique circumstances. It was released by RKO in 1943 but was the product of the cooperation of several studios, which donated the profits to war relief. It was created by twenty-two credited screenwriters—everyone from C. S. Forester and Christopher Isherwood to Alfred Hitchcock and Donald Ogden Stewart—seven directors, and more than a hundred actors, almost all from the British community in Hollywood. The film begins in London during the Blitz (America has not yet entered the war). A young American, Gates Pomfret (Kent Smith), is sent by his father to sell a house they own to its tenant, a distant relative, Lesley Trimble (Ruth Warrick). Gates and Lesley come into immediate conflict because of his typical Americanness. His full name is Trimble-Pomfret, but he's shortened it because they "don't go much for the double-barreled names back home." When Lesley remarks, "Americans haven't much feeling for old houses, have they?" Gates affirms, "Oh, we like them, up to ten years. . . . After that, of course, being a generous people, we turn them over to the termites." When she suggests that some of the value of the house derives from the memories in it, he scoffs at her. They even have trouble communicating: when she mentions the house's *ghost*, he thinks she says *goat* and wonders where it's kept. In the wake of this initial meeting, Lesley, representing the British, seems somewhat foolish for wanting to buy a house that's in imminent danger of destruction because she values its memories, and Gates, representing Americans, seems breezy and superficial, with no appreciation for his family's history or for the past in general. Implied here is a typical American's faith in the future.

A reconciliation develops as Lesley tells Gates the history of the house and the people who lived there—their ancestors—to make him understand why it should be valued. The film then shows us the house's history—from 1804, when the house was built on the foundation of an ancient fort that protected the island from Roman invaders, to 1917, when, as a private boardinghouse, it sheltered England's latest defenders and their families. Throughout, we see the intertwined history of the Pomfrets and Trimbles and the tension between those family members who look forward—building the house, installing indoor plumbing, buying a motorcar, immigrating to America—and those who resist progress. Interestingly, both sides of the family develop American branches. The son of Sir Anthony Trimble-Pomfret (Edward Everett Horton) takes the family business to America (this is Gates's grandfather). Jim Trimble (Brian Aherne), a coal deliveryman who knows how to use his hands, goes to America to make his fortune; his son Ned (Robert Cummings) returns to England as part of the American Expeditionary Force in 1917 (this is Lesley's father). This intertwining suggests that the British and Americans are not discrete nationalities, that they share a common past and cultural identity. Through Lesley's story, Gates comes to appreciate this. But when the house is destroyed by German bombs, Lesley learns from her American relative. When she despairs over her loss, he tells her, "I understand how you feel. You loved an old house, and now it's gone. But the memories you treasured, they're not destroyed. So let's build again." The two have become something of a British-American hybrid, melding a love for tradition and one's heritage with a forward-looking faith in the future. The film seems to offer this combination—an understanding of why Britain needs to be defended and the spirit to win the war and build a peace—as the ideal position for its audience.

Similar themes are explored in *The Canterville Ghost*, a May 22, 1944, MGM release based on a story by Oscar Wilde. The conflict between the English and the Americans is treated more humorously here, but it is nevertheless the impetus for the narrative. A platoon of U.S. Army Rangers is billeted in the castle of the Cantervilles, an aristocratic family whose lineage extends back more than 300 years. The English characters, friendly but formal and self-consciously courteous, are startled by the informality and the lack of class-consciousness of the American soldiers. On arriving at the castle, they greet the butler with democratizing friendliness, shaking his hand, clapping him on the back, and calling him nicknames. At a village tea, the soldiers liven things up by improvising a jazz band and by swing dancing, what one local matron calls "woogie boogie." Even their platoon seems remarkably free of a hierarchy based in rank; they have a sergeant, but a private, Cuffy Williams (Robert Young), seems to be their natural leader. The differences between the Americans and the English are brought home when Cuffy reminds the others that a book they were given says to respect English tradition, as if they were in a land completely foreign from their own.

Like *Forever and a Day*, this film demonstrates that the distinction is not as complete as it might seem. Cuffy, it turns out, is descended from the Cantervilles (he discovers this despite his lack of interest in family research: "We don't go in much for that sort of thing in the States"). This is good news for the ghost of Sir Simon de Canterville (Charles Laughton), whose act of cowardice condemned him to haunt the castle until a kinsman can redeem him with an act of bravery. This shared heritage undercuts the idea of the English and Americans as separate nationalities and emphasizes the importance of family connections; indeed, Sir Simon's cowardice involved not standing up for his brother.

This situation allows the film to undertake an interesting exploration of the value of family heritage. As Sir Simon's curse shows, a sense of kinship is important in terms of family members standing up for one another; a sense of heritage also bestows a feeling of duty. Mrs. Polverdine (Elisabeth Risdon) explains to her charge, the six-year-old Lady Jessica de Canterville (Margaret O'Brien), the meaning of noblesse oblige: "Those of us who are nobly born must prove themselves worthy of it by being ever kind and gracious and thoughtful for others and by living not to take but to give. That is our obligation." Unlike in *Mrs. Miniver* and *This above All*, the aristocracy here is defined by its responsibilities, not its privileges. But the dark side of a sense of heritage is that it can be a burden. It turns out that Sir Simon has never been redeemed because cowardice is hereditary in the Canterville family. He walks Cuffy through the family portrait gallery, telling the story of Canterville after Canterville disgracing himself and his family. Cuffy responds with a typical show of American individualism, saying, "I don't care what the others did. This is Cuffy, see?" But he can't discard his legacy so easily. In two moments of crisis, the first in battle and the second when the Rangers and the castle are threatened by an improbable German "blockbuster" bomb, Cuffy sees the signet ring Sir Simon gave him, a symbol of his family and his heritage, and freezes, unable to act. In the first instance he fails; in the second instance it is only after he shakes off the burden of his family's past that he can act and become a hero. Like *Forever and a Day*, *The Canterville Ghost* argues for the intertwined history of Britain and America, but it seems to suggest that although America needs to value this history, it must be willing to move forward if the two countries are to win the war.

Similar themes run through another MGM picture, *The White Cliffs of*

Dover, released on March 13, 1944. Based on a long poem by Alice Duer Miller (who also contributed to the screenplay of *Forever and a Day*), it tells a story of blatant Anglophilia. A young American woman, Susan Dunn (Irene Dunne), arrives in England with her father (Frank Morgan) for a week's vacation. Full of romantic notions, she is swept off her feet by a baronet, Sir John Ashwood (Alan Marshal), and eventually marries him. Despite several false starts, she never returns to the United States. As in *Forever and a Day* and *The Canterville Ghost*, *The White Cliffs of Dover* establishes conflicts between the British and American characters, but the conflicts here are comparatively insubstantial. In fact, that seems to be the point: although Susan insists that there are differences between England and America and struggles at various points in her life with guilt about abandoning America for England, every time the film introduces an Anglo-American conflict, it's almost immediately glossed over. Mr. Dunn's argument with Col. Walter Forsythe (C. Aubrey Smith) over a chess set the colonel's grandfather took from the White House in 1812 is acknowledged by both men as something of a running joke.[2] Similarly, Mr. Dunn's xenophobia becomes a humorous act he puts on because it's expected of him. When Susan first visits the Ashwood manor, she bristles at the condescending remarks John's family makes about Americans and accuses her hosts of being cold and rude. Lady Ashwood (Gladys Cooper) placates her: "I want you to understand that if there's been anything in my manner to hurt you, it's been nothing to do with John. It's just that, well, perhaps we express ourselves a little differently. . . . The English are anything but effusive. The Scots are worse, and I'm a Scot, you know. So if I've hurt you, my dear, it was in my manner, not in my heart." This is the film's main theme: the differences between the two allies are all in appearance; underneath, they're the same. MGM even stressed this in its advertising: "'The White Cliffs of Dover' has been a symbol of the British spirit, particularly since the heroic Battle of Britain. Behind this symbol is the story of a way of life and the film shows how that way of life dovetails with the American Way."

This theme is further developed in the story of Susan's son John Ashwood II (Roddy McDowall, later Peter Lawford), whose father is killed in World War I. Like the young Lady de Canterville, John learns early that being nobly born entails more duties than privileges. When Susan, sensing a new war brewing, tries to take him to America, he feels that he would be abrogating his duty as lord of the manor, but he makes his argument by making connections to Americans. He asks, "It isn't so very different over there than it is here, is it? You just try and do the thing that's there for you to do." This benevolent view of British aristocracy combines with the democratizing impulse we've seen in several other films. We see class structures breaking down as the senior John marries Susan and as young John woos and apparently marries Betsy (Elizabeth Taylor, who grows up to be June Lockhart), the daughter of a tenant at the manor. John is wounded in the raid at Dieppe (which is ironic, for he was conceived at Dieppe, during one of his father's leaves) and dies in a London hospital where his mother volunteers. Before he dies, Susan looks out the window and describes for him a parade of American and British soldiers, bringing home the film's theme of the lack of difference between the two: "Yes, John, I see them. Your people and my people. Only their uniforms are different. How well they march, John. How well they march together."

Evoking the sense of America's and Britain's shared history, culture, and wartime mission was not difficult for the Hollywood studios. Much more problematic was the presentation of our other major ally, the Soviet Union. Russia, with its vast territory straddling Europe and Asia—a part of both, yet completely neither—had always been difficult for Americans and other Westerners to understand. The Bolshevik Revolution of 1917 and the subsequent creation of the Union of Soviet Socialist Republics, at the time the only Communist country in the world, added to outsiders' confusion. As Winston Churchill famously quipped in an October 1, 1939, radio broadcast, "I cannot forecast to you the action of Russia. It is a riddle wrapped in a mystery, inside an enigma."[3] This sense of mystery, combined with the Soviet government's overt antagonism toward the Western industrial countries, resulted in disconnection rather than connection, difference rather than identification.

For confirmation of this, we need only look at the Hollywood presentation of the Soviet Union in the 1920s, 1930s, and even 1940 and 1941. For much of this time, Soviet characters were all-purpose spies and villains; audiences easily recognized their sinister qualities and threatening demeanor. It was convenient for Hollywood to demonize the Soviets because of the pervasive fear of communism among Americans and, more practically, because the Soviet Union was such a small market for U.S. films. By the 1930s, American films were only infrequently imported into the USSR, partly because of the Soviet government's ideological objections and partly because exhibitors, technologically behind the times, were unable to show movies that required modern projectors. As film historian

Ruth Vasey notes, "The consistent characterization of Russians as villains did not concern the industry because it did not affect profits; it was disregarded by the U.S. State Department because the United States did not recognize the government of the Soviet Union." In short, Vasey argues, "In dollars and cents, Russian indignation was cheap." Shull and Wilt count nine American feature films between 1937 and 1941 with an anti-Soviet bias.[4] One, *Ski Patrol*, a 1940 Universal release, critically depicts the November 1939 Soviet invasion of Finland. Most often, however, these films critique and deflate their Soviet characters and the Soviet Union as a whole through parody. The two best examples of prewar comic representations of the Soviet Union are *Ninotchka* (1939) and *Comrade X* (1940). These films make their digs at the failure of the Soviet system for the average person, and they feature stern, vengeful, and hypocritical commissars, but the focus in both cases is on women who are strong believers in communism. Both films test their beliefs against the joys of a capitalist society, and, not surprisingly, Marxist ideology loses out.

Ninotchka begins its critique with three members of the Russian Board of Trade who have come to Paris to sell the jewels of the royal family. These men, Iranoff (Sig Ruman), Buljanoff (Felix Bressart), and Kopalski (Alexander Granach), are easily seduced by the plenty they see around them. Originally set to stay in a small, run-down hotel, they decide to move to a glamorous one and request the royal suite to further the prestige of the Bolsheviks. They seem to be aware of the irony of Communists enjoying material goods, but they welcome it all, including the cigars, champagne, and French maids helpfully supplied by the White Russian Count Leon (Melvyn Douglas), who really wants to gain possession of the jewels. When they are finally recalled to the Soviet Union, they have reunions to remember the days when a party did not consist of each guest bringing his own egg so that there would be something to eat. They end up as capitalist Russians, abandoning their next political posting in Constantinople in order to open a restaurant. This plot implies that the average Soviet, far from being a rabid ideologue, is, through convenience or fear, only superficially committed to Communist doctrine; given the chance, capitalist virtues such as self-interest and self-indulgence will naturally come to the surface.

Commissar Ninotchka (Greta Garbo), who is sent to Paris from Moscow to investigate the delay in selling the jewels, is, in contrast, a true Communist, thinking only of the state, not of her needs as an individual. Her character becomes the focus for the film's critique of the Soviet Union and how it stunts its people's natural human instincts. Upon her arrival in Paris, Ninotchka is mechanical, emotionless, and humorless. Indeed, she seems suspicious of human interaction. When Count Leon attempts to be romantic with her, she dryly dismisses his advances with a cutting, "Must you flirt?" She shows no interest in the romance of Paris; she confines her curiosity to questions about the engineering aspects of the Eiffel Tower. She even describes herself in mechanistic terms, a "tiny cog in the great wheel of evolution." She uncritically accepts and repeats the Soviet authorities' criticisms of the West and their absurd justifications of their own actions. Speaking of Stalin's purges, she says, "The last massacre was a great success. There will be fewer but better Russians." She is also presented as almost superhuman, climbing all the way to the top of the Eiffel Tower without getting winded. Eventually her dedication to communism is weakened as she discovers that she likes being a woman as well as a commissar. She learns to enjoy life in Paris—the food, the champagne, the clothes—and falls in love with Count Leon. She is conflicted between her love for Leon and her sense of duty to her country. Duty briefly wins out, but having tasted love and life outside the Soviet system, Ninotchka finds Moscow dull and dampening of the human spirit. She is finally ordered to Constantinople and is reunited with Leon and her friends Iranoff, Buljanoff, and Kopalski and thus finds true happiness by defecting.

Comrade X, a 1940 MGM release, is even more critical in its presentation of the Soviet Union. The plot centers on McKinley Thompson (Clark Gable), an American journalist in Moscow who, under the pen name Comrade X, is sending out stories in code to bypass the Soviet censors. This film's Moscow is rife with power struggles among midlevel bureaucrats, complete with assassinations, purges, and hypocritical, lightning-fast ideological shape-shifting. The dissident political philosopher Bastakoff (Vladimir Sokoloff), for example, attains power as police commissar and then arrests and executes his former followers, whom he now sees as treasonous and threatening. While public officials are absorbed in their power plays, the country's infrastructure disintegrates. McKinley's hotel can't provide him with towels—not that he needs them, since there's no water either.

The Ninotchka-like character here is Theodor (Hedy Lamarr)—she has taken on a male name because she is a streetcar motorman, and under Soviet law, only men can hold that occupation; this is another example of the film's take on the through-the-looking-glass absurdity of the Soviet Union. Theodor is a Marxist idealist, never noticing the vanity and hypocrisy around her, never questioning authority, always submitting to the word of the state. Her father (Felix Bressart) knows how dangerous Moscow can be for an idealist, so he blackmails McKinley (he's discovered the secret of Comrade X) into taking Theodor back to America. McKinley persuades her to go by telling her the good she'll do by spreading communism in America. Like Ninotchka, Theodor uncritically believes all she is told by the Soviet government ("I read in the *Pravda* 10 million people starved to death last winter in the United States, and there was nobody to bury them"), she views human relationships unromantically, she denigrates her own femininity (besides being a motorman, she is in a parachute division), and she demonstrates near-superhuman strength, walking with McKinley the seven miles from the end of the streetcar line to central Moscow while reciting *The Iron Law of Overproduction*. She loses faith in her country less through exposure to Western ideas than through the exposure of Bastakoff's duplicity. Nevertheless, at the end of the film, she is with McKinley in Brooklyn, heartily cheering for the Dodgers to murder the Reds.

After the German invasion of the Soviet Union in June 1941 and America's entry into the war the following December, the Hollywood studios were faced with the problem of presenting our new allies positively, not critically. This involved an about-face not unlike Bastakoff's in *Comrade X*. Filmmakers devised several strategies to effect this change in the depiction of the Soviet Union and its people. One of these was to turn qualities for which the Soviets had been criticized into virtues.

This strategy is most easily seen in the character of Sgt. Natalia Moskeroff (Eve Arden) in *The Doughgirls*, an August 30, 1944, Warner Bros. release. Based on a Joseph Fields play of the same name, *The Doughgirls* is one of several film comedies made during the war that focused on the housing crunch in Washington, D.C. Three women, each hoping to be married, share the honeymoon suite of a hotel. Through a series of plot complications, several more people end up moving in with them, including Natalia, described as a Russian Sergeant York who has killed 396 Nazis.[5] Natalia has many of the same characteristics as Ninotchka and Theodor, and in all three films these characteristics are treated humorously, but here, they evoke no criticism. In fact, there are many ways in which they are admirable. Once again, we see that human relations are subordinated to the state, as when Natalia tells of her mother killing 425 Nazis while being pregnant. Natalia celebrates news of the birth of her sister by firing her gun three times: once for the mother, once for the baby, and once for Joe—

Joe Stalin, the father of the country. But here, this dedication to cause and country over family relationships is presented as positive. Once again we see a Soviet woman masculinized, through her clothes and duties, but compared with the frivolous brides-to-be and the other female characters, Natalia earns the viewers' respect. Once again, we see a Soviet woman with something approaching superhuman strength: Natalia takes the dog for a walk and comes back several hours later carrying the dog—she's walked to Baltimore and back—but here, this symbolizes the indomitable Red Army. Natalia also calmly and good-humoredly solves many of the film's crises: she gets the money to pay the hotel bill by tough negotiating at the pawnbroker's, and at a moment's notice, she provides the Russian Orthodox priest to marry the three couples at the end of the film. As we saw in the presentation of the Germans and Italians, the filmmakers used a film stereotype already familiar to American moviegoers, but here they adapted it to elicit praise rather than vilification.

A second strategy filmmakers employed to deal with the problem of presenting the Soviet Union was to defuse the Communist ideology by decontextualizing characters and settings. This strategy involves removing characters from a specific geographic place and sociocultural context and inserting them into a generic, usually rural, setting. Cultural differences then become superficial, and an American-friendly homogeneity can be emphasized. An excellent example of this can be seen in the 1943 MGM production *The Human Comedy.* In one scene Tom Spangler (James Craig) drives his girlfriend, Diana Steed (Marsha Hunt), through a California park on a Sunday afternoon. In a long shot the camera follows the car and the couple past several ethnically distinct groups celebrating the day in ways specific to their country. We see Greeks, Mexicans, Armenians, Russians ("the same the world over," Diana says), and Swedes, each group dressed in its traditional clothing, eating its traditional food, and performing its traditional dances. As they enter the park, Tom says, "Look at them: Greeks, Serbs, Russians, Poles, Spaniards, Mexicans, and all the others, Americans all of them." This melting-pot idea is supported by the underscoring, in which the orchestration blends suggestions of the music of each nationality with "My Country 'Tis of Thee."

The decontextualization strategy is clearly at work in *The North Star,* an October 13, 1943, RKO release, with a screenplay by Lillian Hellman and direction by Lewis Milestone. Set in a small Ukrainian town on the eve of the German invasion, the film gives us characters who look and act much as one imagines Ukrainians looked and acted in the nineteenth century. There are glimpses of tractors, but for the most part, we see the characters riding horses or in horse-drawn carts. In fact, with a few exceptions, mechanization is associated with the Germans. In a scene marking the first sign of the invasion, as a line of horse carts passes a field where shepherds tend sheep, they are bombed and strafed by the Luftwaffe. The only explanation for why the Germans would waste their bombs on these fields is that they are trying to knock out the telegraph lines along the road, but probability aside, the symbolism is striking: a premodern society in which identity and relationships are defined in the family, in work, and in the land is disrupted by a modern society in which technology is associated with destruction.

This interpretation of the conflict is supported by the relatively few references to anything outside the rural world of the film, including the Soviet government and communism. A brief scene is set in Red Army headquarters, where a village representative has gone for weapons, and in another sequence we see a bombardier (Dana Andrews) from the town crash a crippled bomber into some German tanks. Otherwise, the Soviet military is absent; the villagers organize themselves into a guerrilla unit that drives the Germans from the town. Only once or twice is anyone addressed as "comrade." We get only one good look at the Soviet flag flying over the town hall as the Germans strafe it. The commander of the occupying German forces (Tonio Selwart) calls for "the chairman of the Soviet of this collective farm," but elsewhere—as when Doctor Kurin (Walter Huston) reminds the assembled townspeople, "This is our land, our village. We remember we fought another war to make them ours"—there is no indication that *ours* means ownership in a collective rather than in an individual sense. At the end of the film, as the townspeople ride away from their village, which they have set aflame, one young woman (Anne Baxter) says, "We'll make this the last war. We'll make a free world for all men. The earth belongs to us, the people, if we fight for it. And we *will* fight for it." The language and idea here, far from being specific to the Soviet Union, is reminiscent of other "people's war" speeches in such films as *The Great Dictator, So Proudly We Hail!* and *Mrs. Miniver.*

This process of decontextualization moves the film away from the specifics of the Soviet Union and creates a more general situation that can easily be connected to America and Americans. For American viewers, the characters' remarks about having fought a war to win their land connects more to the American Revolution than to the Russian Revolution. Indeed, when a lookout rides through town on a horse shouting, "Burn your houses!

The Germans are coming!" it's hard not to think of Paul Revere. Even the film's score, by Aaron Copeland, suggests American forests and farms, and the characters' folk songs, with music by Copeland and lyrics by Ira Gershwin, have the form and rhymes ("Juliet"/ "school yet") of Broadway show tunes. Like *The Human Comedy*, the film suggests that indications of cultural and national difference are superficial; not far beneath the surface, everyone is like Americans.

Days of Glory, another RKO tribute to the Soviet Union, was released on April 27, 1944. Like *The North Star, Days of Glory* decontextualizes its characters and situation. Again, we are given a rural setting—the underground headquarters of a group of Soviet guerrillas, somewhere behind the German lines. Only one of the characters, Vladimir (Gregory Peck), is a member of the Red Army. The rest, the film stresses, are from everyday walks of life: farmer, blacksmith, factory worker, student, scholar, drunk; even Vladimir, we eventually discover, was an engineer until the German invasion. Again, the official government and Red Army headquarters are mostly absent; headquarters is a far-off place from which orders come, but the characters and the viewers rarely see it. Indeed, this separation of the characters and story from the specifics of the Soviet Union is established at the beginning of the film when the narrator tells us, "Here is the true story, which could have happened in any land, of a little group of free people who lived and loved and fought to drive the invaders from their native soil."

There are some gestures implying Soviet communism here—the characters refer to one another as "comrade" far more often than in *The North Star*—and the film even suggests a sort of collectivism at work among the guerrillas, but this collectivism is both stripped of its ideological significance and expanded to invoke a non-Soviet notion of Russian culture. The simplified collectivism is introduced early in the film: as the guerrillas return to their underground headquarters from their exploits fighting the Germans, they segue into their household duties; everyone has a chore connected to the group's everyday living, and this job is as important as fighting the Nazis. The main complaint against Nina (Tamara Toumanova), a ballet dancer the group has rescued, is that she doesn't know how to cook or sew or do anything that can contribute to their day-to-day life. But this version of collectivism, far from seeming peculiarly Soviet, is similar to the tropes of sacrifice and pulling together used in many World War II movies. This depoliticized collectivism is summed up near the end of the film as two guerrillas argue over which of them will pull the trigger of a cannon aimed at a German tank. When one is mortally wounded, the other (Hugo Haas) puts his hand on the trigger, saying, "It's *our* shot."

But beyond the simple pulling-together theme, the overlapping of military and everyday activities is part of a more complex conflation of work, art, education, and tradition, which the film presents as Russian culture. Songs and literature are as much a part of the guerrillas' everyday lives as fighting and work are. In the evenings they sing folk songs, and Semyon (Lowell Gilmore), an Oxford-educated professor, reads them Pushkin. A religious tradition is indicated by the presence of icons on the walls. Nina, the dancer, had been on her way to the front to entertain the Red Army when she was separated from her troupe and rescued by the guerrillas. The film's emphasis on the presence and self-conscious preservation of culture is reminiscent of the bomb-shelter scene in *Mrs. Miniver.* The integration of culture into every aspect of Russian life is indicated when Vladimir explains to Nina the cultural significance of the dam he'd helped build at Dnepropetrovsk: "Out of the imagination of man it was built, and with the labor of many hands. The whole nation looked to it and waited breathlessly. At last it stood, complete, mighty, and beautiful, bringing light where there'd never been any light before and power that other things might be created. Poets wrote poems to the great dam, composers wrote music, and children all over the land were named for it. It was our own creation, and I helped build it." He articulates the building of the dam in language that suggests artistic creation, and the finished dam inspires literal enlightenment, further artistic creation, and even, in the naming, a sense of identity. The dam also represents Russian sacrifice and stoic determination to defeat the Germans. Vladimir describes helping to destroy the dam so that it won't fall into the hands of the advancing enemy, an incident also mentioned in Frank Capra's entry on the Soviet Union in the Why We Fight series, *Battle of Russia* (1944).

The pervasiveness of this broadly defined culture in Russian life is contrasted with the Nazis, who are, of course, destroyers of culture. Mitya (Glenn Vernon), one of the guerrillas, had been a student studying geology, with the idea of helping to improve Soviet farms, but the invading Germans burned his school. At one point, Nina begins weaving for Mitya a fantasy of the ballet in Moscow, but a German soldier interrupts it. Mitya is eventually captured and hanged, but the film uses this event both to project a future Soviet victory and to predict the incorporation of these current sacrifices into Russian cultural tradition. Nina consoles Mitya's sister (Dena Penn) by telling her this vision of the future: "I saw a big, beautiful, shining medal upon his heart, for he's going to be one of our great, great heroes. In every school of our land his picture will be on a wall, and all the teachers will make beautiful speeches about his bravery on this day of every year. And all the children on the benches will look at Mitya's picture, and they all will envy him for having given up his life for his country so courageously."

MGM's entry in the Soviet-support effort was *Song of Russia*, a December 29, 1943, release. It tells the story of an American conductor, John Meredith (played by Robert Taylor, who was universally derided for his arrhythmic conducting style, which resembles a combination of fencing and swatting a mosquito), who tours the Soviet Union just before the German invasion; falls in love with and marries a Soviet music student-cum-farmer-cum-civilian defense machine gunner, Nadya Stepanova (Susan Peters); and then returns to the United States to promote U.S.–Soviet cooperation. In one sense, the film offers more of a social context in its depiction of the Soviet Union than does *The North Star* or *Days of Glory.* Much of the film is set in urban areas; we also see the operation of a collective farm, and we even see Stalin giving a speech. This social context, however, is ideologically shallow. Collectivization is presented as a happy community working together, rather like a barn raising in the United States. No mention is made of the purge trials, the nonaggression treaty, or the invasion of Poland and Finland. As the reviewer for *Newsweek* summed it up, "MGM performs the neatest trick of the week by leaning over backward in Russia's favor without once swaying from right to left."[6]

In many ways, *Song of Russia* is like *The White Cliffs of Dover.* Each seeks to celebrate the national culture of the country it focuses on, but that culture is presented rather vaguely and disconnected from political and economic contexts. In *Song of Russia*, music—specifically, the music of Tschaikovsky—represents not only Russian culture but also the Russian soul, the Russian national identity. One implication of this metaphor is that the Russian national identity precedes and transcends the Soviet state. Music also represents a democratizing element: Meredith's concerts are attended by citizens from all class levels and professions and are broadcast over the radio to audiences all over the country. Nadya comes from Tschaikowskoye, a small farming community named after the composer, but even here there is a music school and a reverence for music. This reverence provides a means of contrasting the Russians and the Germans. In one clever sequence the camera takes us from a concert hall where Meredith is conducting and Nadya is playing the piano for Tschaikovsky's

Piano Concerto No. 1 across the Russian landscape to a small post where Red Army border guards are listening to the concert on the radio; the camera then tracks across the border to a Nazi post, where the soundtrack introduces martial music that drowns out the Tschaikovsky, as the commanders receive their orders to invade the Soviet Union. After the invasion, when Meredith returns to Tschaikowskoye to join Nadya, he finds the music school destroyed by Nazi bombs; the head of the school (Vladimir Sokoloff) says to him, "Look what they've done to our music."

Similar to *The White Cliffs of Dover*, the characters here invoke differences that separate Soviets from Americans, but the differences are swept away by the film's conflation of nationalities and a movement toward homogeneity. Nadya repeatedly stresses the differences between their cultures as a reason not to become romantically involved with Meredith, and he repeatedly brushes them off until he convinces her to marry him. At the wedding, Meredith's manager, Hank Higgins (Robert Benchley), grouses, "I just can't see it, that's all. He's an American. It's unpatriotic." But after enough vodka, there he is, joining in a Russian dance. The film conflates differences in other ways as well. The early montage of Moscow scenes shows an up-to-date, cosmopolitan city, not unlike Paris or New York. In a New York–style restaurant the performers sing in Russian an American novelty song, "The Music Goes 'Round and 'Round." Later, in another restaurant, another performer sings a supposedly Russian song, "Russia Is Her Name," which, the credits tell us, was written by Jerome Kern and E. Y. Harburg. More pointedly, the film connects Soviet values to Western values. In his speech to the nation, Stalin says, "In this war of liberation, we shall not be alone. We shall have loyal allies in the peoples of Europe and America. Our war, for the freedom of our country, will merge with the struggle of the peoples of Europe and America for their independence, for democratic liberties, and against enslavement by Hitler's fascist armies." Shortly thereafter, the film specifically compares the Soviet Union's fight against the Nazis to the American Revolution. Hank tells Nadya that she's a fool to return to Tschaikowskoye, in the path of the German invasion, rather than to go to America with Meredith. However, he explains, "I come from a small town, too, little place up in New England called Lexington. A lot of fools, like you, fought for that once, died for it, right there on the village green. Someday you'll see my town, you and John. I'm sure of it. It'll still be there because back home, we have a lot of fools like you." At the end of the movie, this theme of discovering common values and experiences underneath the appearance of difference becomes Meredith and

Nadya's purpose, as the villagers of Tschaikowskoye send them to the United States on a mission of "bringing our great countries closer together in this fight for all humanity."

The tropes that these films use to explain America's alliance with the Soviet Union—Russia as victim of German perfidy, Russia's stoic resistance and almost miraculous accomplishments in striking back,[7] the Russian character as grounded in a rural and cultural tradition, the melting-pot similarities between Russia and the United States—are remarkable in their consistency and in what they consistently leave out. We have already seen how these films tend to gloss over the collectivization of farms and how their focus on rural settings allows them to avoid other aspects of the Communist economic system. Not surprisingly, the studios chose to ignore other negative aspects of the Soviet Union's recent past: the purge trials; the Nazi–Soviet nonaggression treaty; the invasions of Poland, Lithuania, and Finland. Such antidemocratic, collaborationist, and territory-grabbing actions certainly did not fit the picture of Russia that Hollywood was trying to conjure; indeed, they suggested that the Soviet Union might have more in common with Nazi Germany than with the United States.[8] Even Frank Capra's *Battle of Russia*, though stressing the resistance to the siege of Leningrad and the breakout from Stalingrad, makes no mention of Stalin's earlier rapprochement with Hitler; in fact, it doesn't even acknowledge the 1917 revolution. Like these other films, *Battle of Russia* tries to connect Russia to a tradition of freedom and democracy much like America's, a connection not supported by the historic record.

The one exception to this strategy of hear no evil, see no evil, speak no evil was Warner Bros.' *Mission to Moscow*, released on May 23, 1943. This was a film adaptation of the memoirs of Joseph E. Davies, President Roosevelt's ambassador to the Soviet Union in the late 1930s. In his book Davies takes great pains to emphasize that although he is a capitalist and an individualist, and therefore in fundamental disagreement with Soviet ideology, he maintained an open mind in dealing with the Russians. He traveled around the country, studied Soviet industry, and came to know the Russian people as flawed but real human beings, not stereotypes. One purpose of his book is to explain the paranoia the Soviets felt in dealing with the West, a paranoia that he thought accounted for many of their actions leading up to the war. Similarly, the film presents Davies (Walter Huston) as an open-minded, straight-talking man who, despite his eagerness to remind his hosts that he is a capitalist, comes to understand and respect the Soviet Union and its people and to recognize the threat that Nazi Germany presents to that country as well as his own.

Mission to Moscow does two things from the outset that distinguish it from other films about the Soviet Union. The titles begin with a shot of a leather diplomatic pouch embossed with the Great Seal of the United States, from which an anonymous hand pulls Davies's handwritten manuscript. A dissolve turns the manuscript into the published book, and another dissolve turns a close-up of the book's title into the film's title. As an off-screen hand opens the book and turns the pages, the film's credits appear pasted directly onto the typescript. This presentation of experience turned into written text turned into published book turned into Hollywood movie suggests that what we're seeing is a representation of the literal, historical truth and something quite different from the narrative, perhaps mythic truths of other films about the Soviet Union. The oddity of what comes before and after the title credits emphasizes both the film's claim to literal truth and its status as a representation of the truth. Before the credits, we see the real Joseph Davies, sitting in what appears to be his office, directly addressing the camera, explaining why he wrote his book and why it is important that Warner Bros. turned it into a film. After the credits, we see Walter Huston portraying Joseph Davies, sitting in what appears to be his office, writing the preface to his book; after finishing the first sentence, he puts down his pen, looks directly into the camera, and states his basic thesis. At first, this bald admission of Hollywood artifice—Huston looks nothing like Davies—is startling. And this is only one of several places where the film seems self-consciously to call attention to its own status as a representation.

The reason for this is suggested in a scene late in the film, when Davies is barnstorming the United States trying to rally support for the Soviet Union after the German invasion. Davies gets off a train, and reporters approach him and ask if the Soviet Union will make a separate peace with Germany. As he answers in the negative, the camera moves in for a close-up of his face, then pulls back to reveal that we're watching this scene in a movie theater—it's a newsreel. In effect, we're looking over the shoulders of other moviegoers, who then begin commenting on his remarks and arguing among themselves about Russia and the extent to which the United States should lend its support. This weird emphasis (by Hollywood standards) on the film's status as representation serves an important function. It creates distance, opens up a space into which can be thrust the audience itself, along with their anticipated reactions and objections to the film's ideas. The film's concern with audience reaction is evident from the beginning—actually, before the beginning—when the real Davies says, "If I were down there in the audience with you, there are certain things that I would want to know about the man who's telling the story." The film attempts to be persuasive in a way the book couldn't be by letting the audience, in effect, talk back to Davies and thus giving him the chance to answer their objections. This is most clearly seen in the climactic rally in Madison Square Garden, where Davies answers and silences the questions of several hecklers. One audience member muses, "I wonder why these things have been kept from us."

This self-consciousness about the film's status as representation and the resulting incorporation of skeptical, dissenting voices serve, paradoxically, to make the film seem more real and, like Davies himself, openminded. It thus can tackle and hope to explain away many of the negative aspects of the Soviet Union that other films simply ignore. We see two instances of the Soviet Union depicted as a police state—Davies's car is followed by the KGB everywhere he goes, and at one point an aide raises the possibility that the U.S. embassy may be bugged—but these are dismissed as examples of the Soviets' justified paranoia. Davies argues that as long as he's always candid with the Soviets, it won't matter if they hear his private conversations. A long sequence showing the first of the purge trials argues that these trials were necessary to root out highly placed Russian fascists who were attempting to turn the country over to Germany.[9] The nonaggression treaty is explained as Stalin's attempt to buy time against the inevitable showdown with Germany. Here the film adopts the U.S. government's interpretation of the treaty as ensuring the Soviet Union's neutrality; both the film and government policy ignored the opportunities the treaty provided for the Soviets' aggression against other countries, especially Poland and Lithuania.[10] The invasion of Finland is rationalized as an attempt to occupy defensive positions against a German invasion.

Although *Mission to Moscow* deserves credit for addressing all these troubling issues about the Soviet Union, because of its simplification of these issues—or, to be less kind, its whitewashing of them—it is probably less successful than the other films we've discussed in defining for American audiences Russia's status as our ally. Even at the time it aroused controversy; reviewers accused it of being uncritical to the point of being propaganda, and history has been harsher. After the war, it was cited as a seminal example of the Communist influence in Hollywood for the House

Un-American Activities Committee, despite the fact that it had been made with the approval of the president and the Office of War Information.[11]

As a group, these films about the Soviet Union are much less successful than those about England in making the case for our alliances. This is probably because the raw materials the filmmakers had to work with were so different. These films demonstrate that although Hollywood magic can do many things, it cannot convincingly rewrite major historical events, nor can it create common ground for divergent cultures.

Similar problems plagued films about our third major ally, China. Although China was the earliest victim of fascist aggression—Japan moved to seize Manchuria in 1931 and began its wholesale war against China in 1937—it was never treated as a full partner in the alliance against the Axis. Nationalist Chinese leader Chiang Kai-shek was only rarely included in the strategy meetings of the Allied leaders, and, from America's point of view, for good reason. Gen. Joseph Stilwell, appointed by President Roosevelt to be Chiang's chief of staff, found confusion and turmoil raging among the Chinese leadership and in the military. He suspected that Chiang, whom he privately referred to as "Peanut," was content to maintain an informal armistice with the Japanese while stockpiling U.S. supplies for an eventual showdown with Mao Tse-tung's Communist forces.[12] So, not surprisingly, there is less focus on China and the Chinese in Hollywood films than there is on England and the Soviet Union. The Chinese are most often used as victims of Japanese violence; indeed, some of the most brutally violent scenes in Hollywood World War II films depict Japanese aggressors and Chinese victims. When the studios attempted to depict the Chinese as a nationality with whom we were allied, they faced two familiar problems: first, how to distinguish our Asian ally (the Chinese) from our Asian enemy (the Japanese); and second, how to present the Chinese as being like Americans.

There are many war films set in China—and many of them are set on the cusp between peace and war—but most of these have little to do with China. Instead, the country serves as an exotic location for the adventures of American or British characters. They are what film historian Bernard F. Dick calls "Yank in the Far East" movies.[13] In *Secret Agent of Japan* (1942) an American nightclub owner in Shanghai inadvertently gets involved with British and Japanese spies. In *Escape from Hong Kong* (1942) the three members of an American vaudeville sharp-shooting act also inadvertently get involved with British and Japanese spies. In *Halfway to Shanghai* (1942) two Americans inadvertently get involved with a murder mystery and Nazi spies on a train. In *Night Plane from Chungking* (1943) an American pilot inadvertently gets involved with Chinese and Japanese spies, has his plane forced down in the jungle, and is captured by and escapes from the Japanese army. And so on. This is not to say that these films do not participate in Hollywood's effort to narrate the war. They all characterize the Japanese as an enemy using the strategies discussed in chapter 3. They frequently present Americans in the process of learning why the enemy must be defeated, in accordance with strategies we've see in many films. In another interesting trope, several of these films, like many other B films and serials, present a German–Japanese alliance in the Far East, in which the Japanese seem subordinate to the Nazis.[14] *Halfway to Shanghai* shows an anti-interventionist newspaper columnist as being actively traitorous, as if all who had opposed American involvement in the war before Pearl Harbor were somehow disloyal.[15] In *Night Plane from Chungking* we're told that a wealthy Chinese woman, Madame Wu (Soo Yong), has burned her estates rather than let them fall into the hands of the Japanese. In *Secret Agent of Japan* a Chinese man (the ubiquitous Victor Sen Yung) who appears to be collaborating with the Japanese turns out to be an agent of Chiang Kai-shek. Nevertheless, it is unusual for a Chinese character to have an important role in these films; the Chinese, like their country, serve as background. Further, these films, unlike the films set in England and the Soviet Union, don't address the issue of China as our ally, as a nation with which and for which Americans need to fight.

Even films that more directly focus on the fighting in China, rather than on espionage, tend to be interested in Americans fighting in China for American or personal interests, not for the Chinese. *Flying Tigers*, a September 23, 1942, Republic release, focuses on one of Gen. Claire Chennault's three American Volunteer Group (AVG) squadrons, which supported the Chinese against the Japanese from September 1941 until they were absorbed into the U.S. Army Air Forces in July 1942. In the film, which borrows many plot elements from *Only Angels Have Wings* (1939), squadron leader Jim Gordon (John Wayne) tries to keep his planes in the air and his pilots alive while fending off Japanese attacks. But the plot really turns on the transformation of one of the pilots, egotistical and selfish Woody Jason (John Carroll). Woody immediately alienates the other pilots with his mercenary attitude. He makes it clear that he's joined the group only for the money. He says, "This is not our home. It's not our fight. It's a business. And boy, I hope business is good." But later, after

Pearl Harbor and after his irresponsibility has led to the death of another pilot, Woody's attitude has changed. He explains to Jim,

> A whole lot of us just don't grow up. We stay kids. The most important thing to a kid is the street he lives on. It's his life, it's his whole world. That was me when I first joined up with you. Hong Kong. Shanghai. Chungking. They didn't mean anything to me. Just a lot of names in a geography book. Not towns where millions of people were being maimed and killed by bombs. But if you call them Texas, Maine, or Michigan— that would have been different. They were my street. That's why I acted the way I did. Not because I was a heel, but because I was still a kid.

Woody's transformation involves two familiar tropes: the American learning why he has to fight; and the narrative connection of places in the Far East with American places, in effect, making them part of America. But this transformation has little to do with China. In fact, beyond a passage from a speech by Chiang Kai-shek praising the Flying Tigers superimposed over a picture of the generalissimo at the beginning of the film, the Chinese presence here is reduced to the background. A doctor is the only Chinese person in a position of authority. The others are in subservient positions—clerks or mechanics—or happy peasants receiving American aid or running onto the field to help push the returning American planes off the runway. As if to underscore that this is a film about Americans, the final image, of Flying Tigers taking off on a new mission, is accompanied by "The Battle Hymn of the Republic."

Similarly, another film about the AVG released late in the war, *God Is My Co-Pilot*, uses the Chinese theater as the stage for an American pilot's transformation. Loosely based on Col. Robert L. Scott's memoir of his time with the Flying Tigers, the film was released by Warner Bros. on February 21, 1945. It is most interested in following Scott (Dennis Morgan) as he achieves his dreams of becoming a pilot, flying in combat, and killing Japanese. It also shows him moving from an apathetic agnosticism through several heavy-handed attempts at conversion by Father "Big Mike" Harrigan (Alan Hale) to a moment of religious enlightenment when he prays to God to let him fly one last mission—a mission to bomb Japan— before he's grounded for his advanced age (he's reached his mid-thirties). Thus the end of the film incongruously brings together Scott's dream (to kill Japanese) and his need (to find religion). General Chennault appears as a character (Raymond Massey), and there are some gestures toward the idea of fighting for the Chinese, but, as in *Flying Tigers*, the Chinese are generally relegated to the background—coolies repairing the runway and giggling nurses.

China, a March 19, 1943, Paramount release, is more interested in presenting China as an ally and does so by some of the same means used in films about England and the Soviet Union, that is, by distinguishing the Chinese as a unique and valuable nationality—especially distinguishing them from the Japanese—and by connecting them to America. The film concerns Mr. Jones (Alan Ladd), an American entrepreneur who demands so much respect that even his friends call him *Mr.* Jones. Along with his companion, Johnny (William Bendix), Jones is driving a truck across China, from the town of Mei-Ki to Shanghai, racing the clock to close a deal to sell oil to the Japanese. Against his will, he gets caught up with a group of Chinese women and their teacher, Carolyn Grant (Loretta Young), who are trying to get to the university at Chun Du, where they can continue their studies.

Mr. Jones, like Woody in *Flying Tigers*, learns over the course of the film why the Japanese must be defeated. He begins as a businessman who's out to make a buck, unconcerned with other people's conflicts. As he says when Carolyn pleads for his help, "This isn't my war. As long as America's neutral, I'm neutral too." Mr. Jones is symbolic of the American attitude toward China before Pearl Harbor, able to separate its humanitarian sympathies for the Chinese from its commercial interests with the Japanese. A Chinese army officer (Beal Wong) says of America's friendship for China, "Sometimes I think it's a curious right- and left-hand friendship. With one hand they give us food and medicines, but with the other they permit men like you to sell oil to the enemy for the planes to kill our people and destroy our towns." Mr. Jones's mercenary attitude is made explicit in his response: "Alright, so you're at war. That's your business. Mine is selling oil, and if the Japs want it, it's *still* my business. At the prices they're offering, it's *good* business." Mr. Jones remains unmoved by Carolyn, although he does agree to stop briefly at the farm belonging to the parents of one of the schoolgirls, Tan Ying (Marianne Quon), to get milk for an orphaned baby (Irene Tso) that Johnny has rescued and christened "Donald Duck." Mr. Jones's turning point comes after the group proceeds and Tan Ying decides to slip off the truck and return to the farm because her parents need her. Mr. Jones and Carolyn drive back to the farm and discover that three Japanese soldiers have killed the parents and Donald Duck and are in the process of raping Tan Ying. Despite their protests that "Japanese and

Americans very good friends," Mr. Jones machine-guns the soldiers in cold blood and afterward reflects, "I just shot three Japs, blew 'em to bits against a wall, and I've got no more feelings about them than if they were flies on a manure heap. As a matter of fact, I kind of enjoyed it." From then on, Mr. Jones not only joins the Chinese in fighting the Japanese; in effect, he symbolically becomes Chinese. The Chinese commandos, with whom he had been in conflict, now adopt him as a "fourth brother."

This symbolic absorption of Mr. Jones is significant in showing that the film is not just about one American learning why the Japanese need to be defeated; it is also about defining the Chinese as a nationality to fight for. This definition seems to be based in the idea of China becoming Westernized: a major distinction between the Chinese and the Japanese in this film is that the Chinese want to become like us. Early in the film, Mr. Jones dismisses the authority of a Chinese army officer by saying, "You give 'em a dime-a-dozen education, teach 'em to eat ham and eggs, and what happens? They think they *are* somebody." By introducing Carolyn and her students shortly after this speech, the film demonstrates how wrong Mr. Jones is in dismissing education. Carolyn is training these women, who will train others and eventually build a new China, which, apparently, will be an Americanized China in its economy, its politics, and its values. When Tan Ying's mother exclaims what a strong farmer and good husband Donald Duck will grow up to be, the students interject, "But first he must be sent to school. He must be taught to read and to write and to think." The ensuing argument makes it clear that whereas the mother represents the old China, which values agriculture, women's traditional role as wife and mother, and wisdom received from one's elders, the students value progress, action, forward-looking women, and critical thinking. The connection between these values and America is made explicit by Carolyn in one of her arguments with Mr. Jones:

> You say you have an appointment in Shanghai. Just how important it is I don't know. But these girls also have an appointment, in Chun Du, and their appointment involves the destiny of China. . . . These girls are students. They're just a few out of many thousands. They're being trained for a very special job: to educate millions of Chinese, to teach them how working together they can build a new China. Mr. Jones, you and I are Americans. Our forefathers fought and died for a new America. These people are fighting for a new China. And if we don't help them now, well, I, for one, am going to stop calling myself an American.

The China we see here shows again and again its movement toward Americanization. Carolyn's assistant, Lin Wei (Victor Sen Yung), is American in his dress (striped T-shirt and windbreaker), speech (a self-conscious formality peppered with American slang), and attitude (he meets Mr. Jones's assertions of authority with a mocking irreverence). Tan Ying tells Mr. Jones that her expectations of him have been formed by seeing "lots of American cinema." When Tan Ying dies, though she is being cared for in a Buddhist temple, Carolyn recites the Twenty-third Psalm. Perhaps the best sign of the triumph of Carolyn's students comes when, after most of the men have been killed in a raid to steal dynamite from the Japanese, the women take their place in setting the dynamite to trigger an avalanche on an advancing Japanese division. After Mr. Jones is killed in the avalanche, one of the women students takes his place in the cab of the truck. These are clearly not the traditional Chinese women Tan Ying's mother valued.

The connection between the Chinese and Americans, as manifested by the Chinese desire to become like Americans, is contrasted to the Japanese. This is seen in the conversation Mr. Jones has with a Japanese gen-

China: Carolyn Grant (Loretta Young), Johnny Sparrow (William Bendix), Mr. Jones (Alan Ladd), and Lin Cho (Philip Ahn) make plans to stop the advancing Japanese.

eral (Chester Gan), as he stalls the division long enough for the dynamite to be set. The general also expresses a desire for things American; he speaks English, was educated in the United States, and loves American cigarettes. But this superficial desire masks a loathing for fundamental American values of freedom and democracy. The general says to Mr. Jones, "You must believe me when I say that, contrary to popular belief, the Japanese people have always held your country in great esteem. . . . Yes, they like it so well that they have finally decided to take it away from you." He tells Mr. Jones about Pearl Harbor and continues, "the fate of Pearl Harbor will be the fate of all so-called free democracies who dare oppose the Imperial Japanese government, because we and our allies, for the ultimate good of all nations concerned, have determined to establish a new world order." This new world order differs from the new China because the latter is based on an ideal of freedom, the most important link between China and the United States, as Mr. Jones makes clear in his final speech: "General, in all the countries that you and your gang have put the finger on, there are millions and millions of little guys just like me, little guys who have never amounted to much but all living our lives under pretty much the same pattern. And the pattern of our life is freedom, and it's in our blood, giving us the kind of courage that you and your gang never dreamed of. And in the end it's that pattern of freedom that's going to make guys like you wish you'd never been born." Ignoring historical reality, the film links the United States and China and all the countries fighting fascism in their valuing of a tradition of freedom and democracy.

China's depiction of young women as being in the vanguard of the movement from agrarianism and tradition to progress and democracy is employed in other films as well. In *Lady from Chungking*, a November 9, 1942, PRC release, the plot centers on the mysterious Kwan Mei (Anna May Wong). Posing as a farm laborer planting and harvesting rice under Japanese supervision, she is actually the leader of the local resistance to the Japanese occupation. Over the course of the movie, she organizes the escape of two pilots of the Flying Tigers and seduces a Japanese general to learn about secret troop movements. In the climax the pilots return with their squadron and support the resistance's attack on a Japanese troop train. The film presents a strong Chinese woman in command of and respected by men; instead of serving as background to the adventures of the American pilots, she rescues them and makes them a part of her plans. (It was also unusual to cast a Chinese American actress in a leading role.) In a striking scene, Kwan Mei is executed by a Japanese firing squad. In the midst of her final speech, the order to fire is given, but though her body falls dead, her translucent spirit remains standing and finishes the speech, as if to illustrate her point. She says,

> You cannot kill me. You cannot kill China. Not even a million deaths could crush the soul of China, for the soul of China is eternal. When I die, a million will take my place, and nothing can stop them, neither hunger nor torture nor the firing squad. We shall live on until the enemy is driven back over scorched land and the armies of decency and liberty are on the march. China's destiny is victory. It will live because human freedom will not perish. Out of the ashes of ruin and old hatreds, the force of peace will prevail until the world is again sane and beautiful.

Kwan Mei implies two battles here: the battle to defeat the Japanese, and the battle to bring about the destiny of a new China marked by freedom.

The most complex presentation of the Chinese as our allies is *Dragon Seed*, a July 18, 1944, MGM release. In a striking departure from its source, the novel by Nobel Prize–winning author Pearl S. Buck, *Dragon Seed* features no European or American characters—only the Chinese and the occupying Japanese. This makes the film—unlike many of the others we've discussed, in which China serves as a background to British and American adventures—uniquely about the Chinese. This may seem an incongruous claim to the contemporary viewer, as none of the major characters is played by an Asian actor; the leads are played by white American actors in varying degrees of makeup (poor Katharine Hepburn looks like she's wearing a mask), with the exception of the Russian Akim Tamiroff and the Turkish Czech Turhan Bey. The Asian actors who do appear, including the stalwart Philip Ahn, have minor roles. Though hard to accept now, this casting created an effect similar to the one created by James Stewart, complete with his midwestern twang, playing a sympathetic German in *The Mortal Storm*: an immediate connection is made between these foreign characters and the American viewers; they may look different, but not far beneath their appearance is someone recognizable and familiar.

This desire to connect the Chinese and Americans informs much of the film's structure and development. As in *China*, we are shown a people who are on the cusp of transformation, changing from a traditional, agricultural, isolated society to a progressive, modern, internationally connected society. This movement from isolation to international brotherhood is signaled in the opening narration. The off-screen narrator (Lionel

Barrymore) tells us, "This is the valley of Ling, as it was in the early summer of 1937. The people who lived here were farmers. They heard there was a world beyond the hills that bounded their little valley, but as yet no one had climbed those hills to see for himself." But he also hints at a connection, perhaps unrecognized, between the family of Ling Tan (Walter Huston) and the outside world; of the family he says, "they were very much like such families in any other land." The theme of isolation is linked to the theme of land possession. Ling Tan's primary motivation throughout the film is to hold on to his land. Early on, when his scholarly cousin (Henry Travers) speaks of the world being round, with different kinds of men who live on the other side, Ling Tan jokes with his wife (Aline MacMahon), "Have you ever thought that somewhere very far below the spot where we stand, our land goes on and on until at last a stranger stands on it?" The wife responds, "I am troubled about that stranger on our land. Somewhere he reaps his grain without telling you. You should ask him for rent."

Both the valley's isolation and the family's landownership are tested by the Japanese occupation. Earlier, when students from the north tried to convince the townspeople of the Japanese threat, they were generally ignored; the troubles of the north seemed disconnected from life in the valley. Thus, when the Japanese begin bombing and then invade the valley, the townspeople are confused and unprepared. Ling Tan refuses to flee before the invading army, saying that he will go only if he can "roll up my land like a cloth and take it with me." Later, the Japanese confiscate his fish, livestock, and rice harvest, telling him, "Nothing is yours." When his wife asks why he did not defy the officer, Ling Tan replies, "Alive, I can hold my land. Dead, I can only hold so much as I am buried in." Eventually, the high command in the mountains (presumably the Communists, though this is never made explicit) sends orders that the farmers are to burn their crops and houses. When Ling Tan objects that his land, his earth, is his country and vows to stay with it, his daughter-in-law Jade (Katharine Hepburn) counters, "But my father, this earth is only your country in peacetime when there is freedom." Ling Tan resists but is finally convinced. As he prepares to burn his house, he muses,

> Third Cousin once said that there is one sun and one moon for all. That is true. All share the sun and moon. Why should we not also all share the Earth? This valley is not the world but only part of the world. And there are others like me whose faces I have never seen. Elsewhere there are

men who love peace and long for good and who will fight to get these things. The stranger is no longer a stranger to me, but a man like me. If I could but know him. If I could but see him. . . . Somehow tonight I feel that there is a power sweeping around the world bringing us all together with that man who is a stranger.

Ling Tan hopes to reclaim his land someday but now recognizes his interconnection with and interdependence on people all over the world.

This emphasis on land is connected to the film's main strategy for distinguishing between the Chinese and the Japanese. The valley dwellers, as we have seen, are associated with the agricultural; indeed, their main use to the occupying forces is to produce food for the Japanese army. They are naive about and confused by technology. The slides the visiting students show are "magic pictures"; the Japanese bombs are "silver eggs." The Japanese, in contrast, are associated with mechanization: planes that drop bombs, cars, motorcycles, and trucks. When the villagers send out a delegation to meet the occupying army, Ling Tan's cousin moans, "But they are machines! How can you talk to machines when they are belching smoke?" Ironically, this association with machines leads to the dehumanization of the Japanese; they are presented as behaving like beasts. On arriving in the town, their first demands are for wine and women. In fact, this film offers one of the most explicit depictions of Japanese atrocities against women: both the mother of Ling Tan's son-in-law (Anna Demetrio) and his daughter-in-law Orchid (Frances Rafferty) are raped and murdered on the first day of the occupation.

The distinction between agricultural and technological is complicated when, after a stream of refugees passes through the valley, a large number of people follow, carrying and dragging the parts of a factory a thousand miles into the mountains, where it will be reassembled.[16] The farmers mock them for carrying metal instead of food, but it becomes clear that this factory and the city that will follow will supply the weapons to defend the land and lead China into a new age. The city people camp overnight on Ling Tan's land, and as the camera shows us their purposeful activity, we hear from somewhere a song: "With our very flesh and blood, let us build a new Great Wall." Jade and her husband, Lao Er (Turhan Bey), decide to leave the valley and go with this group, because, as Jade says, "They seem to have a plan."

As in China and Lady from Chungking, the progress toward a new China is associated here with women—or, more specifically, with one woman,

Jade. We see from the beginning that Jade is the family misfit because of her lack of interest in the traditional roles and duties of women. When she should be preparing her husband's supper and waiting on him after his return from the rice paddies, she is instead in town, listening to the visiting students describe Japanese aggression. When the other villagers reject the students' message, she stands alone in saying that she will help fight the invaders. Her husband, angered by her behavior and frustrated by his inability to relate to her in the way he thinks a husband should relate to his wife, says, "Oh, I wish it were those [ancient] times. I would like to lock you up." Jade responds, "But these are the new times, and I will come and go as I please." Lao Er gradually discovers that a loving relationship with Jade is possible, but only if he sees her as an individual, not as a traditional stereotype. The key moment in this discovery occurs when he agrees to buy her a book. He is shocked that she can read and is concerned about the propriety of her reading in his father's household, but she counters, "There must be changes, even in a household, if there is to be life and growth. . . . [Your mother and father] are of the old, we are of the new." The book Lao Er buys for her is titled *All Men Are Brothers*, and, like her dreams of flying above the valley, it symbolizes her role as a catalyst for the family's and the village's recognition of their connection to the outside world. After the Japanese invasion, Jade and Lao Er are the only ones who can think beyond the family's land and the valley. They follow the city dwellers and their factory, apparently rise to some level of authority in the high command, and are instrumental in persuading Ling Tan to burn his land and embrace his connection with the rest of the freedom-loving world.

As this suggests, unlike in *China*, the older characters in *Dragon Seed* are not associated exclusively with the unthinking acceptance of tradition. The postwar world the film anticipates will need some version of the prewar traditions if freedom and democracy are to be valued. Ling Tan is increasingly concerned about his youngest son, Lao San (Hurd Hatfield), because the war has turned him from a gentle poet into a man who relishes killing. Ling Tan agrees that the Japanese have proved themselves to be not men but beasts, but he asks, "must we too become as beasts?" He fears that men like his son will "not allow peace in the world." He tells his wife, "there is one thing we must remember, old woman, or we have killed ourselves, too. Peace is good. The young cannot remember it, and it is we who must remember and teach them again that peace is man's great food." Again, stenciled over China's actual history is a tradition of valuing democracy, freedom, and peace, which connects China to the United States and the other allies; the real differences between our cultures, traditions, and values are elided in order to create a narrative of sameness and unity in the face of a common totalitarian threat.

We see, then, that Hollywood films about our fighting allies faced different kinds of problems in representing Britain, the Soviet Union, and China as nations to be fought with and fought for. They used a variety of narrative and filmic strategies to a seemingly contradictory end: to show that each of these nations has a unique history and heritage for which it should be valued and that contrasts it with the Nazis and the Japanese; and to show that each nation's history and heritage are not so unique that it can't be seen as being very much like the United States. In the next chapter we show that in Hollywood films about European countries occupied by Nazi Germany, there is little concern with the uniqueness of these nations but quite a bit of emphasis on their similarity to the United States.

5

OUR OCCUPIED ALLIES

Port from Belgium. Ja! Cheese from Yugoslavia. . . . Wine from France. Fish
from Norway. Heaven protect the Führer, he certainly gets together a
wonderful table. . . .
Where did you get that beautiful bird?
We get the bird from all the countries.
　　　—Major Zellfritz (Allyn Joslyn), offering a seductive meal to
　　　Anita Woverman (Joan Bennett), in *The Wife Takes a Flyer*

DRAGON SEED CONTAINS A NUMBER OF SIMILARITIES to another
group of films—those set in European countries conquered and occupied
by Nazi Germany. These films, however, are less interested in explaining
why America should be fighting for these countries and in celebrating the
uniqueness of the featured nation and nationality. Rather, they tend to
focus on two ideas: the horrors of occupation and the possibilities for
resistance. The first idea, as we saw in our discussion of *None Shall Escape*
(see chapter 3), set in occupied Poland, uses the occupation as a way of
defining the Germans as a brutal, inhuman enemy. The second idea, resistance to occupation, is more relevant to our discussion here.

　　Occupation films cover a great deal of geography. Holland is the setting for *The Wife Takes a Flyer* (1942). Yugoslavia is the setting for *Chetniks!*
(1943). Czechoslovakia is the setting for *Hostages* (1943), as well as for
Hangmen Also Die! and *Hitler's Madman*, both released in 1943 and both
about the 1942 assassination of Deputy Reichsprotektor Reinhard Heydrich.
By far, the setting for the greatest number of occupation films is France,

but as a defeated major ally, France is something of a special case, and these films function in a different way, as we will explain later. After France, the country with the most films focusing on its occupation is Norway: *They Raid by Night* (1942); *Commandos Strike at Dawn* (1942); *Edge of Darkness* (1943); *First Comes Courage* (1943); *The Moon Is Down* (1943); and *Son of Lassie* (1945). But unlike the films set in England, the Soviet Union, and China, there is little effort in any of these films to establish the uniqueness of the history, culture, or character of the featured nation. Beyond the characters' names and geographic references, they are fairly interchangeable in terms of plot and characters and their depiction of the occupation and resistance. (Indeed, one film, *The Black Parachute* [1944], is set in an unnamed, apparently fictional occupied country.) In other words, *Hostages*, which is about a group of Czech hostages taken by the Nazis in retaliation for the death of a German officer (who actually committed suicide) and the parallel efforts to get a collaborationist coal baron and a resistance leader released, could just as easily be set in Oslo, Amsterdam, or Paris without any loss of its major themes. Indeed, the execution of hostages is a common trope in occupation films. However, it's hard to imagine *Forever and a Day* set in Moscow or *Dragon Seed* set in rural England without significant rewriting and loss—or at least transformation—of the film's thematic import.

Given this interchangeability, one might wonder why there are so many films about Norway. We think that there are two reasons, which, combined, help us understand the function of occupation films in explaining the war. First, like the United States, Norway had hoped to remain neutral while its larger, more militarily ambitious neighbors fought each other. Also like the United States, Norway had let its armed forces deteriorate in the years after World War I. When Germany invaded on April 9, 1940, using a combination of paratroops and seaborne troops, the attack was completely unexpected by both Norway and its would-be ally Great Britain. That evening, Norwegian fascist leader Vidkun Quisling attempted to take over the government, creating the popular impression that Norway had been betrayed from within. The *Divide and Conquer* film (1943) of Frank Capra's Why We Fight series emphasizes these ideas. It shows, docked in Norwegian harbors, German merchant ships that actually held troops and war supplies waiting to be sprung, Trojan horse–like, on the unsuspecting Norwegians. It goes on to explain that Quisling and other fifth columnists confused the Norwegians' reaction so that German warships and troops were initially unmolested. The narrator sums up, "This was one of the most amazing acts of treachery the world has ever known." These themes of treacherous surprise and betrayal would come to have great resonance for Americans twenty months later, after the attack on Pearl Harbor. In short, the events that brought Norway into the war are strikingly similar to the events that eventually brought America into the war.

The second reason Norway appealed to Hollywood is that, despite being hopelessly outmatched, it resisted the German invasion more stubbornly than most of the better-prepared countries. The Norwegian army, with support from the British, French, and Poles, held out for two months before surrendering (longer than Denmark, Holland, Poland, and even France), and then only after claiming 5,500 German soldiers and more than 200 German planes.[1] Further, King Haakon VII refused to surrender to the Germans or accommodate a Norwegian collaborationist government. He moved his government from Oslo to Trosmo and eventually to exile in England. This stubborn resistance provided another connection to America. The continental United States was never faced with invasion or occupation or even a significant attack during the war, but Americans could imagine themselves suffering such hardships vicariously at the movies, and Norway's stubborn resistance provided the best model for how Americans might imagine themselves behaving. (And such models are important. Historian Philippe Burrin argues that a contributing factor to France's armistice with the Germans was that France had few pop-cultural representations of how to behave under occupation.[2]) Note the implied parallels between Norway and America's self-image in President Roosevelt's famous "look to Norway" speech:

> If there is anyone who still wonders why this war is being fought, let him look to Norway. If there is anyone who has any delusions that this war could have been averted, let him look to Norway. And if there is anyone who doubts the democratic *will* to win, again I say, let him look to Norway.
>
> He will find in Norway, at once conquered and unconquerable, the answer to his questioning.
>
> We all know how this most peaceful and innocent of countries was ruthlessly violated. The combination of treachery and brute force which conquered Norway will live in history as the blackest deed of a black era. Norway fought valiantly with what few weapons there were at hand— and fell. . . .

But the story of Norway since the conquest shows that while a free democracy may be slow to realize its danger, it can be heroic when aroused. At home, the Norwegian people have silently resisted the invader's will with grim endurance. Abroad, Norwegian ships and Norwegian men have rallied to the cause of the United Nations.[3]

Using Norway as a paradigm for why the United States is fighting the war invites a comparison between the two countries, a comparison Roosevelt strengthens with his description of Norway's violation (practically an echo of his "date which will live in infamy") and its rallying to the cause. It takes little imagination to connect Norway's silent resistance and grim endurance with America—should America ever be in the same position. Hollywood seems to have wanted to make the same connections. Thus, the occupation films are not so much a celebration of Norway as they are a demonstration of how resistance against an occupying enemy can be enacted.

The Moon Is Down, based on John Steinbeck's successful novel and play, was released on March 10, 1943, by Twentieth Century–Fox. The film gives us a brief, bucolic look at life in a small Norwegian mining town before the Nazi occupation. But the Germans soon arrive, complete with band (which, in a running joke, repeatedly plays "We're Sailing against England") and a "civilized" commanding officer, Colonel Lanser (Cedric Hardwicke). The local quisling, storekeeper George Corell (E. J. Ballentine), informs Lanser, "I know these people well, and there's no feeling for fight in them." Indeed, the initial reaction to the invasion is repeatedly referred to as confusion. The Germans reach the town during a drill of the local militia, but it seems less drill and more picnic; the militia is wiped out in an ambush. When one militiaman attempts to shoot a paratrooper as he descends, his commander restrains him with the rule of law: "No, no, no. It's supposed to be wrong to shoot them like that. We'll get them on the ground." When Lanser arrives at the mayor's house and attempts to explain the terms of the occupation, he is dumbfounded that the household has been thrown into chaos by a servant's hysterical reaction to the soldiers. The local physician, Dr. Winter (Lee J. Cobb), tries to explain: "I assure you that neither he [the mayor] nor Madame Orden intended any disrespect. It's simply that the people—all of us—have lived at peace so long that we don't quite believe in war. It's not yet real. The temper of a cook *is*. The loss of a good cook is not only real but serious. Well, that's because our sense of values is still occupied with the values of peacetime.

We haven't had time to change. But we'll learn soon, and then we won't be confused. Then we'll know what to do."

The confusion is settled and their education is crystallized in the execution of a miner, Alex Morden (William Post Jr.), who struck and killed a German officer who spit on him. Alex's wife Molly (Doris Bowden) goes to Mayor Orden (Henry Travers) to plead for his life. When she tells the mayor that the people want to be free, he asks her, "Do they know how to go about being free? Do they know what method to use against an armed enemy?" She is uncertain but thinks that the people mustn't be docile: "If they are docile, they're beaten." This idea informs Orden's refusal to legitimate the pretense of a trial. When Lanser speaks of the need for laws to be enforced, Orden replies, "But why go into this nonsense of law? There's no law between you and us. This is war. Don't you know you'll have to kill all of us or we in time will kill all of you? Don't you know that?" He exposes here the charade of the German occupation: the methods of the local administration seek to maintain a veneer of order over the unruly reality of war. The more the Germans can convince the villagers to accept their authority to make laws and issue commands, the more the villagers will be beaten. The less they accept the Germans' authority, the more they are aware of themselves as combatants in a war. Orden makes this new awareness clear in his final words to Alex before his execution:

> Alex, these men are Germans, invaders. They've taken our country by surprise and treachery and force. . . . When it happened we were confused. We didn't know what to do or to think. Yours was the first clear act. Your private anger was the beginning of a public anger. . . .
>
> Go knowing that these men will never again have any rest, no rest at all, until they are gone from Norway or dead. You are making the people one.

Moments after the execution, someone shoots a German officer through a window, and the war is on.

Interestingly, although the film shows some acts of sabotage, courtesy of dynamite air-dropped by the British, most of the resistance is subtler and more personal. Steinbeck's novel and play (which, unlike the film, were set in an unspecified country) had been criticized for presenting the Germans as too human,[4] yet the fact that the German occupiers are human and wish to be treated as such is vital to the Norwegians' resistance. The Germans may confiscate radios, food, blankets, and clothes, but the villagers can deny them one thing: their desire to be recognized as human. In one scene a German soldier approaches a little girl on a breadline. He says, "I've got a little girl back home too, just about your age. But her hair is light, almost yellow. Won't you tell me your name?" When the girl cowers away from him, a captain (Henry Rowland) interrupts, demanding that she answer. He then addresses the people on the line: "There is a limit even to our patience, and I warn you now that you are doing yourselves no service by this persistent attitude of antagonism and surliness toward your protectors. Either you will correct it, and quickly, or we will find some means to impress upon you the error of such an attitude." But his bluster fades as first one man and then everyone on the line begins smiling at him, eerie, mirthless smiles that leave him speechless.

In another scene Lieutenant Tonder (Peter Van Eyck) enters a local pub. When all the locals proceed to leave, he stops them:

> In other countries we have been compelled to take steps to correct such incidents. Customers are not permitted to leave a public place for fifteen minutes after the entrance of a German officer. Perhaps we should do that here.
>
> Or perhaps we can be more sensible. We have neither of us anything to gain by bickering. We have now been here nearly four months, and we shall continue to be here for a long time to come. So perhaps we should accept this fact and try and make the best of conditions. You will return to your tables and continue your discussions.

Tonder's argument seems based in common sense: learning to accommodate each other would be infinitely easier. But the customers refuse to be "sensible." One responds to Tonder's speech by taking out his pocket watch and asking, "Fifteen minutes, Lieutenant?" The customers return to their tables but sit in silence, looking at their watches. When Tonder tries to engage a farmer with memories of his own boyhood on a farm, he responds with one-word answers and pointed stares at the clock. After fifteen minutes, everyone leaves, and Tonder's experiment in peacemaking fails.

Tonder next tries to find companionship with a woman he admires, Molly Morden, not realizing that she is the widow of the man whose firing squad he led. He goes to her house one night, pleading, "Just for a little while, can't we forget the war? Can't we talk together like people?" She resists but ends up chatting and even laughing with him. He says that he wants to make love to her: "A man needs love. Without love, a man dies. His inside shrivels, and his chest feels like dried chip. I am lonely." She spitefully proposes sex in exchange for food, and he is disappointed because she has again altered their connection from a human one to one based in their power relationship. He begs, "Please don't hate me. I didn't ask to come here any more than you asked to be my enemy. I'm only a man, not a conquering man." Molly appears to accept this, to accept him as a human being. She invites him to her bedroom, where she kills him with a pair of scissors.

With this implacable severity, the villagers are merciless in their refusal not only to treat the Germans as human but also to let the Germans think of themselves as human. This refusal is difficult to maintain in the face of both German oppression and the need to be liked, as demonstrated by Tonder and others. This idea is emphasized by the casting of Cedric Hardwicke as Colonel Lanser. His voice is smooth and British accented; he rarely shouts and almost always says "please" and "thank you"; he is educated and demonstrates a distaste for the job he's been given. As a result, he is able to present his requests for cooperation logically and charmingly; it would be easy for the villagers—and the viewer—to think it best for all concerned to accommodate him. Resisting him is hard, but accommodating him would be a sign of the docility Molly warns about. Tonder realizes that as long as the Norwegians refuse to deal with the Germans as humans, they will never be defeated. When a fellow officer claims that the Germans have conquered Norway, Tonder laughs hysterically and says, "Flies conquer the flypaper!" At one point, Mayor Orden tells Lanser, "In all the world yours is the only government and people with a record of defeat after defeat for centuries and every time because you didn't understand people." The film implies that the Germans also don't understand their own needs as people and that this lack of understanding can help lead to their defeat.

Released by Columbia on December 18, 1942, three months before *The Moon Is Down*, *Commandos Strike at Dawn* develops many of the same themes. The film spends more time establishing the quaint and quiet life of the Norwegian fishing village that is its setting. The villagers, mostly fishermen and farming families, are connected with nature. Erik Toresen (Paul Muni) is a scientist, but one who studies the ways of nature: the tides, fish populations and migrations, the weather. He says, "I never feel alone with trees, mountains." The occasion of a folk wedding shows us the harmony of the community and their friendship with a visiting British family—an important point, as the invading Germans will eventually claim that they are protecting Norway from the British. The one discordant note here is sounded by Johan Bergesen (Ray Collins), the local crank who can't stop talking about the threat posed by Hitler and Nazi Germany, and Lars Arnesen (Louis Jean Heydt), the local hotelier who has obvious fascist sympathies. In the kitchen he complains, "That Bergesen. Talk, talk, talk! He should be stopped by law!" to which his wife (Rosemary DeCamp) responds, "You always want to stop something by law. You don't eat enough green vegetables."

These early scenes, and this last dialogue particularly, establish the conflict that develops once the Germans arrive. As in *The North Star* and *Dragon Seed*, the villagers are associated with nature and the enemy with machines; the motorcycles and staff car that bring the Germans into the village are the first mechanized vehicles we have seen. But more important, the Germans announce their arrival with a slew of laws. The occupying colonel (Arthur Margetson) isn't even out of his staff car when he announces, "All is to go on as before. Your industries are now in safe hands. Your culture is protected. Of course, there will be a curfew at 6:30 every night, and any Norwegian found in the streets after that will be shot. No boats are to leave the harbor, under pain of death. Any act of disobedience against the German uniform is punishable by death, at my discretion." In a series of scenes we see the German soldiers burning books; confiscating blankets, radios, and pots and pans; trucking the young men off to work in the mines at Narvik. Meanwhile, the colonel continues to dictate new laws, violations of which are all punishable by death. As in *The Moon Is Down*, this legal mania in pursuit of order is revealed to be a sham. This becomes clear to Erik when Bergesen, who had been arrested the first day of the occupation, returns from his interrogation and torture and says of the Nazis, "No civilized human being could know how bad they are." Erik, who had previously thought that civilians could do nothing against the invaders ("We civilians, it's not exactly our line"), organizes a meeting of potential resisters. He tells them, "For many years, we made a serious mistake: we believed we were living in a civilized world. Today we find that for years, we've been living in a jungle. Regulations were put into effect, and we attempted to live up to them. Now we discover there's only one regulation: kill or be killed. I'm ready to observe that regulation. I've come to ask you how we can change over in this jungle from the murdered Norwegian people to the murdering Norwegian people." When a young woman (Elizabeth Fraser) objects that they can let the British, Americans, and Russians win the war, Erik responds, "Nobody's going to get victory as a gift, Anna. We get only what we earn, and I propose that we earn a great deal."

There follows a montage of the villagers' acts of resistance. Some, like the dynamiting of telephone lines and railroad bridges, are spectacular, but many, as in *The Moon Is Down*, are mundane yet effective: painting an X over official posters; the local minister (Rod Cameron) canceling services for the duration of the occupation, because the church can't serve God and the Nazis; giving the wrong directions to German officers so that they drive over a cliff; schoolchildren defiantly singing the Norwegian national anthem during a German flag raising and then giggling at the impotent sputtering of the Nazi captain (Alexander Knox). Also as in *The Moon Is Down*, all pretense of civilized civil authority breaks down after a young man (Richard Derr) is caught with a radio transmitter and executed in the town square. Shortly thereafter, Erik assassinates the colonel. In retaliation, hostages are taken and executed, and Erik and some others sail to England to join fighters from many other nations.

From this point, the film is primarily interested in action. Erik returns to Norway as part of a British naval and commando task force commanded by Admiral Bowen (Cedric Hardwicke as one of the good guys this time). They destroy a German airfield and rescue the villagers, but Erik and Admiral Bowen's son (Robert Coote) are killed. The conclusions of both *The Moon Is Down* and *Commandos Strike at Dawn* offer interesting messages. In the former, a group of hostages, including the mayor, is executed just as local saboteurs blow up the mine. This suggests an open-ended cycle of resistance and retaliation—vital if the occupied people are not to be beaten, but not a path to winning the war. Similarly, in *Commandos Strike at Dawn* local resistance can accomplish only so much, after which the occupied people must rely on outside forces for their rescue. The methods of resistance celebrated in these films are part of a stoic waiting game, indicative of a refusal to be beaten, but are not in themselves sufficient to bring about the defeat of the occupying enemy.

Edge of Darkness, released by Warner Bros. on March 23, 1943, two weeks after *The Moon Is Down*, takes the occupied Norwegians beyond this ambiguous stalemate. The film opens with a unique narrative frame: A German patrol plane spots the Norwegian flag flying above the headquarters of the occupying forces in the small fishing village of Trollness. Soon a search party steams up the fjord and finds hundreds of dead bodies—both villagers and Germans—at the docks, in the town square, and at the headquarters (a small hotel outside of town). The only living soul is Kaspar Torgersen (Charles Dingle), the owner of the local fish cannery, now insanely babbling that the entire village belongs to him. In the office of Captain Koenig (Helmut Dantine), the late commander of the occupying force, the leader of the search party begins dictating his official report of the incident, and the film begins a flashback to show us how the Norwegians reclaimed their village at such an awful cost.

By mid-1942, the people of Trollness have achieved the type of resistance we have seen in the other films. Captain Koenig explains the trouble to a visiting major (actually a British agent, played by Henry Brandon): "Nothing you can put your finger on. Once in a while a fire breaks out. A boat is sunk. A wire is cut. A shipment of fish is spoiled. The kettle boils." When the major asks for the names of the troublemakers, Koenig replies, "I would have to give you the name of every man, woman, and child." He explains that the Germans have only one man on their side. The major guesses that this one man is the owner of the cannery. "Of course," Koenig confirms. Koenig is confident that no rebellion can possibly succeed: "We're 150 against 800. We could be 150 against 8,000. 80,000! We have guns, and they are afraid to die." This dialogue sets up the basic situation and establishes the film's major themes. As in the other films, the villagers are performing pestering, mundane acts of resistance. As in the other films, the villagers, with the exception of one quisling, are united in their resistance to the occupation. There are two things they need in order to move beyond this stalemate to open rebellion: guns, which will be supplied by the British, and to overcome the fear of death by replacing the notion of the individual with that of the community.

Although the villagers are united in their hatred of the occupiers, the film shows us that there is no real agreement among them on how to resist the Germans. In general, the more focused a person is on himself or herself as an individual, the less willing he or she is to support even modest resistance. The extremes of this idea can be seen in Torgersen, the collaborationist cannery owner, whose desire to protect his personal comfort and personal property puts him in league with the Germans (his selfish greed is seen even in his insanity—he claims the town to be his), and in hotel owner Gerd Bjarnesen (Judith Anderson), who denies every personal need and feeling, even her love for a German soldier, rather than compromise the resistance. A more ambiguous example of this is Dr. Martin Stensgard (Walter Huston playing yet another nationality). He repeatedly asserts that he is a Norwegian and that he loves Norway; he is in conflict with Torgersen, his quisling brother-in-law, because he is profiting at the expense of his country and his countrymen. Yet the doctor is so concerned with keeping his family safe that he disapproves of acts of resistance for fear of the retribution they will bring. This diversity of opinion among the villagers, however, is shown not as a failing but as a strength of democracy. We see them air their differences at a town meeting called to discuss the news that the British are delivering guns to all the towns along the coast, but in a nearby village, the guns were discovered and the people and their town were annihilated. The question, then, is should the people of Trollness accept the guns. The meeting demonstrates both democracy in action and harmonious coordination. The meeting is ostensibly a religious service; children playing outside the church warn of approaching Germans, and the people inside slide seamlessly into a hymn. Tempers run high and there is much arguing, but repeatedly someone will call out, "Every man must speak his mind," and there are reassurances that those who speak against accepting the guns, notably Dr. Stensgard and Pastor Aalesen (Richard Fraser), are not to be considered disloyal. The result is a careful working to a consensus. One farmer (Art Smith) demurs because of the possible loss of individual possessions: "If I lose my farm, there must be a reason for it. The sacrifice of one poor village—what will it accomplish?" Gerd responds with the argument that all concerns about individual property and individuality are irrelevant in a situation such as theirs: "What sacrifice? What are you giving up? Your life? Maybe they'll take that from you whether you fight or not. Your farm? It isn't yours anyway until you fight for it. Your peace? What peace is there when a body of troops can come in the middle of the night and arrest you as a hostage to be shot for something you never did nor ever even thought of, like my father? To live in constant fear. To have blackings at your windows. To talk in whispers. To have guards at your church doors."

The connection between a self-centered focus on the individual and individual possessions and the fear of death is further developed in the subplot of Dr. Stensgard's son Johann (John Beal). In 1940, when the Germans invaded Oslo, Johann in some unexplained way aided the Germans. He has now been called home by his uncle, Torgersen, to help him run the cannery and eventually take it over. But Torgersen also wants him to help betray the villagers' plans to the Germans. After a flashlight is found in the hills where the villagers are hiding the British rifles, Torgersen appeals to Johann with the logic of ownership: "Why, it isn't a question of being a Nazi, Johann, it's a question of protecting what's yours. This cannery is

mine now, but it'll be yours someday. Tomorrow morning, because of this
nonsense on the hill, Koenig is confiscating all the fishing boats. He's afraid
the villagers might use them to get arms. Do you know what that means,
Johann? It means that *our* cannery will have to close. Now, wouldn't it be
better if, quietly and without any fuss, you could find out what they were
doing on that hill?" When Johann refuses this logic, Torgersen shifts to
the threat of death. He reminds Johann what will happen to him if the
villagers find out he is a traitor; further, the Germans now consider him
one of them and will see his refusal to help as traitorous. He warns, "They
don't like traitors either. They shoot them." Johann is persuaded by the
fear of death, but the villagers have been warned by his sister Karen (Ann
Sheridan) and feed him false information. He disgraces himself to the
Germans and is exposed to Trollness as a quisling. Confronted by his family and by the local head of the resistance, Gunnar Brogge (Errol Flynn),
Johann tries to explain himself:

> JOHANN: When the Nazis came into Olso, I had to make a decision,
>   and I thought—
> GUNNAR: You thought of yourself before you thought of Norway.
> JOHANN: Yes.
> DR. STENSGARD: That was in Oslo, but here, that day on the boat,
>   you gave me your word.
> JOHANN: I didn't realize, Father, that once you're in, you can't get
>   out!
> GUNNAR: You can, if you're not afraid to die.

In the end, the focus on possessions and on the individual generates the
fear of death, and, as Koenig notes, if the fear of death can be instilled in a
people, they can be subjugated forever.

Further, the film shows that this fear of death can't be overcome as
long as one is focused on individuality. A person can accomplish nothing
alone. Lars Malken (Roman Bohnen), a shopkeeper who feels that his
contributions to the cause aren't sufficiently appreciated, sneaks into the
German headquarters. When he is caught and the soldiers mock him, he
offers to tell them what he thinks of them, but fear keeps him silent, and
he runs away humiliated. Later, Koenig orders that the house of schoolmaster Sixtus Andresen (Morris Carnovsky) be turned into a blockhouse.
Andresen tells the incredulous Koenig that he forbids the Germans to
come into his house: "You see, I am well past seventy, and at my age, it

would be foolish for me to be like Socrates' enemies and fear death more than I love truth. . . . What you don't understand is that the individual man must stand against you like a rock. . . . If I were afraid, there might be hope for you, but I am not. There are certain things you cannot take away from me. What is mine is mine. Do you think you can stop the working of my brain and my heart?" This is a noble speech, but one that is immediately proved wrong. Koenig throws Andresen down the stairs, drags him out of the hotel, and orders his men to burn the old man's possessions in the public square. The soldiers force him to run a gauntlet, then tie him up and drag him behind a wagon with his furniture, books, and papers, which they torch in the town square. Despite his brave words, Andresen is afraid, and by the time the pastor picks him up and carries him from the square, he is a beaten, dying man. He says to Dr. Stensgard, "Each day we learn a lesson. What is the lesson for today, Stensgard? The individual cannot stand like a rock. Even a rock can be crushed. It's obvious." But Stensgard doesn't learn this lesson. His daughter Karen is raped by a German soldier,

Edge of Darkness: The people of Trollness, Norway (Roman Bohnen, Errol Flynn, and Ann Sheridan in foreground), prepare to storm the German headquarters.

and even after Gunnar, her lover, reluctantly agrees that this is not the time to attack, Stensgard goes out on his own, finds the soldier, and kills him, giving Koenig the excuse he has been looking for to order the execution of all the resistance leaders.

Ironically for Koenig, the impending executions mark the coming together of the villagers; they put aside their individuality and their fear of death and overwhelm the German soldiers in the town square, the harbor, and finally the hotel-headquarters. As rows and rows of people with rifles march toward the town square singing "A Mighty Fortress Is Our God," Gunnar tells Karen, "This time none of them are afraid to die." Indeed, as the villagers close on the hotel, Koenig's Polish mistress (Nancy Coleman) mocks him, "You are frightened." As the headquarters falls, and just before he commits suicide, Koenig writes in a letter to his brother, "Today we own Germany, tomorrow the entire world. We Germans fear nothing in this world. Phrases—slogans. That's all I can write." By rising up as a community, the people of Trollness have turned the tables on their occupiers. The film shows the terrible price the villagers pay to destroy the Germans, as hundreds of people are killed. One is reminded of Mayor Orden's prophecy in *The Moon Is Down*: "you'll have to kill all of us or we in time will kill all of you." The children, many of the women, and the wounded are put on fishing boats to sail for England. The rest of the survivors go to the hills to continue the fight. As Gunnar explains, "These fascists will never drive Norwegians out of Norway. Those of us who come out of this alive will take to the hills, fight on from there until we drive them out." *Edge of Darkness* gives the Norwegians more agency than the other films. It shows us people learning to move beyond acts of resistance (and the condition of victimization they imply) to the status of combatants, striving to drive the Germans out without waiting to be rescued by the British or Americans. The last scene returns to the film's frame: a German soldier takes down the Norwegian flag and raises the Nazi swastika, but before he can get the flag up, he is shot dead by Karen, a sniper in the hills. The implication is that now that the people have arisen, the Germans will never reclaim Trollness.

It is interesting to note the presentation of collaborators in these occupation films. There is usually only one unregenerate collaborator (in *Edge of Darkness* Johann is killed warning the villagers of a trap during the final assault on the German headquarters). The collaborator is usually bourgeois or petit bourgeois: cannery owner, hotelier, shopkeeper. The motivations for collaboration differ, from self-interest to ideological commitment, but they are also irrelevant: the collaborator is a traitor and, as such, is beyond the pale. In *Edge of Darkness*, as Dr. Stensgard pleads with Karen to give Johann a chance to start over, he says, "Why must everything in the world be either black or white?" Karen responds, "Because that's the way the world is these days." But other films present collaborators more ambiguously. In *First Comes Courage*, a September 10, 1943, Columbia release, Nicole Larsen (Merle Oberon) is the mistress of German major Paul Dichter (Carl Esmond) and is consequently ostracized by her entire community.[5] In reality, however, she is using her position to gain information and pass it on to England. The film follows her efforts to help a British commando (Brian Aherne), also her former lover, escape without giving herself away to Major Dichter. In PRC's September 3, 1942, *They Raid by Night*, three commandos (Lyle Talbot, George Neise, and Charles Rogers), two of them British and one Norwegian, parachute into Norway to try to rescue an important Norwegian general (Paul Baratoff). Dalberg (Sven Hugo Borg), who is helping the Nazis in their search for the commandos and who, after their capture and interrogation, is ordered to execute them, ends up helping them escape. As he frees them, he says, "We can't all fight for our native land. We can't all be like you. There are thousands and thousands like myself. We joined the new order only to tear down by night more than they build up by day." In both these films the message seems to be one of caution in making judgments: loyalty can take many forms, including the appearance of betrayal and collaboration.

This ambiguity surrounding collaboration informs many of Hollywood's depictions of France during the war. France, historically an ally of the United States and, in the early months of the war, allied with Great Britain against Nazi Germany, disgraced itself by its rapid capitulation to its invading neighbor in June 1940 and its official policy of collaboration with Hitler's government. Whereas the other European victims of Germany, no matter how helpless, offered some inspiring resistance, France in many ways seemed to welcome the new world order. In the summer of 1940, Parisian companies eagerly sought to do business with the new regime. André Gide, intellectual and author, wrote, "If German domination were to secure us affluence, nine out of ten French people would accept it, three or four of them most cheerfully. . . . To seek agreement with the enemy is not cowardice, but wisdom, as is accepting the inevitable. . . . What would be the point in battering ourselves against the bars of our cage? To suffer less from the cramped nature of the prison, the only thing to do is to keep to the space in the centre." Even more disturbing, some of France's leaders, including World War I hero Philippe Pétain and his second in command, Pierre Laval, used the occasion of the invasion as an opportunity to install a new government based on an ideology very much like national socialism. The Pétain government valorized traditional life: rural occupations and a connection with the land, the primacy of family and country over the individual, praise for motherhood and large families, emphasis on Catholicism not only as a religion but also as a part of the national identity, and deference of individual rights and desires to the state. Veterans were praised, despite the nation's defeat, because in Pétain's portrayal of the national psyche, Jews, Freemasons, Communists, and foreigners were responsible for the problems in French society. Later in the war this list would include Gaullists and Anglo-Saxons. A cult of leadership developed that was codified in the French constitution. Members of the armed forces and magistrates were required to swear allegiance not to France but to Pétain. This is the government that offered an armistice, which Germany accepted as a surrender, and that pursued a policy of collaboration with Hitler. Philippe Burrin describes this policy as being based on the following assumptions and strategies: "France's defeat was definitive and England's was bound to follow soon. In the face of the ineluctable hegemony of Germany, wisdom dictated damage limitation through a show of goodwill and voluntary adhesion to the new order, preferably before England's collapse or, worse, before it sued for a compromise peace."[6]

How was Hollywood to deal with this disgrace and with the confusing proliferation of Frances: German-occupied France, Pétain's Vichy France, de Gaulle's Free France? As Shull and Wilt put it, "France had the singular distinction of being, at various times (and sometimes simultaneously), a fighting Ally, an occupied country, and even an enemy."[7] The confusion over how to understand France can be seen in *Divide and Conquer* of the Why We Fight series, as it attempts to explain why France fell so quickly and so utterly. First, it compares the situation in 1940 with the beginning of World War I in 1914. Then, France stopped the German invasion by following the motto of Marshal Foch: "J'attaque!" Twenty-five years later, the weak-willed French military chose a defensive strategy, relying on the impenetrability of the Maginot Line. The narrator tells us, "In Foch's time the proud spirit of France demanded nothing less than victory and placed its faith in the attack [shots of the French flag billowing in a strong wind and of World War I soldiers going over the top]. In Maginot's time the spirit, no longer proud, asked only to avoid defeat and placed its faith in concrete [shot of the French flag hanging limply as the wind dies down]."

The narrator goes on to tell us that Hitler knew that France was unprepared militarily, but more important, "he knew that France had become a cynical and disillusioned nation." This last assertion is accompanied by newsreel footage of urban riots. The narrator offers several reasons for France's malaise: the loss of 6 million young men in World War I; the failure of the League of Nations, on which France had hung its defensive hopes; a series of political and economic scandals. He sums up, "All had combined to shake the faith of the French people in their democratic ideals, and when a people loses its faith in its own ideals, it is ripe for the insidious words of the devil." The argument seems clear: France fell because of bad military planning, a corruption of national spirit caused by World War I, and ineffectual and self-serving leadership, resulting in a weak and ideologically confused populace. But then, in an odd non sequitur, the film shows us a large cartoon castle, standing on the map of France, and a hand dropping tiny swastikas, which start climbing up the walls of the castle like little bugs. The narrator says, "France still looked like an imposing castle, but Hitler's political termites had so gnawed away the binding of national unity that the castle was ready to crumble." We are then shown scenes, with superimposed titles, of sabotage, fifth columnists, strikes, and riots. So the film carefully moves the blame from France's military leadership to its political and economic leadership to its weak, valueless populace to Hitler. The reasons for its fall are both internal and and external to France, yet neither.

Less bound than Capra was to the facts of historical events, the Hollywood studios still faced the challenge of making sense of a confusing situation in their quest to depict France as a country that America should be fighting for. Complicating the situation early in the war was the Office of War Information's insistence that films not be critical of the Vichy government. The United States maintained diplomatic relations with Vichy, in part so that President Roosevelt would have some influence in convincing Pétain to "instruct his troops not to resist the Allied landings in North Africa."[8] Nevertheless, snide assertions about the French government crept in, particularly in Warner Bros. films. Most famously, the Warners try to have it both ways in the characterization of Vichy official Capt. Louis Renault (Claude Rains) in *Casablanca* (1942). Renault is an opportunist and a realist who understands that the Nazis are in control and that the government he represents is little more than a puppet state. He says, "I blow with the wind. And the prevailing wind happens to be from Vichy." Rains's delightfully ambiguous portrayal makes it seem that Renault and his police force have faith only in tangible things such as money and women. Yet at the end of the film, Renault undergoes an unexpected conversion. He doesn't arrest Rick for killing Major Strasser and allows Victor Laszlo and Ilsa to escape to freedom. Apparently disgusted by the cruel actions of the Nazis in Casablanca and his own complicity with them, he throws a bottle of Vichy water in a wastepaper basket, equating the very name of the water with the collaborationist government.[9] He then accompanies Rick to join the Free French in Brazzaville. Thus the film manages to criticize a representative of the Vichy government—though not too severely, since his portrayal is so charming—and to redeem him.

The need to treat Vichy France diplomatically lessened after the November 1942 American landings in North Africa. Although Adm. François Darlan, the French naval commander, agreed to surrender his ships to the Allied invasion force in late 1942 as a result of an agreement with General Eisenhower, he was unable to assert his authority, especially in Tunisia. The agreement became moot when he was assassinated by a young monarchist on December 24. Pétain, meanwhile, ordered the French troops in Tunisia to fight with the Germans, prolonging the Allies' operations in North Africa.[10] The studios were then freer to be critical of the Vichy government, but this did not solve the problem of how to present France. Despite the collaboration of Pétain's government, France was not really an enemy. Yet, because France had fallen to the invaders and was, after November 1942, an occupied zone, it was not really an ally in the same way that Britain, the Soviet Union, and even China were; even if the enemy was on their soil, they had independent governments and were still battling the invaders. France was not simply an occupied country either, in that before its fall it had been a major ally, and after its fall it adopted an official policy of collaboration rather than resistance. Hollywood's solution was to employ a variety of strategies in the depiction of France, many of which we have already seen in the presentation of our various allies.

One strategy was to separate the idea of France from the actual geographic and governmental France. Perhaps the most complex use of this strategy is found in *Passage to Marseilles*, a February 17, 1944, Warner Bros. release based on the novel *Men without Country* by Charles Nordhoff and James Norman Hall. The confusion of the French situation is mirrored in the film's complex structure: a Chinese box–like series of flashback within flashback within flashback. The narrative frame, set in wartime England, shows a squadron of the Free French air force setting off on a mission. To pass the time until the planes return, the commander, Captain

Freycinet (Claude Rains), tells a reporter (John Loder) the story of how he met the fliers. This begins a flashback to Freycinet's voyage on a freighter carrying nickel ore bound for Marseilles; the freighter picks up five men in a small boat, who turn out to be convicts escaped from Devil's Island. When these men are questioned, they offer yet another flashback, the story of their escape. Within that, one of them, Renault (Philip Dorn), initiates yet another flashback, telling the story of Matrac (Humphrey Bogart). Matrac, a newspaper owner in prewar France, had published editorials warning of the menace of Nazi Germany and attacking the Munich pact. A mob demolished his paper's offices, and he was convicted on a trumped-up charge of murder and sent to Devil's Island. As he says at one point to Captain Freycinet, "I don't care about my country. The France you and I loved is dead, Captain, she's been dying a long time." The story, then, moving from its innermost embedded narrative to its frame, is about how one Frenchman lost his faith in and love for his country and how that faith and love are restored.

This restoration is accomplished through an argument much like the one Prudence makes to Clive in *This above All*, that the imperfections and even the corruption of a country as it exists in the sociohistorical moment must be separated from the ideal potential of the country as it exists in the hearts and minds of its most fervent citizens. *Passage to Marseilles* takes this concept a step further by separating the idea of France from the geographic area known as France. The film's epigraph establishes this theme:

> This is the story of a Free French Air Squadron. It is also the story of France. For a nation exists, not alone in terms of maps and boundaries, but in the hearts of men. To millions of Frenchmen, France has never surrendered.
>   And today, she lives, immortal and defiant, in the spirit of the Free French Air Force as it carries her war to the skies over the Rhineland.

Much of the tension in the film comes from competing ideas of France. This is introduced almost immediately, when Freycinet says to the reporter visiting the Free French air base, "You've come to see some French traitors, as Monsieur Laval would call us." The film then proceeds to offer us many Frances. There is the France that disillusions Matrac, consisting of a corrupt leadership that has betrayed its country's traditional values and embraced the fascism of its neighbor. This corrupt France accounts for the presence of another of the prisoners: Petit (George Tobias), who killed a police officer after he lost his land when it was flooded by the government. There is also the France of the Vichy government, which seeks to collaborate with the Nazis. Two of the other men on the freighter, passenger Major Duval (Sydney Greenstreet) and radio operator Jourdain (Hans Conried), share Pétain's xenophobia, and when France surrenders, they prefer an accommodation with Germany to aligning themselves with England's apparently hopeless cause. Freycinet and the ship's captain (Victor Francen) resist this accommodation; although the new government has ordered the ship, which is midway across the Atlantic, to proceed with its nickel ore to Marseilles, the captain has been secretly adjusting the course to take them to England. The escaped prisoners have mixed feelings: victims of a corrupt justice system, they have no reason to love France, yet their escape had been facilitated by an older prisoner, Grandpere (Vladimir Sokoloff), on the condition that they swear an oath to return home and fight for France. They take the oath, but their allegiance, especially Matrac's, is never clear. Yet when Duval learns of the captain's plan and leads a mutiny, claiming the ship for the Vichy government, the prisoners join with the captain and Freycinet, retaking the ship and then defending it against a Luftwaffe attack. Interestingly, in the Devil's Island flashback, when the prisoners discuss what they love about their country, their statements are very general or abstract, not specifically connected to the actual sociohistorical situation of 1940. One says that he misses the "good French soil," another the nightlife of Paris, another the open countryside. But Renault sees France in terms of its entire historical and cultural tradition: "For me, France will always be the great tradition: Versailles, Joan of Arc, the statues and monuments, Napoleon sleeping in greatness in the Invalide, Place Vendôme." Matrac's love for the idea of France returns as he defends that idea against those—French and German—who would destroy it and as he witnesses the sacrifice of a cabin boy (Billy Roy), who dies with the words, "We'll drive them out of France." This thought that the true defenders of France are not actually *in* France echoes an earlier statement by Matrac's wife, Paula (Michèle Morgan): "It's not just us, *our* lives; it's the life of our country. If we get away, go to America, somewhere, we can do something about it." To fight for our country, we must be somewhere else.

This returns us to the narrative present, where Matrac has been killed during the bombing mission. At his burial, Freycinet reads a letter Matrac had written but had been unable to deliver to his son (still in France) for his birthday. Using a technique we've seen at the conclusion of other films, the letter projects into the future, imagining a time when the war is long over and humans live in peace. Then, this golden age is linked with the idea of France:

My dear son,

Today you are five years old and your father has never seen you. But someday, in a better world, he will. I write you of that day. Together we walk hand in hand. We walk and we look and some of the things we see are wonderful and some are terrible. On a green stretch of ground are ten thousand graves, and you feel hatred welling up in your heart. This was, but it will never be again. The world has been cured since your father treated that terrible abscess on its body with iron and fire, and there were millions of healers who worked with him and made sure there would be no recurrence. That deadly conflict was waged to decide your future. Your friends did not spare themselves and were ruthless to your foes. You are the heir of what your father and your friends won for you with their blood. From their hands you have received the flag of happiness and freedom. My son, be the standard bearer of the great age they have made possible. It would be too tragic if the men of goodwill should ever be lax or fail again to build a world where youth may love without fear and where parents may grow old with their children and where men will be worthy of each others' faith. . . . Au revoir till our work is finished and then, till I see you, remember this, France lives. Vive la France.

In two other films, the idea of France is symbolized by a woman character who is connected to a figure from the French national mythos. *Uncertain Glory*, released on April 24, 1944, by Warner Bros., has a plot inspired by a French classic: *Les Misérables*. Police inspector Marcel Bonet (Paul Lukas) has been tracking master criminal Jean Picard (Errol Flynn) for years. Bonet finally succeeds in capturing Picard, but before he can bring the thief and murderer back to Paris for certain execution, Picard offers a deal: since he is going to die anyway, let him confess to sabotage—the destruction of a bridge—and thus save the 100 hostages the Germans are threatening to kill. Although it seems clear that Picard is playing for time and has no intention of sacrificing himself, Bonet reluctantly compromises his principles and begins tutoring Picard on the act of sabotage so that he can make a convincing confession. Staying a few days in a small village

from which the hostages have been taken, Picard and Bonet meet a naive—almost simple—young woman named Marianne (Jean Sullivan),
whose name recalls the symbol of revolutionary France. Picard escapes
from Bonet and runs away with Marianne, but whatever arguments he
makes against turning himself in are repulsed by Marianne's simple faith
in what is right, in her country, and in him. When he inevitably returns to
Paris to keep his end of the bargain, Bonet asks him why he came back. He
explains, "Maybe it was the look I saw in Marianne's face as she lit a candle.
But there's more to it than that. It's too many things to have a name. I
suppose there's a time when any man, even a man like me, can find something . . . something bigger than himself for which he's ready to die, without question, almost . . . almost happily." The implication is that, in Picard's
case, this something is an idea of France that he learned from Marianne.
When Bonet tells Marianne what has happened, she asks what Picard was
like, "deep in his heart." Bonet replies, "He was a Frenchman."

A second film that uses a woman character as a symbol of the idea of
France is *Joan of Paris*, a January 9, 1942, RKO release. The film focuses
on a group of downed Allied fliers who are hiding in Paris while trying to
get out of France. Their leader is Paul Lavallier (Paul Henreid), a Free
French flyer who has been condemned to death in absentia for leaving the
French military to join de Gaulle in England. The Joan of the title is, like
Marianne in *Uncertain Glory*, a symbol of the unspoiled idea of France and
France's historic and cultural tradition.[11] Joan (Michèle Morgan) is a religious young woman who is compelled to help the fliers because of her
connection with Father Antoine (Thomas Mitchell), who hides the men
in the crypt of his church, and her attraction to Lavallier. Although at first
she is naive about the Nazis and the role that ordinary citizens can play in
defeating them, her love for Paul converts her into first a messenger, then
a martyr. She pretends to agree to lead Herr Funk (Laird Cregar) and the
Gestapo to the pickup point for the Allied fliers but delays the Germans
until the fliers are safely away, knowing that this deception means her
death. During her final confession, Father Antoine encourages her by connecting her to her country: "You will live, Joan. You'll live in the heart of
France, when she's risen again."

This connection is paralleled and reinforced by the film's structure.
The credits are written on the label of a champagne bottle presented to the
viewer by a waiter; the credits change every time overflowing champagne
washes over the label. All this is accompanied by jolly Parisian music.
Next, we see a shot of the Eiffel Tower, followed by a montage of the

bright, neon lights of Paris. We then move into a clip from RKO's 1934 Fred Astaire–Ginger Rogers vehicle, *The Gay Divorcée*, including that film's opening number, a nightclub chorus line singing "Don't Let It Bother You." The scene ends in blackout as a radio announcer says that the Allied invasion of France has begun (an event that isn't referred to again during the film). Finally, we are introduced to Lavallier and his crew trying to avoid capture in the French countryside. This opening sequence seems peculiar and inappropriate to the rest of the film, as if it comes from another movie (and, indeed, some of it does). Yet it allows us to see a movement from an innocent, carefree France to a wartime France. This movement is similar to the transformation in Joan's character. At first, she is a naive girl, aware of the war mostly as an inconvenience. She prays to the statue of St. Joan in her room, asking not for victory or to drive the Germans out, but for a new dress. The first time she delivers a message for Lavallier, he tricks her into it. The second time, she does it willingly and is slightly wounded by Gestapo gunfire. Finally, she knowingly makes her sacrifice. Lavallier, whom she has come to love, thinks that he has missed his chance to escape. Joan meets him in the church, and as he proposes to her, offering a simple life in a small town in the south—a return to innocence—she sees a stained-glass window of St. Joan above her. She takes inspiration from the saint to tell Lavallier that his men are still waiting for him and how to reach them. She says, "You see, I didn't know till tonight. I thought you were just the man I loved. I thought it was only I who needed you. But now France needs you more." She gives up her love and her life to serve her country.

A more complex treatment of a woman as a symbol of France is offered in *Reunion in France*, a December 2, 1942, MGM release. The film begins on the evening of May 9, 1940, the night before the German offensive in the west. We see people in a café, lovers in a garret, and finally Paris's glitterati at a formal dinner, all listening to a French general (Henry Kolker) give a speech assessing the country's war readiness. He says, "Tonight the people of France have reason to be heartened and encouraged. In the north Hitler's army stands helpless and immobilized before our impregnable Maginot Line. Our soldiers are fully equipped and trained to the point of perfection. And behind them, the people of France are confident and united as never before. It is because of our leaders of industry and of labor that our imperishable republic will not only emerge triumphant but will ensure the freedom of Europe for our generation and for the generations to come. France is a great country tonight." He goes on to praise the Committee of Industrial Coordination, which has brought together leaders of various industries, labor, the military, and the government to plan and direct a single, cooperative effort in fighting the war. But this unity, coordination, and cooperation are soon shown to be a sham; France, much as Capra argued in *Divide and Conquer*, is racked with divisions and a lack of focus and resolve that will make the country easy pickings for Hitler.

The sham is revealed through the chairman of the Committee of Industrial Coordination, Robert Cartot (Philip Dorn), and his fiancée, Michele de la Becque (Joan Crawford), a superficial and oblivious heiress. Michele is bored and inconvenienced by the war. She is about to leave for Biarritz and pouts because Robert won't go with her, refusing to understand that his work is important to the defense of France. He, in turn, expresses a cynicism that suggests not all is well in the French government and military. When Michele says that the general is convinced Hitler can't invade France, Robert replies, "Unfortunately, for every general that's right, there's one that's wrong." When she urges him to come away with her, noting that even the prime minister isn't as busy, he says, "that's unfortunately true." More important for the film are the class divisions Michele reveals. Before leaving for the station, she returns to her home, where she has kept a dress designer (Odette Myrtil), a model (Ann Ayers), and a seamstress (Margaret Laurence) waiting for two and a half hours. Not only inconsiderate of their time ("Why is it she never seems to find enough time in which to do absolutely nothing?" snipes the seamstress), she dismisses colors and fabrics she had previously chosen, complains about the quality of material available due to wartime restrictions ("Mademoiselle seems annoyed at the war"), and wonders why the model doesn't see a specialist about a blister on her foot and why she doesn't have her shoes custom-made. After she sweeps from the room, the model asks, "Who does she think she is? Who do they all think they are?" The designer responds, "The glory that was France." This connection between Michele and France is made even more explicit when Robert teases her about a supposed rival: she is "like you in a way: spoiled, selfish, incredibly romantic." He's referring, of course, to France. (As if to emphasize this point, in its British release the film was retitled *Mademoiselle France.*)

Unlike in *Uncertain Glory* and *Joan of Paris*, here a woman stands not for the ideal of France but for all the flaws that resulted in its rapid defeat. Having established this, the film then becomes about Michele's—and France's—transformation. As Michele leaves for Biarritz (so wrapped up in her tearful good-bye to Robert that she is oblivious to a line of refugee children waiting to board the train), the German invasion begins. Starting with a shot of the French flag flying over the train station and the words "Liberté, Egalité, Fraternité" proudly carved at the top of the building, the film takes us into a montage of newspaper headlines documenting the progress of the German forces and the fall of France, newsreel footage of combat and refugees, and shots of Michele suddenly awakened while sunbathing in Biarritz (she later agrees with another character that her situation is "a little like suddenly recovering one's vision"), walking with hordes of others (after her car breaks down) trying to get back to Paris, being strafed by German planes, and sleeping by the side of the road. The montage ends with another shot of the train station, this time with the Nazi flag flying above and "Liberté, Egalité, Fraternité" covered by Nazi banners. In a scene anticipating disaster films of the 1950s, Michele returns to a nearly deserted, lifeless city; the only people she sees are German soldiers, some on duty, some goose-stepping sightseers. Her mansion has been taken over by the Coal Allotment Bureau. She is offered one room, and in the first sign of the collapse of her long-held sense of class, she chooses the concierge's room. Soon she will be working for the dress designer she had earlier kept waiting.

When she first meets Robert after her return to Paris, Michele now projects onto others the faults that had previously been identified with her, especially the selfishness and divisiveness that are harmful to France. Speaking of her hardships while returning to Paris, she says, "It was easier to get away from the Nazis than from the French. Some of them were worse than the Germans, spying on their friends, selling them for a passport, a favor, even a meal. Anything but fight as Frenchmen. What's happened to us, Robert? What's become of France?" She soon discovers what the viewer picked up immediately upon seeing Robert prospering under the occupation: he is a collaborator, designing and building trucks, planes, and tanks for the Germans. In confronting him, Michele urges him to go away with her, saying curiously, "We'll leave Paris and go to France." He understands her literally, wondering what they would live on. But, as in *Passage to Marseilles*, Michele is suggesting that the idea of France can be separated from the physical, geographic space of France and that France as an ideal can be separated from the selfish, divisive, and collaborative actions of individual French people.

Robert and others try to shake her new sense of France by appealing to her sense of class, trying to destroy her vision of a unified France by arguing that she and they are part of an elite that has nothing in common with the mass of people. Robert says to her, "Living is to have today at least what we had yesterday, because we are not equipped for anything else, because it's our destiny. We have been bred and taught to live from the top of the bottle. . . . We weren't born to make sacrifices, we two." Later, a drunken German officer (Ernst Deutsch) who is trying to seduce her says, "You are not the enemy, you never were, you and your kind. You know what it means to be the masters, to live off the weak. . . . Don't fight. Leave that to the little people. They lose when we win. Everything you had you will have again." Nevertheless, Michele sticks to her new vision of herself and her country. She says to Robert, "You told me once I reminded you of France because I was selfish and spoiled. I'm not anymore, and neither is she. Whatever she is now, I am too."

From this new position, Michele becomes involved in a convoluted plot to help an American (John Wayne) flying with the Royal Air Force (RAF) get out of France and back to England. In the process she discovers that Robert is not really a collaborator at all but the head of a network of resisters. One of his agents (Reginald Owen) explains, "The workers in his factories, men on the street, shop girls and teachers and farmers. The greatest organization Cartot ever created. And no one in it knows him as anything but a Nazi lover and an enemy of France." It even turns out that the vehicles his factories are producing for Germany are defective. Michele, who had been planning to leave France, returns to Robert to help him in his struggle. As they stand in the doorway of his mansion, schoolchildren glare at them and spit. Robert says, "We must only begin to worry when they no longer spit at us and our Nazi friends." Michele's transformation is now complete. She was at first a symbol of France divided. She then projected those divisions onto others as she became a symbol of France unified. Finally, by taking on the appearance of a collaborator, she is both working for France and providing a symbol that can unite other French people through their loathing of her. This seems similar to the quisling in They Raid by Night, who argues that many apparent collaborators are really working to tear down by night what they help the Nazis build up by day. Here, at the end of the film, the idea of a unified France is broad enough to include even those who seem to be working with its enemies.

Whereas Reunion in France begins with a vision of an internally divided France, reminiscent of some of Capra's arguments in Divide and Conquer, The Cross of Lorraine goes further, as Capra did, blaming French divisiveness on the betrayal of the country by its leaders and, more important (and paradoxically), on the activities of the Germans. A November

12, 1943, MGM release, the film begins with a montage showing men from all over France, from all classes, levels of education, and professions (including a political prisoner), joining together to defend their country. Even the narrator is one of them, referring to "we" and "us" to reinforce the idea of national unity in the face of an external threat. This unity, however, is quickly destroyed by the German blitzkrieg. The narrator tells us, "Within two short weeks, we were scattered across France like a torn patchwork." Accompanied by newsreel footage of a smiling Marshal Pétain, the narrator tells us of a truce being declared, but because the Germans have destroyed the means of communication, many soldiers never hear of it. What began as a unified army representing a unified country is now a set of isolated individuals. The narrator says, "On a thousand roads a sergeant, a corporal, a private had to decide each for himself what his own lost unit should do." We then cut to a country road at night, where a French colonel and then a German officer use a loudspeaker to encourage French soldiers to surrender. The German assures them that they will be returned home and that side by side the Germans and French will rebuild their country. A small squad surrenders, only to learn later, as a train takes them into Germany and they are marched to a prisoner of war (POW) camp, that they have been lied to and betrayed.

On the train, when they still think that they are going home, there is a great deal of discussion about the repercussions of the surrender: some are appalled and ashamed; some think that initial hard times will give way to a rebuilt and powerful France; one even thinks that German victory is the best thing that could happen to France. These disagreements are presented not as divisive but, like the town meeting in *Edge of Darkness*, as fundamental to a working democracy. After the men reach the POW camp, the real divisions begin, and they are initiated by the Germans. The commandant, Major Bruhl (Tonio Selwart), tells the men, "Those among you who fought us against your better judgment will be recognized and given preferential treatment." Duval (Hume Cronyn), who on the train had spoken in favor of Germany's fascist efficiency, volunteers to serve as a translator and is soon made a capo; his parading of his better treatment—good food, cigarettes, trips to France to assist German officers with their black-market purchases—taunts the men and weakens their resolve. On that first day, with the men having had no food since their surrender, Sergeant Berger (Peter Lorre) appears at the barracks door with a large basket full of bread but throws only one loaf on the floor. The men briefly go mad, fighting one another for the food. Rodriguez (Joseph Calleia), a veteran of the

Spanish civil war, tells them, "Use your head, that's what they want us to do, fight amongst ourselves. That's why they give us this one little loaf." Father Sebastian (Cedric Hardwicke) adds, "When that trick succeeds, you will witness a major victory of the new order." To the men's struggle to survive, then, is added the struggle not to give in to the Germans' attempts to turn them against one another. Major Bruhl explains the logic of this strategy to the prisoner Paul Dupré (Jean-Pierre Aumont) as he pleads to stop an execution: "You thought I would be disturbed by the thought that the prisoners will hate us. Well, we expect that. But we also know that they'll fear us, so they'll work for us. With continued education, their children should like us, and their children's children love us."

The practical goal of these attempts at dividing the prisoners is, as it was at the beginning of the film, to break the group into individuals forced to make lonely choices about whether to collaborate. This inner conflict is best developed in the character of Paul, a lawyer who enlisted in the army when war was declared. He is a reasonable man, confident, at first, of the Germans' common sense if not their humanity; he's sure that they realize that it's in their own best interests to treat defeated France humanely. His confidence is shaken by the treatment of the prisoners, but he is firmly on the side of unity among the POWs. Like them, he gives capo Duval the silent treatment, and he flatly rejects Duval's suggestion that he too could be a capo. But the degradation of being a prisoner, especially the hunger, begins to break him down. He accepts cigarettes from Duval, even scavenging the butts that Duval discards. He wolfs down a fellow prisoner's food seconds after his death. He listens to and believes Duval's reports about how the people back in France are responding to the occupation: "The wise ones are collaborating, getting along fine. The others . . . there aren't very many of them left." After Duval is murdered by the other prisoners, Paul is chosen as the new capo and is clearly conflicted in this role. He hopes to use his influence to make life better for the prisoners; instead, he must struggle with the guilt he feels for the better food, clean uniform, and other privileges that come with his position. He wants to stand with the prisoners and with the French but feels himself slipping into collaboration. As Major Bruhl says to him, "I guess you have discovered if you meet us halfway we are not such brutes after all, hmm?"

Paul is saved from the temptation of gradual collaboration by his need to do something about his comrade Victor (Gene Kelly). As a soldier, Victor was the one most eager to fight the Germans and most devastated by the surrender. In the prison camp he is the cockiest Frenchman, the one most ostentatiously resistant to the rules and the one determined to have his say, even though he knows it means a beating. He finally goes too far and is beaten and tortured until he is little more than a shell of a man. As Major Bruhl says, "You see, we amputated his enthusiasm." He can now be used as one more device to intimidate and divide the prisoners. Major Bruhl explains, "We'll send him back among his comrades, and let them see there's no one the new order can't break." Ever the realist, Rodriguez lays it out for the other men: "It isn't bad being killed. It's much better than to die. Dying—that's what is happening to all of us. Don't you see it? First, our courage burns out, our self-respect, after a while hope. And the carcass lives on. But the man is dead. [To the men] You don't see it, do you? [To Paul] But *you* see it." Paul evidently does see himself in this prisoner's progress, and it leads him to seize the opportunity to help many of the men, including Victor, escape. When 150 Alsatians are released (in exchange for 600 French workers sent into Germany), Paul substitutes many of his friends, planning to rendezvous with them in France and make their way to North Africa to continue the fight. When the now-timid Victor is afraid to go, Paul refuses to go without him, saying, "It's not only Victor. It's all the men who thought the worst that could happen to them will be to die and then discovered that death could be a luxury. . . . I, and all the people like me, we got all the Victors into this. They wanted to fight, and we didn't." Paul recognizes that when he and the other leaders surrendered, it was the first step in a process of collaboration leading to death. Trying to make up for that surrender, he finally manages to get Victor out.

The escaped men meet at the village of Cadignon. Along the way, Victor, still reeling from his torture, imagines that betrayed and occupied France is as divided and as intimidated by the Nazis as the men in the prison camp were. What he and Paul discover is an informal resistance, contingently organized, made up of a unified French people. A teenage boy they meet (Billy Roy) describes this resistance: "Thousands and thousands of us. We're organized too. Our own officers and our own meeting places, the same as any army." At Cadignon, reunited with many of their fellows, Paul and Victor learn that General Cartier has a volunteer army of some 8,000 men in the mountains, and they plan to join him. However, the next day, German soldiers arrive to round up the men of the village for forced labor. Inspired by Paul and a suddenly rejuvenated Victor, the people of the town—men, women, and children—using rocks, coal from their stoves, appropriated weapons, and Molotov cocktails made with gas from the Germans' own vehicles, attack the Nazis. Many of the townspeople are killed, but the Germans are routed. Instead of waiting for the Germans to return, the people propose to burn their homes, as the people did in China and Russia. When some women demur, one mother (Emma Dunn) says, "I know it takes courage to burn our homes, but since when have we been lacking in courage? Come on! Let's scorch the earth! They'll find nothing but ashes when they get here!" The townspeople then march into the mountains to join General Cartier, the burning village in the background transforming into a sunrise as they reach their destination. This film recognizes the divisions in France that led to its defeat, but it also suggests that there are no such divisions on the level of the common, ordinary French people. They may have been betrayed by their leaders, and the Germans may try to divide them, but they will nevertheless unite and find a way to fight.

Another film that makes use of the defeat of the French army to explore the possibilities for resistance is *Paris after Dark*, an October 6, 1943, Twentieth Century–Fox release. After an opening sequence showing the well-oiled resistance operations at a factory in Paris where German tanks are manufactured, the film shows us a group of French soldiers on a train, returning home to Paris after two and a half years of captivity. Like the soldiers in *The Cross of Lorraine*, these men feel betrayed by leaders who surrendered too quickly. One of them (Louis Borell) complains, "Is a man defeated when he didn't even have a chance to fire a shot? Our regiment was ready to die to the last man. I'm still ready to fight." Among the men is Jean Blanchard (Philip Dorn), whose enthusiasm has been amputated (like Victor in *The Cross of Lorraine*). Before the war, Jean was apparently a union activist at the factory, but even though the resistance movement at the factory is organized by former union members and enacted according to union methods, Jean has no interest in joining their activities. Having had fear beaten into him by the Nazis, he thinks that France's best course of action is to suffer the occupation, try not to rock the boat, and do nothing that's likely to bring retribution. When he finds resistance pamphlets that his wife Yvonne (Brenda Marshall), a nurse at the factory hospital and an active member of the resistance, has brought home, he is appalled. He burns them, telling her, "The people responsible for these should be reported so that the rest of us can live in peace." A few days later, when Yvonne's younger brother George (Raymond Roe) is ordered into Germany to work in factories there, Jean tells him, "If you want to live, then obey. There's no other way out. Can you count on the English or the Americans? They will never come. I tell you, New York is a long way from Paris."

Naturally, Yvonne and the other resistance members keep their activities secret from Jean.

Interestingly, Jean's anger is directed not at the Germans but at Dr. Andre Marbel (George Sanders) from the factory hospital, apparently a former opponent of the union but now a leader of the resistance. Jean mistakes Andre and Yvonne's clandestine conversations and late-night meetings for signs that the two are having an affair. Jean confronts Andre, saying, "It was alright for you slackers when the rest of us left for the front. Sitting at home with your bellies full of food, reading the war news in the papers, and to forget about it, taking the wives of the men in the trenches." Later, one of his union comrades (Curt Bois) explains to him, "The doctor used to be against us. Now he's one of our leaders. . . . You know, Jean, resistance to fascism isn't only the workers' privilege. It belongs to everybody, the whole country." Jean seems to make himself a character in the wrong stories: he wants to fight union battles, but the war has collapsed and united the classes; he sees himself in a love triangle, but the other two characters are thinking of their country, not of love. The one story he refuses to see himself in is a war story; he needs to believe that the war is over, at least for him.

Jean's transformation begins after he carelessly tells Michel (Marcel Dalio), a collaborator and informer, about George's plan to escape to England to join de Gaulle. George and several friends (including an uncredited Peter Lawford) are arrested on the road and brought back to the factory, where, after making an impassioned speech, George is shot and killed. Enraged, Jean tracks down and kills Michel. Finally, his eyes opened to the real story he is in, Jean is welcomed into the resistance. His new problem: Yvonne shot the German colonel (Robert Lewis) who killed George, and the Nazis are holding fifty hostages who will be executed if the shooter doesn't surrender. Jean knows what he must do when he hears his father-in-law (Jean Del Val), another man who hoped to get along by not rocking the boat, say, "It is a new kind of war, isn't it? Kill these men in brown shirts, destroy them, or yourself be destroyed." Knowing that he doesn't have long to live—that's why the Germans released him from the POW camp—Jean goes to Andre and offers to surrender himself as the shooter to save the hostages and Yvonne. His explanation marks a new knowledge about France and about the need to resist the Nazis: "You know, I've learned a lot in a few days in Paris. Our people are united, and when they must choose between death and the spirit of freedom, then death becomes a very small matter to them." Like other characters in other occupation movies, Jean learns that there is no accommodating the Nazis: one must kill them and be prepared to die. The French will be defeated only when they stop resisting.

Tonight We Raid Calais, a March 29, 1943, Twentieth Century–Fox release, is another film that examines the dangers of even passive collaboration and the necessity of resistance. The film tells the story of British commando Geoffrey Carter (John Sutton), who is ordered into a French farming community to discover which of several factories is manufacturing antitank guns and to communicate its location to the RAF. When he presents himself to the Bonnard family, the father and mother (Lee J. Cobb and Beulah Bondi) are willing to help, but their daughter Odette (Annabella) refuses: she resents the British because her brother Pierre was killed when the British navy sank the French fleet at Oran. (This mention of armed conflict between the Allies is unusual in a Hollywood film.) She sees this betrayal by the British as typical of their relations with France. She tells Carter, "And why shouldn't I turn an Englishman in, I would like to know? You made us fight for you, then left us alone to be overrun. Well, the Germans are here, on every street corner, in our stores, in our schools, in our houses, and still the English aren't satisfied. They send you and your kind over to make it worse for us, to put our lives in danger." When Carter accuses her of being a traitor to her country, she responds, "A traitor to *my* country, monsieur, or to England?" Indeed, Odette's dislike of Carter is easy to understand: in his single-minded commitment to his mission, he is overbearing. He at first threatens and bullies the Bonnards and later orders the local farmers to burn their wheat to create a flaming bull's-eye around the factory. When Monsieur Bonnard explains about his son's death at Oran, Carter's unsentimental response is, "In war, one is often forced to do things one doesn't like to do."

Odette dislikes the German occupation, but she thinks accommodation and collaboration are the best methods of preserving an acceptably comfortable life. She flirts with German sergeant Block (Howard Da Silva) because he lets the family keep a goat to supply milk for Pierre's orphaned baby. Later, after her mother and father are arrested, she agrees to betray Carter to save them. ("You seem to be very fond of your parents," says the German commander [Reginald Sheffield].) Her father tries to teach her what the Norwegians in *The Moon Is Down* learn: "Someday, perhaps very soon, you'll learn, Odette—and it will be a hard and bitter lesson—surrender only means a slower death with these men. The Nazis give you no quarter, and you can make no deals with them." Odette doesn't realize the truth of her father's words or why the Germans—not the British—are her real enemies until her parents are executed before her eyes, despite her betrayal of Carter. This is her hard and bitter lesson. She manages to get Carter and the women farmers who are helping him out of the German jail and aids them in setting the fire for the bombers. As she admires the planes overhead, Carter reminds her, "They're English." She responds, "I don't care who they are. They're on my side, and they're fighting." Her new position is made clear at the end of the film, when Carter offers to take her and her baby nephew back to England with him. Odette first asserts her sense of nationalism—"This is where I belong"—and then her sense of connection with her country's allies. She asks Carter to take the baby with him and then addresses the child: "Where I am sending you, darling, they won't even speak French, but they are your friends." She charges Carter, "Keep him safe, so he can grow strong in your free country. I don't want him to see what my hands are going to do. And when our job is done, bring him back." What had previously been for her a British fight is now *her* fight and *our* job.

The best occupation film—in our opinion, one of the best films of World War II—is *This Land Is Mine*. Released on March 17, 1943, by RKO, with a screenplay by Dudley Nichols and direction by Jean Renoir, *This Land Is Mine* is set, or so a superimposed title tells us just after the credits, "somewhere in Europe." This is a calculated ambiguity: on the one hand, the setting is clearly France (if we couldn't tell from the characters' names, we would guess from the climactic reading of "The Declaration of the Rights of Man"); on the other hand, since this could be any country, the film's focus is not on nationality but on the issues of occupation, collaboration, and resistance. Moreover, the opening shot shows a town square, and in the background hangs a banner with "Buy War Bonds for Victory" written on it; this imperative, familiar to American viewers from posters, ads, radio shows, and practically every Hollywood movie they saw, subtly suggests that this film could be set in an occupied United States. We have argued that, as a group, the occupation films are less interested in characterizing or valorizing a specific nationality (in contrast to the films about the British, Soviets, and Chinese) than in allowing American viewers the opportunity to vicariously experience how they would behave under occupation. The brilliance of *This Land Is Mine* is that this vicarious experience is complicated by a sophisticated rendering of the operations of power, the insidious possibilities of collaboration, and the price of resistance.

The film's opening sequence, without a word of dialogue, sets up the major thematic tensions. Underneath the titles, the camera focuses on a statue in a town square and then zooms in on it: it's of a World War I soldier falling, frozen in the act of dying for his country. On the pedestal are engraved the words: "1914–1918 In Memory of Those Who Died to Bring Peace to the World." The camera then tilts down to a discarded newspaper on the ground with the headline "Hitler Invades . . . ," the name of the country conveniently torn off. During this camera movement, in the background we see small groups of civilians passing by in some alarm. We then cut to a shot of the large, empty, silent square. A small child leaves a house in the foreground and walks into the street; as we hear the sound of motorized vehicles growing in the background, the child's mother rushes out, picks her up, and runs back into the house, just as the first German motorcycles drive by from the right and trucks with German troops enter from the left. (This is a by-now familiar trope: the Germans' intrusion into a peaceful setting is marked by their mechanization.) There follow several shots of more German motorcycles, trucks, and tanks, plus columns of marching soldiers entering the square; most of these shots feature the World War I statue, the dying soldier gaping with horror at this display of overwhelming force. The point of view then reverses to show us what we couldn't see previously because it was behind us, on the other side of the square: a palatial building, in front of which the soldiers are forming. When the soldiers are in place, a staff car pulls up in front of the building; an officer gets out and, with his aides, enters the building. As he goes in, the soldiers stand at parade rest. After all these long shots, the camera finally gives us a medium close-up, and through a window, we watch the mayor and his staff greet the officer with a salute, which the officer returns. We are then brought inside the room with a close-up in which the German offers the mayor his hand, and the mayor, in surprise and relief, shakes it. This sequence raises questions that are developed throughout the film: In the face of such an overwhelming occupying force and with no native military presence at all, what kind of resistance is possible? Does resisting even make sense? What alternative is there to cooperating with the occupying force? Is collaboration necessarily bad? Is it even possible *not* to collaborate?

The film then apparently jumps forward to a time when the occupation is well established. The plot centers on a schoolteacher, Albert Lory (Charles Laughton), a self-confessed coward. Sickly as a child, Albert continues to be coddled by his mother (Una O'Connor), who has never really

This Land Is Mine: Diffident teacher Albert Lory (Charles Laughton) is coddled by his mother (Una O'Connor).

let him grow up. He has a crush on fellow teacher and next-door neighbor Louise Martin (Maureen O'Hara), but, like an adolescent, he can't work up the nerve to tell her how he feels. When the British bomb the town, he cowers, then nearly breaks down. He can command no respect from his male students. He quails in the face of any authority, from the German soldiers to his mother. But when a handbill appears under the door one morning, headlined "Liberty" and urging, "We must resist," Albert can't bring himself to prudently burn it. Something about its message speaks to him.

Within the tension between fear and resistance lies the potential for collaboration, and the film offers us characters positioned all along the spectrum. As in many occupation films, there is a bourgeois businessman who has thrown in with the Nazis, though in this case his portrayal is more complex. George Lambert (George Sanders) is the manager of the railroad yards. His cooperation with the occupation, coordinating traffic in, out, and through the rail yard and managing the transport of supplies, is based not so much on greed or personal advancement as it is on ideological sympathy with national socialism. He makes his position and his internal conflicts clear in an extended conversation with the commander of the occupation, one-armed Major von Keller (Walter Slezak). After an act of sabotage at the yard, von Keller suggests that Lambert has access to his workers' feelings:

> LAMBERT: Do you think they'd tell me anything? I'm just the man who gives orders around here. They regard anybody who gives orders as an enemy.
>
> VON KELLER: I can remember when we had the same problem in Germany, in the Republic, under capitalism. I fought in the streets for our Führer, Lambert. I killed workers with my own hands. Both hands then. For my class, it was either kill or be killed, but we won, and now we are brothers. Absolute obedience.
>
> LAMBERT: I too fought the unions, Major von Keller, right here in this yard. I was very nearly killed. But you had a leader and were many. We had no leader and were few. That's why you're here.
>
> VON KELLER: But not as your enemy, Lambert.
>
> LAMBERT: If I thought you were, I wouldn't be doing what I am.
>
> VON KELLER: I know that. We're here to help men like you rebuild your own country. Remember what my country was before our Führer? A country without food, without arms, without honor. But the people were not dead. They were only waiting to be told the truth. . . .
>
> LAMBERT: Your ideas are exactly my ideas. I saw how our country was destroyed. False democratic ideas. Women refusing to have children. Strikes in all our factories for a forty-hour week, when your people were working seventy and eighty hours a week. I want the new order for my country. I work for it. But I know that we can't have it until this war is over. I must tell you the truth: I don't like the occupation.
>
> VON KELLER: Neither do I! I'm glad we understand each other. We are both working for this war to be over. Only then can we have a peaceful and united Europe, and only then can your country and men like you regain their dignity and honor. Let us both work for that day. [*Offers his hand, which Lambert accepts and shakes.*]

Lambert admires what he sees as the strongman rule, the discipline, and the clear class distinctions of fascism, but he's also uncomfortable with the lack of independence that comes with the German occupation, and he seems uncomfortable with his own role in that occupation.

Later, Louise, his fiancée, tells him that hostages have been taken in response to an attack on von Keller and the mayor. Not knowing that Louise's brother Paul (Kent Smith) is the attacker, Lambert calls the assailant a criminal and explains his reasoning to Louise: "We all hate this occupation. I stood up to Major von Keller and told him to his face that I didn't like it, but we must face facts. They have the power. If one of us wants to resist and get killed, that's foolish but courageous. He takes the risk and the punishment himself. But the man who secretly resists, with acts of sabotage, is a coward. He escapes and innocent people die." When Louise protests that this would mean the end of the resistance, he responds, "Then we'd have peace. Wouldn't we be better off?"

Lambert's position starts to break down when Albert's mother tells him that Paul is the saboteur and would-be assassin (Albert is one of the hostages, and she is trying to free him). Lambert tells the mayor, who tells von Keller, who gives the order to arrest Paul. However, Lambert's conscience gets the better of him, and he intercepts Paul on the way to his rail-yard shift to warn him. Recognizing the internal battle Lambert is fighting, Paul tells him, "You're looking at yourself, George, and that's what you can't stand." Paul is killed while trying to escape from the rail yard. The next day, von Keller proposes that Lambert find out from Louise who Paul's accomplices were and report that information. Affronted, Lambert asks, "Do you think I'd do *that*?" to which von Keller replies, "I'm sure you will." Feeling guilty about Paul's death, having seen the betrayal and death at the heart of the new order, and finally understanding his role in the occupation, Lambert rejects his collaborative part the only way he can: he kills himself.

The film further complicates the idea of collaboration through other characters. One type of collaborator familiar from other occupation films is the town's mayor (Thurston Hall), shown accepting Major von Keller's hand in the opening sequence. Although this is a simpler characterization than Lambert's, it nevertheless offers an interesting twist. Mayor Manville has apparently decided that the best way to serve the townspeople is with the don't-rock-the-boat philosophy we've seen in other films. It's hinted, late in the film, that in so serving the townspeople, he is also serving himself: he is accused of surreptitiously buying up real estate. Still, in the scene where Lambert comes to turn in Paul, the mayor is given a chance to defend himself in the following dialogue:

MAYOR: They call me a collaborationist. Very well, I am, and you know why.

LAMBERT: It's easy for people in free countries to call us names. But you wait and see how *they* behave when the Germans march in: they'll shake hands, make the best of it.

MAYOR: If they don't, they'll get the worst of it. Between you and me, I do my duty, Lambert. I'm mayor of the town, and my duty is to defend it.

This is an interesting challenge to the American moviegoers watching this film, who are no doubt judging Lambert as weak and the mayor as a bad guy. How *would* they behave if the Germans marched in? How easy is it to just go along, and how hard is it to resist? The film makes it clear that, with a few exceptions, such as Paul, the townspeople are all collaborating in one way or another. Albert makes this point late in the film when he points out that the butcher, who sells black-market meat out the back door at astounding profits, and the hotelier, who boards many German soldiers and sells them champagne at inflated prices, are profiting from the occupation. He says, "I don't blame you for making money, but you should blame yourselves for making the occupation possible." At one point, Major von Keller explains the significance of these collaborators to Albert, and the viewer, in a telling speech:

Lambert was just a tool, very honest, but not very bright. The mayor? . . . He's working for his own interest. But we need them, and we find them in every country we invade. Why, even in Germany we use them. That's the way our party got into power. They're everywhere. And that's why nothing can stop us from winning the world. America feels secure because of her oceans. They think of invasion in terms of armies and airplanes. But they are already invaded. The honest Lamberts and the dishonest Manvilles are waiting to welcome us, just as they did here in Europe. And if any time we need peace, if peace should be a further weapon of conquest, their sincere patriotism will find plenty of arguments for the peace.

The film refuses to let the American moviegoer sit in easy judgment of Lambert and the mayor; von Keller and the film keep insisting that they are not very different from the rest of us. It also spells out here that collaboration, no matter how subtle, how innocuous, is not just aiding the German conquest; it is a weapon of war that the Germans are counting on.

Albert spends the film learning this lesson. As we have seen, early on, he fears the power of the Germans and timidly adopts the don't-rock-the-boat philosophy. At the breakfast table, he rejects the morning paper as being full of lies but then regrets having spoken, even though only his mother is there to hear. His mother complains about the special treatment and food that some people, especially the mayor, receive and about the black-market prices demanded by the merchants, yet she has managed to get a phony prescription for additional milk, and Albert happily but thoughtlessly drinks it. (To be fair, he shares some with the neighbors' cat.) Nevertheless, after all her complaints, the mother concludes, "Ah well. At least we have order. Things are quiet in the town now, thank the Lord, so I suppose we shouldn't complain." Albert apparently agrees. Neither he nor his mother is aware of their own complicity in the black market, and neither is yet aware of how much they have to give up in exchange for order and quiet. The price of this trade is suggested later, when Professor Sorel (Philip Merivale), the schoolmaster, informs Albert and Louise that the occupying authorities are demanding the removal of pages from textbooks. Sorel is resigned and Louise is furious, but Albert accepts the order: "After all, it's only a few pages."

Albert's development is interwoven with the connection between the future of the country and the education of its children. The real point of the occupation, as Major Bruhl points out in *The Cross of Lorraine*, is the shaping of the children. After Albert disgraces himself with his cowardly behavior in front of the students during an air raid, he meets with Sorel, who tries to buck him up and lay out the argument for the necessity of resistance, which is so central to the film. He tells the incredulous Albert, "now, I believe, *we* are the most important people in our country." Pointing out the books that the Germans have ordered destroyed, he goes on to explain why:

These books must be burnt. Very well, then, we must burn them. We can't resist—physically. But morally, within us, we *can* resist. We contain those books. We contain truth. And they can't destroy the truth without destroying each and every one of us. We can keep the truth alive if the children believe in us and follow our example. Children like to follow a leader, and there are two kinds of leaders today. *We* seem weak. We have no weapons. We don't march, except to air-raid shelters. And our heroes are called criminals and shot against the walls. The other leaders have guns, tanks, parades, uniforms. They teach violence, self-love, vanity, everything that appeals to the unformed minds of children. And their criminals are called heroes.

Well, that's a lot of competition for us, Lory. Love of liberty isn't glamorous for children. Respect for the human being isn't exciting. But there's one weapon they can't take away from us: and that's our dignity. It's going to be a fight, Lory, it *is* a fight. But if the children admire us, they'll follow us.

We will win, Lory. Or maybe we'll get shot. But every one of us they execute wins a battle for our cause, because he dies a hero, and heroism *is* glamorous for children.

After Sorel is arrested for authoring the "Liberty" handbills, Louise goes to Major von Keller to plead for his release. In refusing her, von Keller reinforces Sorel's analysis of the importance of children's education, but from the occupying power's side. He says to her, "Your own hostility to me reflects his [Sorel's] teaching, and you pass it on to your children. These ideas are contagion, and the place to stamp them out is in the schools. You can make a child believe whatever you want, and the children of today are the soldiers and mothers of tomorrow. Ten years ago, our German children were like yours, but we National Socialists threw out the Sorels and took over the schools, and look at them now: heroes who have conquered the world!" As if to illustrate these arguments about the classroom as a battlefield for children's minds and thus for the future of the country, just before Sorel is arrested, Albert enters his classroom to find his male students mobbing the class's one Jewish boy (John Donat) and using ink to paint the letter J on his face. At this point, it's clear which side is winning the battle.

After stumbling upon Lambert's body, Albert is arrested for his murder and thus learns his final lessons about the future and about collaboration. The civil courts are one area where the Germans have avoided asserting their power, at least overtly, so when Albert is given a chance to speak in his own defense, he creates a stir by talking about Lambert and the mayor as divided men, profiting from the occupation because they are weak. The fearful prosecutor (George Coulouris), trying to shut Albert up, asks for and receives an adjournment. That evening, von Keller visits Albert in his cell and strikes a deal: Albert will be acquitted (a suicide note will be "found") and thus will not have to finish his speech. The major tells him,

"Lory, I'm glad you decided to live and be a free man. You're a schoolmaster, and you have a great duty: the regeneration of the youth. You must make them ready for the world of tomorrow, and, believe me, it will be a fine world." Albert is initially relieved that his ordeal is over, but the next morning, he watches from his cell window as several hostages, including Professor Sorel, are shot by a firing squad. Sorel hears him call, puts on his glasses, then smiles and waves happily at him as the order to fire is given. This moment is an epiphany for Albert. Everything Sorel had told him earlier becomes truth, and the small, smothered part of him to which the "Liberty" handbill spoke blossoms to overcome his cowardice and give him a clear direction.

That day in court, rejecting the prosecutor's attempt to save him, Albert insists on continuing his defense and, in a beautiful speech, explains his epiphany:

> Last night I had a moment of weakness. Oh, I wanted to live. I had very good reasons to live. Major von Keller told me beautiful things about the future of this world they're building. I almost believed him. But it's very hard for people like you and me to understand what is evil and what is good. It's easy for the working people to understand who the enemy is, because the aim of this invasion and this occupation is to make them slaves. But middle-class people like us can easily believe, as George Lambert did, that a German victory is not such a bad thing. Well, we hear people say that too much liberty brings chaos and disorder. And that's why I was tempted last night by Major von Keller when he came to my cell.
>
> But this morning, I looked out through bars, and I saw this beautiful new world working. I saw ten men die because they still believed in freedom. Among them was a man I loved, Professor Sorel. He smiled and waved at me as if he were telling me what to do. I knew then I had to die. And the strange thing is, I was happy.

He goes on to connect Paul's sabotage to the kind of heroism Sorel advocated as necessary to shape the future of the country:

> Paul was a soldier, without glory, but in a wonderful cause. I see now that sabotage is the only weapon left to a defeated people. And so long as we have saboteurs, the other free nations who are still fighting on the battlefront will know that we are *not* defeated. Oh, I know that for every German

killed, many of our innocent citizens are executed, but the example of
their heroism is contagious, and our resistance grows.

Oh, it's very easy to talk about heroism in the free countries, but it's
hard to talk about it here where our people are starving. The hard truth
is: the hungrier we get, the more we need our heroes. We must stop
saying sabotage is wrong, that it doesn't pay—it does pay. It makes us
suffer, starve, and die. But though it increases our misery, it will shorten
our slavery. That's a hard choice, I know, but even now they are bringing
more troops into the town because of the trouble that has started. And
the more German soldiers there are here, the less they have on the fighting fronts. Even an occupied town like this can be a fighting front too.

And the fighting is harder. We not only have to fight hunger and the
tyrant—first we have to fight ourselves. The occupation, any occupation
in any land, is only possible because we are corrupt.

Collaboration of any kind, even the innocuous, don't-rock-the-boat kind,
aids the German conquest and robs the country of its future.

In making his speech, Albert becomes the kind of hero he is calling
for. He is acquitted by the civil court, but knowing that he will be arrested
by the Germans, he returns to his classroom, where his formerly unruly
and disrespectful students stand when he enters. In the few moments he
has before the German soldiers come for him, he reads to his students
from "The Declaration of the Rights of Man." He tells them of the men
from all classes and all walks of life who came together to compose the
document, and then he goes on: "Now other men are trying to destroy this
book. Maybe this copy will be burned, but they can't burn it out of your
memories. You'll have to rewrite it someday. That's why you young people
are so important: you're the new nation." Before he can finish reading, the
soldiers arrive. He says to his students, "Good-bye, Citizens," and leaves
Louise to continue the lesson as the film fades out. If the students are
representative of the future of the country, the lessons Albert has learned,
his transformation, and his heroism have swung them away from the influence of the Nazis. The new world they will be working for will be based
on the ideals of freedom.

This Land Is Mine is the best example of what most occupation films,
in one way or another, were trying to do: let Americans walk in the shoes
of people in occupied countries. In this way, U.S. viewers could vicariously suffer with the occupied people and experience the brutality of the
Nazis. More important, however, they could see the types of behavior ex-

hibited by occupied people and ask themselves how they would behave if the United States were conquered and occupied. They also learned that the home front could be a fighting front and that ordinary people could be as important in defeating fascism as soldiers—important lessons for their own lives. Whereas occupation films made these points through indirection, other films more overtly addressed the issues of how American men and women could best participate in the war effort. We look at these films in the next chapter.

6

AMERICAN MEN AND WOMEN

Hero, baloney! Nobody's a hero in this country. All of us guys are the same. We've got homes, wives, and kids. . . . So we don't like anybody who pushes us around.
—Joe Smith (Robert Young) in *Joe Smith, American*

After Pearl Harbor, I says to myself, now, what can a doddering old fool like me do—nothing, I says. And then I thought: I've got a house, and I can cook, and if the girls of this town can do a man's job, I can do a woman's.
—"Mother" Henry (John Philliber) in *Ladies of Washington*

WE HAVE SEEN HOW HOLLYWOOD FILMMAKERS defined the Germans, Italians, and Japanese as our enemies and the British, Soviets, other Europeans, and Chinese as our allies. This still leaves us with the issue of how Americans were defined to American moviegoers. How were Americans supposed to see themselves, and how were they to behave? In this time of war, how were they to perform the role of American? The answer, in terms of U.S. popular culture during the war years, seems to have depended on one's gender: both men and women were told that they had vital roles to perform, but they were very different roles—very different

216

from each other and from prewar constructions of masculinity and femininity. Just as Hollywood had a storeroom full of stock German, Italian, Asian, and Russian types that filmmakers could draw on to construct viewers' understanding of our enemies and allies, it also had stock representations of the masculine and the feminine. Unlike the stereotypic ethnic representations, however, the existing film stereotypes of American men and women tended not to serve the needs of the war effort. But, as film critic Mick LaSalle writes, "Different fears bring about different fantasies and those fantasies create different heroes."[1] During the war years, filmmakers transformed male and female role models to the point that the qualities valued in each were practically reversed from prewar films.

In one sense, a man's role during the war—that is, the role promoted by popular culture—might seem obvious: to be willing to fight and, if necessary, die for his country. Indeed, we've already cited a number of films—*Air Force* and *China* among them—that focus on an American male character's education: He moves from a state of selfishness and indifference to an awareness of why the war is being fought, why the enemy must be defeated, and how he can contribute to that defeat. He learns that the primary virtue of a man in wartime is sacrifice—sacrifice of time, of youth, of health, of life, of individuality. But this education, which essentially results in the submersion of the male character's individuality into a homogeneous cause, runs counter to an idea of American masculinity that is at least as old as our country. From Benjamin Franklin's autobiography to Frederick Jackson Turner's frontier thesis to R.W. B. Lewis's conception of the American Adam, American men have been represented in ways that stress their autonomy, their independence, and their ability to encounter, come into conflict with, and overcome and remake their environment— natural or social. Central to the mythos of the American male is the charismatic frontiersman who moves into a new territory, faces the challenges of nature and the original inhabitants and tames them, creates a safe and ordered environment into which others can move, but then bristles at the rationalized and rule-bound society they engender. He remains always an outsider to his environment. This mythos of autonomy, independence, and individuality is manifested in one way or another in American culture from James Fenimore Cooper's Leatherstocking to Horatio Alger's rags-to-riches heroes to F. Scott Fitzgerald's Gatsby. In time, this mythos was also manifested in Hollywood films' presentation of the male hero. As LaSalle argues about pre–Production Code films of the early 1930s, "More than anything else, movies of this time emphasized the primacy of the individual and the importance of individual concerns, treating the government as a malign, or at best neutral, force. Shady characters, sly operators, and fast-talking con men were often heroes, if for no reason but that they were individualists making their way in the world. Meanwhile, anyone representing organized power, such as business or government, was part of the problem. That's why private detectives were almost always good guys, while policemen were usually nuisances."[2] The heroes of detective films, adventure films, Westerns, and gangster films typically function as individuals coming into conflict with and perhaps overcoming, perhaps succumbing to, some societally generated system.

The presentation of women in American popular culture has been very different. Women tended to be valued for their looks, for their ability to reproduce, and for their talent for caregiving. They tended to be dependent on men, waiting for them and waiting on them. They tended to be the recipient of sexual attention but rarely initiated it. American popular culture has offered exceptions to these stereotypes, of course, independent, strong, aggressive women—Nathaniel Hawthorne's Hester Prynne, for example—but with dismaying frequency they tended to learn their lessons, to be tamed, or to be punished for transgressing their expected roles. Film critic Jeanine Basinger notes that this traditional presentation of women was adopted by Hollywood: "If it is true, as many suggest, that Hollywood films repressed women and sought to teach them what they ought to do, then it is equally clear that, in order to achieve this, the movies had to bring to life the opposite of their own morality. To convince women that marriage and motherhood were the right path, movies had to show women making the mistake of something else." Thus films often showed women involved in all sorts of activities from flying planes to running companies, but in the last five minutes, they invariably gave it up for love. What is most obvious about a woman's role, especially in films that were identified as "women's pictures," is that everything is "translated into the terms of a woman's daily life. World War I is not about the Allies versus the Kaiser. It's about how unmarried women become pregnant when they have sex. The Depression is not about an economic collapse. It's about runs in stockings, no money for carfare, and being forced out on the streets. Natural disasters like earthquakes and cholera epidemics are defined by miscarriages and dying children. Everything is couched in terms of what are presumed to be the major events of a woman's life: love, men, marriage, motherhood, and all the usual 'feminine' things."[3]

We can see both the male and female constructions of gender being reinforced in a film released just months before America entered the war, Warner Bros.' *The Maltese Falcon* (1941). Written and directed by John Huston, this was Hollywood's third adaptation of Dashiell Hammett's novel and the most faithful. Faced with a number of problems—among them, the murder of his partner, being implicated in that murder and another, and the mysterious nature and whereabouts of the black bird—the film's hero, Sam Spade (Humphrey Bogart), acts on his own, outside the legal structures of society. At one point, he forcefully explains this to the district attorney: "Now both you and the police have as much as accused me of being mixed up in the other night's murders. Well, I've had trouble with both of you before. And as far as I can see, my best chance of clearing myself of the trouble you're trying to make for me is by bringing in the murderers all tied up. Now the only chance I've got of catching them and tying them up and bringing them in is by staying as far away as possible from you and the police because you'd only gum up the works." Throughout the film, Spade leaps back and forth across the boundaries of socially accepted legal, ethical, and moral behavior. He instructs his lawyer to bribe the coroner regarding his partner's inquest. He risks arrest rather than reveal his client's name and the nature of the case, but he blithely takes on multiple clients involved in the same case in a clear conflict of interest. He has been having an affair with his partner's wife, whom he dumps as soon as she's a widow. Despite this seeming nihilism, at the end of the film we discover that Spade has his own private code. As he prepares to turn in the woman he may love for his partner's murder, he tells her, "You'll never understand me, but I'll try once and then give it up. When a man's partner's killed, he's supposed to do something about it. It doesn't make any difference what you thought of him. He was your partner, and you're supposed to do something about it." Spade resolves his conflicts, but he does so independently, operating by his own rules, trying to please no one but himself.

While Sam Spade serves as an example of the male as hero, the woman he may or may not love, Brigid O'Shaughnessy (Mary Astor), is an example of all a woman is not supposed to be. Rather than having the name of her father or a husband, she goes by a number of names—Miss Wonderly, Miss Leblanc, Brigid O'Shaughnessy—suggesting that she isn't owned by any man. When angered, she hits and kicks, but she's more likely to put on an act of helplessness to trick men, including Spade, into helping her. That it is a performance is stressed over and over again by Spade's responses to her pleas: "You're good. You're *very* good." In fact, far from being dependent on men, she uses them and then disposes of them, setting one man up to be killed and murdering Miles Archer, Spade's partner, herself. Moreover, she is sexually aggressive. The film implies that she frequently has sex with men, including Spade, to get what she wants. When Spade sees through her routine—what he calls her schoolgirl manner—she immediately becomes sexually available. When she says, "I haven't lived a good life. I've been bad. Worse than you can know. . . . I won't be innocent," it's less a confession than an advertisement. Of course, Brigid is punished for her independence and aggression (and her murderous ways). Spade turns her over to the police, and the film emphasizes her punishment by showing the elevator cage closing, cell-like, in front of her.

Another example of an independent woman who is punished is found in MGM's *Woman of the Year* (1942). Tess Harding (Katharine Hepburn) is a celebrated and influential newspaper columnist. She speaks dozens of languages, is an expert on the international situation, especially the situation in Europe, and even engages in informal diplomacy. Her marriage to Sam Craig (Spencer Tracy), a sportswriter, founders because he can't stand playing second fiddle to his accomplished wife. The film ends with an extended comic sequence in which Tess tries to win Sam back by cooking his favorite breakfast. She is ridiculed and humiliated because she doesn't know how to cook. But this failure restores the equilibrium of the male-female relationship and presumably saves the marriage.

Generalizations are dangerous, but in general, it seems that Hollywood films valorized independent, powerful men but excoriated independent, powerful women in favor of man-dependent, passive women.

We can begin to see how male characters were transformed in Hollywood's World War II films by studying a series of films, most from early in the war, that draw on the tradition of gangster films. Gangster films had been popular at least since the early 1930s, and one reason for the popularity of the gangster hero—a popularity that many social commentators found troubling—was that he fit so precisely into the myth of the American male. As LaSalle writes, "the gangster was . . . the era's mythic, iconic role. Through the gangster, Hollywood found itself able to say everything it really wanted to say about men, the law, and society in general." Paul Muni's eponymous character in *Scarface* (1932), Edward G. Robinson's Rico in *Little Caesar* (1931), and James Cagney's Tom Powers in *The Public Enemy* (1931) are the best examples of a pattern that is repeated in dozens of 1930s Hollywood films. A young man of obscure and humble origins, facing a hostile social environment, turns to crime as an opportunity to advance himself; he achieves power and money and, even though he is punished for his crimes, goes out in a blaze of glory. This is the fundamental narrative of American individuality. As LaSalle says of Rico, "He was Andrew Carnegie or the young Ben Franklin, but twisted."[4]

It isn't surprising that when the United States entered World War II, Hollywood quickly made use of the gangster film, one of its most popular genres, to tell stories about the war. The earliest of these, *All through the Night*, was released by Warner Bros. on January 28, 1942, less than two months after Pearl Harbor. It was obviously in production before the attack, intended to argue the danger that Nazi Germany presented to the United States, and it was quickly modified to reflect U.S. involvement. An effective combination of comedy and drama, the film focuses on gangster Gloves Donahue (Humphrey Bogart), who is ruthless enough to control most of the rackets in midtown Manhattan but loyal to his friends and devoted to his mother (Jane Darwell). When his mother's friend (and the baker of his favorite cheesecake), Mr. Miller (Ludwig Stossel), is murdered in his shop, Gloves drops everything to investigate. While following Leda Hamilton (Kaaren Verne), a beautiful woman who comes to the shop asking for Miller, Gloves stumbles on to another murder (for which he is blamed), as well as a nest of Nazi spies led by Hall Ebbing (Conrad Veidt) and the sadistic murderer Pepi (Peter Lorre). Unable to convince the police of the danger, Gloves gathers his gang and a rival gang, breaks up a meeting of fifth columnists, rescues Leda, and prevents Ebbing from accomplishing his mission of blowing up a new U.S. battleship in New York Harbor.

The film's plot incidents are held together by Gloves's transformation from a traditional gangster, firmly placed in the mythos of the American male, into the kind of American needed to win the war. He begins the film unconcerned about the world around him; a self-made success, he thinks he owes society nothing and wants only to be left alone by the police, district attorneys, and politicians. In the film's first scene, Gloves dismisses his henchmen's arguments about the war, but his lieutenant, Sunshine (William Demarest), objects, saying, "This is serious business, Gloves. Don't you think it's time you got your mind out of the sports section and onto the front page?" Gloves replies, "I can't be bothered. That's Washington's racket. Let them handle it." But his encounters with the fifth columnists force Gloves to reconsider his indifference. In a showdown with Ebbing about midway through the film, Gloves is forced to defend

All through the Night: Gloves Donahue (Humphrey Bogart) is more interested in the sports pages than the battlefields of Europe. His henchmen include Jackie Gleason, Phil Silvers, and William Demarest.

his relationship to society. Ebbing says, "It's a great pity, Mr. Donahue, that you and I should oppose each other. We have so much in common. . . . You are a man of action. You take what you want, and so do we. You have no respect for democracy; neither do we. It's clear we should be allies." Gloves responds, "It's clear you are screwy. I've been a registered Democrat ever since I could vote. I may not be model citizen number one, but I pay my taxes, wait for traffic lights, and buy twenty-four tickets regular to the Policemen's Ball. Brother, don't get me mixed up with no league that rubs out innocent little bakers." Gloves also is forced to overcome his conviction that Nazism can't happen here. He tries to dismiss Nazi threats by making the distinction between Nazi Germany and democratic America, saying, "This is Broadway, not Berlin." And he states, "This is a free country. Nobody has to do anything they don't want to do." But then he finds out that Leda has been compelled to work for Ebbing because her father is being held hostage in Dachau.

Gloves's transformation is signaled in a speech he gives to his gang and a rival gang. He says,

> I got a firsthand report tonight on what it's like on the other side from that Hamilton babe, and brother I'm telling you we got to watch our steps. Those babies are strictly no good from way down deep. They're no bunch of petty racketeers trying to muscle in on some small territory. They want to move in wholesale, take over the whole country. . . . They'll tell you what time you get up in the morning and what time you go to bed at night. They'll tell you what you eat, what kind of clothes you can wear, what you drink. They'll even tell you the morning paper you can read. . . . Why don't you read the papers? It's on the front page every day.

As a result of this speech, both gangs, two Oklahoma businessmen who were about to be clipped in a card game, and Gloves's black valet all join to fight the Nazi threat. Later, in a final showdown with Ebbing, Gloves asks, "You don't think you can sink one of them big boats all by yourself, do you?" Ebbing replies, "Why not? One man, if he's inspired, can change the world." Ebbing is proved wrong, of course, defeated by ordinary Americans (well, ordinary gangsters) joining together. In the film's final scene, when Leda tries to paint Gloves as a hero, telling the press that he's her white knight, he rejects the label, warning the reporters, "Anybody who prints that can expect the usual trouble."

The film presents an interesting double reversal. First, Gloves moves from the position of a typical movie hero, independent and in conflict with his environment, to a position that recognizes interdependence and the social environment's interconnection with the individual. Second, Ebbing, the Nazi, takes on the qualities that are traditionally associated with film heroes and the myth of the American male: autonomy of the individual, conflict with the social environment, and confidence that a strong individual can overcome that environment. The result is a movie not only at odds with its filmic tradition but also internally confused. We can see that the Runyonesque tone of the film and the comic casting (Jackie Gleason and Phil Silvers are among the supporting actors), at first apparently so inappropriate to the subject matter, are necessary to mask the anomaly of gangsters, who make their living breaking the law, as champions of democracy. Nevertheless, the contradiction occasionally breaks through, such as when Gloves, earlier an advocate of the free press, threatens the reporters with "trouble"; the film wants us to find censorship both outrageous and humorous.

A similar thematic development can be found in another gangster film, *Lucky Jordan*, a November 16, 1942, Paramount release. Here, the title character (Alan Ladd) is a New York racketeer trying desperately to avoid the draft. He has so little regard for the war that he uses a "Salvage for Sailors" building as a front for one of his gambling operations. When his lawyer suggests that he owes it to his country to serve in wartime, he snaps, "I don't owe anything to anybody. Everything I got in this country I got the hard way, and there was plenty of guys trying to keep me from getting it." The war's biggest impact on him, he thinks, is that the Santa Anita racetrack has been closed. Sent to boot camp, Lucky is soon fed up and deserts, stumbling by chance into an attempted robbery of some plans for tank armor engineered by his former lieutenant, Slip Moran (Sheldon Leonard), on behalf of a Nazi spy ring. Lucky ends up with the plans and decides to take advantage of his good fortune and sell them himself. Jill Evans (Helen Walker), a canteen worker whose car Lucky hijacks during his desertion, tries to make him see how he's involved in the war: "You think this war hasn't anything to do with you, but it has. The whole world's involved and everybody in it. If we lose, we'll end up slaves, Nazi slaves. That means you too." Lucky admits that he'd prefer the United States to win the war, but not enough to fight himself. He says, "It's like a fight at the Garden. You might want the guy in the purple pants to win. You might even bet a few bucks on him. But you don't want him to win bad enough that you climb up into that ring and get your face bashed in helping him." Lucky stands on his autonomy from society and from every other person.

He begins to change when he develops a personal relationship. While trying to make a deal to sell the plans, he hides out with an elderly alcoholic woman, Annie (Mabel Paige), whom he had hired to pretend to be his dependent mother when he met with the draft board. As Annie fixes him meals and shares her fantasies that Lucky is really her son and is an officer in the army, a kind of mother-son relationship develops, at first jokingly, eventually sincerely. When Slip's men beat up Annie while looking for the plans, Lucky realizes for the first time what the stakes are. He says, "I'll take care of Slip for this. I'll take care of those foreign lugs too. . . . This stuff they want so bad's going where it will hurt them most: right back to the army." Lucky spends the rest of the film trying to recover the plans and rounding up Slip and the spy ring. As in *All through the Night*, the Nazi leader (John Wengraf) tries to compare American gangsters to

Nazis: "I've read about American gangsters. And it seemed to me that their viewpoint and ours were quite similar. I was told that when they wanted something, they took it. So do we. When somebody stood in their way, he was eliminated. We understand that technique thoroughly." Lucky responds, "Don't try to put me in your class, squarehead. I've knocked around a little, but alongside of you, I'm a Sunday school teacher." When Lucky tells the spies that he's going to give the plans back to the army and go back into the army himself, another of the leaders (Miles Mander) asks, "Why should you give up $100,000 for the sake of a country that considers you an enemy of society?" Lucky responds, "Maybe it's because I don't want to see that country run by a bunch of guys who go around beating up old women. Till I ran up against you, *Nazi* was just a word in the newspaper to me. Now it's another way to spell *cockroach*." Like Gloves Donahue, Lucky rejects independence and embraces society when he learns the true nature of the Nazi threat. And like Gloves, after he has captured the Nazis and recovered the plans, Lucky is not put into the role of hero. Jill suggests that after what he's done, the army will give him a medal. But the last we see of him, Lucky is a military prisoner, digging trenches to pay for his desertion. Again, the traditional notion of a hero is subjugated to an idea of the community.

This same narrative pattern is followed, but with an even more explicit connection to the mythos of American masculinity, in *Mr. Lucky*, a 1943 RKO release. In this film, set before the U.S. entry into the war, Joe Adams (Cary Grant), the owner of a crooked gambling ship, takes on the name of a dead Greek crewman to avoid the draft and schemes to hold a gambling benefit for a war-relief organization, after which he intends to cheat the organization of the profits. In the process, he romances one of its blue-blooded leaders, Dorothy Bryant (Laraine Day).

Like Gloves Donahue and Lucky Jordan, Joe begins with no sense of responsibility to society. In objecting to being drafted, he specifically connects himself to the autonomy and self-responsibility of the American rags-to-riches narrative: "This isn't my war. I had my war, crawling out of the gutter the hard way. I won that war. . . . I don't recognize any other war." Later, Dorothy drives Joe from New York to her Maryland estate, where they view the portraits of her ancestors (both sides of her family go back to the American Revolution). Her grandfather has been trying to have Joe arrested, and Dorothy threatens to marry Joe unless he calls off the police. For Joe, this brings into the foreground the differences between Dorothy's privileged background and his hardscrabble one. He says,

You think the worst thing that could happen to you is to marry me? To people like you, folks like me are animals. We're so bad. And you're so very good. What do you expect: credit for it? How could you be anything else with what you had to start out with? You ought to be horsewhipped if you didn't turn out right. And what are you so high and mighty about? What did you ever do? He's [indicating a portrait] the guy who made all your dough for you, and he was born in a log cabin. You know where I grew up? In a one-room shack with a dirt floor. You talk about this side of your family and that side of your family. As far as I know, we only had one side and it was awful poor. Lots of times there wasn't what-for to eat. That's why I ran away when I was nine. I got tired of being hungry and seeing my old lady go hungry until she died.

Joe's autonomy is evidenced both in his lack of personal relationships and in his desire to play the hero. Like Lucky Jordan, Joe doesn't trust most of his subordinates, though he does like being the boss. At the war-relief organization, where he volunteers while he tries to sell Dorothy on his benefit idea, his relationships with the various women tend to be confused and contradictory; he calls one society matron both "Mother" and "Toots." He also enjoys being seen as the white knight, saving the women from greedy businessmen who stand in the way of their work. He fools one man with a trick coin to get the organization a load of blankets for free, and he knocks out a deliveryman so that the women can get some medical supplies unloaded. As the only man in the organization, he relishes being the hero for the women.

Joe's experiences in the organization, however, confuse his idea of masculinity and put him in a position to establish two life-changing personal connections. As a volunteer at the war-relief organization, Joe, who is unhappy being subordinate to anyone, must take orders from women. His first assignment is to learn to knit, a decidedly unmasculine activity. Adding to this gender reversal, he refers to Dorothy as a guy. Indeed, as his relationship with Dorothy changes from antagonism to love, she tends to play the male role—she's the aggressor and the one in charge. Joe must be convinced that she's sincere and not just using him; he's the one who seems compromised after their night together and feels the need to confirm that their feelings are real. The other personal connection Joe makes is with the mother of the Greek crewman whose identity he has stolen. He receives a letter from the man's mother and asks the priest (Vladimir Sokoloff) at a Greek church to translate it. He learns that the Germans invaded the mother's town and that all the men, including her other sons, were killed defending it. She writes, "Not one of our men lived, but a hundred Germans died, and Greek honor lived for an added hour." After reading the letter, the priest asks Joe to pray with him and says, "We beseech Thee to bring consolation to the heart of this mother and to all the mothers of this war-torn world. And to the hearts of their sons bring courage and the will to oppose evil, as this woman hath brought it to her son Joseph, who in Thine eyes is the brother of all men."

Because of these new personal connections—to Dorothy and to the Greek mother—and because of this new sense of connection to a larger world struggle, Joe decides to throw over his plan to bilk the war-relief organization, fighting his own mutinous gang to do so. He uses his gambling ship to transport the organization's supplies to Europe and joins the merchant marine, serving under a captain who was once his employee. Like Gloves Donahue, Joe resists the hero's role in the film's ambiguous ending. Joe's story has been told in flashback from a frame in which Dorothy waits at the end of a pier at night for Joe to return, as is apparently her habit. The romance of the scene is undercut when Joe does return—not from the sea but from downtown New York, where he has been celebrating between voyages. Dorothy sees him and runs to him, but Joe's reaction seems far from happy—in fact, he seems to consider running away. Although Joe has earned the right to "get the girl," the film suggests that the world of larger relationships and responsibilities must take precedence, at least for the time being.

Some B films use the same basic narrative as *All through the Night*, *Lucky Jordan*, and *Mr. Lucky*: gangsters or criminals, who feel that they owe nothing to society, learn why it is important to fight the Nazis; in the process, they learn that they have a responsibility to society and to the world and that, to fulfill this responsibility, they need to join with others. In *Seven Miles from Alcatraz*, released by RKO in 1942, two convicts (James Craig and Frank Jenks) escape from Alcatraz, hold the inhabitants of an island lighthouse captive, and, when Nazi saboteurs arrive on the island, are willing to make deals with them. But when they learn that the Nazis can't be trusted and see how they treat the weak and the helpless, the convicts fight them and disrupt their plan. The convicts are returned to Alcatraz, but with a recommendation that they be given an early release so they can join the army. In *Hitler—Dead or Alive*, a 1943 Charles House release, three hoods, headed by Steve Matchick (Ward Bond), take an airplane manufacturer up on his offer of a million-dollar reward for killing

Hitler. Improbably, they parachute into Germany and discover that this isn't just another hit. Although they initially have no political commitment to their job—one gets the impression they would kill anybody for a million dollars—by the time they meet Hitler (Bobby Watson), they understand why he's such a threat. They decide to hold him hostage while an end to the war is negotiated, personal gain being replaced by a desire to save the world. When they are all captured, the Gestapo officers don't recognize Hitler because the hoods have shaved his mustache and cut his hair, and he's shot while trying to escape. Waiting for his own execution, Steve sees small children being lined up against a wall and shot, and he realizes that Hitler's death won't end the war. He says, "War among men is one thing, but when it comes to butchering kids, there ain't a guy in the world, I don't care who he is, who will stop fighting for one minute until this rotten breed of Nazis is wiped clear off the face of the earth." He has learned that the Nazis as a whole must be defeated and that the rest of the world needs to join together to do it.

Casablanca, released by Warner Bros. on November 27, 1942, works out the issue of masculinity in a wartime setting in a more sophisticated way than these other films do. Drawing on the gangster-movie hero, it asks what the role of a man should be in the present war and ends by redefining the notion of a hero.

Rick Blaine (Humphrey Bogart) certainly participates in the film tradition of the mythos of the American male as represented in gangster films. Like Gloves Donahue, his origins are obscure and probably humble. He runs an illegal gambling casino but is loyal to his employees. Unlike Gloves and the other gangsters, however, Rick isn't naive about the Nazis. He has fought against fascism in Spain and Ethiopia. But presumably because of the disappointment of those defeats and, more specifically, his rejection by Ilsa (Ingrid Bergman) at the end of their Paris love affair—an end marked significantly by the arrival of the Wehrmacht—Rick has tried to withdraw into himself. Rick's losses in politics and in love seem to overlap to create the psychologically wounded man we meet at the beginning of the film. He has declared his autonomy from the people and the world around him. He justifies himself by saying repeatedly, "I stick my neck out for nobody." In fact, he says it so often, one wonders if he's trying to convince himself. Clearly, his actions give the lie to his words: the aforementioned loyalty to his employees or, more blatantly, his generosity to the couple from Bulgaria. The wife, Annina (Joy Page), confides her problem to Rick: She and her husband (Helmut Dantine) have escaped the Nazi occupation of Bulgaria but now lack the money to purchase an exit visa. Her husband is gambling away the rest of their money, and she is considering a sex-for-visa deal with Captain Renault (Claude Rains). Rick is obviously angry when he hears her story—angry at the injustice, angry at a world where the powerful bully the weak, and angry at his inability to change that world. His rude dismissal of Annina (he says, "Go back to Bulgaria," and "Everybody in Casablanca has problems. Yours may work out") is an attempt to mask with indifference his anger, frustration, love of justice, and hate for bullies. The mask falls off completely, at least for a moment, when he lets the husband win the money he needs to buy the visas. The mythos of the American male—the self-reliance, the autonomy, the potential to change the world—is, in the presentation of Rick's character, disqualified as a way of defining how a man should act in a world threatened by Nazis.

How, then, should a man act? The film offers a number of potential roles for men, models that Rick and the male moviegoing audience could follow. One is Louis Renault, the Vichy prefect of police. Whereas Rick has withdrawn into himself, Renault has become a chameleon, willing to repress whatever beliefs he has in favor of a superficial compliance with the dominant political power. As he tells Major Strasser (Conrad Veidt), "I have no convictions." Renault is able to adapt to whatever political or social situation arises; he can be anything from a brutal enforcer of Vichy and Nazi policies for Major Strasser to a world-weary cynic for Rick, from a bon vivant for the ladies to a prude shocked—shocked!—by the gambling in Rick's saloon. But Renault becomes each of these things with self-conscious superficiality, knowing that he is momentarily playing a necessary or useful role, and knowing that others know so as well. (Major Strasser repeatedly questions his loyalty, correctly, as it turns out.) The problem here in terms of how a man should act is that when a man can slide among so many superficially adopted roles, the roles become separated from the notion of identity. Is there a real Louis Renault under his multitude of masks, or are there only the masks?

Resistance leader Victor Laszlo (Paul Henreid) is another inadequate role model for masculine behavior, though he is the opposite of Captain Renault. Where Renault is too protean, Laszlo is too static. As we saw in the introduction, Laszlo is presented as an ideal leader: he is steadfast, unswerving, willing to sacrifice his personal feelings, including his love for Ilsa, to the greater cause. Although he is stiff and formal, he is a charismatic figure who draws others to him, brings them together, focuses their resistance to the Nazis, and makes them better and stronger than they would be without him. But it is this charisma, the mystique of leadership, that makes him static; if he were less certain, more changeable, more human, viewers could better identify with him, but then he would be a less effective leader. As it is, he is someone to admire, but asking viewers to model themselves on him would be akin to modeling themselves on FDR or Churchill. The film presents him as an icon, not as someone that Rick, or any of us, could be like.

Surprisingly, it is Ilsa who is the key to Rick's transformation. When she comes to his room, she offers the model of behavior that, by the end of the film, Rick follows. She pleads, threatens, and finally makes love to Rick in order to get the exit visas. This is not a selfish act, for we know that she would stay behind if Laszlo could go on. And she doesn't do it for the simple love of her husband—the extent to which she loves him is ambiguous, to say the least. She acts out of devotion to the cause; she knows that getting Laszlo to America is necessary to defeat the Nazis. Ilsa's motivation here is famously uncertain: Does she still love Rick? Or is she only pretending to love Rick out of love for Laszlo? To a great extent, the question is irrelevant. What Ilsa does isn't motivated by what Ilsa needs or wants but by what the world needs. Her individuality is subsumed into a sense of responsibility to others and to the world, and her sense of herself is actively joined with others in a vitally important cause.

At the airport, when Rick tells her that "the problems of three little people don't amount to a hill of beans in this crazy world," he demonstrates that he has learned her lesson, and in the process, he redefines the film hero and expectations for the American male. He acknowledges his interconnection with and responsibility to society and the world, and he acknowledges the relative unimportance of the individual in times like these. In joining Renault and the Free French at Brazzaville in "a beautiful friendship," Rick acknowledges the necessity of being part of a group. Thus, in the course of the film, Rick moves from the dead end of the gangster hero as a manifestation of the mythos of the American male to a new kind of American male, the kind needed if the United States is to win the war.

The reversals in expectations in terms of gender roles for women were even more radical than those for men. When Hollywood films presented women very differently from prewar characters, they were to a great extent reflecting obvious changes in the ways American women were functioning in society during the war. Before U.S. entry into the war, films tended to value women for their appearance and their caregiving skills and tended to limit their domain to the home. But during the war, women were needed to work in many areas from which they had traditionally been excluded, and Hollywood films were expected to help their audiences understand how this could be so. Between 1942 and 1945, 350,000 women served in uniform in the WAVES (Women Accepted for Volunteer Emergency Service), the WACs (Women's Army Corps), and the Army and Navy Nurse Corps. The majority of them served either stateside or in zone-of-the-interior billets, but about 60,000 women were stationed overseas. In addition, women were called on to fill jobs in the defense industry and in many other industries—jobs that became available because of the combination of the wartime industrial buildup and the loss of male workers to the armed forces. As one historian sums up, "millions of women found employment in jobs ranging from welders and machine setters to taxi drivers, railroad conductors, and farm workers." The Office of War Information encouraged women to work and endorsed emphasizing this message not only in films but also in advertisements and radio broadcasts. Kate Smith, for example, in an announcement for the OWI, said, "Friends, it would be impossible for me or anyone else to overemphasize the importance of women in this war. Actually, millions of American women are working now in aircraft factories and war plants of all kinds. But even more of us women are needed. The fact is women are needed for all kinds of jobs in many parts of the country."[5]

This is not to say that Hollywood transformed its presentation of women overnight or completely. Most female characters in the films produced during the war years function in traditional ways: as mothers and fiancées agonizing over their men in the armed forces (*The Sullivans* [1944], *The Human Comedy* [1943]), as objects of desire pursued by sailors and soldiers (*Abroad with Two Yanks* [1944], *Bride by Mistake* [1944]), and the corners of love triangles (*Gung Ho!* [1943], *The Fighting Seabees* [1944], *Crash Dive* [1943]). Indeed, many films of the *Stage Door Canteen* (1943) and *Hollywood Canteen* (1944) type suggest that a young woman's most important contribution to the war effort was providing company and an implied sexual comfort to servicemen. We discuss this theme more fully in chapter 7.

Nevertheless, there are many films in which this traditional presentation of women is critiqued and alternative presentations are offered. *To Have and Have Not*, an October 18, 1944, Warner Bros. release adapted from Ernest Hemingway's novel, does both. The traditional woman is

Hellene de Bursac (Dolores Moran), a stylish and attractive Frenchwoman who has accompanied her husband, a Free French agent, on a mission to rescue a resistance leader from Devil's Island. The film makes it clear that she is beautiful and wants to take care of her husband—traditionally valued attributes—but that otherwise, she is basically useless. When she and her husband are transported to Martinique by Harry Morgan (Humphrey Bogart), and later when Morgan operates to remove a bullet from her husband, Hellene tries to give orders, but everyone ignores her. When Morgan tells her to help during the operation, she grows squeamish and eventually faints. The next morning, Morgan asks her why she came along on the mission, and she explains, "I loved him. I wanted to be with him. . . . There's another reason. They told me to come, our people did. They said no man was much good if he left someone behind in France for the Germans to find and hold. . . . I told them I'd only be in the way, that I could do no good, that I was afraid. But the worst of it is that it's been so hard for him to have me along, because I've made him that way too. Now he's afraid." Her experiences to this point have taught her that what she has to offer—love, care, beauty—are of no help to her husband in wartime; moreover, her dependence and passivity are a drag on her husband's efforts.

Hellene is contrasted to a different kind of woman represented by Marie Browning (Lauren Bacall), a.k.a. Slim. She is attractive, but she is also tough; she expects no man to take care of her, she lets no man control her, and she can be slapped without flinching. When Hellene faints during the operation, Slim coolly takes her place. She is sexually aggressive, both when she is attracted to a man, as she is to Morgan, and when she needs to get some money for a meal or a drink. Although there is a sexual tension between Slim and Morgan, their relationship is founded on a shared worldview and a mutual respect that transcends gender. His nickname for her—Slim—is gender neutral. She's as likely to light his cigarette as he is hers, and when she does ask for a light, he tosses her the matches; there are no formal courtesies between them. The morning after the operation, she follows Morgan to his room and uncharacteristically offers to take off his shoes, make him breakfast, and fix him a bath. He turns down all these offers ("Look, when I get ready to take my shoes off, I'll take them off myself"), until he realizes that she is parodying Hellene and her supposed attractions. Morgan rejects both the real Hellene and the parody Hellene in favor of a woman who can take care of herself and join him in his adventures.

This development of the old idea of woman to the new one is explored more complexly in two home-front movies: *Since You Went Away* and *Tender Comrade*. *Since You Went Away*, a self-consciously prestigious film written and produced by David O. Selznick, was released by United Artists on July 19, 1944. The film establishes its narrative and thematic thrusts before the first line of dialogue is spoken. The opening credits roll over a shot of a fire burning gloriously in a fireplace, indicating that this will be a story about those who keep the "home fires burning" while the men are off at war. Contrasting with this mood of warm coziness, the next shot is of the Hilton home in a driving rain with the following words superimposed: "This is a story of the Unconquerable Fortress: the American Home . . . 1943." The shot then dissolves briefly to a close-up of a star hanging in the window and then again to the inside of the home, a close-up of a well-used easy chair, now empty. The camera tilts down to show us a no-longer-young bulldog asleep at the foot of the chair, then pans past a discarded box marked "Military Raincoats—Rush" and moves toward a desk calendar showing Tuesday, January 12. It then pans to a crumpled Western Union telegram addressed to Capt. Timothy Hilton and reading, "Proceed January Twelve to Camp Claiborne Louisiana"; the background music briefly plays "You're in the Army Now." The camera continues across the desk past a fancy fountain pen and holder to a small fish mounted on a plaque inscribed, "Caught by Anne and Tim Hilton on Their Wedding Trip, August 25, 1925." Next we see two bronzed baby shoes on top of a neatly stacked pile of papers and finally a family photo of a wife and two daughters. The camera ends its tour of the room by returning to the star hanging in the window, and we see a car pulling up. The dog waddles to the window but, apparently not seeing the person he was expecting, goes back to his spot to sleep.

This sequence of shots, really the best moment in the film, establishes two ideas. The first comes from the contrast between the neat arrangement of the room, its very order implying the history of this family, and the two items suggesting disorder: the uniform box and the crumpled telegram. The war, we see, has upset the order and routine of this home and has in a real sense disrupted the story of this family. The second, connected idea is that this is a film about absence. This opening scene is all about what isn't there: Tim Hilton, the husband, gone off to war. Indeed, Tim never appears in the film. When the family tries to meet him between trains as he's on his way overseas, they are delayed and miss him. About halfway through, he is reported missing in action. And at the end, on Christmas Eve, when it turns out he's alive, the news comes via a cablegram read over the telephone, not even his own voice. This absence established at the beginning tells us that the rest of movie will explore the way the women he's left behind—a wife and two daughters—adjust to the challenges of his absence and how they negotiate new roles for themselves as women.

Up until his enlistment, Anne Hilton (Claudette Colbert) has occupied the privileged position of an upper-middle-class woman. The film shows her struggling to adjust to new, not very glamorous roles during her husband's absence. Interestingly, many of these new roles are motivated by financial concerns. For example, the allotment checks she receives from the army are only a fraction of Tim's salary as an advertising executive, so she has to let their maid (Hattie McDaniel) go and take over the house-cleaning and cooking duties herself—apparently a new experience. She also has to take care of the household finances, even asking the grocer for credit, something she's never had to think about before. Eventually, both to bring in extra money and to help alleviate the housing shortage, she takes in a boarder (Monty Woolley), putting her in the unusual and frequently unpleasant role of combination maid and landlord. Tim's absence also brings about challenges in her personal life. Anne must be both mother and father to their two daughters, trying to handle the problems that arise from their rapid wartime maturation in ways that she thinks Tim would approve of. She must also negotiate the sexual tension that develops between her and Tony Willet (Joseph Cotten), finding a balance between needed male companionship and faithfulness to her husband. She finally must find a way to contribute to the war effort beyond the limits of her home. Early on, when Tony asks her why she doesn't get a job, Anne replies wistfully, "What on earth could I do?" But later she realizes that giving up a husband to the army and keeping the home fires burning are not really sacrifices, so she becomes a welder at a shipyard. Anne's progress demonstrates not only the ways that women need to transform their traditional roles in order to contribute to the winning of the war but also how the war has moved one person from a socially privileged position to an admittedly less comfortable one, making her, in the process, a richer, more socially aware human being and an integral part of society.

Similarly, Tim and Anne's daughters find ways to negotiate the new social circumstances. The older daughter, Jane (Jennifer Jones), postpones her dream of a college education to become a nurse's aide. In this volunteer position, she works with the unpleasant results of the war, physically and psychologically mangled men, and she helps prepare them to become reintegrated into American society. The younger daughter, Bridget (Shirley Temple), does everything a teenager can to help the war effort, from planting and maintaining a victory garden to organizing scrap drives to rolling bandages and selling war stamps.

Nevertheless, at one point Bridget's frustration breaks out: "Oh Mother, it's just terrible! My not doing anything about the war at all!" It's this frustration at the way the war has intruded on and disrupted the family's life that motivates all the Hilton women to move into their new roles. They act, hoping to help end the war more quickly so that things can return to normal, but they're barely aware of how their actions are changing them and making a return to their prewar life impossible. The changes in them and the impossibility of returning to the way things were are made clear by the character of Emily Hawkins (Agnes Moorehead), who resists the changes brought by the war and in fact barely acknowledges the war at all. Recently divorced, she has no man to sacrifice to the armed services. Thus she remains caught up in the preoccupations of the traditional and stereotypical upper-class woman: her appearance, possessions (she admits hoarding), and gossip. As the Hilton women adjust more and more successfully to the new social circumstances caused by the war, Emily seems increasingly frivolous, trivial, and, eventually, evil. Early in the film, at a dance at the local army base, Tony shakes his head in wonder at all the eager young men. He explains to Anne, "They expect to come back to something. . . . Something like they left—only better. I hope they don't get too many surprises." The end of the film suggests that because of the changes taking place in the people—especially the women—left behind on the home front, the servicemen won't be coming back to the society they knew, but perhaps to something better. Whereas the film began with the disruption of the family, it ends with the formation of a new, ad hoc family. Gathered for the Christmas Eve celebration are the Hilton women, their former maid Fidelia, their boarder (a retired army colonel), Tony and a fellow naval officer, a friend of Anne's from the shipyard (a Polish woman), a friend of Bridget's who, until this point, had been shy to the point of muteness, and a recovering soldier Jane has been working with. This scene implies that the postwar family and, by extension, U.S. postwar society will be a more complex, informal, inclusive, democratic structure than it had been before the war, and that this is a good thing.[6]

Tender Comrade also shows a community of women forming an ad hoc family and, in the process, developing from prewar to postwar women. Like *Since You Went Away*, it focuses on a group of women trying to adjust to the absence of the men in their lives. Directed by Edward Dmytryk from a screenplay by Dalton Trumbo, *Tender Comrade* was released by RKO on December 29, 1943. It ends up dealing with many of the same issues raised in *Since You Went Away*, though less subtly and with a more pronounced ideological vision of the postwar world.

Here, four women who work at a Douglas Aircraft plant in Southern California decide to pool their money and rent a house together rather than separately renting unsatisfactory apartments. Jo (Ginger Rogers) has just sent her army sergeant husband off to an unknown overseas station. Helen (Patricia Collinge), the oldest of the four, has both a husband and a son in the army. Doris (Kim Hunter), the youngest, married her GI only moments before he had to leave with his unit. Barbara (Ruth Hussey) is married to a sailor on the *Yorktown*. In the absence of their men, these women not only become factory workers and joint heads of a household but also reject traditional women's activities, especially cooking and cleaning. As Jo says, "Housekeeping isn't our racket." After all, she argues, "It seems to me we got this house in order to enjoy it. We work eight hours a day as it is. If we have to work another eight hours to keep this dump going, we might as well go back to where we were." They decide to hire a housekeeper. Beyond running the house, they have to take responsibility for their decisions regarding their relationships with men. They frequently discuss the ethics of dating while one's husband is in the service; only Barbara sees no harm in it, though she learns her lesson when her husband is reported missing after the *Yorktown* is sunk. They must also make their own decisions regarding their relationships with society at large: At what point does hoarding become unacceptable? Should they accept an extra pound of bacon from the butcher? All these issues, and many others, are resolved after meetings, discussions, and votes.

This is all very different from Jo's prewar life with her husband Chris (Robert Ryan), which we see in several flashbacks throughout the film. Although in the narrative present Jo idealizes her relationship with Chris (note their androgynous names), in the flashbacks we see frequent arguments, some of them caused by Jo's immaturity, but some of them caused by their different understanding of each person's role in the relationship. Chris, anticipating the U.S. entry into the war, has begun working nights to build up savings for Jo, in case he's drafted. Not knowing this—Chris made the decision unilaterally—Jo resents having to spend so much time alone. Then, on a rare night together, when Jo tries to divert his attention from a magazine, Chris rejects her in the roles of seductress, pouting child, and nurse (removing a splinter from his finger) to complain about her failures as a housekeeper. But many of these complaints are actually about his loss of control over the household; that is, Jo doesn't keep things arranged as he desires: "My suit isn't back from the cleaners, and this one looks like a rag, and that's because you didn't send the other suit to the cleaners when you were supposed to. And my socks are always in the top drawer instead of in the middle drawer where I keep begging you to put them. And my nightshirt's never on the same hook at night as where I put it in the morning." Jo responds, with some justification, "I'm just a cheap substitute for a housekeeper. All you want is somebody to work and slave and scrub and cook and order the groceries and take care of the laundry and the pressing and clean the house and dust the furniture and lay out your clothes and scrub the bathtub and then sit with her hands folded in the evenings and watch you read!" When Chris finally explains why he's working nights, Jo offers to get a job to help increase their income, but Chris rejects that option out of hand. He sees his wife functioning in a very traditional role and refuses to consider her in any other.

Chris is like the young soldiers over whom Tony shakes his head in *Since You Went Away*, imagining the postwar world. Saying good-bye to Jo, Chris tells her what their life will be like when he comes home: "They'll be holding my job for me, and we'll go right ahead with our plans. Everything will be the same. Except that I'll be crazier about you, because I've been away from you for a little while." Together, they imagine a perfect house, with a barbecue and a garden, and a son. But the postwar world as it is being formed by Jo and her housemates will be far different from the traditional, patriarchal one Chris expects. Several times, the women refer to their living arrangement as a democracy, but it goes beyond that to a kind of collectivism. The authority in the house is spread among all the inhabitants, and decisions are made through meetings, consensus building, and votes. Even when one of the women claims that a decision is personal and none of the others' business, circumstances prove her wrong. For example, when Barbara decides to date other men, despite her friends' disapproval, she immediately hears the radio report of the *Yorktown's* sinking; in wartime, personal decisions have far-reaching ramifications. The collectivism is introduced when they decide to hire a housekeeper. Unlike Chris, who considered Jo's housework important only to the extent that it supported his more important work, the women make their housekeeper Manya (Mady Christians) a full member of the group. They decide to pool their four salaries, pay their bills from the pool, and split the remaining money among the five of them. Soon, the collectivism extends beyond money. When Manya's husband sends home a medal he's earned for valor, Doris wonders where they should put it. When Manya starts to protest, Doris says, "You don't think we're going to let Manya keep this all to herself, do you? It's part ours—share and share alike." This idea of joint ownership extends further. After Jo gives birth to a son, all five women act as his mother, all jumping out of bed, for example, when he cries in the night. Similarly, when Doris's husband Mike (Richard Martin) visits during a leave, all the women prepare for him their husbands' favorite dishes. Not surprisingly, when Dmytryk and Trumbo were accused during the McCarthy years of working Communist propaganda into their films, *Tender Comrade* was exhibit A.

The film ends with Jo receiving the news of Chris's death. In a long—and aesthetically unsuccessful—speech to her son, she makes it clear that Chris's sacrifice was important in helping to build a new world. But it is also clear that although it's important to remember him, his presence isn't necessary. In the new world being created by Jo and the others, women can make their own decisions, run their own social systems, and live independently of men.

The same gender-role negotiations that we see in these home-front films can also be seen in films focusing on women in battlefield situations. *Cry "Havoc,"* a November 9, 1943, MGM release adapted from the play *Proof through the Night*, is usually described as a film about army nurses on Bataan, but this misses the point. The voice-over at the beginning emphasizes that only two of the main characters are actually in the army; the rest are civilians—Americans, British, and one Filipino caught in the Philippines when the Japanese attacked—who have volunteered to help the American-Philippine defense by becoming nurses' aides. Most of these women come from backgrounds where they functioned in the traditional female gender roles, focusing on appearance and caregiving: one was a waitress (Ann Southern); one was the fashion writer for a Manila newspaper (Ella Raines); one was a burlesque dancer (Joan Blondell); and one was a southern belle (Diana Lewis) who, when asked what she can do, says, "Back home where I come from, women aren't allowed to do a blessed thing." The film then follows these women as they learn both how to serve the war effort—they become adept at assisting and, at times, taking over for the trained nurses—and, as in *Tender Comrade*, how to negotiate power and responsibility in a community without men. Interestingly for a combat film, the only men who appear are extras, the wounded men the women care for; the only important male character, the officer in charge of communications, appears only once on screen, in a long shot. So the women are left on their own to develop a working relationship that combines elements of the army hierarchy with the authority that comes from mutual respect, understanding, and friendship. At the end, as they almost serenely surrender to the Japanese, they understand not only how they have contributed to eventual American victory but also how they have had to transform themselves, from traditional women to wartime women, in order to make this contribution.

A more sophisticated treatment of these ideas can be found in *So Proudly We Hail!* (1943). In chapter 2 we saw how this movie worked to make the war in the Pacific relevant to Americans. But by focusing on women in a combat situation—this time, a group of army nurses who leave the United States in peacetime and end up as part of the delaying action on Bataan and Corregidor—the film also shows the tension that exists between the traditional gender expectations for women and the new expectations that arise during the war. This is perhaps most baldly shown in the character of Joan O'Doul (Paulette Goddard). Joan begins the film as a frivolous flirt, a woman who relishes her sexual desirability and is willing to use it to advance herself or occupy the center of attention. Her appearance is her identity. When we first see her at the transport's embarkation, she is desperately trying to keep her two fiancés from meeting. On the slow voyage toward Hawaii, she writes letters to seemingly dozens of beaus. (When she innocently asks someone for the date, we are cued to the imminence of the attack on Pearl Harbor.) For a dress-up Christmas party after the ship has been diverted to the Philippines, she stands out wearing a slinky black negligee. After the nurses arrive at a field hospital not far from the front lines on Bataan, they are given men's uniforms to wear and "GI underwear" to sleep in, but Joan continues to sleep in the negligee because it "keeps her morale up." It clearly gives her a sense of identity in an increasingly defeminizing situation. But this running joke soon turns to tragedy. When the field hospital is ordered to evacuate farther behind the collapsing front lines, Joan delays the departure of the last truck while she runs back to her bunk to grab the negligee. She's gone only a moment, but it's long enough for a Japanese patrol to approach, kill three soldiers, and trap the nurses in a small building. By trying to hold on to the symbol of her desirability, Joan has put them all in danger. The message is clear: in such a situation, traditional notions of femininity are inappropriate and potentially fatal.

One of the trapped nurses, Olivia D'arcy (Veronica Lake), has also been struggling to balance her feelings as a woman with her duties as a wartime nurse. Olivia was not one of the original group of nurses; she was picked up after her own transport was torpedoed and sunk. The other nurses are put off by her intensity and unfriendliness until they find out that her fiancé was a pilot killed by Japanese strafing during the attack on Pearl Harbor. With cold Electra-like fury, she vows revenge, even while recognizing the conflict between her personal feelings as a wronged woman and her duty as a nurse: "I'm going to kill Japs, every blood-stained one I can get my hands on. . . . That doesn't sound nice coming from a nurse, does it? We're supposed to be angels of mercy. We're supposed to tend to the wounded and take care of the sick. We're supposed to be kind and tender and serve humanity in the name of humanity. What humanity? Jap humanity?" When the nurses reach the field hospital, Olivia asks to be assigned to the ward with the Japanese wounded, apparently intending to kill them, but her sense of ethics as a nurse overcomes her desire for revenge.[7]

One of the other trapped nurses (Lorna Gray) argues that rather than be captured by the Japanese, the women should all kill themselves. She says, "I was in Nanking. I saw what happened to the women there. . . . When the Red Cross protested, the Japanese called it the privilege of serving his Imperial Majesty's troops. It's an honor—an honor you die from." Only Olivia sees a way to turn this desirability into a weapon. Leaving the others, she pretends to surrender while clutching a hand grenade inside her shirt; she becomes a human bomb, killing the Japanese who crowd around her, and saving her friends. Interestingly, Veronica Lake, a Hollywood bombshell, was photographed very severely throughout the film, her hair pulled tightly back in a bun and her face only lightly made up. At this point, however, her sexuality is emphasized: her hair falls down in the familiar Veronica Lake style, and she undoes several buttons on her shirt. Her action seems to offer a response to Joan's frivolous sexuality and a balance to her own earlier unchanneled fury for personal revenge. Hers is an untraditional, aggressive sexuality that functions not to murder aimlessly and emotionally but to save others.

The tension between the traditional woman and the new, wartime woman is most fully developed in the character of Janet Davidson (Claudette Colbert). "Davey" is the leader of the nurses and, as such, has a strong sense of her responsibilities. She leads by example—she is mature, self-confident, and reliable—but she also leads as a friend, acting as cheerleader, confessor, and comforter. Although she is indulgent of her nurses' relations with men, she resists having any emotional attachments of her own. When John Summers (George Reeves), a medical technician in whom she is guardedly interested, makes a play for her, she argues that she can't become involved in a relationship because she must dedicate herself to helping to win the war. In response to his pleas, she tells him, "There's no time, no time for anything personal. . . . I can't love you, I won't permit myself to. . . . Because I've got a job to do." Nevertheless, she falls for John and then must try to balance her feelings for him with her sense of duty. When John briefly visits the first field hospital on Bataan, Davey spends the night with him in a foxhole, not finding out until morning that her commanding officer has been looking for her. The commanding officer, Captain McGregor (Mary Servoss), makes her abrogation of duty explicit: "Davidson, I discovered you went out with Lieutenant Summers. I'm warning you, if there's a repetition of anything like this, I shall order you to pack up and recommend a dishonorable discharge." Thereafter, the tension continues to build for Davey. She manages to follow orders and get her nurses evacuated to Corregidor, arranges a hasty operation for John after he is wounded, and then gets both of them to Corregidor too. Later, when John volunteers to go to Mindanao in a desperate attempt to bring back supplies, Davey informs Captain McGregor that she is going to break regulations and marry him, which she does, but only after receiving tacit permission.

The tension between love and duty finally becomes too much for Davey when she and the other nurses are ordered to Australia before John returns. At the dock, she becomes hysterical and refuses to go: "I won't take orders. I'm not in the army anymore. When I married, I broke regulations. It meant I was out. You can't make me go." The combination of these overflowing emotions, McGregor's claim that John's party is officially considered lost, and the concussion of a nearby shell burst puts Davey in a coma. Symbolically, her mental breakdown comes because she has been unsuccessful in reconciling her traditional duties to her lover/husband and her new duties to the nurses in her charge, to the army, and to her country. There is a hint of hope at the film's end, however, when Davey comes out of the coma as a doctor reads her a final letter from John; psychologically, the letter offers some closure. But the difficulty the other nurses have in readjusting to simply being women—relearning how to walk in high-heeled shoes, trying to regain their figures—suggests that Davey's healing process and her struggle to redefine her identity as a woman will not be easy.

So Proudly We Hail! offers one character who seems to combine the traditional woman and the new wartime woman successfully: Captain McGregor. As a commanding officer, her persona is no-nonsense, yet the nurses affectionately call her "Ma." We see evidence of both sides of her leadership strategy. But beyond this, she is a mother in fact. Her son is an army pilot in the Philippines. We see the pride she takes in him and in her grandson, and we see her sorrow when her son dies in the army hospital. Her role as mother does not seem to interfere with her role as captain, and vice versa, because she understands that these two roles are not in conflict but mutually supportive. After her son dies, McGregor briefly breaks down, but in a moment she recovers herself, assures Davey, "It's over," and prepares to return to her duties—duties she connects to her family. Both her husband and her son died fighting for what they believed in, and she tells Davey, "It's a pattern that will go on, I suppose, until we do make the world a decent place to live in." McGregor as mother and as "Ma" is doing her part to make this kind of world.

The changes Hollywood filmmakers made in the presentation of gender-appropriate roles for men and women during the war led to some curious results, depending on how they were combined. *A Guy Named Joe*, released by MGM on December 24, 1943, offers the narrative combination of a man who has to learn to be part of a team, not a hero, and a woman who is independent and aggressive. This leads to some interesting gender reversals.

The first part of the film focuses on Pete Sandidge (Spencer Tracy), a hotshot American bomber pilot stationed in England. The conflict in which Pete is involved is established in the film's opening shots. First, we see a group of English children gazing through the air-base fence as Pete's squadron is returning from a mission. One says, "I'll bet you he's the best pilot in the whole world." There's an immediate cut to Pete's commanding officer, Nails Kilpatrick (James Gleason), complaining, "He's a grandstanding windbag. You can't trust him with a motorcycle much less an airplane." Clearly, Pete likes to play the hero, but he's in an army where heroes are less valued than groups of men working together. The film hammers this point home. Nails dresses down Pete for that morning's mission, during which he dropped his bombs on a railroad roundhouse from such a low altitude that debris from the blast, including a train whistle, was blown through his plane. Nails says, "You seem to want to end [the war] in the next three or four days all alone. . . . When you're up with your squadron, you're supposed to lead the squadron, not lone-wolf it. You've got a lot of lives and a lot of planes under your control. I expect you to stay where you belong. . . . What are you trying to be: a hero?" Pete, however, refuses to play by the rules. He tells Nails, "When a tough job comes up, I won't make a report of it, and I won't assign it to somebody else: I'll do it myself." His girlfriend Dorinda Durston (Irene Dunne), a pilot in the Army Air Transport Command, also berates him for his reckless flying. She asks him, "When are you going to stop being a dime-store hero?" Later, when she's trying to convince him to take a training assignment back in the States, she loses her temper: "What makes you think you're a flier? You belong back in 1925 in a flying circus. I can just see you now out at the fairgrounds doing loop-the-loops. You never stayed with your squadron in your whole life. You're a lone wolf in a service where men fly together. You've got hero-hunger, and better men than you come a dime a dozen."

Pete learns this lesson very slowly; in fact, he doesn't learn it completely until after he dies. Shortly after his showdown with Dorinda, while on a reconnaissance mission, he spots a German aircraft carrier.[8] His copilot suggests bombing it, and Pete is tempted but declines: "This is a job for headquarters to figure out. What are you trying to do, be a hero?" But after his plane is disabled and his crew has bailed out, he decides to take out the carrier by himself. He flies in low and makes a direct hit, but once again he is caught in the concussion from his own blast. He tries to save the plane but can't. It catches fire and crashes into the ocean, and Pete dies. He finds himself in a Pentagon-like heaven populated with deceased pilots whose job it is to return to earth, unseen and unheard, to help the young men who are learning to fly. The commanding officer (Lionel Barrymore) attacks Pete's confident assertion of his own individuality: "You are not under the impression that you learned to fly all by yourself, are you? . . . You were helped by every man since the beginning of time who dreamt of wearing wings, by pioneers who flew pieces of wire and pasteboard long before you were born, by every pilot that ever crashed into the ground in order that others could stay up in the sky. . . . And now it's your turn to pass that along to the next man." He has to make this point again to Pete later: "It isn't just you as an individual helping your man as an individual. It's all of us working together for the future, every man that ever flew." We know that Pete has finally learned this lesson by the speech he makes to Dorinda (who can't hear him): "This thing that's going on is bigger than you and me. It's bigger than any of us. We don't count, Dorinda. We're just nothing. And yet, if we do the job we're supposed to do, we can be great people."

Dorinda, in contrast, knows from the beginning of the film that, if women are to contribute to the war effort, they must free themselves from the confines of their traditional roles. Pete, interestingly, is constantly trying to make Dorinda act like a traditional woman. He doesn't approve of her or any woman being a pilot. Near the beginning of the film, he gives her a fancy party dress to wear on their date, instead of her uniform. Although their relationship is of some duration, it is apparently the first time he's seen her dressed up. He says, "It makes me realize you're a girl instead of a sky-flying cowboy." When she threatens to transfer to Australia unless he takes an assignment as an instructor, he tries to settle the matter by ordering her not to. He blithely dismisses her concerns about his safety by reciting an old poem: "Men must work, and women must weep." Dorinda rejects all these attempts to place her in a traditional role. Not only is she a pilot; she is, in some of their friends' opinions, a better—and more risk-taking—pilot

A Guy Named Joe: Ghostly pilots Dick Rumney (Barry Nelson) and Pete Sandidge (Spencer Tracy) look after Ted Randall (Van Johnson), who seems to be doing fine with Dorinda Durston (Irene Dunne). Al Yackey (Ward Bond) looks on.

than Pete is. She is also sexually aggressive. Pete complains that she dances too close to him, and then she proposes to him. Later, she responds enthusiastically to the attempts of Ted Randall (Van Johnson), ghostly Pete's charge, to pick her up. She is criticized in many of the same ways Pete was—for making a risky landing, for trying to win the war all by herself—but not in the same terms: whereas others were concerned that Pete was hurting the war effort by being a lone wolf, here they are concerned with Dorinda's personal safety and well-being.

Like "Ma" McGregor in *So Proudly We Hail!* Dorinda negotiates a connection between her personal life and her war work. Her friends worry that she hasn't been able to let go of her grief for Pete, yet she uses that grief productively, doing important work for the war effort in the Pacific after her transfer. She and Ted gradually develop a love relationship, but it doesn't interfere with either of their jobs. Indeed, after she changes her mind and tells Ted that she can't accept his marriage proposal because she's still in love with Pete, she finds out that Ted has volunteered for a dangerous mission. Fearing that her depressing news may affect his ability to perform the mission successfully, she tries to rectify what she's done, to make sure that her personal feelings haven't hurt him or hindered the war effort.

These two different presentations of gender roles come together in the film's climactic sequence. Dorinda, fearing that Ted won't succeed in his mission because of her refusal and that she'll lose another man in her life, steals his plane and sets off to perform the mission—bombing a Japanese ammunition dump—herself. She attempts exactly the lone-wolf, heroic action for which Pete was criticized. Ghostly Pete accompanies her and, through a kind of muted mental telepathy, tries to convince her to turn back. His argument is based on both what he's learned about the interconnectedness of all the men and events in the war effort and his old assumption that she's simply not a good enough pilot and will fail. He says, "Everything you're doing is against orders, Dorinda. It doesn't make any sense. Now look, Dorinda, I know you're a great little flier, but you're not a fighter pilot. You know a lot more depends on this job than just blowing up an ammunition dump. Suppose you don't make the grade. Did you ever stop to think of that? You'll tip off the whole show. Guys hundreds of miles from here will be dying just because you got scared and stopped running away from yourself." Luckily, the doubts Pete raises don't make her turn back. She flies in low, hits her target, and rides out the concussions caused by her bombs and the exploding ammunition. She is able to fly out of the same kind of situation that killed Pete.

Dorinda, by being everything the war needs a woman to be—independent, aggressive, confident—pulls off a heroic action. This seems especially significant in a film in which the male characters have repeatedly been told not to be heroic. The thematic logic of the film insists that the mission presented here could be done only by a woman. Interestingly, at the end of the film, the male characters—who have been encouraged to suppress their individuality and to be team players rather than lone wolves—become strangely feminized. Ted, anxiously awaiting Dorinda's return and then running across the field to hug her after she lands, seems to be playing the role of the lonely wife. Pete plays the role of a ghostly Stella Dallas, releasing Dorinda from his love so that she can go to Ted, sacrificing himself for her happiness. This is an intriguing reversal. In becoming the kind of man and woman the war effort demands, the main characters in this film develop traits that put them close to the traditional presentation of the opposite sex.

These changed gender roles, as presented in World War II films, anticipate changes in the postwar world—the corporate-conformist culture of the 1950s and the feminist movement of the 1960s and beyond. Although Hollywood would return, of course, to its male heroes and would try to put the stopper back in the bottle by once again relegating women to roles as sex objects and housekeepers, ambiguity in and contention about gender roles would remain both in movies—postwar film noirs and anti-heroic Westerns—and in the culture at large. In the next chapter we examine how the ambiguity and contention beneath the seeming homogeneity of the home front and its war effort became the subject of some wartime films.

1

HOME-FRONT ANXIETIES

After all, Potter, some people like George had to stay at home.
Not every heel was in Germany and Japan.
—Uncle Billy (Thomas Mitchell) to Mr. Potter
(Lionel Barrymore) in *It's a Wonderful Life*

SO FAR, WE HAVE BEEN CONCENTRATING on what Hollywood films of the World War II era had in common—the narrative conventions, character types, and tropes by which, en masse, they made the war understandable and communicated ideas about the war, America's place in it, our enemies, our allies, and each American's role in fighting it. Taken together—and together with other forms of pop culture and public discourses—these films helped construct the reality of the war for millions of Americans. Perhaps this is one of the reasons that retrospectively we tend to think of the World War II era as a time of unusual unity, of Americans pulling together in a common purpose. However, as we saw at the end of the previous chapter, the various narratives working together to create the impression of unity didn't always succeed in covering up issues of contention and public anxieties that always exist in a society, but especially in wartime. Some films—primarily B movies or movies by strong-minded, quirky directors—either by accident or by design looked beneath the facade and became *about* the contention and anxiety in wartime America.

These B movies were low-budget, quickly made, usually action-oriented films. This describes much of the product of the so-called poverty-row studios—Columbia, Republic, Universal, PRC, Monogram—and the programmers, films designed to fill the second half of a double bill, by the major studios. Many of the films we've examined have been B movies. Compared with bigger-budget, more prestigious films, they tend to make their points about the war more simply and bluntly—for example, Twentieth Century–Fox's *Little Tokyo, U.S.A.*, discussed in chapter 3. However, perhaps because they were made so quickly or because the studio heads, the Hays Office, and the Office of War Information (OWI) paid them less attention, B movies sometimes depicted war-related problems in American society in ways that other films tended to avoid.

And there were problems. Historian Allan Nevins, writing in 1946, offered this assessment of the domestic social upheaval resulting from the war:

> It has been a war in which big business has gotten bigger, while tens of thousands of small industrial plants have suffered acutely (with their managers and employees) from the high-speed mobilization. It has been a war in which the country has had to increase its forty-five millions of gainfully employed to sixty-five or seventy millions, which has meant working millions of semi-fit people long hours. Literally millions of workers have been moved by irresistible economic forces from one section of the country to another; millions have been shifted, or have restlessly shifted themselves, from one industry to another—the labor turnover at certain places and times has reached 30 per cent a month. Multitudes of families have been uprooted, and multitudes of children hurried into jobs. The result has been a painful strain on family ties, and a spectacular increase in juvenile delinquency. Crimes against the person—murder, rape, assault—have sharply risen. The population has had to adjust itself to the jamming of cities, the dislocation of transport, the pinch of a thousand shortages, the unpredictable shift of prices, the intrusion of government into new spheres. It has seen some groups enriched and others impoverished. The violence and confusion of these changes test many people severely even if they never see a gun.[1]

The problems Nevins outlines here—overcrowding and inadequate housing, shortages of goods and rationing, sudden urban growth and concomitant crime, and increased juvenile delinquency—are all addressed in Hollywood films, although they were often treated comically.

For example, one problem that affected many Americans was the housing shortage. Thousands of people were suddenly relocated to metropolitan or military-base areas after December 7, 1941, due to military service, government service, or war-industry work. This relocation, combined with shortages of materials to build new homes and apartment complexes (material that was going to the war effort), resulted in overcrowding, eccentric and ad hoc living arrangements, and strained social services. Although this was a serious problem, Hollywood tended to use the housing shortage for its comic potential. We have already discussed overcrowding as the premise for *The Doughgirls* (1944) and *Tender Comrade* (1943), but there were many other such comedies. The most famous, and probably the best, is *The More the Merrier* (1943), in which dollar-a-year man Charles Coburn wheedles his way into Jean Arthur's Washington apartment, invites Joel McCrea to move in too, and then plays matchmaker. Another Washington comedy, *Government Girl* (1943), begins with another dollar-a-year man, Sonny Tufts, unable to get a hotel room. But when he sits down in a hotel lobby, he attracts the attention of dozens of beautiful women made desperate by the man shortage.[2] It also depicts the difficulty of getting around Washington, with seven or eight people sharing a cab and full-to-bursting buses, and it features a subplot in which soldier James Dunn and Anne Shirley are newlyweds searching desperately for a place to consummate their marriage. In *Standing Room Only* (1944) secretary Paulette Goddard cancels boss Fred MacMurray's Washington hotel room, after which the two of them pose as husband and wife *and* take jobs as a butler and a maid so as to have a place to live until Fred can close a government contract. In *Johnny Doesn't Live Here Anymore* (1944) a man going into the service sublets his Washington apartment to Simone Simon but forgets to tell her that he has given keys to all his friends. In *Without Love* (1945) inventor Spencer Tracy moves into the Washington home of widow Katharine Hepburn. In *San Diego, I Love You* (1944) inventor Edward Everett Horton and family have trouble finding a place to live. In *Pillow to Post* (1945) oil saleswoman Ida Lupino pretends to be army lieutenant William Prince's wife in order to get a room in a motor court near San Diego. In *Three Is a Family* (1944) Marjorie Reynolds and her children move into her parents' New York City apartment after her serviceman husband ships out. She is soon joined there by her brother and his pregnant wife plus a serviceman buddy and his pregnant wife. Tipsy maid Hattie McDaniel remarks, "All these people living in one apartment, just like Harlem!" The studios clearly saw in the housing shortage situation an opportunity for comedy, especially romantic comedy, with unmarried men and women shown in uncommon and risqué proximity. The tone of most of these films is summed up by the narration at the beginning of *Ladies of Washington*, a 1944 Twentieth Century–Fox comedy-mystery programmer: "Wartime Washington: where the housing situation is so acute that there is a waiting list for park benches. Wartime Washington: where Republicans are sharing rooms with Democrats, and even isolationists are doubling up." The reality, of course, was not so amusing. Overcrowding frequently put pressure on family structures and overwhelmed local civic structures.

A connected problem was the shortage of gasoline, food, and other materials, such as metal and rubber. To ensure enough supplies for the military and a fair distribution of food on the home front, the Office of Price Administration established a complicated but generally effective system of rationing. As historian and veteran of the Washington bureaucracy Henry F. Pringle described it:

> Americans—at least American women—learned to use a new form of currency: ration stamps and tokens. Americans accustomed themselves to little butter and almost no beef. They got along without bacon. As the war continued, shortages developed in cheaper clothes, leather goods of all kinds, kitchen utensils, paper, and other commodities. Nobody suffered, except possibly during the short-lived scarcity of whisky and cigarettes. But America at war was curiously different from America at peace. Store clerks, cooks, and nursemaids flocked to the war plants. The old American custom of quick, efficient, courteous service was abandoned for the duration. Instead of being always right, the customer was always wrong.
>
> "Don't ya know there's a war on!" was the snarling answer to any complaint.[3]

Pringle's amused tone reflects the nature of most Hollywood films on the topic of rationing. Most home-front films manage to get in a couple of references to rationing, either to show characters setting a good example or to make a few jokes. One film, *What a Blonde* (1945), sets up a country-house farce involving lingerie manufacturer Leon Errol, a priggish textile executive, an actress who pretends to be Errol's wife, Errol's unexpectedly returning real wife, and a bevy of chorus girls all staying overnight at Errol's house because of gas and meat rationing (really!).

Another problem, which developed as a result of absent fathers in the military and mothers working in war plants, was unsupervised children. There was a great deal of concern about the war's effect on both small children and adolescents. Child-development experts Anna W. M. Wolf and Irma Simonton Black wrote that placing small children in child care or with relatives while their parents were away fighting or working threatened long-term psychological consequences: "If there is one thing that nations at war have learned it is that continuous separation from their mothers is one of the most destructive experiences a young child can have." Older children, Wolf and Black noted, were frequently left on their own to wander the streets while their mothers worked: "While these children are obviously not so dependent upon their mothers as the younger ones, they are usually better off with a little less cash and a little more care." The war made children, especially adolescents, grow up faster; many teenage boys quit school to go to work, and many teenage girls became inappropriately involved with servicemen on leave. The lack of supervision and the pressure to grow up too fast, combined with the rapid growth and overcrowding of many cities, led to an increase in juvenile delinquency rates. Wolf and Black quoted Arthur H. Crowl of the FBI as defining the problem this way:

> Before any boy or girl has broken the law . . . some adult has committed a more serious fault, some parent has been negligent in his responsibility or some social agency has failed to fulfill completely its purpose. Before any child strays from the path of the right, the adult generation has forgotten that the most solemn obligation anyone can assume in the eyes of God and man is to guide and direct a child along the proper paths of life. And when an adult places anything ahead of that responsibility, it is akin to criminal negligence. . . . The American home today may be excused to some extent for failure to carry out its responsibilities. But the community cannot be excused and it must accept its added responsibilities.[4]

Again, however, Hollywood's depiction of young people in its home-front films tends to ignore or treat lightly the effects of the war. Some films focusing on young people were able, paradoxically, to show teenagers how they could contribute to the war effort while indulging their fantasies of stardom. In *Johnny Doughboy* (1942) temperamental teenage movie star Jane Withers is convinced by her fan-club-president double to join a group of has-been child stars (including several of the Our Gang kids) in a tour to entertain the troops. In *Song of the Open Road* (1944) temperamental teenage movie star Jane Powell learns to be one of the gang when she joins the U.S. Crops Corps, an actual organization that sent adolescents out to pick crops while farmworkers were serving the country in other ways. In *Youth on Parade* (1942) students at a small private college put on a show that will propel some of them into show-business careers but also sends a message about college students' important contribution to the war effort and to the forthcoming peace. Its finale is a production number based around the song "You Gotta Study, Buddy," by Jule Styne and Sammy Cahn. Sassy leading lady Ruth Terry sings, "You gotta study, buddy. We need brains. 'Cause pen and ink and guys who think can build more planes."

When juvenile delinquency was treated on the screen, the badness was only paper thin and easily reformable, as in several Dead End Kids (a.k.a. East Side Kids) comedies. In *Flying Wild* (1941) reprobate Leo Gorcey initially refuses to join his comrades working at an airplane factory but is redeemed when he helps them break up a sabotage and smuggling ring. In *Let's Get Tough!* (1942) the Kids vandalize a Chinese shop, thinking that it's Japanese, but then help uncover and defeat a cell of the Black Dragon Society. In *Kid Dynamite* (1943) Gorcey's authority is undermined when one of the other Kids joins the army; he tries to force the new recruit into committing a crime, is knocked out for it, and then joins the navy. In an earlier film, *The Dead End Kids on Dress Parade* (1939), Gorcey is a delinquent who is admitted to a prestigious military school as a favor to his dying father. He rebels against authority, alienates the other cadets, decides too late that he wants to be friends, but eventually becomes a hero and a leader. This plot is probably drawn from the 1932 *Tom Brown of Culver*, which was remade as *The Spirit of Culver* in 1939, with Jackie Cooper as the delinquent; the plot was recycled again in *Junior Army* (1942), with Billy Halop as the delinquent and several other Kids making appearances. The recurring message seems to be about the beneficial effects of military service on young men rather than an exploration of delinquency.

The majority of home-front films, then, treated their material in such a way that the real social problems caused by the war were not developed seriously. Perhaps it was considered harmful to the war effort to dwell on these problems. Perhaps helping audiences to laugh at these problems was a way to alleviate their anxiety. Nevertheless, there were a few B films that directly addressed some of these problems in ways that make them stand out from the more typical and conventional movies discussed in the previous chapters.

The MGM programmer *Main Street after Dark* (1944) is about crime in an unnamed city that has grown rapidly because of the influx of soldiers and sailors since the beginning of the war. The film begins at the home of the Dibson family; they have just learned that the older son, Lefty (Tom Trout), is coming home. On leave, we wonder, from the fighting front (there's a star hanging in the window)? No, from prison, where he's been serving a three-year term for robbery. It turns out that everyone in the family is involved in one crooked scheme or another. Lefty's wife, Jessie Belle (Audrey Totter), is a dime-a-dance girl and, it's suggested, a prostitute on the side. She and the younger son, Posey (Dan Duryea), practice cons on Jessie's servicemen customers, everything from picking their pockets to renting them nonexistent hotel rooms and offering to put their valuables in nonexistent hotel safes. The little sister Rosalie (Dorothy Morris) has left school, where she was in frequent trouble for stealing from her classmates, and is being trained in the dime-a-dance routine by Jessie. All the family's activities are overseen by Ma (Selena Royle). The criminal possibilities for such a family are described by Keller (Hume Cronyn), a pawnbroker and fence, when he hears that Lefty is coming home: "There is grain alcohol, whiskey, nylon hose, gasoline ration books. In fact, there are any number of opportunities now, Ma, for a young man with gumption and one who isn't afraid to work." This is a weird, corrupt version of the American Dream. On the other side is police lieutenant Lorrgan (Edward Arnold), who is coordinating with the military police and shore patrol to clean up crime in the city. As he explains to a group of victimized servicemen, "First, you must realize, that in every large city, times like these bring out Paddy-rollers, pickpockets, muggers, and bunco artists of all sorts, and their favorite target is the man in uniform." He goes on to say, "Every light-fingered tramp within the radius of 500 miles has moved in here since this was made an embarkation point." By the end of the film, Lorrgan has executed a huge sweep of the city's criminals and the Dibson family is in jail (or dead—Posey is accidentally shot by his own brother), but the happy ending is undercut by Lorrgan's narration, over shots of the Dibsons at various prison activities, suggesting that the problem of urban crime has not been solved: "Well, ladies and gentlemen, that's our story, primarily the story of pathetically misdirected energy. With the same or even with less effort than they gave to crime, not only Ma Dibson and her brood but thousands of the men and women who fill our penitentiaries could have made an honest living—even a better living. Fortunately, for many of them, the temporary restraint of prison offers a new hope through education to social responsibility. Why they don't realize this, well, that's the mystery of all criminology. We admit we don't know. Perhaps *you* can tell *us*."

Allotment Wives, a 1945 (just postwar) Monogram release, depicts a different kind of racket preying on servicemen. Army colonel Pete Martin (Paul Kelly) is called in by the Office of Dependency Benefits to investigate women who marry multiple servicemen to collect their allotment checks and to cash in on their life insurance should they be killed. Instead of a few heartless, unscrupulous women, Pete discovers a widespread criminal organization that controls its female employees like pimps do their prostitutes. As in *Main Street after Dark*, the circumstances of the wartime home front have generated a new kind of social corruption and a new opportunity for organized crime.

Columbia's *The Racket Man* (1944) focuses on a charming gangster, Matt Benson (Tom Neal), who is drafted, goes gladly into the service, but soon clashes with army discipline. He buckles down to military life after a fight he starts costs his sergeant his stripes. Rather than being sent overseas, however, he is asked to go undercover into his old gangland life to help defeat organized crime's trafficking in rationed goods. Mr. Burton (Warren Ashe), the government agent who recruits him, explains, "Men like you aren't picked like this by accident. There's a job on the outside, a very important job, one you're so well fitted for it would be hard to get somebody to replace you. If you went across it'd be just one of you against one of the enemy. But over here on the home front, we're facing a serious problem: a home-front enemy that menaces the war effort with its greed for gain. I'm talking about the mobs, the modern racketeers, the black-marketeers, the element that you were so well acquainted with in civilian life." When he returns to his gang, Benson discovers that his trusted lieutenant, Toby Sykes (Douglas Fowley), has not only taken over the business but also expanded it into the black market. Benson uses his underworld contacts to help federal agents break up black-market activities until he is killed in a shoot-out with Toby. Far different from the comedies that treat violations of rationing with a wink and a giggle, this film presents the black market as a huge, well-organized extension of crime syndicates; here the illegal selling of essential goods, such as meat and gas, poses a serious threat to America's ability to make war.

The black market is presented in a similar way in two other films, both about the illegal trade in automobile tires. In *Tomorrow We Live* (1942), an Atlantis release and surely one of the worst movies ever made, a father and daughter who run a diner in the desert are blackmailed by mob boss Ricardo Cortez to help him with a black-market tire operation. Unlike *The Racket Man's* Tom Benson and the lovable gangsters we saw in chapter 6, who may be criminals but will have no truck with the fascists threatening democracy, Cortez is presented as a dictator, intolerant and power-mad. Here, the black-marketeering gangster is as much of a threat as any fascist dictator. In Warner Bros.' *The Last Ride* (1944) a gang steals tires off cars and then sells inferior tires back to their owners. Early on, one customer (Jack La Rue) compares buying illegal tires to Prohibition: there's no harm in bending the rules to get something that the government is artificially restricting. But the rest of the film demonstrates exactly where the harm is. Drivers die when the inferior tires blow out, the gang kills potential witnesses against them, and bribes corrupt the highest levels of the police force. The film shows that although defying rationing regulations on the individual level may seem trivial, these individual actions take place in the context of expanding criminal organizations that hurt both the war effort and the home front.

Boss of Big Town, released by PRC in 1942, examines this same idea in the area of food distribution. Michael Lynn (John Litel), the head of the central farmers' market for a large city, is approached by gangster Kenneth Craig (John Miljan) with a proposition: establish one wholesaler for each kind of produce (milk, eggs, lettuce, etc.), thereby controlling the prices and creating a hefty profit for the gang and Lynn, if he goes along. When he refuses, the gang turns to violence, ruining produce, sabotaging equipment, and attacking farmers. Lynn, of course, fights back. When he finally confronts the gang's mastermind, he finds that it's his own boss, Jeffrey Moore (H. B. Warner), who had been publicly fighting the racketeers. Lynn says, "You're pretty smug, Moore, making that great talk over the radio: *you're* for the people. *I'll* say you are—you're for what you can get out of them. Talk about the fifth column, you invented a new one: the *sixth* column. With food one of the most important items for our morale, you stand behind the flag, cheating the people, racketeering babies. They ought to hang you for treason, and they will. Oh, you might get me, Moore, but you'll never get 130 million people, 130 million that hate you and your kind and everything you stand for." Behind this entire plot is the premise that the fair distribution of food to the public is vital to the country's ability to fight the war, but this fair distribution is something that we must fight for, since some corrupt people will always seek to enrich themselves at others' expense.

Rationing (1944), an MGM comedy, manages both to critique the red tape connected with rationing and to condemn those seeking to evade the rationing system and those looking to profit by subverting it. Set in the small town of Tuttleton, the film begins by focusing on the conflict between Ben Barton (Wallace Beery), the local grocer and butcher, and his longtime neighbor and antagonist Iris Tuttle (Marjorie Main), who is postmistress and head of the local rationing board. The tone of the film is set early when Ben, bringing supplies back to his store, runs out of gas. He asks Cash Riddle (Howard Freeman), the local gas station owner, for some gas without coupons; Cash says sure, but at fifty cents a gallon, a huge markup. Thus the film pairs the inconvenience of the rationing system with the temptation to circumvent it. Ben expresses both sides of this problem in two speeches. Early on, venting his frustration to Iris about regulations and the forms to be filled out, he says, "Let's see. Do I get this right? I file this number 2 form which I don't understand in a file which I can't buy on a form that you haven't received as yet just so I can sell something that I've run out of to a fella with a ticket that he ain't got. If it keeps up, I'll wind up in a lunatic asylum that they haven't built yet." Just then a farmer (Milton Parsons) comes in with a stack of papers and asks if he can butcher his pig. Ben says, "What's the matter with you, Hank? Why, you look like you lost twenty pounds. You been ailin'?" Hank laconically responds, "Nope. Just been filling out forms." In a later sequence set in Washington, we see that confusing bureaucracy is not just a small-town problem. Ben is sent from agency to agency by receptionists who don't really listen to what he's asking for. But in his second speech Ben makes it clear that despite the confusion and inefficiency and the seeming absurdity, rationing is being done for a good reason. When a frustrated shopper (Sarah Edwards) asks how she and her husband can have a good meal, Ben answers, "That is very simple. First of all, you take a steak away from a marine down in Guadalcanal, and you cook it with some potatoes that should go to one of the coast guardsmen on the Aleutian Islands. Then you add some fresh vegetables from the mess of our troops down in northern Africa, and add a couple of pounds of butter that you were going to send to some sailors on a submarine, with two cups of coffee that belongs to an aviator in the South Pacific." When Ben finds out that Cash, his new partner, has been helping gangsters buy and sell black-market meat, he turns down a huge bribe and helps smash the operation. The red tape may be infuriating, but the importance of the war effort short-circuits any temptation Ben might feel to circumvent the rationing system. The criticism here of New Deal bureaucracy has its sting, but the film clearly shows that the real villains are the people—gangsters and everyday, small-town folks—who seek more than their share, hoard, and try to profit from the shortages.

The most interesting of these B movies about war-related social problems are the ones focusing on young people. Monogram's *Are These Our Parents?* (1944) tells the story of two adolescents from two different classes. Terry Salisbury (Noel Neill) is a spoiled rich girl who seems to have everything she wants—except her mother's attention. Her mother Myra (Helen Vinson) is a much-married sexual predator who, with her business manager George Kent (Lyle Talbot), seems to be involved in shady schemes to profit from inside information about domestic war construction. Terry is so desperate for her mother's attention that, in the first few minutes of the film, she rejects a dress George has sent on Myra's behalf, runs away from her boarding school, goes dancing and drinking in a roadhouse, outdrives two motorcycle cops when the roadhouse is raided, abandons her car, hitchhikes a ride home, and tries to vamp Hal Bailey (Richard Byron), the young man who picks her up. Once home, she refuses to be sent to another school and tries to begin a relationship with a bad-news nightclub owner (Ivan Lebedeff), one of her mother's former flames. Terry is precociously self-aware of her problem and where it might lead. In explaining why she left school, she says to her mother,

> I want to be with you. It seems to me as if I've never had you. I want you. I need you. I want to pal with you. Jehoshaphats, mother, there are things a girl just can't talk over with governesses and teachers. . . .
>
> I am out of hand, but I'll be even more so if you don't keep me around and keep an eye on me. . . .
>
> Why don't you spank me and put me to bed? At least if you spanked me, I'd know you love me.

Hal is in many ways Terry's opposite. He's from a working-class family, and he has applied himself assiduously to his studies and his afternoon job at a service station in preparation for enlisting in the army air forces. He seems the very picture of a good kid, yet he too has trouble at home. His father (Anthony Warde), a foreman at a defense plant, is being paid good money for the first time in his life, and it has a bad effect on him. When we first meet him, he doesn't have time to help Hal with his math homework because he has a date with a floozy (Robin Raymond), whom he subsequently marries. He spends his nights drinking and begins skipping work so he can go to the track and gamble. Even good kids need a parent's guidance and a strong role model; even with the best of intentions they lack experience and wisdom. When Hal tries to intervene in a confrontation between Terry and the nightclub owner, the nightclub owner is killed by a gunshot, and Hal and Terry go on the run.

The film's diagnosis of the problem of juvenile delinquency is made explicit near the conclusion. First, a police detective (Addison Richards) scolds Hal's and Terry's parents and a group of adults who witnessed their escape for taking a lineup of young suspects too lightly. Echoing FBI agent Crowl, he says, "This is not done for your entertainment. This is a solemn and sad occasion. Sad because it wouldn't be necessary unless you, as a community, were shirkers. But for the guiding hand of good parents, but for the environment of good citizens, but for the grace of God, it would be *you* on parade." Second, Hal and Terry find a temporary home with an older couple (Ian Wolfe and Emma Dunn) who, although they know the kids are fugitives, treat them like their own children, giving them attention and love and helping them reorient themselves morally. After some time with the couple, Hal and Terry are ready to return to their families and take responsibility for their actions.

Faces in the Fog, a 1944 Republic release, makes similar points in a similar way. Here the two adolescents, Mary Elliott (Jane Withers) and Joe Mason (Eric Sinclair), are next-door neighbors whose parents present a set of contrasts. Whereas Dr. Mason (John Litel) is wise, good-natured, commonsensical, and a caring parent, Tom Elliott (Paul Kelly) is hard-headed, hard-drinking, quick-tempered, and a stern disciplinarian. While still suffering from the shakes from the previous night's partying, he calls his wife Cora (Lee Patrick) to arrange a new party and another evening away from their children. Cora interrupts her afternoon bridge party to take his call, then goes into the backyard to chase away her son Les (Bob Stebbins) and his friends because they are making too much noise building a clubhouse. Her attitude toward her children is made clear in two statements. She says to her son, "I don't care where you play so long as you get out of here." Seconds later, when Mike (Richard Byron), a neighborhood teen, drives up and asks if Mary's home, she answers, "No, she's still at school—or somewhere." The unsupervised Les and his friends go off with the older Mike to steal lumber for their clubhouse; later, they play with a gun Les has taken from his father's desk, and he is accidentally shot in the arm. In contrast, that same evening, Dr. Mason and his wife (Dorothy Peterson) host a party, with dancing and hot dogs, for the local teenagers. It's here that Mary and Joe begin to go steady.

Mary and Joe are both good kids, but again, they lack the wisdom and experience to make good judgments. Mike, while out with a bunch of kids who are drinking and driving too fast, hits a pedestrian. Joe takes the man to a hospital, is blamed for the accident, and loyally but stupidly refuses to tell who's really responsible. Joe is expelled from school, and he and Mary decide to elope. Tom Elliott, having been informed by Mike that Joe and Mary have checked into a motel, tracks them down and shoots Joe, wounding him badly. But Mary convinces Joe not to tell anyone that they're married, so her father will be acquitted. Later, after the trial and after Joe joins the army, Mary is arrested for perjury. The jury at Elliott's trial debate what causes juvenile delinquency—whether a lack of supervision or kids who are just bad—but one juror, Miss Harvey (Virginia Brissac), traces the problem's origin to a basic lack of understanding between parents and their children:

> I don't believe there are any bad children. Some are weak and misguided. Others are frustrated. Others are just plain lonely. I don't think we grownups give the average child credit for the common sense he really has. We look upon him as one of immature intellect. We say, "Oh, you wouldn't understand. You're just a child." But they do understand, gentlemen. They understand more than you think. And they want to be understood. . . .
>
> I say that if complete understanding existed between children and parents, things like this wouldn't happen.

For such a complete understanding to exist, parents would need to spend time with their children, guide them and get to know them, recognize that war makes children grow up faster, and provide them with models through their own behavior and judgment.

The RKO programmer *Youth Runs Wild* (1944) similarly focuses on a star-crossed teenage couple, but it also does a better job than the other films of putting the problem of young people during wartime into a broader social context. The film begins with a montage of headlines about juvenile delinquency—"Nab Youngsters in Theft Ring," "Juveniles Cause Dance Hall Riot," and so on—over shots of young people engaged in dancing, drinking, fighting, and public necking. Interestingly, the montage ends with shots of defense plants and hundreds of workers going in and out of them. We then segue into the neighborhood where the main action is set, and we see a truck carelessly back into and knock over a sign that reads, "Drive Slowly: We Love Our Children." Even as it tells its main story, the film continues to drive home its point about this wartime society's disregard for its children. In the background of one scene, a child walks down the street calling for a younger child, "Dorothy, Mother wants you." Neither the child nor the mother has any idea where Dorothy is. Later, we see a crying baby locked in a car overnight in the parking lot of a war plant while its mother presumably works.[5] At another point, a small child wandering into the street forces a driver to veer and run into a group of children around an ice-cream truck.

The film makes sure that the viewer understands the actions of its teenage characters in the context of this society-wide abandonment of children. The teenage lovers here are Frankie Hauser (Glenn Vernon) and Sarah Taylor (Vanessa Brown, here billed as Tessa Brind). Frankie, up until now a good kid and a good student, is starting to go bad. His parents both work at a defense plant all night and sleep all day, so they rarely have time for him; they leave him messages on a chalkboard inside the front door. Frankie is frustrated at his lack of money for a good time or to spend on Sarah, but more generally he is frustrated at having no place in a wartime society. He says at one point, "Everybody's doing something but me. All I do is go to school." He begins skipping school to work at a service station. We see him sneaking into the movies without paying. Finally, he joins some other boys stealing tires from cars parked at a defense plant; they are caught and taken to juvenile court. Sarah is more aggressively ignored by her parents, also defense workers (Ben Bard and Elizabeth Russell). They disregard the meals she's made and swipe away the table setting she's carefully prepared. They want her to either stay home and watch her younger sisters so that they can go out drinking or go out so that they can host a party. They even forget her birthday. Out in the city on her own, Sarah takes up with a minor racketeer and his moll (Lawrence Tierney and Bonita Granville), gets involved in a shooting, and becomes a B-girl in a notorious local bar. Frankie and his friends come looking for Sarah and start a fight in the bar, and the moll is accidentally killed. The court sends Frankie to a forestry camp, and he goes happily, apparently realizing that this is an important second chance.

Like *Are These Our Parents?* and *Faces in the Fog*, this film recognizes that the problems connected with young people are a community responsibility. After the car hits the children at the ice-cream truck, Danny (Kent Smith), a convalescing soldier who is married to Frankie's sister Mary (Jean Brooks), says, "there's more to war than fighting. What it does to kids, that's just as much our job." Mary reminds him, "But they want people to work in defense factories, Danny. They can't work and take care of their kids at the same time." Danny comes up with an idea: he and Mary start a playground and clubhouse in the Hausers' backyard, a place where children can be taken care of while their parents are working. Danny also takes responsibility for the boys who were caught stealing tires. By becoming their pal and their mentor, he provides the adult role model they so desperately need. At the end of the film, after Frankie is sent to forestry camp, Danny challenges Sarah to take their local idea and make it a community project. Sarah notes that she doesn't really fit in anyplace, and Danny responds, "That's because you've grown up too fast. I think it's a lucky break. It means you can see both sides, and that's when you can really help people." Accompanied by a montage of shots of young people engaged in healthy and useful activities, Danny tells Sarah about teenagers around the country who have helped establish recreation centers and teen activities. He says, "Men and women work eagerly to help youth help itself. Our government knows that juvenile citizenship spreads faster than juvenile delinquency." Sarah leaves the backyard with a glow in her eyes and a purpose.

The social anxiety inspired by questions about how America will change because of the war is also reflected in several major studio productions that stand out for their treatment of serious social issues, their rejection of the fundamental narratives of war propagated by Hollywood during the war years, and their subversion of the narrative conventions of the Hollywood World War II film. Many of these films created controversy because of the critical eye they cast on the war effort, but that they were made at all—despite the watchful eyes of studio executives, the Hays Office, and the OWI—suggests that they reflect the uncertainty that existed in society at large. That they stand out even now as different from other wartime films demonstrates just how successful Hollywood was in creating a homogeneous picture of American society at war.

The Miracle of Morgan's Creek, a January 5, 1944, Paramount release, with screenplay and direction by Preston Sturges, is surely the funniest film of the war (and, in our opinion, one of the funniest films ever), but it is also probably the most subversive film of the war.[6] The target of its subversion is the wartime romance—the carpe diem sexual encounter between the about-to-depart serviceman and young woman left behind that is the basis for dozens of films from *Stage Door Canteen* (1943) to *Since You Went Away* (1944) to *The Clock* (1945). The wartime romance narrative implies that since the young serviceman is going overseas to fight for his country, the young woman, who can't fight, can nevertheless serve her country by providing the soldier (sailor, marine) with some last-minute loving. Indeed, at the end of *The Clock*, after she has said good-bye to Robert Walker—the man she's known only a few hours but who is now her husband—and put him on a train that will take him toward some theater of operations, Judy Garland walks out of Pennsylvania Station teary-eyed but proud, chin in the air as if to say, I've done my bit. This is not to say that these films aren't effective, but they can be troubling in what they don't say or in what's between the lines: that a man about to risk his life to defend his country deserves a sexual sendoff, and it's the patriotic duty of any real American woman to give it to him. This idea is expressed especially blatantly in a nightclub number, by Mack Gordon and Harry Warren, near the beginning of *Iceland* (1942):

> Listen little lady, it's the order of the day,
> Issued by the highest of authority.
> Fellows in the service simply can't be turned away.
> You know that defense must get priority.
> So if you're patriotically inclined,
> Heed the call to arms,
> And keep this thought in mind:
>
> You can't say no to a soldier,
> A sailor or a handsome marine.
> No, you can't say no if he wants to dance.
> If he's going to fight, he's got a right to romance.
> So get out your lipstick and powder.
> Be beautiful and dutiful too!
> If he's not your type, then it's still OK.
> You can always kiss him in a sisterly way.
> Oh, you can't say no,
> No, you've got to give in,
> If you want him to win for you.

The Miracle of Morgan's Creek introduces small-town girl Trudy Kockenlocker (Betty Hutton), who has completely bought into the wartime romance mythos. Morgan's Creek is home to an army boot camp, and Trudy is among the most popular girls with the soldiers because of her commitment to sending them off with a smile, a dance, and a kiss. As her sister Emmy (Diana Lynn) puts it, "You've *got* to kiss the boys good-bye." After her father, the local constable (William Demarest), reads an editorial warning about the trouble all the soldiers in town can cause for young girls, he forbids Trudy to go to that evening's farewell festivities. Trudy tries to enlist her erstwhile boyfriend Norval Jones (Eddie Bracken)— who isn't in the army because at moments of stress he sees spots—to pretend to take her to the movies so she can go dancing with the soldiers. Her argument is a hybrid of romantic and patriotic discourse: "They're fine, clean young boys from good homes and we can't send them off maybe to be killed and rockets' red glare, bombs bursting in air, without anybody to say good-bye to them, can we?" She tells him what he should say: "I want you to say, 'Trudy, it's your bounden duty to say good-bye to our boys, to dance with them, to give them something to remember, something to fight for.'" (That Trudy is an uncritical mouthpiece for societal discourse is established when we first see her in a record store lip-syncing a song.) Norval is unconvinced but agrees to the deception anyway.

The film follows the deception and the logic of the wartime romance mythos to their illogical and absurd conclusions. Trudy comes back from her night out at eight o'clock the next morning, suffering from the effects of too much champagne and a concussion she sustained while dancing. She gradually remembers, and confides to Emmy, that she married one of the soldiers, whose name she can't remember ("It had a *z* in it. . . . Like 'Ratzkiwatzki'"), but since they didn't give their real names to the justice of the peace, there's no marriage license and no way to track down her husband. Since there's also no way to track *her* down, Trudy can pretend that it never happened—until a few weeks go by and it becomes clear that she's pregnant. Trudy and Emmy (who, though only fourteen, is in many ways more worldly-wise than her sister) need to come up with a scheme that will allow Trudy to avoid the shame of unwed motherhood. It is here that the film reveals the contradictions and hypocrisy of a small town in wartime. Even though the culture at large expects young women to subscribe to the wartime romance mythos, it is ready to condemn them for its results. The film shows the potential for shame by emphasizing the atmosphere of surveillance in Morgan's Creek. Constable Kockenlocker is always stationed in the middle of town directing traffic, and the streets are patrolled by the MPs from the local boot camp. The rest of the citizenry, self-appointed busybodies, is constantly watching and listening. Sturges's long tracking shots, following Trudy and Norval or Trudy and Emmy as they walk through town, always reveal people in the background—on the streets, on the sidewalks, on their front porches—watching, and the characters are always aware of the possibility of being overheard. When Trudy and Emmy go to the town doctor (Torben Meyer) and lawyer (Al Bridge) for help, one of their concerns is that these men not tell anyone. Passersby observe and make judgments, offer unsolicited advice, and ask personal questions, all the time presuming their right to know and meddle.

Inevitably, the busybodies win. There follows a complicated plan in which Norval, in a World War I–era cavalry uniform, is going to marry Trudy under Ratzkiwatzki's name so that Trudy can then get an annulment and marry Norval for real, all before the baby comes. Of course, the plan falls apart: Norval signs his own name (not Ratzkiwatzki's) to the marriage license and is arrested on a variety of charges, including corrupting a minor and impersonating a serviceman. Kockenlocker, finally finding out the true situation and what Norval has tried to do for Trudy, helps him escape and thus loses his job. As Trudy's due date draws near, Norval is a fugitive, Kockenlocker is without a job, and the family has moved to a farm outside of town to escape the shame.

The film further develops its attack on societal hypocrisy by revealing that the foundations on which both the wartime romance mythos and the approbation toward unwed mothers are based are bogus. The final section of the film presents the miracle of the title—and not just in the fact that Trudy gives birth to sextuplets, all boys. As she nears the end of her pregnancy, it's Christmastime. To make sure that we don't miss the symbolism, Kockenlocker tries to cheer up the despondent Trudy by saying, "You've got to have more confidence in the Almighty, or whatever it is that makes the wheels go 'round. Alright? It's almost Christmas. Where was He born? In a cowshed." Then Emmy interrupts her playing of "Silent Night" to point out that their cow, Bessie, has gotten into the house. These parallels point toward the nature of the townspeople's hypocrisy: the Christianity they use to justify their moral judgment of Trudy began with the miracle birth of a child from a woman made pregnant by an absent and unknown father.

That the town's judgment is based on a shallow appreciation of principle is further seen after Trudy gives birth to the six boys, and those who were ready to condemn her now celebrate her. Her "immoral" behavior is forgotten in light of the fame Morgan's Creek will attain from her unprecedented progeny. The film uses the worldwide attention the births receive to mock the wartime romance mythos—the idea that young women who tend to the sexual needs of the boys about to go overseas are somehow serving the war effort. In a montage showing the press response to the births, one headline reads, "Nature Answers Total War: Platoon Born in the Midwest." We see the angry reaction of Mussolini (Joe Devlin) when an aide brings him the news, then the headline, "Mussolini Resigns: 'Enough Is Sufficiency,' Screams Il Duce." Similarly, Hitler (Bobby Watson) has a temper tantrum on hearing the news, after which we see the headline, "Hitler Demands Recount." That the births could have this kind of effect on the war is funny but also blatantly silly.

Finally, the factitiousness of all moral and patriotic standards is made clear by the narrative's frame: the local newspaper editor (Victor Potel) telling Trudy's story over the phone to Governor McGinty (Brian Donlevy) and The Boss (Akim Tamiroff), characters from Sturges's *The Great McGinty* (1940) making cameo appearances here. Eager that nothing spoil the windfall this represents for the state (and, under the table, for them), they easily solve the problems that have been vexing the main characters for the entire film; they use their power to rearrange the facts to create a new "reality." McGinty orders the editor to get Norval out of jail. When he asks how, McGinty answers, "By dropping the charges, you dumb cluck." McGinty and The Boss attack the men bringing the charges against Norval: the justice of the peace who almost married Trudy and Norval has his license revoked; the banker who claims that Norval robbed him has his bank's charter canceled. Norval wasn't impersonating a soldier at all, McGinty says, "That was a State Guard uniform. . . . As a matter of fact, he's a colonel in it. I'm bringing him his commission tomorrow." The Boss adds, "Retroactive as of last year." The editor brings up the problem of the marriage, but McGinty dismisses it:

> McGINTY: What's the matter with the marriage? She's married to Norval Jones. She always has been. The guy married them, didn't he? The boy signed his right name, didn't he?
> EDITOR: But he gave his name as "Ratzkiwatzki."
> McGINTY: He was trying to say "Jones." He stuttered.

Meanwhile, The Boss gets on another phone to persuade a friendly judge to annul the marriage to Ratzkiwatzki "retroactively." At the heart of this reconstruction of Trudy's story is, of course, money. McGinty tells The Boss, "You better get right down to Morgan's Creek. Buy up a few choice corners, maybe some hotel sites, they'll need some. And the bus franchise will be very valuable."

At a time when most movies accepted as a given the principles of patriotism, Christianity, universal morality, and justice, *The Miracle of Morgan's Creek* calls them all into question. Such principles serve a social purpose, but all are disposable if the chance to make a profit comes along. Throughout the film, whenever Norval hears any news that unexpectedly shatters his sense of the world—for example, when Trudy tells him that she's married and that she's pregnant—his condition comes on and he sees spots. At the end of the film, when Norval visits Trudy in the hospital and finds out about the six boys, he sees spots again, but this time the spots fill the screen, and we in the audience see them too. This is an indication that the film has tried to shake us out of our sense of the world as defined through Hollywood film narratives. The film's humor helps disguise its cynicism about American social institutions and the so-called principles that support them.

Lifeboat, released by Twentieth Century–Fox on January 11, 1944, and directed by Alfred Hitchcock from a screenplay by Jo Swerling, based on an unpublished John Steinbeck novella,[7] similarly subverts the conventions of the Hollywood World War II film to explore the question of what fighting the war is doing to American society. As we saw in chapter 1, Hitchcock's *Foreign Correspondent* helped define the European war to Americans. He also made *Saboteur* (1942), in which Robert Cummings is falsely accused of sabotaging a defense plant and must clear himself by exposing the real saboteurs, a nest of German spies and fifth columnists. This film participates fully in the Hollywood propaganda effort, especially in one scene in which a blind man gives a speech about the importance of fighting for democracy and another in which the "freaks" of a circus choose democracy over the intolerance of a Hitler-like midget. But Hitchcock was too independent to follow the conventions of wartime films too closely. One propaganda film that Hitchcock made for the British was rejected for not being in line with the official version of the war.[8] *Lifeboat* uses the official discourses and narratives about the war but slowly reveals them to be charades, eventually dangerous charades that generate a problematic new society.

As the film opens, a merchant marine vessel torpedoed by a U-boat is sinking, but not before its gun crew sinks the U-boat. Survivors gather in a lifeboat: Connie Porter, a famous American correspondent (Tallulah Bankhead); C. J. Rittenhouse, a millionaire industrialist (Henry Hull); Kovac, an American sailor and Communist Party member (John Hodiak); Stanley Garrett, a British sailor (Hume Cronyn); Gus Smith, an American sailor with a bad leg wound (William Bendix); Alice MacKenzie, a nurse on her way to London (Mary Anderson); Mrs. Higgins, a suicidal, shell-shocked Englishwoman with a dead baby (Heather Angel); Joe Spencer, the African American ship's steward (Canada Lee); and, problematically, Willy, the captain of the sunk U-boat (Walter Slezak). The Allies' representatives bicker over whether to allow Willy to remain on board, uncomfortably deciding to do so. When the Allies can't decide on a leader, Willy, having gained their trust by amputating Gus's gangrenous leg, steps forward. Thanks to secreted water, energy pills, and a compass, Willy appears to be a superman; the others capitulate and let him row them toward his supply ship. When Gus discovers the hidden water, Willy casually and cruelly pushes the amputee overboard. Finally understanding the true nature of this Nazi, the Allies join together to beat him brutally and then throw him over the side. Too weak to row, they wait for the German supply ship to pick them up and make them prisoners, but at the last moment, an American ship appears and sinks the supply ship. The film ends with the survivors waiting for their imminent rescue.

On one level, the film seems to participate in the same narrative understanding of the war that Churchill put forth in his "Their Finest Hour" speech: the conflicts—Christianity versus heathenism, civilization versus

Lifeboat: U-boat captain Willy (Walter Slezak; far left) is able to divide and almost conquer the other survivors (from left: John Hodiak, Tallulah Bankhead, Henry Hull, William Bendix, Heather Angel, Mary Anderson, Canada Lee, and Hume Cronyn).

barbarism, order and rule of law versus chaos and lawlessness—and the narrative resolution—victory through teamwork and sacrifice. The civilized merchant marine and the civilian passengers, transporting Red Cross packages, are torpedoed and have their lifeboats shelled by the barbarous German U-boat. When the survivors debate whether to throw Willy overboard, Rittenhouse argues from a self-consciously democratic and Christian position: "We are perfectly willing to abide by the decision of the majority. That's the American way. But if we harm this man we are guilty of the same tactics that you hate him for. On the other hand, if we treat him with kindness and consideration, we might be able to convert him to our way of thinking. That's the Christian way." Stanley even worries about the ramifications of the Geneva Convention: "He's a prisoner of war and has to be treated as such. The way it's done is to hang on to him till we're picked up, then turn him over to the proper authorities. Till that time, we represent the authorities." This concern with law, rules, and fair play is contrasted to Willy's deceit: hiding the compass, not sharing his water and energy tablets, and killing Gus. Kovac, who stubbornly refuses to trust Willy and repeatedly argues for killing him, is made to seem intolerant, the antithesis of the values for which the Allies are fighting.

As the story proceeds, it illustrates Churchillian messages about resolving these dichotomies through sacrifice and cooperation. The self-indulgent Connie learns sacrifice by having the material possessions she prizes so much—her camera, her mink coat, her typewriter—stripped from her. At one point, referring to a bracelet, she says, "I wouldn't take it off for anyone or anything in the world." But later, as she tries to inspire the others not to give up, she offers the bracelet to use as fish bait and eventually loses it, too. Similarly, the survivors begin their ordeal separated by their many differences: upper class and working class, capitalist and Communist, men and women, black and white, British and American. They even argue over their favorite baseball teams. Willy is able to exploit these differences to gain control of the boat, and it isn't until the differences are overcome and the survivors join together that Willy is defeated.

Beneath this surface compliance with the official narrative understanding of the war, however, is a critique of that narrative. Churchill's clear conflicts are confused in this film, and his resolutions are made unappealing. The unexpectedly subversive nature of the film is suggested in the long opening shot. As the merchant marine vessel's smokestack submerges, the camera pans across the detritus: Red Cross packages, a chess board, a *New Yorker* magazine—all symbols of the civilized superiority of the Allies—

and then a body. A woman? A baby? Hitchcock himself? No, a German sailor. This is unexpected and unsettling. Are we supposed to feel sympathy for the dead man, even though he is one of the enemy? Are we supposed to connect the dead German to the images of culture and civilization we previously saw in the water? The film seems to be signaling the viewer that what the official narratives of the war present as conflicts, binary oppositions, are deconstructable; that is, the opposing terms of each conflict are not as completely opposite as the official narrative needs them to be. Once we see that the two terms are not opposite at all but are, at least in some ways, alike, the Churchillian version of the war is no longer so persuasive. For example, the climactic American shelling of the German supply ship and its longboat is uncomfortably similar to the initial U-boat sinking of the merchant marine ship. Kovac even announces, "Well, that settles the score." We wonder why one is more barbarous than the other. If the two sides wage war in the same manner, can one really be said to be good, Christian, and civilized and the other bad, heathenish, and barbaric?

In this context Joe functions not as a symbol of pulling together (as characters from racial and ethnic minorities frequently function in World War II films[9]) but as a deconstructive principle; his presence serves to expose as false the assumptions behind the official narratives about the war, especially the assumptions about the superiority of America over its Axis enemies. That Joe is not really an equal member of the group is made clear by what the upper-class characters call him—Connie calls him "Charcoal," and Rittenhouse, habituated by Pullman porters, can't understand that his name is not George. And all the survivors order Joe around. In the speech quoted earlier Rittenhouse makes the case for the Allies' superiority based on their democratic and Christian nature, but when the survivors begin democratically deciding whether to throw Willy overboard, the process is undercut by Joe's surprised question, "Do I get to vote, too?" and Rittenhouse's uncomfortable reply: "Why . . . certainly." We are reminded that back home in the arsenal of democracy, Joe probably doesn't get to vote. Later, when Mrs. Higgins's baby is buried at sea, only Joe can remember and recite the Twenty-third Psalm; Rittenhouse, who had declared himself and the others Christian, can manage only the first line. And after Willy's death, when Joe, indicating heaven, asserts, "We still got a motor," both Rittenhouse and Connie mock him. Most significant, Joe is the only one who does not join the group in killing Willy. Instead, he tries unsuccessfully to pull Alice away, then retreats to another part of the boat.

We see that this is not a triumphant pulling together. The survivors are animal-like as they scream and claw at Willy; they pound at him with their fists, an oar, and finally the shoe from Gus's amputated leg. Joe's presence reminds us that this kind of pulling together results in mobs and lynchings. Who are the barbarians now?[10]

Lifeboat ends ambiguously, not only in terms of its plot—as many wartime films do—but also in its decidedly muted sense of triumph. After the German supply ship is sunk and as the survivors wait to be picked up by the friendly vessel, a sailor from the supply ship is pulled aboard in a scene that echoes Willy's entrance into the lifeboat. Rittenhouse, previously the advocate of democracy, Christianity, and fair play, now hysterically insists that the man be put overboard, shrieking, "You can't treat them as human beings! You've got to exterminate them!" When the scared sailor threatens the survivors with a gun and must be disarmed by Joe, the others agree that this new experience confirms the lesson they learned from Willy: that Germans will return kindness with treachery. Earlier, after killing Willy, Rittenhouse had wondered, "To my dying day, I'll never understand Willy or what he did. First, he tried to kill us all with his torpedoes. Nevertheless, we fished him out of the sea, took him aboard, shared everything we had with him. You'd have thought he'd have been grateful. All he could do was plot against us. And he let poor Gus die of thirst. What do you do with people like that?" Again, at the end, Kovac asks, "What are you going to do with people like that?" Stanley replies, "I don't know. I was thinking of Mrs. Higgins and her baby. And Gus." Connie, in the film's last line, says, "Well, maybe they can answer that," apparently referring to their dead comrades. But how can they answer anything regarding our relations with our enemies? The lack of closure undercuts the happy narrative resolution Churchill promised: perhaps the conflict isn't so neatly defined, perhaps pulling together isn't so easy, and perhaps the Nazis can't be defeated unless we're willing to become like them. The film implicitly asks us: How will we deal with our enemies after the war is over? And what kind of people will we have become by the time we achieve victory?[11]

Christmas in Connecticut is also concerned with the anticipated postwar world, but more specifically with the American home front. It was released by Warner Bros. on June 20, 1945, between the end of the war in Europe and the Japanese surrender, when eventual victory was assured and a war-weary public was looking forward to peace and a return to normal. It is this notion of "normal" that propels the film's plot. Whereas the official narratives about the war focus on home-front sacrifice and team-work, *Christmas in Connecticut* explores the social anxieties operating beneath the surface of the public discourse, anxieties about what the returning servicemen will find when they come home and what kind of women will greet them.

The plot focuses on a sailor, Jefferson Jones (Dennis Morgan), who spends eighteen days adrift in a lifeboat after his destroyer is torpedoed. He eventually lands in a hospital, where, in order to get a good meal, he proposes to his nurse (Joyce Compton). When Jeff begins to get cold feet, his would-be fiancée decides that he needs a taste of real home life and arranges for him to spend the Christmas holiday at the farm of Elizabeth Lane (Barbara Stanwyck), columnist for *Smart Housekeeping*, a national women's magazine. Unbeknownst to anyone, Elizabeth's descriptions of homey farm life, a husband and child, and delicious dinners in her "Diary of a Housewife" column are created in her midtown Manhattan apartment, drawn from memories of a friend's farm, the recipes of a Hungarian chef, and an active imagination. When her publisher, Alexander Yardley (Sydney Greenstreet), insists that she entertain Jeff and himself for the holidays, Elizabeth agrees to marry longtime beau John Sloan (Reginald Gardiner), in return for the use of his farm and his participation in the charade. Thus, Christmas Eve finds Jeff and Yardley at Sloan's farm expecting everything they have read about in Elizabeth's columns; Sloan trying to get Elizabeth alone long enough for a judge to marry them; and the Hungarian chef, Felix (S. Z. Sakall), in the kitchen doing the cooking. Before long, Elizabeth and Jeff fall in love.

These and other levels of illusion and deception are significant in terms of the serviceman's expectations about life back home after the war. The film begins with Jeff in the lifeboat, dreaming of the meal he will have after being rescued. But in the hospital he is frustrated when the doctors put him on a diet of milk and raw eggs. In desperation, he proposes to his nurse to get steaks and chops, but he can't even keep his dream meal down. This desire for a good meal leads Jeff to project his notion of the perfect peacetime life onto the Elizabeth Lane columns he reads. Here is everything he's fighting for, everything he hopes to return to at war's end: a comfortable, rustic life; a nurturing and caring helpmate; plentiful and delicious food provided by his ideal woman—just like the life Alvin York returned to in *Sergeant York*. As Jeff sums it up, "Elizabeth Lane is a marvelous woman: a good housekeeper and a great cook." He imagines her older and motherly, but the Elizabeth Lane he envisions is just another dream. The real Elizabeth Lane writes of rolling lawns, a glowing fireplace, and a roast goose dinner, but she looks out over city rooftops, is warmed by a noisy steam radiator, and eats sardines for breakfast. This conflict between the dream of the ideal and the reality suggests a larger societal anxiety over what kind of woman will exist in the postwar world: traditional housekeeper and cook, combination sex object and idealized mother, or working woman without the so-called womanly skills.

Yardley shares Jeff's vision of Elizabeth Lane as the feminine ideal, but he imagines putting that ideal to use in creating a very different kind of postwar world. He too believes in the fantasy Elizabeth Lane that has been created through the columns. In fact, he and Jeff seem to have memorized the columns and thus know more about the make-believe Elizabeth than the real Elizabeth does. Their expectations for the weekend have been shaped by those columns, and Yardley is dictatorial in having his expectations met: Elizabeth doing the cooking, Elizabeth flipping him his breakfast pancake, Elizabeth walking her cow to bed in the barn. For Yardley, it is important that the reality behind the image be genuine, because he plans to profit from that image. By manipulating the columns' nostalgia for a traditional life (home, values, family, food), he intends to encourage returning servicemen and their new wives to purchase products to help them replicate that life. Yardley even encourages Sloan to impregnate Elizabeth with a "second" child (she already has an imaginary one), preferably by September, in the short term to boost circulation, but in the long term to encourage others to have babies and thus buy the baby products advertised in Yardley's magazines. But the life that Yardley is encouraging consumers to have is an inferior replica of the nostalgic ideal. He and Sloan discuss a home-design column to serve the anticipated postwar housing boom; however, they imagine not the homey farm of Elizabeth's column but housing tracts thrown up as quickly as possible: prefabricated, plastic, synthetic dwellings. Yardley wants to use the Elizabeth Lane ideal to profit off the desire it creates and the new suburban, baby-boom America that would be its antithesis.

John Sloan, Elizabeth's architect husband-to-be, is not seduced by the Elizabeth Lane ideal; he knows and wants the real Elizabeth, but he wants to change her. For him, she is another ornament for his perfectly decorated house. He wants her to give up any semblance of independence so that she will fit into his rigidly ordered world. He disapproves of the Elizabeth who is so independent that she buys herself a mink coat rather than wait for some man to give her one. She must learn to follow Sloan's timetable, to respect the placement of Sloan's knickknacks, to be subservient to Sloan's ideas. Sloan becomes emblematic of those who expect women, especially women who went to work during the war, to return to their former roles of serving men in various ways after the war.[12] Early in the film, when Elizabeth is faced with losing her job, Sloan reminds her, "You have another job waiting for you, if you want it: the job of being Mrs. John Sloan."

The film resolves these conflicts superficially on the level of plot, but not in a way that relieves the social anxiety they create. In a series of complications, Elizabeth and Jeff are arrested for wandering off in a horse-drawn sleigh after a dance, and Yardley, seeing the baby he thinks is Elizabeth's taken away by its real mother, reports a kidnapping to the police and the press. When Elizabeth and Jeff return home at dawn, she explains the kidnapping caper, but Yardley attacks her for dallying with Jeff. He says, "My public believe in *you*, Mrs. Sloan. Millions of women in these United States pattern their daily lives after that feature and you're going to live up to their ideals or my name isn't Alexander Yardley." When Elizabeth confesses the charade, Yardley fires her; she has subverted his ideal and undercut his plans for the future. Similarly, Sloan, disgusted with the chaos Elizabeth has brought into his little world and by his failure to remake her identity, ends their engagement:

SLOAN: I must say, the way you've been behaving isn't exactly . . .
ELIZABETH: . . . as the wife of John Sloan, the prominent architect, *should* behave?

For her part, Elizabeth insists that she's tired of being told what to do by everyone—and, presumably, being told what to *be*. Throughout the film, she struggles with the challenge of maintaining her autonomous identity in the face of the expectations of the patriarchal Yardley, the motherly and nourishing Felix, the prissy Sloan, and the fantasizing, nostalgic Jeff. An independent career woman, Elizabeth has become entangled in a trap that she helped build. On the one hand, she has rejected most of the social expectations of how women are supposed to act. She can't cook. She can't diaper a baby. She desires neither to grab nor to be grabbed by a man (remember her self-bought mink coat). The most important thing in her life is her job: writing the Elizabeth Lane column. But on the other hand, her column has helped perpetuate expectations about the way she, and presumably all women, should act. Her conundrum is that in order to keep what is most important to her, her job, she must eschew her own identity and become her own creation, the traditional Elizabeth Lane, who would never have an outside job. This problem is made concrete in the deal she makes with Sloan: in order to keep her job, she agrees to marry Sloan, who insists that, as his wife, she cannot keep her job.

Elizabeth and Jeff's pairing seems to be a restatement of the traditional ideal. Brought together by the purveyor of good food, Felix, their union suggests a rejection of both Sloan's identity-snatching view of the future and Yardley's crassly commercial view in favor of the traditional ideal of home and fundamental values that Jeff has been after from the outset. The film seems to suggest that returning servicemen will be able to participate in the ideal life they have been fighting to preserve. And, since Elizabeth turns down Yardley's attempt to rehire her, this implies that the war's working women are prepared to become postwar wives. But Felix's final line, "She can't cook, but what a wife!" suggests that the postwar woman will not be the same woman she was before the war. In addition, there are many unanswered practical questions: Without Elizabeth's income, what will they live on? Where will they live—Elizabeth's Manhattan apartment? If so, what becomes of Jeff's ideal of home then? Moreover, the film is peppered with examples of women leaving behind their traditional roles: Yardley's daughter can't come home for Christmas because she can't get away from her government job; Elizabeth's mink coat is delivered by an African American woman in a stylish uniform; Sloan's house becomes an informal day-care center for the children of women working at local defense plants; and, at the Christmas night dance, nearly as many women as men are in military uniforms. Thus the film's happy ending seems to be a faux resolution: the ideal of home is a fantasy, and American women will not be fulfilling traditional, constrictive expectations in the postwar world.

Hail the Conquering Hero, written and directed by Preston Sturges and released by Paramount on June 7, 1944, also anticipates the postwar world, but here the concern is how the returning servicemen will affect the country. This film's plot, like *Christmas in Connecticut*'s, is propelled by a series of deceptions and illusions. Woodrow Lafayette Pershing Truesmith (Eddie Bracken)—a name, like Jefferson Jones, suggesting a combination of the heroic and the mundane—has been raised in the shadow of his marine sergeant father, a hero killed in World War I. So Woodrow's discharge from the Marine Corps for chronic hay fever makes him feel like a failure. Rather than go back to Oakridge and disappoint his family and fiancée, he

Hail the Conquering Hero: Encountering homecoming anxieties, Woodrow Truesmith (Eddie Bracken) is flanked by the reception committee chairman (Franklin Pangborn) and the sergeant (William Demarest).

writes that he has been sent overseas, then gets a job in a San Francisco shipyard. He tells his story to six marines on leave who decide to take him home, say that he has been honorably discharged after heroic service, and reunite him with his mother. The deception steamrolls, however, when the group finds Mrs. Truesmith (Georgia Caine), the fiancée (Ella Raines) (now engaged to another man), the mayor (Raymond Walburn), four bands, and the rest of the town waiting at the train station for what they presume to be a hero. In the wild celebration that follows, the town pays off Mrs. Truesmith's mortgage, proposes building a statue of Woodrow and his father shaking hands, and nominates Woodrow to run for mayor. Woodrow's efforts to reveal the deception are overwhelmed by the marines' creative new lies.

On the most basic level, the film deals with the question of what a hero is. One view is presented at the beginning of the film when the broke marines try to talk a bar manager (Paul Porcasi) into taking a fake war souvenir, a tooth taken from Admiral Yamatoho after his seppuku, as payment for food and drink. The manager pulls out an array of souvenirs from previous servicemen-patrons and says,

> You wouldn't like to buy the flag they buried him in, would you? I can let you have it very reasonable. I have it in several sizes. MacArthur's suspenders. The first bullet to land in Pearl Harbor. You can take your pick. A piece of a Japanese submarine. If you look at it this way, it becomes a German submarine. And this way, it's piece of a shell that *just missed* Montgomery. Here we have the seat of Rommel's pants. And last but not least, we have a button from Hitler's coat, although, that one I don't personally believe.

He doesn't understand that heroics can't be represented by the tangible souvenirs servicemen collect; the souvenirs are imperfect signifiers pointing toward but unable to represent inexpressible wartime experiences. To the manager, the heroics represented by the faux souvenirs are just debris to be discarded, and the stories behind them are hooey to be disregarded. In a civilian setting, wartime heroics are at best irrelevant, at worst annoying. The opposite view is presented by the townspeople of Oakridge. They see the superficial signs of heroism (he was gone and now he's back with medals) and project an idea of heroism onto Woodrow that takes on a life of its own. Woodrow, of course, protests that he's not a hero, but even the real marines shake off this projected idea of heroism as not representing the truth of their actions or their experiences. As the sergeant (William Demarest) says, "I've been a hero, you could call it that, for twenty-five years. And does anybody ever ask me what I done? And if they did, I could hardly tell them, I've told it so different so many times. . . . [Referring to a local statue of a general] All everybody else knows is he's a hero: he's got a statue in the park and the birds sit on it. Except I ain't got no birds on me, I'm in the same boat." What the public craves in its heroes, stories of danger and valor, are just that—stories that may entertain but can't contain the truth of wartime experience. This is made clear in the myriad stories about Woodrow's heroics that the marines cheerfully make up to entertain his crowd of supporters. The sergeant orders one marine to tell a real story about him and another marine, "Only *you* got to be Smitty, *he's* got to be you, and you *both* got to come out alive." The marines act out Paul Fussell's argument that soldiers often engage in verbal subversion because of their "conviction that optimistic publicity and euphemism had rendered their experience so falsely that it would never be readily communicable."[13]

Neither of the views of the returning servicemen—irrelevant or heroic—recognizes the reality of their actions; the film suggests that the returning servicemen won't be understood by means of the public's various notions of heroism and so won't be easily assimilated back into society. We discuss this anxiety further in chapter 8.

A second conflict centers around the returning servicemen's relations with women. After creating his story about going overseas, Woodrow wrote to his fiancée, Libby, to say that he had fallen in love with someone else and thus set her free. She is now engaged to the mayor's son, Forrest (Bill Edwards), who is 4F because of (you guessed it) chronic hay fever. But with Woodrow's return, Libby's feelings become confused; she puts off telling Woodrow about her engagement and gets swept up in the town's heromania. This represents the common fear of the men who stayed behind for whatever reason: Will their wartime work pale beside that of the returning heroes, the men who served and saw action? Will the returning heroes steal the girlfriends, fiancées, and wives of the men who stayed at home? Forrest wonders whether appropriating women will be considered their right, like a trophy of war. He asks Libby, "Do you want me to offer you to him like the keys to the city on a silver platter?" And within this is another conflict: what will women's roles be after the war? Libby, like many women, went to work during the war years, but when Forrest suggests that she will have to give up her job, she objects:

FORREST: You weren't going to stay on as father's secretary anyway, after our marriage. . . .

LIBBY: What was I going to do? Stay home and weave?

FORREST: You might stay home and take care of your children, with the servant problem the way it is.

And when Forrest says that having children is what marriage is for, Libby bristles, "I suppose so, if you look at it from a purely unromantic standpoint, like a breeding farm." Like John Sloan, Forrest sees being a wife as a profession (in this case, a servant) and a duty (to propagate the species).

Both these conflicts contribute to the most important conflict created by Woodrow's return: the distribution of power in Oakridge. The entrenched power is represented by the aptly named Mayor Noble (he even has a suit of armor decorating his baronial office). Noble has apparently been mayor for many years and is emblematic of the blending of political and industrial power (in every speech he plugs his chair factory—"seats of all descriptions") for the gain of a self-appointed elite. When a populist fervor results in Woodrow's nomination for mayor, Noble sees the danger to the status quo represented by the returning servicemen, not just in Oakridge but throughout the country. He says, "Soldiers coming back at moments like this [just before an election] can upset a political balance it has taken years to adjust." He is clearly referring to the power he has established at the expense of the people he is supposed to serve. He reveals his contempt for and fear of the people when he says, "There you see one of the fallacies (I wouldn't want this to go any further, you understand) of the democratic principle: they can vote for anybody they like. . . . The poor misguided voters, without a brain to bless themselves with." He derides Woodrow's ability to lead and his right to participate in the distribution of power, saying, "What he does best he does in Guadalcanal." And he fears what the hordes of homecoming servicemen will do to his "political balance." He says, "In a few years you won't be able to swing a cat without hitting a few heroes."

But the political balance that has been so profitable for Mayor Noble and his cronies has been revealed by the disruption of the status quo during the war years to be unstable and corrupt. This is established very early on at the train station, where chaos reigns: four bands play at once, the mayor's speech is repeatedly interrupted, and the mayor's son's fiancée takes off her engagement ring so that she can pretend to be Woodrow's girl. The problems with the political and the social status quo are best articulated by Judge Dennis (Jimmy Conlin) as he tries to talk Woodrow into running for mayor:

> There's something rotten in this town, nothing you can put your finger on exactly, but a kind of something you can feel. It's like the town was selfish. Everybody thinking about little profits and how not to pay the taxes and reasons for not buying bonds and not working too hard and not working at night because it's nicer in the daytime, all things that are alright in peacetime, things you used to call thrift and relaxation that made many a fortune, but things that are plain dishonest in wartime. The motto of this town is "Business as usual," but a lot of us feel wartime ain't a usual time and that business as usual is dishonest. That's why we need an honest man for mayor. An honest man who'll wake us up and tell us the truth about something he knows all about.

The film suggests that the current dispensation of political, social, and cultural power is self-serving and corrupt and that the return of the servicemen—unassimilable and ready to disrupt political, social, and sexual structures—is an opportunity to reconstitute the distribution of power and all manner of intellectual assumptions. The film articulates anxiety over the threat to the status quo but clearly sides with the troublemakers.[14]

The resolution of these conflicts is confused by the basic indefinability of *hero*. Woodrow finally reveals the deception in a scene of public humiliation, but with the sergeant's help, the town reconfigures its notion of the heroic to include such a confession. Thus on the level of plot, everything is set right: Woodrow will run for mayor and presumably win; the Truesmith family unit is restored; Woodrow gets Libby back; and, most important, Woodrow becomes the hero he felt he was always meant to be. He says to the departing marines, "I knew the marines could do almost anything, but I never knew they could do anything like this." And he receives the answer, "You got no idea." And here lies the problem: the marines' intervention in Woodrow's problems seems miraculous; they are dei ex machina who appear out of the fog in San Francisco and disappear into the steam of a departing locomotive. This suggests that the conflicts about postwar America and the impact of returning servicemen are resolvable only through fantasy or divine intervention. Like *Christmas in Connecticut*, the happy ending of the plot is belied by wish-fulfillment fantasy and unanswered questions.[15]

These films, then, form a minipattern of sub rosa resistance, not to the war but to the official narratives about the war that most Hollywood films gladly promulgated. This resistance is significant in two ways. First, it reveals something that most movies concealed: the disjunction between the discourses of the official narratives about the war and the reality of the war, or at least of wartime life. In fact, most movie narratives were premised on this concealment. Second, this resistance reveals the divisive social anxieties that existed beneath the narratives of homogeneity, cooperation, and sacrifice. Anxieties about race and class divisions, the fit of homecoming servicemen into American society, the role of women in the postwar world, and what America had turned itself into by fighting this war would become more overt subjects for Hollywood films after the war.

8

POSTWAR FILMS
IN THE POSTWAR WORLD

We're all excited around here. My brother just got the
Congressional Medal of Honor. The president just decorated
him.
Yes, well, I guess they do those things.
　　　—George Bailey (James Stewart) and bank examiner
　　　　Carter (Charles Halton) in *It's a Wonderful Life*

The thing that scares me most is that everybody's going to try
to rehabilitate me.
　　　—Sgt. Al Stephenson (Fredric March) in
　　　　The Best Years of Our Lives

AS WE SAW IN THE LAST CHAPTER, as the end of the war approached,
some Hollywood films began reflecting anxieties about what the postwar
world would be like. By the time the war ended in September 1945, films
about the war had begun inexorably to change. It was no longer necessary
for them to make the war understandable; they began to use the war as a
setting to pursue other purposes. At the end of *Casablanca*, Rick famously
tells Ilsa, "it doesn't take much to see that the problems of three little
people don't amount to a hill of beans in this crazy world." The films

produced during the war confirm this—they are full of unresolved love stories and incomplete life stories. The individuality of the characters' loves and lives is subordinate to the drama of the war. After September 1945, however, the war becomes a background against which other dramas can be played out. Lewis Milestone's *A Walk in the Sun* (1945) uses a platoon in a nameless action in the Italian campaign to explore the psychology of men in combat. Lillian Hellman's *The Searching Wind* (1946) sets the intergenerational struggles of an American family against the rise of fascism and the coming of the war. By 2001 this kind of film had degenerated into *Pearl Harbor*, a multimillion-dollar special-effects spectacular in which the real-life dramas of the Battle of Britain, the attack on Pearl Harbor, and the Doolittle raid are all reduced to background for the insipid love relationships of three shallow characters. This film is the apotheosis of Rick's statement: the problems of these three little people surely *don't* amount to a hill of beans, but that didn't stop someone from spending an awful lot of money to tell their story.

Broadly speaking, films about the war produced after September 1945 use the same narratives, discourses, character types, and tropes that made the war understandable to the American moviegoing public to engage the new, postwar world. We look at two types of postwar films: the social film, which deals with the return of the serviceman to American society, and the international film, which, in arguing that the war isn't really over, seeks to prepare Americans for the new cold war.

As we saw in chapter 7, such war-years films as *Hail the Conquering Hero* and *Christmas in Connecticut* address social anxieties about the return of the American serviceman to civilian life. That such anxieties existed is evidenced by many popular publications: Jack Goodman's *While You Were Gone*, a collection of essays on all aspects of American life—politics, social issues, art, sports (James Thurber even writes on "What the Animals Were Up To")—designed to help the returning serviceman catch up on what was happening in America while he was overseas; Maxwell Droke's *Good-by to GI: How to Be a Successful Civilian*, a book to help the serviceman readjust to civilian life; Dixon Wecter's *When Johnny Comes Marching Home*, a book that looks at the returning World War II serviceman in the context of the aftermath of previous American wars; and psychologist Franklin Fearing's "Warriors Return: Normal or Neurotic?" on the fear that returning servicemen will be mentally unstable and hard to fit back into society. As the war ended, films about the returning servicemen proliferated. How would their experiences in the war change them? Would they come back different people? How would they fit back into the family and social structure? One film, *Snafu* (released by Columbia in late 1945), based on a Broadway play, engages this anxiety by imagining the returning serviceman as the "child" he would have been before joining up, the typical teenager who enters the service and goes to war, and the man who comes back—someone his family doesn't recognize.

A year prior to the beginning of the action, fourteen-year-old Ronald Stevens (Conrad Janis) had run away from the home of his parents, Ben and Madge (Robert Benchley and Vera Vague). One night at the movies, they see a shot of Ronald in a newsreel feature on the army in the South Pacific. Madge orders her husband, "You go to the army and tell them to send that child home immediately." As local excitement builds about the return of a veteran, Madge insists that Ronald is still a child who will return to his typical American teenage life. She tells one reporter, "We hope Ronald will be able to come home as though nothing had happened." Ben concurs: "The way things were, that's the way they're going to be." They are, of course, wrong. For one thing, the returned Ronald, now fifteen and a sergeant, thinks of himself as a man, not a child. He complains, "Why did you have to go and do it, Mom? Why couldn't you leave me alone? How do you think I felt? There's a battle going on. It's plenty rugged. Right in the middle of it, the C.O. calls me in and says, 'Sergeant, your momma wants you.' Me, in Colonel Terrigan's Terrors, the toughest outfit in the islands. The C.O. calls me in and says, 'Your mother wants you.' How would you feel?" The souvenirs he has brought home hint at what he has been through, experiences far removed from the typical American teenager's: a Japanese sword, taken from the body of an officer who had committed hara-kiri; a Japanese regimental flag with ominous stains ("that stuff here, that's not dirt, that's Jap blood!"); a bugle won in a crap game; a grass skirt given to him by a friendly native woman ("They give you anything they got. If they had a shirt, they'd give it to you"); a pickled cannibal head. Still, among all the family, friends, neighbors, and public officials there to greet Ronald when he comes home, only Josephina (Eva Puig), the maid, sees that he is not a child: "You wear the clothes of a man. You *are* a man."

It soon becomes clear that things are not going to be the way they were. Ronald rises at 5:00 every morning and plays reveille on his bugle. Friends from the service drop in to stay. When planes from the local airfield pass over, Ronald yells, "Air raid!" and dives for cover. When approached from behind, he's likely to respond with a judo throw. When Ben wants to have a serious talk about his behavior, Ronald takes the lead and ends up offering his father advice on his marriage. He has his own money and wants his independence. Madge reminds Ben that everything is supposed to go back to the way it was and says, "I imagine you're happy that our son has learned to hang around bars, that he's become a gambler." Ben responds, "I was talking about the kid that left here, not about an army sergeant." Madge worries about how this unfamiliar son will fit into society: "It'd be alright if there were just the two of us. We're his parents. We love him. We understand him. We can get used to all this blood and guts. . . . But what happens when he gets out among people?" Through a series of complications—and because they still think of him as a child—Ben and Madge become convinced that Ronald has terrorized the dormitory of a women's college and stolen $1,000 to buy a car. When an army colonel (Winfield Smith) shows up, they assume that he's there to arrest Ronald. Instead, he talks to them about the problems of readjusting servicemen, including problems caused by how others perceive them:

> In time, you know, he'll stop being the glamorous figure who fascinates you with stories of far places and strange people. He'll cease to be the center of attention. What happens then? . . . He'll be just another citizen trying to find a place for himself. And he should have no difficulty if you are prepared for it, if he's met with trust and not suspicion. Some people warn us that because our soldiers have been trained to kill that they'll come back tough and dangerous, go around breaking the laws, taking what they want, attacking people. Why, you know how ridiculous this is in terms of your own son. Instead of worrying about the problems of the readjusted soldier, perhaps there ought to be more thought given to the problems of the readjusted civilian.

Ronald returns, and all the confusion is cleared up, after which the colonel presents him with the Silver Star for gallantry in action. For the first time, his parents look at him with pride for what he's accomplished and what he's become. But the confidence of the colonel's words is undercut when a plane buzzes low overhead and the colonel dives for cover, dragging a neighbor with him.

Even before the end of the war, some films made use of this strategy of presenting the returning soldier as a stranger. In Columbia's *The Impatient Years* (1944) Lee Bowman and Jean Arthur, swept up in a whirlwind romance, marry just before he ships out. When he returns, they are like strangers and quickly get on each other's nerves. Before a judge will grant them a divorce, however, he insists that they re-create their meeting, quick courtship, and marriage in San Francisco. The trick works, and they fall in love again. In PRC's *When the Lights Go on Again* (1944) a corporal on leave from combat in the Pacific gets amnesia when his cab is in an accident. He returns to his hometown not recognizing anything or anyone. His parents and wife employ various stratagems to help him remember who he is and who they are.

Released in April 1945, just as the war in Europe was ending, Republic's *Identity Unknown* also uses amnesia to dramatize the problem of the returning serviceman. As we meet the soldier (Richard Arlen) on a U.S.-bound hospital ship, we find out that he has lost his memory. He was one of four men holed up in a French farmhouse, cut off from the American lines, and bombed by the Germans. When U.S. troops moved forward, they found this soldier and three dead men, their dog tags scattered. Thus the army knows that he's one of four men, but nobody's sure which one. Told to choose a temporary name for himself, the soldier hears another man playing "When Johnny Comes Marching Home" on the harmonica and chooses "Johnny March." Back in the United States, on his way to a hospital, Johnny notices that the train has pulled into the hometown of one of the four men he might be. On an impulse, he gets off the train and begins a journey on which he visits the homes of each of the four men, hoping to discover which is *his* home.

As he visits each of his potential families, he quickly discovers that he is not that man, but he also discovers the hole that each man's death has left in his family: absent husband, absent father, absent brother, absent son. In each case the family member has given in to despair, and in each case Johnny helps rebuild the broken relationship and restore hope. His message to one widow (Cheryl Walker), who wants to move to another town to get away from the memories of her husband, is that it's vital to embrace and cherish the past but not to become lost in it. He says, "Now what do you want to do, move out of town, give up your friends, give up your home, because it reminds you of Mac? Sally, it should remind you of Mac. He fought for this. He gave his life so that you could live. . . . You can't stop living just because you were hurt. These surroundings are part of you, part of your life. You've got to love them again: the pictures that Mac helped you hang and the chair next to the fireplace where he always smoked his pipe." When he says that both of them have smashed-up lives to rebuild,

Sally is skeptical. She says, "What have you got to rebuild? You came back. All you have to do now is pick up where you left off." Johnny's situation, though an extreme one, makes it clear that this is not so. Speaking of himself, Johnny explains to Sally that he has to discover his past, not so he can take up where he left off but so he can build his future.

This is his message for each of the families he visits. The last family, the Andersons (Forrest Taylor and Sara Padden), are about to auction off their Iowa farm because of the memories of their lost son. Johnny, sensing that this is wrong, helps stop the auction by addressing the would-be bidders:

> You see, this just wasn't a farm to [Mr. Anderson]. It was something far more precious, something that he and his son had built together. Now that son is gone. But as long as this farm endures, something of that boy will remain to give hope and consolation to two hearts: his father's and his mother's. Mr. Anderson doesn't see it that way now, but he will. For there isn't anything more important in the whole world than the love of a mother and a father for a boy that's gone, unless it's the happiness they may still find in keeping faith with that boy's ideals, especially when keeping faith with those ideals means helping to feed the millions of hungry kids who are waiting for the things this farm can produce.

The bidders tactfully and quietly file out. Given his insistence that the past must be known and used to create the new postwar world, it is appropriate that when Johnny discovers his true identity (it turns out that he was a pilot attempting to drop supplies to the men in the farmhouse and was caught in an explosion), he learns that he was a history professor. The film suggests that we should not expect the returning servicemen simply to pick up where they left off; they will have to struggle to come to terms with their past and struggle to combine that past with their wartime experiences to help build a new American society and a new world.

A film that offers a similar message in an unusual way is *The Courage of Lassie* (MGM, 1946). Here, the collie Bill (Lassie), through a series of complications, is separated from his owner, Kathie (Elizabeth Taylor), and becomes a war dog for the army. Bill becomes a hero in the Aleutians, running through enemy fire while wounded to bring help to his pinned-down platoon, but he also gets the canine equivalent of shell shock; he recognizes no one and attacks every person he sees. Back in the States, Bill escapes from the train that's taking him to an army rehabilitation hospital, winding up near Kathie's home. But this violent, war-shaken Bill quickly becomes a local sheep-killing terror; he even attacks Kathie, until something in him recognizes his owner and he snaps back to himself. Nevertheless, the owners of the sheep demand that he be destroyed, and he is brought before a judge (Harry Davenport). Kathie's friend Harry McBain (Frank Morgan) tries to defend Bill, but the evidence seems overwhelming until Harry finds the army identification tattoo inside Bill's ear. From this, he is able to find out about the dog's record and make a final plea to the judge in which he explicitly connects Bill's experiences to those of his son Gary and other returning servicemen. After reading Bill's record, he says:

> This letter I made my notes on is from my boy, Gary. He's in an army hospital in New York, and from what he writes I guess that he's going through something like what Bill here went through. And it just occurred to me that perhaps a lot of our boys will be coming back not quite ready to take up where they left off. They'll have gone through more than most of us could ever think of, and they're going to need patience and love and understanding from us. And most of all, perhaps, they'll need time. You know, they didn't become soldiers in a day, and we can't expect them to become civilians in a day either.
>
> And Bill here, he went through the fight too, and he's no less a soldier 'cause he can't talk. But he found a big love and a big understanding from a little girl, and he's come through his bad time. Your honor, I know dogs, and I can swear to you that Bill here is a good citizen now. And so I ask you, on his record as a first-class soldier, to give him a break.

Of course, Bill is reunited with Kathie. Again we see the idea that war has changed the servicemen, that they can't just come back home and be who they were before they left.[1]

Films made during the war, including *Since You Went Away* (1944), in which war widow Jennifer Jones becomes a nurse at an army hospital; *Dr. Gillespie's Criminal Case* (1943), in which Keye Luke is a doctor helping a taxi driver who lost his legs at Pearl Harbor; and *Thirty Seconds over Tokyo* (1944), which explores Ted Lawson's concern that his wife won't accept him with scars and a missing leg (see chapter 2), sometimes addressed the rehabilitation of the wounded back into society—a more specific and blatant way of dealing with the returning-veteran anxiety we've been discussing. As the war was ending and immediately afterward, this theme became more common. The narrative pattern here—serviceman comes home maimed or disabled (that is, changed), angrily resists his reintegration into society, but finally, often through the help of a good woman, accepts his situation and looks toward the future—maps easily onto the plots of the other films we've been looking at. In *The Enchanted Cottage* (RKO, 1945), an updated version of a 1924 film based on a stage play, aviator Robert Young returns from the Pacific with a useless arm and a scarred face. To escape the world, he lives in an old honeymoon cottage in New England and marries Dorothy McGuire, the homely housekeeper. But through the magic of the love contained in the cottage, the two come to look beautiful to each other, and he gains the courage to reenter the world. More realistic, *Pride of the Marines* (1945) follows John Garfield, blinded during a horrifying banzai charge on Guadalcanal, as he swings between self-pity and denial but finally learns to accept his disability and fit into society. These films reassure their audiences that the men injured in the war, physically or psychologically, can return to society, but they also warn that these men will be changed.

All these themes are developed in more sophisticated ways in the best homecoming movie—indeed, one of the best movies of all time—*The Best Years of Our Lives*. Released in November 1946 by Samuel Goldwyn, with a screenplay by Robert E. Sherwood and direction by William Wyler, *The Best Years of Our Lives* follows three servicemen as they return to their hometown of Boone City. Like the other films we've looked at, this one is about the difficulties of veterans returning to society, but unlike the others, it is also about postwar American society as seen through the eyes of the veterans: what has changed, what hasn't changed, and what, in the end, the servicemen were fighting for. The tension between these two narrative points of view is established immediately as we see how difficult it is for the servicemen simply to get home. Capt. Fred Derry (Dana Andrews) tries to get a commercial flight to Boone City but is told that all flights are booked for several weeks and is pushed aside by a prosperous businessman (Ralph Sanford), obviously no veteran, and his golf clubs. The businessman has a reservation and doesn't mind paying extra for his overweight baggage, but there's no room for the veteran. Fred is directed to the army's Air Transport Command (ATC), where servicemen, if they don't mind waiting and aren't too picky about where they end up, can be flown along with cargo. A corporal (Blake Edwards) signs up for a flight to Cleveland, and when Fred comments that Cleveland is a nice town, the corporal responds, "Yeah, but Detroit's where I live." Fred finally gets a flight home, and as the plane approaches Boone City, he notes, "Well, the old hometown hasn't

The Best Years of Our Lives: Homer Parrish (Harold Russell), Peggy Stephenson (Teresa Wright), Fred Derry (Dana Andrews), Milly Stephenson (Myrna Loy), Uncle Butch (Hoagy Carmichael), and Al Stephenson (Fredric March) enjoy the servicemen's first night home.

changed very much, has it?" As they fly over the local country club, he comments, "People playing golf, just as if nothing had ever happened." This disjunction between the veterans' wartime experiences and those of the home front provides the main conflict for each of the three servicemen's stories.

Of the three returning servicemen, sailor Homer Parrish (Harold Russell) seems most familiar from earlier homecoming films. Badly burned when his aircraft carrier was sunk, Homer had his hands amputated and replaced with hooks. But two things make Homer different from disabled veterans in other films. First, Wyler took a risk in casting Russell, who was not an actor but an actual veteran with a genuine disability. In Russell, the viewer must encounter the disturbing reality of war's consequences. Wyler's risk paid off, as Russell turns in a beautifully affecting performance for which he received two Academy Awards, one honorary and one for Best Featured Actor. Second, when we meet Homer, he has apparently already gone through the process of acceptance and adjustment that constitutes the plot of other disabled-veteran films. At the ATC terminal and on the flight to Boone City, others are disturbed by his hooks, but Homer is cheery, casual, and quite adept, taking a pen to sign his name and striking matches to light his traveling companions' cigarettes. As he explains how he lost his hands, he shows no resentment or self-pity: "They took care of me fine. They trained me to use these things. I can dial telephones, I can drive a car, I can even put nickels in a jukebox. I'm alright." But he also reveals his concern that his girlfriend, Wilma (Cathy O'Donnell), won't be able to accept him with the hooks. Although they are about the same age, he says, "Wilma's only a kid. She's never seen anything like these hooks." *He* can deal with what has happened to him, but because his experiences now are so different from Wilma's, *she*, he imagines, will not. As the film goes on, we see that Homer's acceptance of his disability is, to a great extent, public bravado. In public, with strangers, he can be nonchalant and make up amusing stories about what happened to him, but with his family and Wilma—people who knew him before he lost his hands—he is clumsy, angry, and sullen. Privately, he can't believe that he can be loved, only pitied. To make this point once and for all, he challenges Wilma to help him get ready for bed. She, and finally the audience, sees him for the first time without his hooks and how helpless he is. When Homer forgives her for being shocked and disgusted and not knowing what to say, she responds, "I know what to say, Homer. I love you, and I'm never going to leave you. Never," and kisses him. Her words and her gawky, innocent, teenage sexual desire, which is emphasized by the bedroom setting, convince Homer that he is loved. He finally achieves an emotional healing to match his physical rehabilitation.

The second returning serviceman is Al Stephenson (Fredric March, in an Academy Award–winning role), a sergeant in the infantry who served in the Pacific. He seems to challenge the pattern of all the other film veterans we've discussed by being able, apparently, to pick up where he left off before the war. He hasn't been wounded, like Homer, nor does he have the recurring nightmares that haunt Fred. He returns to a sound and loving family: wife Milly (Myrna Loy), daughter Peggy (Teresa Wright), and son Rob (Michael Hall). He goes back to work at the local bank, the Cornbelt Trust Company, and is given both a promotion, to vice president in charge of small loans, and a raise. Yet his excessive drinking suggests that his readjustment is not as smooth as it appears. The problem is hinted at during a meeting with his boss, Mr. Milton (Ray Collins), who explains the reasoning behind his promotion: "Your war experience will prove invaluable to us here. See, we have many new problems, this GI Bill of Rights, for instance. It involves us in consideration of all kinds of loans to ex-servicemen. We need a man who understands the soldier's problems and, at the same time, who's well grounded in the fundamental principles of sound banking. In other words, *you*." Al, however, cannot reconcile these two parts of himself—the banker he was and the U.S. army sergeant he has become—as easily as Milton thinks. He reveals the tension in a comment to Milly as they talk about his returning to work: "Last year it was kill Japs, and this year it's make money."

His internal struggle is best seen when an ex-Seabee, Mr. Novak (Dean White), applies for a loan to buy a farm. The son of a sharecropper, Novak sees this as his chance to own land of his own. He has dreams of helping to feed a hungry world. But he has no collateral and only the vaguest understanding of what's required to take out a loan. When he senses Al's reluctance, he asserts his rights under the GI Bill, saying, "You see, Mr. Stephenson, I don't feel this is asking the bank for a handout. I feel this is my right." But the banker in Al snaps back, "Your loan would be administered through this bank, which would put up half of the $6,000 you require. Now, that involves risk for this bank, Mr. Novak." At this point, Al sees Homer, who often appears as a sort of wartime conscience for the other characters, and has a brief conversation with him. When he returns to Novak, the ex-sergeant is thoroughly in control of the banker, and Al tells him that he'll get the loan: "You look like a good risk to me." Later, when another banker, Mr. Prew (Charles Halton), complains about the loan to Milton, Al defends his decision, arguing, "You see, Mr. Milton, in the army I've had to be with men when they were stripped of everything in the way of property except what they carried around with them and inside them. I saw them being tested. Now, some of them stood up to it and some didn't. But you got so you could tell which ones you could count on. I tell you this man Novak is OK. His collateral is in his hands and his heart and his guts. It's in his right as a citizen." Milton chooses not to pursue the matter, but he reminds Al, "We have every desire to extend a helping hand to returning veterans, whenever possible, but we must all remember that this is not our money we're doling out: it belongs to our depositors. We can't gamble with it." Al's answer to Milton and his reconciliation of banker and sergeant come in a somewhat drunken speech at a dinner given by the bank to honor his wartime service:

> I want to tell you all that the reason for my success as a sergeant is due primarily to my previous training in the Cornbelt Loan and Trust Company. The knowledge I acquired in the good old bank I applied to my

problems in the infantry. For instance, one day on Okinawa, a major comes up to me, and he says, "Stephenson, you see that hill?" I said, "Yes sir, I see it." "Alright," he said, "you and your platoon will attack said hill and take it." So I said to the major, "But that operation involves considerable risk. We haven't sufficient collateral." "I'm aware of that," said the major, "but the fact remains that there's the hill, and you are the guys who are going to take it." So I said to him, "I'm sorry, major. No collateral, no hill." So we didn't take the hill. And we lost the war. . . .

I love the Cornbelt Loan and Trust Company. There are some who say that the old bank is suffering from hardening of the arteries and of the heart. I refuse to listen to such radical talk. I say that our bank is alive, it's generous, it's human. And we're going to have such a line of customers seeking *and getting* small loans that people will think we're gambling with the depositors' money. And we will be. We'll be gambling on the future of this country.

The third returning serviceman, Fred Derry, probably has the most difficult time finding his place in postwar America. Although of the three men he achieved the highest rank in the military hierarchy (he was a bombardier in the army air forces), in civilian life he is from the lowest socioeconomic bracket. His father and stepmother (Roman Bohnen and Gladys George), Wyler's camera shows us, live on the other side of the tracks—literally. One guesses that Fred had no formal education after high school, and his job before going into the service was a soda jerk at the local drugstore. Considering that Dana Andrews was thirty-seven and looked it, we can conclude that prewar Fred was not on the fast track to success. Just before he was sent overseas, Fred married a girl he met while training in Texas, Marie (Virginia Mayo), who subsequently moved to Boone City, but she knows Fred only as an officer. During the plane ride home, Fred confides to Al his dream for a new life, a dream similar to Jefferson Jones's in *Christmas in Connecticut* and Alvin York's: "All I want's a good job, with a mild future, and a little house big enough for me and my wife." Al responds, "Well, I'd say that's not too much to ask," but, as the film shows us, it is.

Fred finds that his officer's uniform and his wartime experience carry little weight when he's looking for a job. This is made clear in his interview with Mr. Thorpe (Howland Chamberlain), the new manager of the drugstore where he used to work:

THORPE: What are your qualifications, your experience?

FRED: Two years behind a soda fountain and three years behind a Norden bombsight.

THORPE: Yes. But while in the army, did you have any experience in procurement?

FRED: No.

THORPE: Purchasing or supplies? Materials?

FRED: No, I didn't do any of that. I just dropped bombs.

THORPE: Did you do any personnel work?

FRED: No.

THORPE: But as an officer you surely had to act in an executive capacity. You had to command men, be responsible for their morale.

FRED: No, I was only responsible for getting the bombs on the target. I didn't command anybody.

THORPE: I see. I'm sure that work required great skill, but unfortunately, we've no opportunities for that with Midway Drugs.

Thorpe offers Fred the position of assistant floor manager, with soda fountain duties, but Fred rejects this out of hand. As the weeks pass, however, his bankroll disappears, and no other jobs present themselves. Finally he swallows his pride and becomes Boone City's oldest soda jerk. His dream of a good job seems to have been only a dream.

Similarly, his dream of a happy home with his wife turns out to have been a fantasy. While Fred was away, Marie worked at a nightclub and apparently had a very good time. For her, the war years were a party, and she doesn't see why the party has to end. She resists all of Fred's efforts to put the war behind them and begin a domestic life: she complains when he wants to stop wearing his officer's uniform; she pouts when he wants to have dinner at home; when Fred's drugstore income can't support a wild nightlife, she takes up with other men and goes back to her nightclub job. From Marie's perspective, during the war she had a job, was independent, and lived as she liked, and she sees no reason to give that up to become dependent on and subservient to a man whom she's rapidly coming to see as a loser. On his side, Fred begins to see that life with Marie won't be the loving, domestic relationship he dreamed of, and he becomes more and more attracted to Al's daughter, Peggy. Though younger than Marie, Peggy is more emotionally mature, and her job at a local hospital marks her nurturing, caring, supportive personality. She seems to represent for Fred both his domestic dream and the perpetual unavailability of that dream.

After an encounter with Al, Fred ends his relationship with Peggy; soon after this, Marie leaves him (her parting shot: "You'll get a good job someplace else. There are drugstores *everywhere*"), and he resolves to leave Boone City and start again elsewhere.

While waiting for a flight out, Fred wanders to the part of the airfield where hundreds of B-17s wait to be junked. In the film's cinematic climax, we follow him through the piles of plane parts and watch him climb up into a bomber and sit in his old bombardier's position, the one place in his life he has ever fit, had a clear purpose, and been successful. Like the B-17s, he's of no use to society now that the war's over, and like them, there's nothing to do with him but discard him. At this low point, he's interrupted by the foreman (Al Bridge) of the crew disassembling the planes, who explains that they're being turned into material to build prefabricated houses. Desperate, Fred talks his way into a job with the salvage men and, like Al, finds his place with those building the new America.

That Homer ends up marrying Wilma and that Al and Fred, in different ways, commit themselves to building America suggest a faith in the country's future that seems strikingly lacking among the characters who didn't go overseas. Among them, pessimism reigns. Rob Stephenson reports that his high school physics teacher lectures "that we've reached the point where the whole human race has either got to find a way to live together or else—." Wilma's father (Don Beddoe) anticipates bad economic times and drones, "Next year, in my opinion, we'll see widespread depression and unemployment." Homer's Uncle Butch (Hoagy Carmichael) reassures Homer on his first night home that his family and everything else will settle down, "unless we have another war. Then none of us have to worry because we'll all be blown to bits the first day." Milton lectures Al about the uncertain economic situation, ruinous taxes, and the complications presented by the GI Bill. In the film's most blatant example, an Axis sympathizer (Ray Teal), reading a newspaper headlined "Senator Warns of New War," accosts Homer as he eats a sundae at Fred's soda fountain, telling him that he lost his hands in a sucker's war: "We let ourselves get sold down the river. We were pushed into war. . . . The Germans and the Japs had nothing against us. They just wanted to fight them Limeys and them Reds. And they would have whipped them too, if we didn't get deceived into it by a bunch of radicals in Washington. . . . We fought the wrong people, that's all." It's against this background of gloom and doom that Homer's marriage, Al's speech to the bankers, and Fred's decision to go into salvaging seem so important: they are all commitments to building the future. Perhaps without even being conscious of it, the three veterans have a vision of the possibility of America that many of the other characters, the ones who didn't serve, seem to have lost. Interestingly, though, the film doesn't present the triumph of this vision without qualification: after his speech, Al is aware that the next time there's a questionable loan, he'll have to fight the same battle all over again; Fred tells Peggy as he embraces her at the end of the film that their life will be a struggle. The film leaves us with the traditionally order-restoring ritual of marriage, but the social conflict between the visionaries and the pessimists, the builders and the naysayers, is left unresolved.

The two themes developed in homecoming movies made and released at the war's end and immediately thereafter—civilian anxiety over how ex-servicemen will fit into society and the ex-servicemen's responsibility to help build a new postwar America—continued to appear in films released in subsequent years. Some films used the returning veterans' situation for comedy or pathos. In *Dear Ruth* (1947), for example, returned soldier William Holden tries to woo the woman he thinks he was corresponding with during the war, only to find out that the letters were written by her little sister. *Apartment for Peggy* (1948) focuses on the difficulties faced by married veteran William Holden (again) as he attends college under the GI Bill. Many films from this period, however, exaggerate the anxiety over the returning serviceman; that is, the ex-serviceman is presented as a threat to a well-ordered civilian society. This anxiety is revealed as early as *The Thin Man Goes Home* (1944), in which a murder weapon is revealed to be a serviceman's souvenir from the Pacific. One is reminded of how Arthur Conan Doyle's Sherlock Holmes mysteries reflected Britain's anxieties over its colonial holdings; Doyle's murders are often committed via exotic animals, poisons, or weapons brought back to England from the far-flung reaches of the British Empire.

In other postwar movies, the ex-serviceman himself is the threat. In *The Blue Dahlia* (1946) veteran navy flier William Bendix, who suffered a head injury during the war, responds to loud music with violent rages and is suspected of murdering Alan Ladd's unfaithful wife. In *High Wall* (1947) former bomber pilot Robert Taylor, who (you guessed it) suffered a head injury during the war, is accused of murdering (right again) his unfaithful wife. He's eventually exonerated, but the other characters—police and psychiatrists and even Taylor himself—automatically assume he's guilty because of his wounded-veteran status. As an aside, both these films also deal with the serviceman's anxiety over an unfaithful wife or girlfriend, something that films made during the war rarely addressed. In *Act of Violence* (1949) crippled veteran Robert Ryan monomaniacally stalks Van Heflin, who he thinks betrayed him and other POWs. In all these films the serviceman's wartime accomplishments are downplayed or dismissed, and the threat he poses to society is emphasized. Earlier films examined how the war changed men—those who returned were not the same men who had left—but here that change is so extreme and the danger so great that reintegration into society is no longer an issue: the crazy returned veteran must be put away in prison, hospitalized, or killed.

The flip side of this theme is the nature of the society that returning veterans come home to and how they can help improve it. In the years after the war—coincident with the rise of film noir and its pessimistic, cynical tone—films about postwar American society became increasingly dark. Returned veterans find corruption and evil at the heart of America's social system, every bit as bad as the forces they were fighting overseas during the war. These veterans find out that the war isn't really over; there are still battles to be fought at home. In *Crossfire* (1947) sergeant Robert Mitchum collaborates with the police to catch an anti-Semitic soldier, Robert Ryan, who murdered civilian Sam Levene. In *Dead Reckoning* (1947) paratrooper Humphrey Bogart, trying to track down a buddy who's absent from a ceremony where he's supposed to receive the Medal of Honor, finds organized crime, murder, and blackmail; the source of this evil is a woman, Lizabeth Scott, who appears to be an innocent victim. In *All My Sons* (1948), based on Arthur Miller's play, defense manufacturer Edward G. Robinson's pilot son kills himself when he learns that his father knowingly sold defective airplane parts to the government. In *Key Largo* (1948) ex–army major Humphrey Bogart, visiting a dead buddy's family, stumbles onto an organized-crime plot to smuggle counterfeit money into the United States. As late as *Bad Day at Black Rock* (1955), one-armed veteran Spencer Tracy uncovers the prejudice-inspired killing of a Japanese farmer in a desert town under the dictatorial control of rancher Robert Ryan. The America of these films is one of rotted social institutions, far-reaching criminal organizations, selfish and corrupt industry, debilitating prejudice, and long-dead innocence. The servicemen and veterans here are war-weary and take up their new battles not with the enthusiasm of Fred Derry and Al Stephenson but with a Sisyphean sense of exhaustion. The war is not over, nor is it likely ever to be.

This idea of the war not being over is central to what we're calling the postwar international films. These films, most of them set in Europe during or just after the war, can be categorized in two ways: first, those films that argue that, even though the war is over, Nazism is not dead and is still a threat to the United States; and second, those films that use World War II to address issues connected to the emerging cold war with our former ally, the Soviet Union.

Even before the war in Europe had officially ended, Hollywood was warning of a continued Nazi threat. *The Master Race* (1944) projects forward to the end of the war in Europe and shows us specially trained German officers entering the civilian population of displaced persons in order to undermine the Allies' attempts to rebuild. In March 1945 Warner Bros. released *Hotel Berlin*, a revamped wartime version of *Grand Hotel* (1932). Here a variety of Nazis, civilians, resistance fighters, and officers and soldiers on leave are the clientele of the titular hotel as Berlin prepares to fall to the advancing Allied troops. In one subplot several Nazis prepare to be smuggled into the United States by submarine to surreptitiously carry out Hitler's plan for global conquest. As their leader, Henry Daniell, explains, "This time we shall be anti-Nazis, poor refugees who escaped from Germany. . . . Americans forgive and forget easily. But we must spread rumors and create dissension and distrust. They will not remain united for long." As the film ends, the men head into the city, a spectacular air raid going on, to begin their journey. The film is pointedly ambiguous: we never find out whether they're stopped or might be walking among us now. This idea is developed further in the postwar film *The Stranger* (1946). Here, Nazi Orson Welles has managed to escape to America and set himself up as a teacher at an exclusive New England prep school, where he waits until the time is right to resuscitate the cause. In a wonderful scene he reveals himself to suspicious federal agent Edward G. Robinson by casually remarking during a dinner-party conversation about the future of Germany, "But Marx wasn't a German. Marx was a Jew." In Alfred Hitchcock's *Notorious* (1946) federal agent Cary Grant enlists the aid of Ingrid Bergman, the disgraced daughter of an American Nazi agent, to go to Brazil and investigate a cell of scientists from the German chemical cartel IG Farben who are up to no good with uranium ore.

If Nazis are at work in the New World, it shouldn't surprise us to find them in Europe as well. In *A Foreign Affair* (1948), some of which was filmed on location in bombed-out Berlin, U.S. officials coerce soldier John Lund to continue his romance with cabaret singer Marlene Dietrich in order to bring her jealous, most-wanted Nazi lover out of hiding. In *Berlin Express* (also filmed on location, mostly in Frankfurt, 1948) an underground of militaristic, nationalistic Germans (interesting how *underground* now refers to the bad guys) kidnaps German diplomat Paul Lukas to prevent him from pursuing his plans for a united Germany allied with its former enemies. Something of a United Nations joins forces to rescue him: American Robert Ryan (at last, not a crazy veteran), Englishman Robert Coote, Frenchwoman Merle Oberon, and Soviet lieutenant Roman Toporow. Although the film seems to want to argue for the possibility of a peace based on an alliance of the former Allies and their reformed enemy, its plot stresses the problems that are likely to prevent such an alliance. Not only are the Americans, British, and Russians still hostile toward the Germans (amid the ruins of bombed-out Frankfurt, when an underground member speaks of their determination to build the Germany they deserve, Ryan snarls, "I think you've got that now"), but they are also antagonistic toward one another. Their moment of unity in rescuing Lukas is only a moment. At the beginning of the film, when a carrier pigeon is shot, the narrator (Paul Stewart) intones, "That's right. The dove of peace was a pigeon, a dead pigeon." With discord rife among the victors and the neo-Nazis boasting, "We are still at war," the possibilities for a lasting peace seem slim indeed.

This continued emphasis on the Nazi threat, even after the war's end, might be explained by Hollywood's reluctance to let go of a good villain, and Nazis certainly make great villains, even today. But other ideas are at work as well. These films warn against American complacency, the kind of we've-done-our-bit isolationism that marked the national mood after the First World War. These films suggest that we can't turn our back on the world, because the same conditions and activities that led to the rise of Nazism after World War I may be found in the wake of World War II. Moreover, we need to be on guard against internal threats that could lead to totalitarianism at home. In short, by stressing that the war isn't really over and that there are still enemies out there—or, more disturbingly, in our own country—these films help prepare the intellectual atmosphere for the burgeoning cold war; they prepare their audiences to think of our former ally the Soviet Union as a new foreign enemy and to fear Communist sympathizers insidiously working against America from within.

Connected with this, many of the combat-oriented films released in the years just after the war seem to use the war against Germany as a way of examining the new cold war against the Soviet Union; rather than being discussed directly, the cold war is displaced onto the familiar conventions and tropes of the World War II film. For example, two films, *O.S.S.* (1946)

and *13 Rue Madeleine* (1947), celebrate the wartime activities of the Office of Strategic Services, America's main espionage agency and the forerunner of the CIA, just as Congress and the Truman administration began debating the need for and appropriateness of continuing the office's mission in peacetime. In *O.S.S.* an officer (Joseph Creshaw) training new agents makes the case this way: "We're late—400 years. That's how long ago the other major powers started *their* O.S.S. We've only got months to build the first central intelligence agency in our history. A worldwide organization that will beat the enemy at its own game. Not *your* kind of game. You don't know each other. You're here under assumed names. But you're all average, decent Americans. Americans aren't brought up to fight the way the enemy fights. We *can* learn to become intelligence agents and saboteurs if we have to, but we're too sentimental, too trusting, too easygoing, what's worse, too self-centered." A British liaison officer (Gavin Muir) adds, "Forget everything you've ever been told about fair play and sportsmanship. Forget everything except your country's fighting for its life." With this, "America the Beautiful" begins playing on the soundtrack. This scene works masterfully: it compliments Americans on their inherent decency and then insists on the necessity of throwing over that decency to survive in a nasty world. The "enemy" here, in terms of the film's plot, is Nazi Germany, but in the unspoken terms of its postwar context it is Soviet Russia.

Another kind of displacement is at work in two other films, *Command Decision* (1948) and *Twelve O'Clock High* (1949). The focus of both these films is a character study of the commanders (Clark Gable and Gregory Peck, respectively) responsible for planning missions in the early months of the U.S. bombing war against Germany. They struggle with balancing the necessary sacrifice of men and planes against the damage inflicted on the enemy. But along with the character study is a celebration of the efficacy of the U.S. bombing strategy: it's sad that men were lost, but through our successful high-altitude bombing of enemy targets, we were able to bring Germany to its knees. (This same argument is made subtly in *A Foreign Affair* and *Berlin Express*, where on-location footage shows us up close the damage the American and British air forces were able to inflict.) This argument, however, is in conflict with our government's own postwar conclusions. Arthur Schlesinger Jr., a member of the postwar U.S. Strategic Bombing Survey team, reports its conclusion "that strategic bombing was considerably overrated as a decisive weapon."[2] Yet the newly independent air force (no longer a part of the army) and, more specifically, the Strategic Air Command, formed in March 1946, were given the main responsibility of defending postwar America and protecting its interests abroad, a responsibility that grew even heavier after the Soviet Union tested its first atomic bomb in 1949.[3] In one sense, *Command Decision* and *Twelve O'Clock High* work similarly to *Bombardier* (1943), in that they argue for the accuracy, efficiency, and effectiveness of high-altitude bombing. They're using an idea about the virtues of high-altitude bombing in World War II that the audience already accepts—thanks in part to wartime movies like *Bombardier*—but in a new postwar context. Implicitly, the film asks the audience to connect what it already accepts about airpower in the old war, whether or not those beliefs are backed up by facts, to the role of airpower in the new cold war.

That this technique of displacement can be effective is testament to how well wartime films established the fundamental narratives, characters, and images by which the American public came to know the war. Firmly established in the American unconscious, they can be used to connect what audiences already believe about World War II to other conflicts and other situations. This displacement can be used in two ways. The first, as we saw earlier, is to place World War II narratives and narrative techniques in a more contemporary context and encourage the audience to view this new context through the frame provided by what they know about World War II. This method has probably become less effective over time. Although President Nixon supposedly ordered the invasion of Cambodia after seeing *Patton* (1970), 1960s World War II movies were not successful in persuading many people to think of the Vietnam War in terms of World War II. The second method of displacement is to apply the narrative techniques of World War II films to the narratives of other conflicts. This is most evident in movies about the Korean War—*I Want You* (1951), *Battle Circus* (1953), *The Bridges at Toko-Ri* (1954)—but it also shows up as late as *The Green Berets* (1968), John Wayne's attempt to sell the Vietnam War.

To our minds, these films are unsuccessful in trying to duplicate the effects of films made during World War II. Films made during the war were, as we've shown in this book, remarkably successful propaganda (in Edward Bernays's conception of the term), in that they contributed mightily to manipulating Americans' understanding of the war, America's place in it, our enemies, our allies, and each individual's contribution to the war effort in similar ways. But this success was also fostered by a moral imperative behind the war, inspired by the nature of fascism, the danger faced by our own country, and the worldwide threat to concepts and practices that most Americans value. This moral imperative was demonstrably lacking in later conflicts such as Korea and Vietnam, and without it, the narrative techniques and rhetorical tropes are a structure without support. World War II films' great speeches about how the future of the world hinges on this conflict are still moving and effective; the same rhetoric in *The Bridges at Toko-Ri* rings hollow.

The narratives and rhetoric of World War II will likely continue to be used by public officials, the media, and the entertainment industry to try to persuade us to think about the world in certain ways. It's important, then, for us to understand how these narratives and this rhetoric worked in their most popular and effective manifestation: the Hollywood film. This is important not only historically—that is, to understand how 1940s Americans' knowledge of the war was constructed—but also in contemporary society. Our knowledge of the past shapes (or can be used to shape for us) our understanding of the present and our expectations of the future. The better we understand where that knowledge came from—how it was constructed and transmitted—the better we can participate in the public discourse as self-aware, critically thinking members of a democratic society.

NOTES

INTRODUCTION

1. We draw here on Ernest Bormann's symbolic-convergence communication theory. See his *The Force of Fantasy*.

2. *New York Times* columnist Frank Rich opined, "If cable has taught us anything during 'War in Iraq,' it is this: battalions of anchors and high-tech correspondents can cover a war 24/7 and still tell us less about what is going on than the mere 27 predigital news hounds who accompanied the American troops in Normandy on D-Day" ("The Spoils of War Coverage," 1).

3. Lingeman, *Don't You Know There's a War On?* 177, 206.

4. Pagliarini, Letter, 11.

5. Schlesinger, *A Life in the Twentieth Century*, 146, 155.

6. Fyne, *The Hollywood Propaganda of World War II*, 5.

7. Bernays, *Propaganda*, 101, 20.

8. Tye, *The Father of Spin*, 52.

9. Bernays quoted in Tye, *The Father of Spin*, 24, 40.

10. Tye, *The Father of Spin*, 95.

11. For more on this, see Foucault's *The Order of Things*, especially chapters 7–10; Lyotard's *The Postmodern Condition;* and White's *The Content of the Form.*

12. Churchill, "Their Finest Hour," 314.

13. The Why We Fight series was produced by the War Department and directed by Frank Capra between 1942 and 1945. These seven documentaries were created to explain to those in the armed forces why it was necessary to fight and win the war. The first in the series, *Prelude to War*, was released to the general public and won the 1942 Academy Award for Best Documentary. See Capra, *The Name above the Title*, 326–43; Dick, *The Star-Spangled Screen*, 2–9; and Barsam, *Nonfiction Film*, 183–91. The other titles in the series were *The Nazis Strike* (1943), *Divide and Conquer* (1943—nominated for an Academy Award for Best Documentary), *Battle of Britain* (1943), *Battle of Russia* (1944), *Battle of China* (1944), and *War Comes to America* (1945).

14. Or, as Elmer Davis of the Office of War Information put it during congressional hearings in 1943, "We stick to the truth abroad as well as at home. We tell a true story to every area but to each one we tell the kind of story that will best suit our interests" (quoted in Bishop, "An American Voice," 34).

15. Harmetz, *Round Up the Usual Suspects*, xiii.

16. Harmetz, *Round Up the Usual Suspects*, 56.

17. Harmetz, *Round Up the Usual Suspects*, 258–59.

18. Koppes and Black, *Hollywood Goes to War*, 21; Dorothy B. Jones, "The Hollywood War Film," 13.

19. Koppes and Black, *Hollywood Goes to War*, 3.

20. Hampton, *History of the American Film Industry*, 299; Production Code quoted in Vizzard, *See No Evil*, 367; Hays quoted in Wiley and Bona, *Inside Oscar*, 25. See Vizzard, 366–81, for the complete Motion Picture Production Code that was formally adopted by the Association of Motion Picture Producers, Inc. (California) and the Motion Picture Association of America, Inc. (New York) in March 1930. The Code was revised several times and was eventually replaced by a film rating system in the 1960s.

21. Production Code quoted in Vizzard, *See No Evil*, 367.

22. Roeder, *The Censored War*, 20; Fussell, *Wartime*, 191–92.

23. Joint Army and Navy Public Relations Committee quoted in Roeder, *The Censored War*, 8; BPR memo quoted in Roeder, 20; Koppes and Black, *Hollywood Goes to War*, 72–80; Dick, *The Star-Spangled Screen*, 127–28.

24. Koppes and Black, *Hollywood Goes to War*, 119; Roeder, *The Censored War*, 20; Friedrich, *City of Nets*, 233.

25. See Bishop and Mackay, "The Federal Government Reports on Defense," for a discussion of the genesis of the Office of War Information (OWI). Its forerunner was the National Emergency Council (NEC), which was formed by President Roosevelt as a supercabinet to coordinate government agencies fighting the Depression. The NEC was replaced in September 1939 by the Office of Government Reports, with Lowell Mellett as director. However, other agencies were also distributing government information. The Division of Information, for example, "furnished idea sheets, mat services, a weekly magazine, posters, pamphlets, leaflets, placards, radio programs from spot announcements to quizzes and dramas, movies and coordinated campaigns" (Bishop and Mackay, 7). Eventually, because of numerous agencies overlapping in terms of public relations and propaganda, Roosevelt signed the order to create the Office of War Information in June 1942, with Elmer Davis, a novelist and short-story writer as well as a distinguished radio commentator for CBS, as its first director. Among the agencies contained under this office were the Office of Facts and Figures of the Office of Emergency Management, directed by poet and librarian of Congress Archibald MacLeish; the Division of Information of the Office of Emergency Management, headed by Robert Horton of Scripps-Howard; the Office of Civilian Defense, headed by Fiorello H. La Guardia; and the Foreign Information Service, directed by playwright Robert E. Sherwood. The Foreign Information Service became the Overseas Branch of the OWI but had problems of control, such as, "1) setting unified objectives and 2) physically controlling output, whether film, radio, publications or news service, to see that each item contributed to OWI objectives" (Bishop, "An American Voice," 29).

26. Braverman, *To Hasten the Homecoming*, 139; Jacobs, "World War II and the

American Film," 10; *Government Information Manual for the Motion Picture Industry* quoted in Koppes and Black, *Hollywood Goes to War*, 66–67, and Lingeman, *Don't You Know There's a War On?* 191.

27. Jones, "The Hollywood War Film," 2–3.

28. Letter quoted in Friedrich, *City of Nets*, 211.

29. See Koppes and Black, *Hollywood Goes to War*, 113–41, for a detailed description of the increase in power of the Overseas Branch of the OWI.

1. BEFORE PEARL HARBOR

1. Ketchum, *The Borrowed Years*, 224; Chadwin, *The Hawks of World War II*, 31; FDR quoted in Goodwin, *No Ordinary Time*, 187; Koppes and Black, *Hollywood Goes to War*, 19.

2. Ketchum, *The Borrowed Years*, 511; Doenecke, *The Battle against Intervention*, 37.

3. Rosten, *Hollywood*, 140, 162.

4. Nye quoted in Cole, *Senator Gerald P. Nye*, 186, and Woll, *The Hollywood Musical Goes to War*, 4. See Shull and Wilt for a list of movies mentioned by Nye and other anti-interventionists as being pro-war (*Hollywood War Films*, 411). The list includes *Escape* (1940), *Flight Command* (1940), *Foreign Correspondent* (1940), *The Great Dictator* (1940), *Man Hunt* (1941), *The Man I Married* (1940), *The Mortal Storm* (1940), *Mystery Sea Raider* (1940), and *Sergeant York* (1941).

5. Nye quoted in Koppes and Black, *Hollywood Goes to War*, 41; Lindbergh quoted in Dear and Foot, *The Oxford Companion to World War II*, 30; Warner quoted in Woll, *The Hollywood Musical Goes to War*, 7; Rosten, *Hollywood*, 78.

6. Production Code quoted in Vizzard, *See No Evil*, 370; Friedrich, *City of Nets*, 50; *Hollywood Reporter* quoted in Shindler, *Hollywood Goes to War*, 1; Koppes and Black, *Hollywood Goes to War*, 39. In surveying American films made between 1937 and 1941 by nine studios—Columbia, MGM, Monogram, Paramount, RKO, Twentieth Century–Fox, United Artists, Universal, and Warner Bros.—we found that of approximately 1,956 films, only about 6.2 percent were connected at all with world conflict. Counted were films set in China or somewhere in Europe, including Spain and dealing with the Spanish civil war; those that focused, however loosely, on fascism; those that seemed to show the might of the U.S. military; and general spy films. The number of films connected to war more than doubled between 1940 and 1941, but the percentage was still modest: 5.35 percent in 1940 and 11.8 percent in 1941. The Hays Office contended that in 1940 about 5 percent of American films were connected to political events (Koppes and Black, 20). Shull and Wilt have similar figures for war-related films from the 1937–1941 period, but they also discuss "discernable biases" and "topical references" as contributing to the overall "slide towards belligerency" (*Hollywood War Films*, 11); see part 1 of their book for examples and discussion.

7. See Glancy, *When Hollywood Loved Britain*, for a detailed discussion of Hollywood films that focus on British themes. He notes that in addition to the sympathy

of Anglophiles for beleaguered Britain, "'British' films drew consistently high earnings in the domestic market, but they also earned exceptionally high foreign grosses, and the additional foreign revenue often resulted in substantial profits" (68).

8. Wylie, *Keeper of the Flame*, 22.

9. See Karr, "The Dark Truth and the Silver Screen," for a more detailed discussion of Nazi-sponsored organizations, youth camps, and activities in the United States. In addition, a 1939 mystery novel, *Crooked Shadow* by Kurt Steel, focuses on a Nazi youth camp on Long Island.

10. Karr, "The Dark Truth and the Silver Screen," 90.

11. Film historian Bernard F. Dick, in *The Star-Spangled Screen*, discusses the background to these Spanish civil war films and the process by which they became politically neutered (15–20). He concludes, " For the studios the question was not 'What are the characters' politics?' but 'Will the picture play Peoria?'" (16).

12. *Variety* quoted in Karr, "The Dark Truth and the Silver Screen," 90.

13. Gilbert, *The First World War*, 475; Wood, *Howard Hawks*, 165.

14. Hitchcock quoted in Truffaut, *Hitchcock*, 98. In the Truffaut interviews, when Hitchcock talks about his films in relation to the war, it is to point out how they were criticized for hurting the war effort. For example, the U.S. Navy complained that *Saboteur* implied that the *Normandie* had been sabotaged (106), and reviewers and columnists such as Dorothy Thompson complained that *Lifeboat* made the German character seem too superior to the characters from the Allied countries (113). Hitchcock explains his decision to return to England to make two propaganda shorts by saying, "I felt the need to make a little contribution to the war effort. . . . I knew that if I did nothing I'd regret it for the rest of my life" (115); this suggests that he didn't consider his Hollywood films much of a contribution.

15. Harris and Lasky, *The Films of Alfred Hitchcock*, 95.

16. In *Espionage Agent* spies also use the cover of a peace organization.

17. There's a similar sort of Anglo-American alliance between British and American intelligence services in the 1941 films *International Lady* and *Man at Large*.

18. A newspaper reporter's awakening to represent America's learning why it needs to fight was a frequently used trope. For examples, see Claudette Colbert in *Arise, My Love* (1940), Don Ameche in *Confirm or Deny* (1941), and Robert Young in *Journey for Margaret* (1942).

19. McGilligan, *Fritz Lang*, 256–58.

20. The creators of *Man Hunt* were fairly faithful to their source but made the film more explicitly political than the novel. *Rogue Male* focuses on the main character's attempts to go it alone as the prey in a big-game hunt. The film specifies that Hitler is the intended target, while the novel mentions only the "head of a nation" (Household, 23) that the protagonist is stalking. The protagonist contends for most of the book that he was stalking for sport, but finally, under intense stress, he admits in his diary that he was trying to kill because a woman he loved had been taken and shot for "Reasons of state" (Household, 224).

21. Humphries, *Fritz Lang*, 81–85.

22. Maland, *Chaplin and American Culture*, 164, 166.

23. Clausius, *The Gentleman Is a Tramp*, 129.

24. Flom, *Chaplin in the Sound Era*, 131.

25. See Flom, *Chaplin in the Sound Era*, 142–44, for a sample of these reactions.

26. Maland, *Chaplin and American Culture*, 175–76; Milton, *Tramp*, 379 (Milton's muckraking and mean-spirited biography of Chaplin tries to make the case that at this point in his career Chaplin's films were essentially reporting the Communist Party line); Smith, *Chaplin*, 115.

2. THE WAR IN THE PACIFIC

1. Weinberg, *A World at Arms*, 260; Dear and Foot, *The Oxford Companion to World War II*, 855. Weinberg points out that these materiel losses were less significant than they seemed: most of the ships were repaired and returned to duty. More important, the Japanese had miscalculated the U.S. response to a surprise attack, inadvertently inspiring the United States to refuse to negotiate anything short of unconditional surrender (261–62).

2. Weinberg, *A World at Arms*, 312–14.

3. Weinberg, *A World at Arms*, 338.

4. Weinberg, *A World at Arms*, 344.

5. Young, "Captain Ed Dyess," 16.

6. Pentagon spokesman quoted in Schultz, *The Doolittle Raid*, 204–5.

7. Schultz, *The Doolittle Raid*, 277.

8. British resentment at the Yanks' claiming credit for British accomplishments has survived the war. It arose again with regard to *U-571* (2000), which depicts Americans capturing the German Enigma encryption machine, thus overlooking years of British code-breaking work.

9. They also, of course, define the Japanese as an enemy; we look closely at this in chapter 3.

10. This is based on an actual incident. A group of B-17s was scheduled to land at Hickam Field on Honolulu on Sunday morning, December 7. The planes arrived, unarmed and nearly out of fuel, and were attacked by both Japanese fighters and U.S. antiaircraft batteries but managed to land safely.

11. Dick, in *The Star-Spangled Screen* (206), explains the criticism Warner Bros. received from the press and the OWI over this film's unsubstantiated claim of fifth columnists working in Hawaii. *December 7th*, John Ford and Gregg Toland's strange documentary about the U.S. entry into the war (edited version released in 1943; complete version finally released in 1991), similarly establishes the threat posed by Hawaii's Japanese population but then belatedly admits that these people are, for the most part, loyal.

12. This is a fictionalization; many marines survived and were taken prisoner (Wukovits, "The Fight for Wake," 46–47). But the image of the marines fighting to the last man makes the connection to past American desperate stands that much stronger.

13. The liberation of Cabanatuan is the subject of Hampton Sides's *Ghost Sol-*

diers. Interestingly, Sides presents this as an untold story, but *Back to Bataan* told it only months after it happened.

14. See Jewell and Harbin, *The RKO Story*, 184. The rationing of some goods and materials began before the United States entered the war. RKO apparently made a deal with the army air forces for a larger share of some rationed materials in exchange for a celebratory film. Some of the delays in the production of *Bombardier* were due to the army's changing its mind about the nature of the film.

15. Schultz writes, "They learned that the highly secret Norden bombsight was not accurate for a low-altitude mission. A simpler bombsight, dubbed the 'Mark Twain,' was installed in each B-25. It had been designed by Captain [C. Ross] Greening and built at Elgin [Field] for a cost of twenty cents each. Not only was the new sight accurate, it was also easy to use" (*The Doolittle Raid*, 66).

16. Sherman, "The Secret Weapon," discusses the history of the Norden bombsight and the myths about its accuracy.

17. See Lawson, *Thirty Seconds over Tokyo*, 38. In the film version of *Thirty Seconds over Tokyo*, Ted Lawson's character (Van Johnson) also speaks of a submarine in Tokyo Bay radioing back the positions of barrage balloons, an interesting case of fictional narrative continuity between films.

18. This seems to have been based on an actual incident. On September 11, 1942, aboard the submarine *Seadragon*, pharmacist's mate Wheeler Lipes performed an emergency appendectomy on sailor Darrell Dean Rector, using makeshift cutlery. Reporter George Weller's account of the operation in the *Chicago Daily News* won a Pulitzer Prize (Goldstein, "George Weller").

19. Morella, Epstein, and Griggs, *The Films of World War II*, 208.

20. This is apparently based on an incident from the Battle of the Coral Sea. During the attack on and sinking of the Japanese aircraft carrier *Shoho*, the U.S. planes' communications were "patched into the American ships' public address systems so that the crews could identify with the action going on 184 miles to the northwest" (Deac, "Battle beyond the Horizon," 47).

21. Costello, *The Pacific War*, 358.

3. OUR ENEMIES

1. Royko quoted in Terkel, *"The Good War,"* 138.

2. Barnes quoted in Morella, Epstein, and Griggs, *The Films of World War II*, 36.

3. Interestingly, in the novel Martin is a Communist; in the film he takes umbrage at being called a Red, a change that enhances his Americanness.

4. See Shirer, *The Rise and Fall of the Third Reich*, 234–40, for the Nazi co-optation of churches, including replacing the Bible with *Mein Kampf* as the sole book on the altar and removing the cross "from all churches, cathedrals and chapels . . . superseded by the only unconquerable symbol, the swastika" (240). The 1943 film *First Comes Courage* depicts a surreal Nazi wedding in which all the religious objects and symbols are replaced with Nazi paraphernalia.

5. Shull and Wilt, *Hollywood War Films*, 51.

6. Berlin notes the similar characterizations of the two detectives ("Mr. Moto," 68).

7. Moeller, "Pictures of the Enemy," 30–32.

8. Roosevelt, *The Public Papers and Addresses*, 10:514–15.

9. Cooper, *The Deerslayer*, 232.

10. Shull and Wilt, *Hollywood War Films*, 249.

4. Our Fighting Allies

1. The film's credits call this character Uncle Wilbur, but on the soundtrack he's distinctly called Wilfrid.

2. At least the film acknowledges that the British and Americans have been at war with each other. *War Comes to America* (1945), the final installment of the Why We Fight series, manages to talk its audience through the American Revolution without ever mentioning whom the colonists were rebelling against.

3. Churchill, Broadcast, 199.

4. Vasey, *The World According to Hollywood*, 242, 54; Shull and Wilt, *Hollywood War Films*, 52.

5. Natalia is probably based on Ludmilla Pavlichenko, a sniper who killed 311 Germans and visited the United States in 1942 (Gallico, "What We Talked About," 34). The trope of the Russian superwoman is present in less exaggerated form in many other films, often in passing. In *Corvette K-225* (1943), a celebration of the Canadian navy, the Russian merchant ship in the convoy is captained by a Russian woman. At the end of *Action in the North Atlantic* (1943) an American merchant ship arriving in Murmansk is greeted by female Russian dockworkers.

6. *Newsweek* quoted in Morella, Epstein, and Griggs, *The Films of World War II*, 176.

7. In *Counter-Attack* (1945) the Soviets secretly build a bridge across a river at night, keeping it just below the surface of the water. When their counterattack begins, their tanks seem to be miraculously rolling across the water.

8. Before Germany's June 1941 invasion of the Soviet Union, American pop culture sometimes equated Nazi Germany and Communist Russia. A 1940 comic-book-style exposé, *Hitler and Stalin: The Murder Men and Their Plot to Rape the World*, supposedly written anonymously by an American foreign correspondent, graphically details Nazi and Soviet crimes and "the detailed plans by which Adolf Hitler and Josef Stalin believe they will shove democracy from the face of the earth and establish in its place a world dictatorship" (3). The 1940 rerelease of Warner Bros.' *Confessions of a Nazi Spy* mentions the Soviet invasion of Finland as being the same as Nazi aggression.

9. In his book the real Davies notes his increasing skepticism about the trials as they continued. .

10. Dear and Foot discuss how recently disclosed documents explode the buying-time theory of the nonaggresssion treaty. See *The Oxford Companion to World War II*, 780–82.

11. Neve, *Film and Politics in America*, 71. See Koppes and Black, *Hollywood Goes*

to War, 188–209, for background on bringing *Mission to Moscow* to the screen and the critical reaction to it.

12. See Costello, *The Pacific War*, 237 and passim, for an account of Stilwell's frustrations in trying to get the Chinese to fight.

13. Dick, *The Star-Spangled Screen*, 103.

14. Among the films that show German–Japanese collaboration in the Far East are *Escape from Hong Kong* (1942), *Lure of the Islands* (1942), *Remember Pearl Harbor!* (1942), *Secret Agent of Japan* (1942), *Submarine Alert* (1943), and *Two-Man Submarine* (1944). *Wings over the Pacific* (1943) goes so far as to feature a dogfight between an American and a German over a Pacific island. Even more unintentionally hilarious is a German colonel's (John Wosper) explanation of the plan to unite Germany and Japan after the defeat of the Soviet Union in *Miss V from Moscow* (1942): "Our submarines will presently shut off all American supplies to Russia, and this timed to coincide with our grand offensive on the east to join our yellow Aryan brothers."

15. Another film, *Spy Ship* (1942), presents an America First–type group as being led by traitors in the employ of Germany and Japan.

16. *China Sky* (1945), based on another novel by Pearl S. Buck, mentions the transport and rebuilding of factories in the mountains as well. This detail is also celebrated in *Battle of China* (1944), the sixth entry in the Why We Fight series.

5. Our Occupied Allies

1. Dear and Foot, *The Oxford Companion to World War II*, 823.

2. Burrin, *France under the Germans*, 44.

3. Roosevelt, *The Public Papers and Addresses*, 11:377–78. Roosevelt's speech is used as a voice-over at the end of *Edge of Darkness*.

4. Morella, Epstein, and Griggs, *The Films of World War II*, 111–12.

5. Stokker confirms the antagonism toward such women, called *tyskertös* ("German whore"). She writes, "Even more despised than the Nazis, their leaders, and the occupying soldiers were the Norwegian women who befriended them" (*Folklore Fights the Nazis*, 57).

6. Burrin, *France under the Germans*, 28; Gide quoted in Burrin, 26; Peschanski et al., *Collaboration and Resistance*, 47, 173, 56; Burrin, 80. Marcel Ophüls's 1969 documentary *The Sorrow and the Pity* explores the difficult topic of collaboration during the German occupation of France. Many of the people Ophüls interviews reveal that they were more collaborative than they later wanted to admit.

7. Shull and Wilt, *Hollywood War Films*, 212.

8. Kennedy, *Freedom from Fear*, 581. Also, Cook maintains that Roosevelt disliked de Gaulle so much that he preferred "to continue an unnecessarily sympathetic and friendly diplomatic relationship with . . . the defeated, collaborationist, pro-Nazi Vichy government" ("'Send him back to Algiers,'" 35). See also Weinberg, *A World at Arms*, 728, and Stafford, *Roosevelt and Churchill*, 256, on Roosevelt's antipathy to de Gaulle.

9. The Office of War Information prohibited Warner Bros. from showing the film in North Africa. Robert Riskin, screenwriter of such classics as *Meet John Doe* and *It Happened One Night*, became head of the motion-picture division of the Overseas Branch of the OWI. Although he was told that the North African situation was under control by January 1943, several Frenchmen who had seen the film advised him that the picture might cause resentment there (Harmetz, *Round Up the Usual Suspects*, 284–86).

10. Weinberg, *A World at Arms*, 432–36.

11. A play on Joan of Arc's name appears in a Judy Canova comedy *Joan of Ozark*. This 1942 Republic film features Canova as a sharp-shooting mountain girl who foils Axis agents and scores a musical success singing "The Lady from Lockheed." Her heroism is most evident at the end of the film when she flies up to retrieve an unbroken champagne bottle from a newly christened bomber and then drops the bottle, which has been filled with explosives by enemy agents, on a conveniently passing Japanese submarine.

6. American Men and Women

1. LaSalle, *Dangerous Men*, 113.

2. LaSalle, *Dangerous Men*, 106.

3. Basinger, *A Woman's View*, 6, 14–15.

4. LaSalle, *Dangerous Men*, 45, 57.

5. Litoff and Smith, *We're in This War, Too*, 29, 81; Braverman, *To Hasten the Homecoming*, 22; Smith quoted in Braverman, 22.

6. The theme of ad hoc families being formed to fill the gaps in traditional families disrupted by the war occurs in many films. In both *The Human Comedy* (1943) and *Happy Land* (1943) a family loses a son in action, but at the end a pal of the dead son with no family of his own arrives on the scene and is welcomed into the family as a kind of replacement. In *Sunday Dinner for a Soldier* (1944) a poor grandfather and his four grandchildren invite a sergeant (John Hodiak) from a nearby airfield to dinner. As the day progresses, the sergeant, who ran away from his own broken home when he was fifteen, becomes like a member of the family. The film ends with him signing over his allotment check to them and bragging to the other men in the bomber command about his new family. Frequently the ad hoc family is created through formal or informal adoption. In *Journey for Margaret* (1942) the pregnant wife of an American war correspondent assigned to London (Laraine Day and Robert Young) is wounded in a bombing raid, miscarries, and is left unable to have children. While working on a story, the correspondent meets two British war orphans (Margaret O'Brien and William Severn) traumatized by the loss of their parents in the bombing. By adopting the children and bringing them to America, the couple begins a healing process for the children and themselves. In *The Pied Piper* (1942) a curmudgeonly British gentleman (Monty Woolley) is on vacation in the south of France when the war breaks out. As he makes his way across France trying to get home, he at first unwillingly, then paternally (or perhaps

grand-paternally), picks up orphans from a number of nations—even one from Germany—and manages to get them to England. In *The Amazing Mrs. Holliday* (1943) missionary Ruth Kirke (Deanna Durbin) brings eight orphans—American, European, and Asian—to the United States from China, but in order to get them into the country, she pretends to be the widow of an elderly and wealthy owner of a steamship line (Harry Davenport) who she thinks died when their ship was torpedoed. Ruth says of the children, "we're not really related, but they're just like a family." A new nontraditional family is formed when the elderly owner shows up alive, gives his approval to the marriage of Ruth and his son, and adopts the children himself. In *Tish* (1942) a small-town girl (Susan Peters) goes to Canada to join the man she's secretly married to, who is ferrying bombers to England, but she dies in childbirth after finding out that he's missing in action. Spinster Tish (Marjorie Main), who thinks the child is illegitimate, claims that she's the child's mother to protect the girl's reputation and her nephew, whom she wrongly suspects is the father. Her two spinster friends (Zasu Pitts and Aline MacMahon) join her in the deception and in caring for the baby. Finally, the pilot (Richard Quine) shows up alive, clears up the confusion, and, before he heads off to join the army, insists that Tish be the child's mother while he is away. Underlining the unusual nature of the family being formed here, Tish says at one point, "This is going to be the only baby in the world with three mothers." All these films expand the possible compositions of the family unit, and in several of them the role of head of the family is filled untraditionally: by an old man, by a woman, or by a community of women.

7. One of the nurses evacuated from Corregidor, Eunice Hatchitt, served as technical adviser for *So Proudly We Hail!* She called attention to those aspects of the film that she felt trivialized or misrepresented the nurses' work. In particular she was appalled by Olivia's character and the implication that the nurses did not treat Japanese patients with the same care and compassion they extended to other patients. The film was a box-office success, but the real Bataan nurses hated it and blamed Hatchitt for its misrepresentations of their experience (Norman, *We Band of Angels*, 125–29).

8. This was an odd choice by the filmmakers, since Germany didn't have any aircraft carriers (see Schuster, "The European Axis Powers"; Taylor, "Germany's Aircraft-Carrier Development"). Even Pete finds the news surprising. He says, "I never saw a German carrier, did you?"

7. HOME-FRONT ANXIETIES

1. Nevins, "How We Felt about the War," 7–8.

2. The man shortage is also treated in *Get Going* (1943), in which employee Grace McDonald pretends to be a spy to attract the attention of personnel investigator Robert Paige.

3. Pringle, "The War Agencies," 179–80.

4. Wolf and Black, "What Happened to the Younger People," 70, 76, 84.

5. In *Beautiful but Broke* (1944) Joan Davis and her all-girl band see babies left

unattended in cars outside a defense plant and interrupt the journey to their first gig to help establish a day-care center.

6. Curtis recounts the difficulty Sturges had getting the script approved by the Paramount front office, the Hays Office, and the War Department Pictorial Board. Even the Catholic League of Decency demanded changes for the film to earn a "Morally Objectionable in Part for All" rather than a "Condemned" rating (*Between Flops*, 179–81, 184).

7. Hitchcock thought Steinbeck's screenplay version of his novella "incomplete" and assigned the rewrite to MacKinley Kantor (whose book-length poem *Glory for Me* was the basis for *The Best Years of Our Lives* [1946]). Hitchcock was also displeased with this treatment and reassigned the story to Jo Swerling (Truffaut, *Hitchcock*, 113). Although Swerling gets credit for the screenplay, Hitchcock obviously was deeply involved in the final script. In a short-story version of *Lifeboat* that was published in *Collier's*, Hitchcock is listed as the author, along with Harry Sylvester, based on "an original screen story by John Steinbeck" (Hitchcock and Sylvester, "Lifeboat," 16). Steinbeck didn't like the movie and asked his agent to have Twentieth Century–Fox remove his name from the film because "the picture seems to me to be dangerous to the American war effort" (quoted in Millichap, *Steinbeck and Film*, 85).

8. Hitchcock directed two short films, *Bon Voyage* and *Aventure Malgache*, in London in 1944 for the British Ministry of Information. The films were stories about the French resistance acted by the Molière Players, a French company that had taken refuge in England (Spoto, *The Art of Alfred Hitchcock*, 508). The films were supposed to be shown in France, in areas where the Germans were losing ground, to help the French people appreciate the resistance. However, *Aventure Malgache* was never released, possibly because it showed how divided the Free French were (Truffaut, *Hitchcock*, 116).

9. Many war films show combat groups with a diverse ethnic or regional representation to stress that all were "acting together . . . against the enemy" (Jones and McClure, *Hollywood at War*, 17). There are several instances when African American characters function in this way. See, for example. Oliver Cromwell Jones (Ben Carter) in *Crash Dive* (1943), who starts the film as a mess steward and eventually risks his life to help McDonnell (James Gleason) blow up a German installation, and Wesley Epps (Kenneth Spencer) in *Bataan* (1943), who "dies as heroically as the other soldiers in the face of the overwhelmingly superior Japanese force" (Koppes and Black, *Hollywood Goes to War*, 180). In *This Is the Army* (1943) Joe Louis is asked if he feels nervous about joining the army. He replies, "I just quit worrying the day I got into uniform. All I know is I'm in Uncle Sam's Army and God's on our side."

10. In the *Collier's* short story there is even more violence on the part of the Allied characters. Mrs. Higgins rakes her fingers over Willy's face when she finds out that her baby is dead. Kovac knocks out Willy to frisk him and then finds the compass. In the scene where Willy is beaten up and thrown overboard, Alice attacks Willy first, then Joe hits him with a rabbit punch before Kovac and Rittenhouse

lunge at him. Stanley stamps on his face, Kovac twists his neck, and Connie stabs him to death with the knife used to cut off Gus's leg. There are other interesting differences between the film and the short story. In the story Willy doesn't take an active part in Gus's death. Gus announces to Willy that he's going for a swim and Willy replies, "Sure, why not, Gus." He does nothing to stop Gus and later tells Stanley, "No use waking the others, and no one will miss Gus" (Hitchcock and Sylvester, "Lifeboat," 58). Also, in the story there is no second German who tries to get on the boat. In Steinbeck's novella Joe tries to save Willy after he has been pushed overboard (Koppes and Black, *Hollywood Goes to War*, 310–11).

11. Reactions to the movie as propaganda were mixed. Bosley Crowther, in a January 23, 1944, review in the *New York Times*, states that the film "sold out the democratic ideal and elevated the Nazi 'Superman'" (quoted in Koppes and Black, *Hollywood Goes to War*, 309). Both Fyne (*The Hollywood Propaganda of World War II*, 79) and Dick (*The Star-Spangled Screen*, 206) comment on the moral ambiguity of the Allied characters' actions. Harris and Lasky see the film "as a sharp allegory of democracy's all-but-suicidal acquiescences to Hitler's bullying in the thirties and wartime forties" (*The Films of Alfred Hitchcock*, 119). François Truffaut told Hitchcock that he originally thought the film "intended to show that everyone is guilty" but later decided he was mistaken (Truffaut, *Hitchcock*, 113). Hitchcock called the film "a statement telling the democracies to put their differences aside temporarily and to gather their forces to concentrate on the common enemy, whose spirit was precisely derived from a spirit of unity and of determination" (quoted in Truffaut, *Hitchcock*, 113).

12. Among the questions asked about women workers at the beginning of the war were, "What sort of work should women do; . . . would they be willing to return to the home when the war was over; and, if no to the last, would they take a job from some returning GI?" (Lingeman, *Don't You Know There's a War On?* 159). Some books and films attempted to assure men that the traditional status quo would be restored when the soldiers returned. Toward the end of *The Gals They Left Behind*, a fictional series of wartime letters written to overseas husbands, one of the narrators writes, "We have started a strict regime of cold creaming at night, dining with lighted candles, and filling up the cracks in our hands with lotion" (Shea, *The Gals*, 112), indicating that the woman the soldier has been dreaming of will be there when he gets back. As far as Hollywood was concerned, "Popular war movies of the years 1941–1945 disclosed an ambivalence toward women's roles and status that would continue to permeate American society through the post-war era. According to these films, women could perform the usual work of men efficiently and competently, but they chose to do so only in a national emergency, for their deeper commitment was to their husbands, families, and homes" (Baker, *Images of Women in Film*, 133).

13. Fussell, *Wartime*, 268.

14. Other films show a similar disruption of entrenched power. In *A Medal for Benny* (1945) the town fathers of Pantera, California—all of them white, middle-class businessmen—are ecstatic when a local boy wins the Medal of Honor, but

they can't understand why the name is unfamiliar to them. The name they think is Benny Martin is actually Benny Martín, a troublemaking kid from the Mexican slums. Their attempts to hide this from the governor and a general representing the president backfire and end up exposing the assumptions of their politics of privilege. In *A Stranger in Town* (1943) a Supreme Court justice (Frank Morgan), vacationing incognito, joins with a young lawyer who is about to go into the service to expose and reform the corrupt power structure of a small town. And in the just-postwar *Colonel Effingham's Raid* (1945) William Eythe and a group of soldiers from a small southern city about to ship out warn the town fathers that their corrupt ways had better be cleaned up by the time they return.

15. The film was received well by contemporary critics (Curtis, *Between Flops*, 191). Koppes and Black find the "ambiguous view of military heroism" and the ending artistically unsatisfying but note that the OWI praised it as "a good picture of working democracy in America today" (*Hollywood Goes to War*, 174).

8. Postwar Films in the Postwar World

1. Other war films use war dogs to represent men going off to war. See *War Dogs* (1942), *My Pal Wolf* (1944), and *A Boy, A Girl, and a Dog* (1946).

2. Schlesinger, *A Life in the Twentieth Century*, 350–51.

3. Hollywood's postwar celebration of the air force as our protection against the Soviet threat reaches its zenith in *Strategic Air Command* (1955).

BIBLIOGRAPHY

Baker, M. Joyce. *Images of Women in Film: The War Years, 1941–1945.* Ann Arbor: UMI Research Press, 1980.

Barsam, Richard Meran. *Nonfiction Film: A Critical History.* New York: Dutton, 1973.

Basinger, Jeanine. *A Woman's View: How Hollywood Spoke to Women, 1930–1960.* New York: Knopf, 1993.

Berlin, Howard M. "Mr. Moto: A Character Sketch." *Classic Images* (Feb. 2004): 67–69.

Bernays, Edward L. *Propaganda.* New York: Horace Liveright, 1928.

Bishop, Robert L. "An American Voice: Uncertain Beginnings." In *Mysterious Silence, Lyrical Scream: Government Information in World War II. Journalism Monographs* 19 (1971): 22–39.

Bishop, Robert L., and LaMar S. Mackay. "The Federal Government Reports on Defense, 1939–1942." In *Mysterious Silence, Lyrical Scream: Government Information in World War II. Journalism Monographs* 19 (1971): 1–21.

Bormann, Ernest G. *The Force of Fantasy: Restoring the American Dream.* Carbondale: Southern Illinois UP, 1985.

Bottome, Phyllis. *The Mortal Storm.* Boston: Little, Brown, 1938.

Braverman, Jordan. *To Hasten the Homecoming: How Americans Fought World War II through the Media.* Lanham: Madison Books, 1996.

Buck, Pearl S. *Dragon Seed.* New York: John Day, 1942.

Burrin, Philippe. *France under the Germans: Collaboration and Compromise.* Trans. Janet Lloyd. New York: New Press, 1996.

Capra, Frank. *The Name above the Title.* New York: Macmillan, 1971.

Chadwin, Mark Lincoln. *The Hawks of World War II.* Chapel Hill: U of North Carolina P, 1968.

Churchill, Winston. Broadcast, London, 1 Oct. 1939. In *Never Give In! The Best of Winston Churchill's Speeches.* Ed. Winston S. Churchill. New York: Hyperion, 2003. 199–201.

———. "Their Finest Hour." In *Blood, Sweat, and Tears.* New York: Putnam's, 1941. 305–14.

Clausius, Claudia. *The Gentleman Is a Tramp: Charlie Chaplin's Comedy.* New York: Peter Lang, 1989.

Cole, Wayne S. *Senator Gerald P. Nye and American Foreign Relations.* Minneapolis: U of Minnesota P, 1962.

Cook, Don. "'Send him back to Algiers—in chains if necessary.'" *Military History Quarterly* 6.3 (1994): 34–41.

Cooper, James Fenimore. *The Deerslayer.* 1841. New York: Signet, 1980.

Costello, John. *The Pacific War: 1941–1945.* New York: Quill, 1982.

Curtis, James. *Between Flops: A Biography of Preston Sturges.* New York: Harcourt, 1982.

Davies, Joseph E. *Mission to Moscow.* 1941. Rev. ed., New York: Pocket, 1943.

Deac, Wil. "Battle beyond the Horizon." *WWII History* (May 2003): 42–49.

Dear, I. C. B., and M. R. D. Foot, eds. *The Oxford Companion to World War II.* Oxford: Oxford UP, 1995.

Dick, Bernard F. *The Star-Spangled Screen: The American World War II Film.* 1985. Lexington: UP of Kentucky, 1996.

Doenecke, Justus D. *The Battle against Intervention, 1939–1941.* Malabar: Krieger, 1997.

Droke, Maxwell. *Good-by to GI: How to Be a Successful Civilian.* New York: Abingdon-Cokesbury Press, 1945.

Fearing, Franklin. "Warriors Return: Normal or Neurotic?" *Hollywood Quarterly* 1.1 (1945): 97–109.

Flom, Eric L. *Chaplin in the Sound Era: An Analysis of the Seven Talkies.* Jefferson: McFarland, 1997.

Foucault, Michel. *The Order of Things: An Archaeology of the Human Sciences.* 1970. New York: Vintage, 1994.

Friedrich, Otto. *City of Nets: A Portrait of Hollywood in the 1940s.* New York: Harper & Row, 1986.

Fussell, Paul. *Wartime: Understanding and Behavior in the Second World War.* New York: Oxford UP, 1989.

Fyne, Robert. *The Hollywood Propaganda of World War II.* Metuchen: Scarecrow, 1994.

Gallico, Paul. "What We Talked About." In *While You Were Gone: A Report on Wartime Life in the United States.* Ed. Jack Goodman. New York: Simon & Schuster, 1946. 28–63.

Gilbert, Martin. *The First World War: A Complete History.* New York: Holt, 1994.

Glancy, H. Mark. *When Hollywood Loved Britain: The Hollywood "British" Film, 1939–45.* Manchester: Manchester UP, 1999.

Goldstein, Richard. "George Weller, 95; Won a Pulitzer Prize in '43." *New York Times,* Dec. 29, 2002, 1:34.

Goodman, Jack, ed. *While You Were Gone: A Report on Wartime Life in the United States.* New York: Simon & Schuster, 1946.

Goodwin, Doris Kearns. *No Ordinary Time: Franklin and Eleanor Roosevelt, The Home Front in World War II.* New York: Simon & Schuster, 1994.

Hampton, Benjamin B. *History of the American Film Industry from Its Beginnings to 1931.* 1931. Rev. ed., New York: Dover, 1970.

Harmetz, Aljean. *Round Up the Usual Suspects: The Making of "Casablanca"—Bogart, Bergman, and World War II.* New York: Hyperion, 1992.

Harris, Robert A., and Michael S. Lasky. *The Films of Alfred Hitchcock.* Secaucus: Citadel Press, 1976.

Hitchcock, Alfred, and Harry Sylvester. "Lifeboat." *Collier's* (Nov. 13, 1943): 16–17, 52–58.

Hitler and Stalin: The Murder Men and Their Plot to Rape the World. New York: Country Press, 1940.

Household, Geoffrey. *Rogue Male.* Boston: Little, Brown, 1939.

"How to Tell Your Friends from the Japs." *Time* (Dec. 22, 1941): 33.

Humphries, Reynold. *Fritz Lang: Genre and Representation in His American Films.* Baltimore: Johns Hopkins UP, 1989.

Jacobs, Lewis. "World War II and the American Film." *Cinema Journal* 7 (Winter 1967–1968): 1–21.

Jewell, Richard B., and Vernon Harbin. *The RKO Story.* New York: Arlington House, 1982.

Jones, Dorothy B. "The Hollywood War Film: 1942–44." *Hollywood Quarterly* 1.1 (1945): 1–19.

Jones, Ken D., and Arthur F. McClure. *Hollywood at War: The American Motion Picture and World War II.* New York: Castle, 1973.

Karr, Kathleen. "The Dark Truth and the Silver Screen: A Nazi Underground Operated in Depression America." *WWII History* (Sept. 2002): 24–29, 89–90.

Kennedy, David M. *Freedom from Fear: The American People in Depression and War, 1929–1945.* New York: Oxford UP, 1999.

Ketchum, Richard M. *The Borrowed Years, 1938–1941: America on the Way to War.* New York: Random House, 1989.

Koppes, Clayton R., and Gregory D. Black. *Hollywood Goes to War: How Politics, Profits and Propaganda Shaped World War II Movies.* Berkeley: U of California P, 1987.

LaSalle, Mick. *Dangerous Men: Pre-Code Hollywood and the Birth of the Modern Man.* New York: St. Martin's, 2002.

Lawson, Ted. W., with Robert Considine. *Thirty Seconds over Tokyo.* New York: Random House, 1943.

Lewis, Sinclair. *It Can't Happen Here.* Garden City: Doubleday, Doran, 1935.

Lingeman, Richard R. *Don't You Know There's a War On? The American Home Front 1941–1945.* New York: Putnam's, 1970.

Litoff, Judy Barrett, and David C. Smith, eds. *We're in This War, Too: World War II Letters from American Women in Uniform.* New York: Oxford UP, 1994.

Lyotard, Jean-François. *The Postmodern Condition: A Report on Knowledge.* Trans. Geoff Bennington and Brian Massumi. Minneapolis: U of Minnesota P, 1984.

Maland, Charles J. *Chaplin and American Culture: The Evolution of a Star Image.* Princeton: Princeton UP, 1989.

McGilligan, Patrick. *Fritz Lang: The Nature of the Beast.* New York: St. Martin's, 1997.

Millichap, Joseph R. *Steinbeck and Film.* New York: Ungar, 1983.

Milton, Joyce. *Tramp: The Life of Charlie Chaplin.* New York: HarperCollins, 1996.

Moeller, Susan D. "Pictures of the Enemy: Fifty Years of Images of Japan in the American Press, 1941–1992." *Journal of American Culture* 19.1 (1996): 29–42.

Morella, Joe, Edward Z. Epstein, and John Griggs. *The Films of World War II: A Pictorial History of Hollywood's War Years*. Secaucus: Citadel Press, 1973.

Neve, Brian. *Film and Politics in America: A Social Tradition*. London: Routledge, 1992.

Nevins, Allan. "How We Felt about the War." In *While You Were Gone: A Report on Wartime Life in the United States*. Ed. Jack Goodman. New York: Simon & Schuster, 1946. 3–27.

Nordhoff, Charles, and James Norman Hall. *Men without Country*. Boston: Little, Brown, 1942.

Norman, Elizabeth M. *We Band of Angels: The Untold Story of American Nurses Trapped on Bataan by the Japanese*. New York: Random House, 1999.

Pagliarini, Florence. Letter. *Films of the Golden Age* (Summer 2004): 11.

Peschanski, Denis, et al. *Collaboration and Resistance: Images of Life in Vichy France, 1940–1944*. Trans. Lory Frankel. 1988. New York: Abrams, 2000.

Pringle, Henry F. "The War Agencies." In *While You Were Gone: A Report on Wartime Life in the United States*. Ed. Jack Goodman. New York: Simon & Schuster, 1946. 165–86.

Remarque, Erich Maria. *Flotsam*. Trans. Denver Lindley. Boston: Little, Brown, 1941.

Rich, Frank. "The Spoils of War Coverage." *New York Times*, April 13, 2003, sec. 2:1, 15.

Roeder, George H., Jr. *The Censored War: American Visual Experience during World War II*. New Haven: Yale UP, 1993.

Roosevelt, Franklin D. *The Public Papers and Addresses of Franklin D. Roosevelt*. Ed. Samuel I. Rosenman. Vols. 10 and 11. New York: Harper, 1950.

Rosten, Leo C. *Hollywood: The Movie Colony, The Movie Makers*. New York: Harcourt, Brace, 1941.

Schlesinger, Arthur M., Jr. *A Life in the Twentieth Century: Innocent Beginnings, 1917–1950*. Boston: Houghton Mifflin, 2000.

Schultz, Duane. *The Doolittle Raid*. New York: St. Martin's, 1988.

Schuster, Carl O. "The European Axis Powers Attempted but Failed to Employ Aircraft Carriers." *World War II* (Nov. 2001): 22–32.

Scott, Robert L., Jr. *God Is My Co-Pilot*. New York: Scribner's, 1943.

Seghers, Anna. *The Seventh Cross*. Trans. James A. Galston. Boston: Little, Brown, 1942.

Shea, Margaret. *The Gals They Left Behind*. New York: Ives Washburn, 1944.

Sherman, Don. "The Secret Weapon." *Air and Space* (March 1995): 78–87.

Shindler, Colin. *Hollywood Goes to War: Films and American Society 1939–1952*. Boston: Routledge & Kegan Paul, 1979.

Shirer, William L. *The Rise and Fall of the Third Reich: A History of Nazi Germany*. New York: Simon & Schuster, 1960.

Shull, Michael S., and David Edward Wilt. *Hollywood War Films, 1937–1945: An Exhaustive Filmography of American Feature-Length Motion Pictures Relating to World War II*. Jefferson: McFarland, 1996.

Sides, Hampton. *Ghost Soldiers: The Forgotten Epic Story of World War II's Most Dramatic Mission*. New York: Doubleday, 2001.

Smith, Julian. *Chaplin*. Boston: Twayne, 1984.

Spoto, Donald. *The Art of Alfred Hitchcock: Fifty Years of His Motion Pictures*. Garden City: Dolphin, 1979.

Stafford, David. *Roosevelt and Churchill: Men of Secrets*. Woodstock: Overlook, 1999.

Steel, Kurt. *Crooked Shadow*. 1939. Cleveland: World, 1943.

Steinbeck, John. *The Moon Is Down*. New York: Viking, 1942.

Stokker, Kathleen. *Folklore Fights the Nazis: Humor in Occupied Norway, 1940–1945*. Madison: Fairleigh Dickinson UP, 1995.

Taylor, Blaine. "Germany's Aircraft-Carrier Development Masked a Hidden Struggle between Admiral Erich Raeder and Marshal Hermann Göring." *WWII History* (May 2003): 22–27.

Terkel, Studs. *"The Good War": An Oral History of World War II*. New York: Pantheon, 1984.

Tregaskis, Richard. *Guadalcanal Diary*. New York: Random House, 1943.

Truffaut, François, with Helen G. Scott. *Hitchcock*. New York: Simon & Schuster, 1967.

Tye, Larry. *The Father of Spin: Edward L. Bernays and the Birth of Public Relations*. 1998. New York: Owl, 2002.

Vasey, Ruth. *The World According to Hollywood, 1918–1939*. Madison: U of Wisconsin P, 1997.

Vizzard, Jack. *See No Evil: Life Inside a Hollywood Censor*. New York: Simon & Schuster, 1970.

Wecter, Dixon. *When Johnny Comes Marching Home*. Cambridge: Riverside Press, 1944.

Weinberg, Gerhard L. *A World at Arms: A Global History of World War II*. Cambridge: Cambridge UP, 1994.

The White Cliffs of Dover. Advertisement. *Good Housekeeping* (May 1944): 2.

White, Hayden. *The Content of the Form: Narrative, Discourse, and Historical Representation*. Baltimore: Johns Hopkins UP, 1987.

White, W. L. *They Were Expendable*. New York: Harcourt, Brace, 1942.

Wiley, Mason, and Damien Bona. *Inside Oscar: The Unofficial History of the Academy Awards*. 4th ed. New York: Ballantine, 1993.

Wolf, Anna W. M., and Irma Simonton Black. "What Happened to the Younger People." In *While You Were Gone: A Report on Wartime Life in the United States*. Ed. Jack Goodman. New York: Simon & Schuster, 1946. 64–88.

Woll, Allen L. *The Hollywood Musical Goes to War*. Chicago: Nelson-Hall, 1983.

Wood, Robin. *Howard Hawks*. Garden City: Doubleday, 1968.

Wukovits, John. "The Fight for Wake." *WWII History* (May 2002): 36–47.

Wylie, I. A. R. *Keeper of the Flame*. New York: Random House, 1942.

Young, Donald J. "Captain Ed Dyess Was a Fighter Pilot, Infantryman, Bataan Death March Survivor and Hero." *World War II* (Feb. 2002): 10–16.

Young, James R. *Behind the Rising Sun*. Garden City: Doubleday, Doran, 1943.

FILMOGRAPHY

Above Suspicion. Dir. Richard Thorpe. Perf. Joan Crawford, Fred MacMurray, Conrad Veidt, and Basil Rathbone. MGM, 1943.

Abroad with Two Yanks. Dir. Allan Dwan. Perf. William Bendix, Dennis O'Keefe, and Helen Walker. United Artists, 1944.

Act of Violence. Dir. Fred Zinnemann. Perf. Van Heflin, Robert Ryan, and Janet Leigh. MGM, 1949.

Action in the North Atlantic. Dir. Lloyd Bacon. Perf. Humphrey Bogart, Raymond Massey, Alan Hale, and Sam Levene. Warner Bros., 1943.

Adventure in Washington. Dir. Alfred E. Green. Perf. Herbert Marshall, Virginia Bruce, Gene Reynolds, and Ralph Morgan. Columbia, 1941.

Adventures of Smilin' Jack. Dir. Lewis D. Collins and Ray Taylor. Perf. Tom Brown, Marjorie Lord, Keye Luke, and Philip Ahn. Universal, 1943.

Air Force. Dir. Howard Hawks. Perf. John Garfield, John Ridgely, Gig Young, Arthur Kennedy, and Harry Carey. Warner Bros., 1943.

All My Sons. Dir. Irving Reis. Perf. Edward G. Robinson, Burt Lancaster, and Mady Christians. Universal, 1948.

All Quiet on the Western Front. Dir. Lewis Milestone. Perf. Lew Ayres, Louis Wolheim, and John Wray. Universal, 1930.

All through the Night. Dir. Vincent Sherman. Perf. Humphrey Bogart, Conrad Veidt, and Kaaren Verne. Warner Bros., 1942.

Allotment Wives. Dir. William Nigh. Perf. Kay Francis, Paul Kelly, and Otto Kruger. Monogram, 1945.

The Amazing Mrs. Holliday. Dir. Bruce Manning. Perf. Deanna Durbin, Edmond O'Brien, Barry Fitzgerald, and Harry Davenport. Universal, 1943.

An American Romance. Dir. King Vidor. Perf. Brian Donlevy, Ann Richards, and Walter Abel. MGM, 1944.

Apartment for Peggy. Dir. George Seaton. Perf. Jeanne Crain, William Holden, and Edmund Gwenn. Twentieth Century–Fox, 1948.

Are These Our Parents? Dir. William Nigh. Perf. Noel Neill, Richard Byron, Helen Vinson, Lyle Talbot, and Ivan Lebedeff. Monogram, 1944.

Arise, My Love. Dir. Mitchell Leisen. Perf. Claudette Colbert, Ray Milland, and Walter Abel. Paramount, 1940.

Assignment in Brittany. Dir. Jack Conway. Perf. Jean-Pierre Aumont, Susan Peters, Richard Whorf, and Signe Hasso. MGM, 1943.

Aventure Malgache. Dir. Alfred Hitchcock. Perf. Molière Players. British, 1944.

Back to Bataan. Dir. Edward Dmytryk. Perf. John Wayne, Anthony Quinn, and Beulah Bondi. RKO, 1945.

Background to Danger. Dir. Raoul Walsh. Perf. George Raft, Brenda Marshall, Sydney Greenstreet, and Peter Lorre. Warner Bros., 1943.

Bad Day at Black Rock. Dir. John Sturges. Perf. Spencer Tracy, Robert Ryan, Anne Francis, Dean Jagger, Walter Brennan, Ernest Borgnine, and Lee Marvin. MGM, 1955.

Bataan. Dir. Tay Garnett. Perf. Robert Taylor, George Murphy, Thomas Mitchell, and Lloyd Nolan. MGM, 1943.

Battle Circus. Dir. Richard Brooks. Perf. Humphrey Bogart, June Allyson, Keenan Wynn, Robert Keith, and Philip Ahn. MGM, 1953.

Battle of Britain. Dir. Frank Capra. Why We Fight series #4. War Department, 1943.

Battle of China. Dir. Frank Capra. Why We Fight series #6. War Department, 1944.

Battle of Russia. Dir. Frank Capra. Why We Fight series #5. War Department, 1944.

Battleship Potemkin. Dir. Sergei Eisenstein. Perf. Alexander Antonova, Vladimir Baarsky, and Grigori Alexandrov. Russian, 1925.

Beasts of Berlin, a.k.a. *Hitler, Beast of Berlin.* Dir. Sherman Scott. Perf. Alan Ladd, Roland Drew, and Greta Granstedt. PDC, 1939.

Beautiful but Broke. Dir. Charles Barton. Perf. Joan Davis, Jane Frazee, Judy Clark, and John Hubbard. Columbia, 1944.

Behind the Rising Sun. Dir. Edward Dmytryk. Perf. Tom Neal, Margo, J. Carrol Naish, and Robert Ryan. RKO, 1943.

A Bell for Adano. Dir. Henry King. Perf. Gene Tierney, John Hodiak, William Bendix, and Richard Conte. Twentieth Century–Fox, 1945.

Berlin Express. Dir. Jacques Tourneur. Perf. Merle Oberon, Robert Ryan, Charles Korvin, and Paul Lukas. RKO, 1948.

The Best Years of Our Lives. Dir. William Wyler. Perf. Fredric March, Myrna Loy, Dana Andrews, Teresa Wright, Virginia Mayo, Harold Russell, and Hoagy Carmichael. Goldwyn, 1946.

Betrayal from the East. Dir. William Berke. Perf. Lee Tracy, Nancy Kelly, Richard Loo, and Philip Ahn. RKO, 1945.

The Big Parade. Dir. King Vidor. Perf. John Gilbert, Renee Adoree, and Hobart Bosworth. MGM, 1925.

The Black Parachute. Dir. Lew Landers. Perf. Larry Parks, John Carradine, and Jonathan Hale. Columbia, 1944.

Blockade. Dir. William Dieterle. Perf. Henry Fonda, Madeleine Carroll, Leo Carrillo, and John Halliday. United Artists, 1938.

The Blue Dahlia. Dir. George Marshall. Perf. Alan Ladd, Veronica Lake, William Bendix, Howard Da Silva, and Hugh Beaumont. Paramount, 1946.

Bombardier. Dir. Richard Wallace. Perf. Pat O'Brien, Randolph Scott, Anne Shirley, and Eddie Albert. RKO, 1943.

Bon Voyage. Dir. Alfred Hitchcock. Perf. John Blythe and the Molière Players. British, 1944.

Boss of Big Town. Dir. Arthur Dreifuss. Perf. John Litel, Florence Rice, and H. B. Warner. PRC, 1942.

A Boy, a Girl, and a Dog. Dir. Herbert Kline. Perf. Jerry Hunter, Sharyn Moffett, Harry Davenport, and Lionel Stander. W. R. Frank, 1946.

Bride by Mistake. Dir. Richard Wallace. Perf. Laraine Day, Marsha Hunt, Edgar Buchanan, and Alan Marshal. RKO, 1944.

The Bridges at Toko-Ri. Dir. Mark Robson. Perf. William Holden, Grace Kelly, Fredric March, and Mickey Rooney. Paramount, 1954.

British Intelligence. Dir. Terry Morse. Perf. Boris Karloff, Margaret Lindsay, Maris Wrixon, and Holmes Herbert. Warner Bros., 1940.

Broken Lullaby, a.k.a. *The Man I Killed.* Dir. Ernst Lubitsch. Perf. Lionel Barrymore, Nancy Carroll, Phillips Holmes, and Zasu Pitts. Paramount, 1932.

Buck Privates. Dir. Arthur Lubin. Perf. Bud Abbott, Lou Costello, Lee Bowman, Alan Curtis, Jane Frazee, and the Andrews Sisters. Universal, 1941.

Burma Convoy. Dir. Noel M. Smith. Perf. Charles Bickford, Evelyn Ankers, Cecil Kellaway, Keye Luke, and Turhan Bey. Universal, 1941.

Calling Philo Vance. Dir. William Clemens. Perf. James Stephenson, Margot Stevenson, Henry O'Neill, and Edward Brophy. Warner Bros., 1940.

The Canterville Ghost. Dir. Jules Dassin. Perf. Robert Young, Charles Laughton, and Margaret O'Brien. MGM, 1944.

Casablanca. Dir. Michael Curtiz. Perf. Humphrey Bogart, Ingrid Bergman, Claude Rains, and Paul Henreid. Warner Bros., 1942.

Caught in the Draft. Dir. David Butler. Perf. Bob Hope, Dorothy Lamour, and Eddie Bracken. Paramount, 1941.

Charlie Chan at the Olympics. Dir. H. Bruce Humberstone. Perf. Warner Oland, Keye Luke, Katherine De Mille, and Pauline Moore. Twentieth Century–Fox, 1937.

Charlie Chan in Panama. Dir. Norman Foster. Perf. Sidney Toler, Jean Rogers, Victor Sen Yung, Mary Nash, and Lionel Atwill. Twentieth Century–Fox, 1940.

Chetniks! Dir. Louis King. Perf. Philip Dorn, Anna Sten, and Martin Kosleck. Twentieth Century–Fox, 1943.

China. Dir. John Farrow. Perf. Loretta Young, Alan Ladd, and William Bendix. Paramount, 1943.

China Sky. Dir. Ray Enright. Perf. Randolph Scott, Ruth Warrick, Ellen Drew, Philip Ahn, and Anthony Quinn. RKO, 1945.

Christmas in Connecticut. Dir. Peter Godfrey. Perf. Barbara Stanwyck, Dennis Morgan, Reginald Gardiner, Sydney Greenstreet, and S. Z. Sakall. Warner Bros., 1945.

Citizen Kane. Dir. Orson Welles. Perf. Orson Welles, Joseph Cotten, Everett Sloane, Agnes Moorehead, and Dorothy Comingore. RKO, 1941.

The Clock. Dir. Vincente Minnelli. Perf. Judy Garland, Robert Walker, James Gleason, and Keenan Wynn. MGM, 1945.

Colonel Effingham's Raid. Dir. Irving Pichel. Perf. Joan Bennett, Charles Coburn, William Eythe, and Allyn Joslyn. Twentieth Century–Fox, 1945.

Command Decision. Dir. Sam Wood. Perf. Clark Gable, Walter Pidgeon, Van Johnson, Brian Donlevy, and Charles Bickford. MGM, 1948.

Commandos Strike at Dawn. Dir. John Farrow. Perf. Paul Muni, Anna Lee, Lillian Gish, and Cedric Hardwicke. Columbia, 1942.

Comrade X. Dir. King Vidor. Perf. Clark Gable, Hedy Lamarr, Felix Bressart, and Oscar Homolka. MGM, 1940.

Confessions of a Nazi Spy. Dir. Anatole Litvak. Perf. Edward G. Robinson, Francis Lederer, Paul Lukas, and George Sanders. Warner Bros., 1939.

Confirm or Deny. Dir. Archie Mayo. Perf. Don Ameche, Joan Bennett, Roddy McDowall, and John Loder. Twentieth Century–Fox, 1941.

Conspiracy. Dir. Lew Landers. Perf. Allan Lane, Linda Hayes, and Robert Barrat. RKO, 1939.

Corregidor. Dir. William Nigh. Perf. Elissa Landi, Otto Kruger, and Donald Woods. PRC, 1943.

Corvette K-225. Dir. Richard Rosson. Perf. Randolph Scott, Ella Raines, and Barry Fitzgerald. Universal, 1943.

Counter-Attack. Dir. Zoltan Korda. Perf. Paul Muni, Marguerite Chapman, and Larry Parks. Columbia, 1945.

The Courage of Lassie. Dir. Fred Wilcox. Perf. Elizabeth Taylor, Frank Morgan, Tom Drake, and Harry Davenport. MGM, 1946.

Crack-Up. Dir. Malcolm St. Clair. Perf. Peter Lorre, Brian Donlevy, Helen Wood, and Ralph Morgan. Twentieth Century–Fox, 1937.

Crash Dive. Dir. Archie Mayo. Perf. Tyrone Power, Dana Andrews, Anne Baxter, and James Gleason. Twentieth Century–Fox, 1943.

The Cross of Lorraine. Dir. Tay Garnett. Perf. Jean-Pierre Aumont, Gene Kelly, Cedric Hardwicke, Hume Cronyn, and Peter Lorre. MGM, 1943.

Crossfire. Dir. Edward Dmytryk. Perf. Robert Young, Robert Mitchum, Robert Ryan, and Gloria Grahame. RKO, 1947.

Cry "Havoc." Dir. Richard Thorpe. Perf. Margaret Sullavan, Joan Blondell, Ann Southern, and Fay Bainter. MGM, 1943.

Dangerous Moonlight, a.k.a. *Suicide Squadron.* Dir. Brian Desmond Hurst. Perf. Anton Walbrook, Sally Gray, and Derrick de Marney. RKO/Republic (British), 1941.

Dawn Patrol. Dir. Howard Hawks. Perf. Richard Barthelmess, Douglas Fairbanks Jr., Neil Hamilton, and Frank McHugh. Warner Bros., 1930.

Dawn Patrol. Dir. Edmund Goulding. Perf. Errol Flynn, Basil Rathbone, David Niven, Donald Crisp, and Barry Fitzgerald. Warner Bros., 1938.

Days of Glory. Dir. Jacques Tourneur. Perf. Gregory Peck, Alan Reed, Maria Palmer, Lowell Gilmore, and Tamara Toumanova. RKO, 1944.

The Dead End Kids on Dress Parade. Dir. William Clemens. Perf. Leo Gorcey, John Litel, and Huntz Hall. Warner Bros., 1939.

Dead Reckoning. Dir. John Cromwell. Perf. Humphrey Bogart, Lizabeth Scott, and Morris Carnovsky. Columbia, 1947.

Dear Ruth. Dir. William D. Russell. Perf. Joan Caulfield, William Holden, Mona Freeman, and Edward Arnold. Paramount, 1947.

December 7th. Dir. John Ford and Gregg Toland. Perf. Walter Huston, Harry Davenport, and Dana Andrews. U.S. Navy/Twentieth Century–Fox, 1943.

Desperate Journey. Dir. Raoul Walsh. Perf. Errol Flynn, Raymond Massey, Ronald Reagan, Nancy Coleman, Alan Hale, and Arthur Kennedy. Warner Bros., 1942.

Destination Tokyo. Dir. Delmar Daves. Perf. Cary Grant, John Garfield, Alan Hale, and John Ridgely. Warner Bros., 1943.

Destination Unknown. Dir. Ray Taylor. Perf. Irene Hervey, William Gargan, Sam Levene, Turhan Bey, and Keye Luke. Universal, 1942.

Dive Bomber. Dir. Michael Curtiz. Perf. Errol Flynn, Fred MacMurray, Ralph Bellamy, and Alexis Smith. Warner Bros., 1941.

Divide and Conquer. Dir. Frank Capra. Why We Fight series #3. War Department, 1943.

Doomed to Die. Dir. William Nigh. Perf. Boris Karloff, Marjorie Reynolds, and Grant Withers. Monogram, 1940.

The Doughgirls. Dir. James V. Kern. Perf. Jane Wyman, Ann Sheridan, Alexis Smith, Eve Arden, Jack Carson, and John Ridgely. Warner Bros., 1944.

Dr. Gillespie's Criminal Case. Dir. Willis Goldbeck. Perf. Lionel Barrymore, Van Johnson, Keye Luke, Donna Reed, and Margaret O'Brien. MGM, 1943.

Dragon Seed. Dir. Jack Conway. Perf. Katharine Hepburn, Walter Huston, Turhan Bey, Aline MacMahon, and Akim Tamiroff. MGM, 1944.

Edge of Darkness. Dir. Lewis Milestone. Perf. Errol Flynn, Ann Sheridan, and Walter Huston. Warner Bros., 1943.

Ellery Queen's Penthouse Mystery. Dir. James P. Hogan. Perf. Ralph Bellamy, Margaret Lindsay, Charley Grapewin, and Anna May Wong. Columbia, 1941.

The Enchanted Cottage. Dir. John S. Robertson. Perf. Richard Barthelmess, May McAvoy, and Ida Waterman. First National, 1924.

The Enchanted Cottage. Dir. John Cromwell. Perf. Robert Young, Dorothy McGuire, Herbert Marshall, and Mildred Natwick. RKO, 1945.

Enemy Agent. Dir. Lew Landers. Perf. Richard Cromwell, Marjorie Reynolds, Helen Vinson, Philip Dorn, and Robert Armstrong. Universal, 1940.

Escape. Dir. Mervyn LeRoy. Perf. Norma Shearer, Robert Taylor, Conrad Veidt, and Philip Dorn. MGM, 1940.

Escape from Hong Kong. Dir. William Nigh. Perf. Don Terry, Leo Carrillo, Andy Devine, and Marjorie Lord. Universal, 1942.

Escape to Glory, a.k.a. *Submarine Zone.* Dir. John Brahm. Perf. Constance Bennett, Pat O'Brien, Melville Cooper, Edgar Buchanan, and John Halliday. Columbia, 1940.

Espionage Agent. Dir. Lloyd Bacon. Perf. Joel McCrea, Brenda Marshall, George Bancroft, and Jeffrey Lynn. Warner Bros., 1939.

Exile Express. Dir. Otis Garrett. Perf. Anna Sten, Alan Marshal, Jerome Cowan, and Harry Davenport. Grand National, 1939.

Faces in the Fog. Dir. John English. Perf. Jane Withers, Eric Sinclair, and John Litel. Republic, 1944.

A Farewell to Arms. Dir. Frank Borzage. Perf. Gary Cooper, Helen Hayes, and Adolph Menjou. Paramount, 1932.

The Fighting Seabees. Dir. Edward Ludwig. Perf. John Wayne, Susan Hayward, Dennis O'Keefe, and William Frawley. Republic, 1944.

The Fighting 69th. Dir. William Keighley. Perf. James Cagney, Pat O'Brien, George Brent, and Jeffrey Lynn. Warner Bros., 1940.

First Comes Courage. Dir. Dorothy Arzner. Perf. Merle Oberon, Brian Aherne, and Carl Esmond. Columbia, 1943.

First Yank into Tokyo. Dir. Gordon Douglas. Perf. Tom Neal, Barbara Hale, Marc Cramer, and Richard Loo. RKO, 1945.

Five Graves to Cairo. Dir. Billy Wilder. Perf. Franchot Tone, Anne Baxter, Akim Tamiroff, and Erich von Stroheim. Paramount, 1943.

Flight Command. Dir. Frank Borzage. Perf. Robert Taylor, Ruth Hussey, Walter Pidgeon, and Paul Kelly. MGM, 1940.

Flying Tigers. Dir. David Miller. Perf. John Wayne, John Carroll, Anna Lee, and Paul Kelly. Republic, 1942.

Flying Wild. Dir. William West. Perf. Leo Gorcey, Bobby Jordan, and Donald Haines. Monogram, 1941.

A Foreign Affair. Dir. Billy Wilder. Perf. Jean Arthur, Marlene Dietrich, John Lund, and Millard Mitchell. Paramount, 1948.

Foreign Correspondent. Dir. Alfred Hitchcock. Perf. Joel McCrea, Laraine Day, Herbert Marshall, and George Sanders. United Artists, 1940.

Forever and a Day. Dir. René Clair, Frank Lloyd, Victor Saville, Edmund Goulding, Cedric Hardwicke, Robert Stevenson, and Herbert Wilcox. Perf. Brian Aherne, Robert Cummings, Ida Lupino, Charles Laughton, Herbert Marshall, Ray Milland, and C. Aubrey Smith. RKO, 1943.

The 49th Parallel, a.k.a. *The Invaders.* Dir. Michael Powell. Perf. Anton Walbrook, Eric Portman, Leslie Howard, Raymond Massey, Laurence Olivier, and Glynis Johns. Columbia (British), 1941.

Four Sons. Dir. Archie Mayo. Perf. Don Ameche, Eugenie Leontovich, Mary Beth Hughes, and Alan Curtis. Twentieth Century–Fox, 1940.

Freedom Radio, a.k.a. *A Voice in the Night.* Dir. Anthony Asquith. Perf. Clive Brook, Diana Wynyard, and Raymond Huntley. Columbia (British), 1941.

The Gay Divorcée. Dir. Mark Sandrich. Perf. Fred Astaire, Ginger Rogers, Edward Everett Horton, Alice Brady, and Erik Rhodes. RKO, 1934.

Get Going. Dir. Jean Yarbrough. Perf. Robert Paige, Grace McDonald, and Vera Vague. Universal, 1943.

God Is My Co-Pilot. Dir. Robert Florey. Perf. Dennis Morgan, Raymond Massey, Andrea King, Alan Hale, Dane Clark, and Richard Loo. Warner Bros., 1945.

Government Girl. Dir. Dudley Nichols. Perf. Olivia de Havilland, Sonny Tufts, and Anne Shirley. RKO, 1943.

Grand Hotel. Dir. Edmund Goulding. Perf. Greta Garbo, John Barrymore, Joan Crawford, Wallace Beery, and Lionel Barrymore. MGM, 1932.

Grand Illusion. Dir. Jean Renoir. Perf. Jean Gabin, Pierre Fresnay, and Erich von Stroheim. French, 1937.

The Great Dictator. Dir. Charles Chaplin. Perf. Charles Chaplin, Paulette Goddard, Jack Oakie, and Reginald Gardiner. United Artists, 1940.

Great Guns. Dir. Monty Banks. Perf. Stan Laurel, Oliver Hardy, Sheila Ryan, and Dick Nelson. Twentieth Century–Fox, 1941.

The Great McGinty. Dir. Preston Sturges. Perf. Brian Donlevy, Muriel Angelus, Akim Tamiroff, and Allyn Joslyn. Paramount, 1940.

The Green Berets. Dir. John Wayne and Ray Kellogg. Perf. John Wayne, David Janssen, Jim Hutton, and Aldo Ray. Warner Bros., 1968.

Guadalcanal Diary. Dir. Lewis Seiler. Perf. Preston Foster, Lloyd Nolan, William Bendix, and Richard Conte. Twentieth Century–Fox, 1943.

Gung Ho! Dir. Ray Enright. Perf. Randolph Scott, Alan Curtis, Noah Beery Jr., J. Carrol Naish, and Robert Mitchum. Universal, 1943.

A Guy Named Joe. Dir. Victor Fleming. Perf. Spencer Tracy, Irene Dunne, Van Johnson, Ward Bond, and Lionel Barrymore. MGM, 1943.

Hail the Conquering Hero. Dir. Preston Sturges. Perf. Eddie Bracken, William Demarest, Freddie Steele, Ella Raines, and Raymond Walburn. Paramount, 1944.

Halfway to Shanghai. Dir. John Rawlins. Perf. Kent Taylor, Irene Hervey, and George Zucco. Universal, 1942.

Hangmen Also Die! Dir. Fritz Lang. Perf. Brian Donlevy, Walter Brennan, Anna Lee, Gene Lockhart, and Dennis O'Keefe. United Artists, 1943.

Happy Land. Dir. Irving Pichel. Perf. Don Ameche, Harry Carey, Frances Dee, and Harry Morgan. Twentieth Century–Fox, 1943.

Hell's Angels. Dir. Howard Hughes. Perf. Ben Lyon, James Hall, and Jean Harlow. Howard Hughes, 1930.

High Wall. Dir. Curtis Bernhardt. Perf. Robert Taylor, Audrey Totter, Herbert Marshall, and Dorothy Patrick. MGM, 1947.

Hitler—Dead or Alive. Dir. Nick Grinde. Perf. Ward Bond, Bobby Watson, Dorothy Tree, Warren Hymer, and Paul Fix. Charles House, 1943.

The Hitler Gang. Dir. John Farrow. Perf. Bobby Watson, Martin Kosleck, Victor Varconi, and Luis Van Rooten. Paramount, 1944.

Hitler's Children. Dir. Edward Dmytryk and Irving Reis. Perf. Bonita Granville, Tim Holt, and Kent Smith. RKO, 1943.

Hitler's Madman. Dir. Douglas Sirk. Perf. John Carradine, Patricia Morison, Alan Curtis, and Ralph Morgan. MGM, 1943.

Hollywood Canteen. Dir. Delmar Daves. Perf. Bette Davis, John Garfield, Joan Leslie, Robert Hutton, Dane Clark, and Janis Paige. Warner Bros., 1944.

Hostages. Dir. Frank Tuttle. Perf. William Bendix, Luise Rainer, Roland Varno, Oscar Homolka, and Hans Conried. Paramount, 1943.

Hotel Berlin. Dir. Peter Godfrey. Perf. Helmut Dantine, Andrea King, Raymond Massey, Peter Lorre, and Henry Daniell. Warner Bros., 1945.

The Human Comedy. Dir. Clarence Brown. Perf. Mickey Rooney, Frank Morgan, James Craig, Marsha Hunt, Fay Bainter, Van Johnson, and Ray Collins. MGM, 1943.

I Want You. Dir. Mark Robson. Perf. Dana Andrews, Dorothy McGuire, Farley Granger, and Peggy Dow. RKO, 1951.

Iceland. Dir. H. Bruce Humberstone. Perf. Sonja Henie, John Payne, Jack Oakie, and Felix Bressart. Twentieth Century–Fox, 1942.

Identity Unknown. Dir. Walter Colmes. Perf. Richard Arlen, Cheryl Walker, Roger Pryor, and Bobby Driscoll. Republic, 1945.

The Impatient Years. Dir. Irving Cummings. Perf. Jean Arthur, Lee Bowman, and Charles Coburn. Columbia, 1944.

International Lady. Dir. Tim Whelan. Perf. Ilona Massey, George Brent, and Basil Rathbone. United Artists, 1941.

International Settlement. Dir. Eugene Forde. Perf. George Sanders, Dolores Del Rio, Leon Ames, John Carradine, and Keye Luke. Twentieth Century–Fox, 1938.

International Squadron. Dir. Lothar Mendes. Perf. Ronald Reagan, James Stephenson, and Olympe Bradna. Warner Bros., 1941.

It Happened One Night. Dir. Frank Capra. Perf. Clark Gable, Claudette Colbert, and Walter Connolly. Columbia, 1934.

It's a Wonderful Life. Dir. Frank Capra. Perf. James Stewart, Donna Reed, Lionel Barrymore, and Thomas Mitchell. Liberty, 1946.

Joan of Ozark. Dir. Joseph Santley. Perf. Judy Canova, Joe E. Brown, Eddie Foy Jr., and Jerome Cowan. Republic, 1942.

Joan of Paris. Dir. Robert Stevenson. Perf. Michèle Morgan, Paul Henreid, Thomas Mitchell, May Robson, Laird Cregar, and Alan Ladd. RKO, 1942.

Joe Smith, American. Dir. Richard Thorpe. Perf. Robert Young, Marsha Hunt, and Harvey Stephens. MGM, 1942.

Johnny Doesn't Live Here Anymore. Dir. Joe May. Perf. Simone Simon, James Ellison, William Terry, Minna Gombell, Alan Dinehart, and Robert Mitchum. Monogram, 1944.

Johnny Doughboy. Dir. John H. Auer. Perf. Jane Withers, William Demarest, and Henry Wilcoxon. Republic, 1942.

Journey for Margaret. Dir. W. S. Van Dyke. Perf. Robert Young, Laraine Day, Margaret O'Brien, Fay Bainter, and Nigel Bruce. MGM, 1942.

Junior Army. Dir. Lew Landers. Perf. Freddie Bartholomew, Billy Halop, and Huntz Hall. Columbia, 1942.

Keep 'Em Flying. Dir. Arthur Lubin. Perf. Bud Abbott, Lou Costello, Carol Bruce, and Martha Raye. Universal, 1941.

Keeper of the Flame. Dir. George Cukor. Perf. Spencer Tracy, Katharine Hepburn, Richard Whorf, Margaret Wycherly, Howard Da Silva, and Forrest Tucker. MGM, 1942.

The Kennel Murder Case. Dir. Michael Curtiz. Perf. William Powell, Mary Astor, Eugene Pallette, and Ralph Morgan. Warner Bros., 1933.

Key Largo. Dir. John Huston. Perf. Humphrey Bogart, Edward G. Robinson, Lauren Bacall, Lionel Barrymore, and Claire Trevor. Warner Bros., 1948.

Kid Dynamite. Dir. Wallace Fox. Perf. Leo Gorcey, Bobby Jordan, Huntz Hall, and Sammy Morrison. Monogram, 1943.

Ladies of Washington. Dir. Louis King. Perf. Trudy Marshall, Ronald Graham, and Anthony Quinn. Twentieth Century–Fox, 1944.

Lady from Chungking. Dir. William Nigh. Perf. Anna May Wong, Harold Huber, and Mae Clarke. PRC, 1942.

The Last Ride. Dir. Ross Lederman. Perf. Richard Travis, Jack La Rue, Eleanor Parker, and Charles Lang. Warner Bros., 1944.

Last Train from Madrid. Dir. James P. Hogan. Perf. Dorothy Lamour, Lew Ayres, Gilbert Roland, and Anthony Quinn. Paramount, 1937.

Let's Get Tough! Dir. Wallace Fox. Perf. Leo Gorcey, Huntz Hall, Bobby Jordan, Sammy Morrison, Tom Brown, and Philip Ahn. Monogram, 1942.

Lifeboat. Dir. Alfred Hitchcock. Perf. Tallulah Bankhead, William Bendix, Walter Slezak, John Hodiak, Hume Cronyn, Henry Hull, and Canada Lee. Twentieth Century–Fox, 1944.

Little Caesar. Dir. Mervyn LeRoy. Perf. Edward G. Robinson, Douglas Fairbanks Jr., and Glenda Farrell. Warner Bros., 1931.

Little Tokyo, U.S.A. Dir. Otto Brower. Perf. Preston Foster, Brenda Joyce, and Harold Huber. Twentieth Century–Fox, 1942.

The Lone Wolf Spy Hunt. Dir. Peter Godfrey. Perf. Warren William, Ida Lupino, Rita Hayworth, and Virginia Weidler. Columbia, 1939.

The Lost Squadron. Dir. George Archainbaud. Perf. Richard Dix, Mary Astor, Erich von Stroheim, and Joel McCrea. RKO, 1932.

Lucky Jordan. Dir. Frank Tuttle. Perf. Alan Ladd, Helen Walker, Marie McDonald, and Sheldon Leonard. Paramount, 1942.

Lure of the Islands. Dir. Jean Yarbrough. Perf. Robert Lowery, Big Boy Williams, Ivan Lebedeff, and Margie Hart. Monogram, 1942.

Main Street after Dark. Dir. Edward Cahn. Perf. Edward Arnold, Audrey Totter, Dan Duryea, Hume Cronyn, and Selena Royle. MGM, 1944.

The Maltese Falcon. Dir. John Huston. Perf. Humphrey Bogart, Mary Astor, Sydney Greenstreet, and Peter Lorre. Warner Bros., 1941.

Man at Large. Dir. Eugene Forde. Perf. George Reeves, Marjorie Weaver, and Steven Geray. Twentieth Century–Fox, 1941.

Man Hunt. Dir. Fritz Lang. Perf. Walter Pidgeon, George Sanders, and Joan Bennett. Twentieth Century–Fox, 1941.

The Man I Married, a.k.a. *I Married a Nazi.* Dir. Irving Pichel. Perf. Joan Bennett, Francis Lederer, and Lloyd Nolan. Twentieth Century–Fox, 1940.

The Man Who Wouldn't Talk. Dir. David Burton. Perf. Lloyd Nolan, Onslow Stevens, and Jean Rogers. Twentieth Century–Fox, 1940.

Manila Calling. Dir. Herbert I. Leeds. Perf. Lloyd Nolan, Carole Landis, and Cornel Wilde. Twentieth Century–Fox, 1942.

The Master Race. Dir. Herbert J. Biberman. Perf. George Coulouris, Stanley Ridges, Osa Massen, Nancy Gates, and Lloyd Bridges. RKO, 1944.

A Medal for Benny. Dir. Irving Pichel. Perf. Dorothy Lamour, J. Carrol Naish, and Arturo de Cordova. Paramount, 1945.

Meet Boston Blackie. Dir. Robert Florey. Perf. Chester Morris, Rochelle Hudson, and Richard Lane. Columbia, 1941.

Meet John Doe. Dir. Frank Capra. Perf. Barbara Stanwyck, Gary Cooper, and Edward Arnold. Warner Bros., 1941.

The Miracle of Morgan's Creek. Dir. Preston Sturges. Perf. Eddie Bracken, Betty Hutton, William Demarest, Diana Lynn, and Brian Donlevy. Paramount, 1944.

Miss V from Moscow. Dir. Albert Herman. Perf. Lola Lane, Noel Madison, and Howard Banks. PRC, 1942.

Mission to Moscow. Dir. Michael Curtiz. Perf. Walter Huston, Ann Harding, Oscar Homolka, George Tobias, and Gene Lockhart. Warner Bros., 1943.

The Moon Is Down. Dir. Irving Pichel. Perf. Cedric Hardwicke, Henry Travers, and Lee J. Cobb. Twentieth Century–Fox, 1943.

The More the Merrier. Dir. George Stevens. Perf. Jean Arthur, Joel McCrea, and Charles Coburn. Columbia, 1943.

The Mortal Storm. Dir. Frank Borzage. Perf. James Stewart, Margaret Sullavan, Frank Morgan, and Robert Young. MGM, 1940.

Mr. Lucky. Dir. H. C. Potter. Perf. Cary Grant, Laraine Day, Charles Bickford, and Gladys Cooper. RKO, 1943.

Mr. Smith Goes to Washington. Dir. Frank Capra. Perf. James Stewart, Jean Arthur, Claude Rains, and Edward Arnold. Columbia, 1939.

Mr. Wong in Chinatown. Dir. William Nigh. Perf. Boris Karloff, Marjorie Reynolds, and Grant Withers. Monogram, 1939.

Mrs. Miniver. Dir. William Wyler. Perf. Greer Garson, Walter Pidgeon, Dame May Whitty, Teresa Wright, Reginald Owen, Henry Travers, and Richard Ney. MGM, 1942.

Murder over New York. Dir. Harry Lachman. Perf. Sidney Toler, Marjorie Weaver, Robert Lowery, and Victor Sen Yung. Twentieth Century–Fox, 1940.

My Pal Wolf. Dir. Alfred Werker. Perf. Sharyn Moffett, Jill Esmond, and Una O'Connor. RKO, 1944.

Mystery Sea Raider. Dir. Edward Dmytryk. Perf. Carole Landis, Henry Wilcoxon, and Onslow Stevens. Paramount, 1940.

Mystery Ship. Dir. Lew Landers. Perf. Paul Kelly, Lola Lane, and Larry Parks. Columbia, 1941.

Nation Aflame. Dir. Victor Halperin. Perf. Noel Madison, Lila Lee, and Norma Trelvar. Independent, 1937.

Navy Secrets. Dir. Howard Bretherton. Perf. Fay Wray, Grant Withers, and Dewey Robinson. Monogram, 1939.

The Nazis Strike. Dir. Frank Capra. Why We Fight series #2. War Department, 1943.

Nick Carter, Master Detective. Dir. Jacques Tourneur. Perf. Walter Pidgeon, Donald Meek, Rita Johnson, and Henry Hull. MGM, 1939.

Night Plane from Chungking. Dir. Ralph Murphy. Perf. Ellen Drew, Robert Preston, Otto Kruger, Victor Sen Yung, and Steven Geray. Paramount, 1943.

Night Train to Munich. Dir. Carol Reed. Perf. Rex Harrison, Margaret Lockwood, and Paul Henreid. British, 1940.

Ninotchka. Dir. Ernst Lubitsch. Perf. Greta Garbo, Melvyn Douglas, Ina Claire, Bela Lugosi, Sig Ruman, and Felix Bressart. MGM, 1939.

None Shall Escape. Dir. Andre de Toth. Perf. Alexander Knox, Marsha Hunt, and Henry Travers. Columbia, 1944.

North of Shanghai. Dir. Ross Lederman. Perf. James Craig, Betty Furness, and Keye Luke. Columbia, 1939.

The North Star. Dir. Lewis Milestone. Perf. Anne Baxter, Dana Andrews, and Walter Huston. RKO, 1943.

Notorious. Dir. Alfred Hitchcock. Perf. Cary Grant, Ingrid Bergman, and Claude Rains. RKO, 1946.

Objective, Burma! Dir. Raoul Walsh. Perf. Errol Flynn, William Prince, Henry Hull, and George Tobias. Warner Bros., 1945.

Only Angels Have Wings. Dir. Howard Hawks. Perf. Cary Grant, Jean Arthur, Richard Barthelmess, Rita Hayworth, and Thomas Mitchell. Columbia, 1939.

O.S.S. Dir. Irving Pichel. Perf. Alan Ladd, Geraldine Fitzgerald, and Patric Knowles. Paramount, 1946.

Panama Patrol. Dir. Charles Lamont. Perf. Leon Ames, Charlotte Wynters, and Adrienne Ames. Grand National, 1939.

Parachute Battalion. Dir. Leslie Goodwins. Perf. Robert Preston, Edmond O'Brien, Harry Carey, Nancy Kelly, and Buddy Ebsen. RKO, 1941.

Paris after Dark. Dir. Leonide Moguy. Perf. George Sanders, Philip Dorn, and Brenda Marshall. Twentieth Century–Fox, 1943.

Passage to Marseilles. Dir. Michael Curtiz. Perf. Humphrey Bogart, Claude Rains, Michèle Morgan, Philip Dorn, Sydney Greenstreet, George Tobias, and John Loder. Warner Bros., 1944.

Passport to Destiny. Dir. Ray McCarey. Perf. Elsa Lanchester, Gordon Oliver, and Lloyd Corrigan. RKO, 1944.

Patton. Dir. Franklin Schaffner. Perf. George C. Scott, Karl Malden, and Stephen Young. Twentieth Century–Fox, 1970.

Pearl Harbor. Dir. Michael Bay. Perf. Ben Affleck, Josh Hartnett, Kate Beckinsale, and Cuba Gooding Jr. Touchstone, 2001.

The Pied Piper. Dir. Irving Pichel. Perf. Monty Woolley, Anne Baxter, Roddy McDowall, and Otto Preminger. Twentieth Century–Fox, 1942.

Pillow to Post. Dir. Vincent Sherman. Perf. Ida Lupino, William Prince, and Sydney Greenstreet. Warner Bros., 1945.

Pimpernel Smith, a.k.a. *Mister V.* Dir. Leslie Howard. Perf. Leslie Howard, Mary Morris, and Francis L. Sullivan. United Artists (British), 1941.

Pittsburgh. Dir. Lewis Seiler. Perf. John Wayne, Marlene Dietrich, and Randolph Scott. Universal, 1942.

Prelude to War. Dir. Frank Capra. Why We Fight series #1. War Department, 1942.

Pride of the Marines. Dir. Delmer Daves. Perf. John Garfield, Eleanor Parker, Dane Clark, John Ridgely, and Rosemary DeCamp. Warner Bros., 1945.

The Public Enemy. Dir. William Wellman. Perf. James Cagney, Jean Harlow, Eddie Woods, and Beryl Mercer. Warner Bros., 1931.

The Purple Heart. Dir. Lewis Milestone. Perf. Dana Andrews, Farley Granger, Sam Levene, Richard Conte, Richard Loo, and Benson Fong. Twentieth Century–Fox, 1944.

The Racket Man. Dir. D. Ross Lederman. Perf. Tom Neal, Hugh Beaumont, and Larry Parks. Columbia, 1944.

Rationing. Dir. Willis Goldbeck. Perf. Wallace Beery, Marjorie Main, and Donald Meek. MGM, 1944.

Remember Pearl Harbor! Dir. Joseph Santley. Perf. Don Barry, Alan Curtis, Fay McKenzie, and Sig Ruman. Republic, 1942.

Return of the Vampire. Dir. Lew Landers and Kurt Neumann. Perf. Bela Lugosi, Nina Foch, Frieda Inescort, and Roland Varno. Columbia, 1943.

Reunion in France. Dir. Jules Dassin. Perf. Joan Crawford, John Wayne, and Philip Dorn. MGM, 1942.

The Road Back. Dir. James Whale. Perf. Richard Cromwell, John King, Slim Summerville, Louise Fazenda, and Andy Devine. Universal, 1937.

The Road to Glory. Dir. Howard Hawks. Perf. Fredric March, Warner Baxter, and Lionel Barrymore. Twentieth Century–Fox, 1936.

The Roaring Twenties. Dir. Raoul Walsh. Perf. James Cagney, Priscilla Lane, Humphrey Bogart, and Gladys George. Warner Bros., 1939.

Saboteur. Dir. Alfred Hitchcock. Perf. Robert Cummings, Priscilla Lane, Norman Lloyd, and Otto Kruger. Universal, 1942.

Sahara. Dir. Zoltan Korda. Perf. Humphrey Bogart, Bruce Bennett, J. Carrol Naish, Rex Ingram, Lloyd Bridges, and Dan Duryea. Columbia, 1943.

Salute to the Marines. Dir. S. Sylvan Simon. Perf. Wallace Beery, Fay Bainter, Reginald Owen, and Keye Luke. MGM, 1943.

Samurai. Dir. Raymond Cannon. Perf. Paul Fung, Luke Chang, and Sung Li. Cavalcade, 1945.

San Diego, I Love You. Dir. Reginald LeBorg. Perf. Edward Everett Horton, Louise Albritton, Jon Hall, Eric Blore, and Irene Ryan. Universal, 1944.

Saving Private Ryan. Dir. Steven Spielberg. Perf. Tom Hanks, Edward Burns, and Matt Damon. Dreamworks/Paramount, 1998.

Scarface. Dir. Howard Hawks. Perf. Paul Muni, Ann Dvorak, George Raft, and Boris Karloff. Universal, 1932.

The Scarlet Pimpernel. Dir. Harold Young. Perf. Leslie Howard, Merle Oberon, and Raymond Massey. British, 1935.

The Searching Wind. Dir. William Dieterle. Perf. Robert Young, Sylvia Sidney, Ann Richards, and Dudley Digges. Paramount, 1946.

Secret Agent of Japan. Dir. Irving Pichel. Perf. Preston Foster, Lynn Bari, Steven Geray, and Victor Sen Yung. Twentieth Century–Fox, 1942.

Sergeant York. Dir. Howard Hawks. Perf. Gary Cooper, Walter Brennan, Joan Leslie, and George Tobias. Warner Bros., 1941.

Seven Miles from Alcatraz. Dir. Edward Dmytryk. Perf. James Craig, Bonita Granville, Frank Jenks, and Cliff Edwards. RKO, 1942.

The Seventh Cross. Dir. Fred Zinnemann. Perf. Spencer Tracy, Signe Hasso, Hume Cronyn, and Jessica Tandy. MGM, 1944.

Shadows over Shanghai. Dir. Charles Lamont. Perf. Linda Gray, James Dunn, and Ralph Morgan. Grand National, 1938.

Sherlock Holmes and the Secret Weapon. Dir. Roy William Neill. Perf. Basil Rathbone, Nigel Bruce, and Lionel Atwill. Universal, 1942.

Sherlock Holmes and the Voice of Terror. Dir. John Rawlins. Perf. Basil Rathbone, Nigel Bruce, Hillary Brooke, and Henry Daniell. Universal, 1942.

Sherlock Holmes in Washington. Dir. Roy William Neill. Perf. Basil Rathbone, Nigel Bruce, Marjorie Lord, and Henry Daniell. Universal, 1943.

Since You Went Away. Dir. John Cromwell. Perf. Claudette Colbert, Jennifer Jones, Joseph Cotten, Monty Woolley, Shirley Temple, Robert Walker, and Hattie McDaniel. United Artists, 1944.

Ski Patrol. Dir. Lew Landers. Perf. Philip Dorn, Luli Deste, Stanley Fields, and Samuel S. Hinds. Universal, 1940.

Smashing the Spy Ring. Dir. Christy Cabanne. Perf. Ralph Bellamy, Fay Wray, and Regis Toomey. Columbia, 1938.

Snafu. Dir. Jack Moss. Perf. Conrad Janis, Robert Benchley, and Vera Vague. Columbia, 1945.

So Ends Our Night. Dir. John Cromwell. Perf. Fredric March, Margaret Sullavan, Frances Dee, and Glenn Ford. United Artists, 1941.

So Proudly We Hail! Dir. Mark Sandrich. Perf. Claudette Colbert, Paulette Goddard, Veronica Lake, George Reeves, and Sonny Tufts. Paramount, 1943.

Somewhere I'll Find You. Dir. Wesley Ruggles. Perf. Clark Gable, Lana Turner, and Robert Sterling. MGM, 1942.

Son of Lassie. Dir. S. Sylvan Simon. Perf. Peter Lawford, Donald Crisp, June Lockhart, Nigel Bruce, and Leon Ames. MGM, 1945.

Song of the Open Road. Dir. S. Sylvan Simon. Perf. Jane Powell, Bonita Granville, W. C. Fields, and Edgar Bergen and Charlie McCarthy. United Artists, 1944.

Song of Russia. Dir. Gregory Ratoff. Perf. Robert Taylor, Susan Peters, John Hodiak, Robert Benchley, and Felix Bressart. MGM, 1943.

The Sorrow and the Pity. Dir. Marcel Ophüls. Swiss, 1969.

The Spirit of Culver. Dir. Joseph Santley. Perf. Jackie Cooper, Freddie Bartholomew, Andy Devine, Tim Holt, and Henry Hull. Universal, 1939.

Spy Ship. Dir. B. Reeves Eason. Perf. Irene Manning, Craig Stevens, Maris Wrixon, and Tod Andrews. Warner Bros., 1942.

Stage Door Canteen. Dir. Frank Borzage. Perf. Cheryl Walker, William Terry, Lon McCallister, Marjorie Riordan, Katharine Hepburn, Paul Muni, Gypsy Rose Lee, Count Basie, and Edgar Bergen and Charlie McCarthy. United Artists, 1943.

Standing Room Only. Dir. Sidney Lanfield. Perf. Fred MacMurray, Paulette Goddard, Edward Arnold, and Roland Young. Paramount, 1944.

The Story of Dr. Wassell. Dir. Cecil B. De Mille. Perf. Gary Cooper, Laraine Day, Signe Hasso, and Dennis O'Keefe. Paramount, 1944.

The Stranger. Dir. Orson Welles. Perf. Orson Welles, Loretta Young, Edward G. Robinson, and Richard Long. International, 1946.

A Stranger in Town. Dir. Roy Rowland. Perf. Frank Morgan, Richard Carlson, and Jean Rogers. MGM, 1943.

Strategic Air Command. Dir. Anthony Mann. Perf. James Stewart, June Allyson, Frank Lovejoy, and Barry Sullivan. Paramount, 1955.

Submarine Alert. Dir. Frank McDonald. Perf. Richard Arlen, Wendy Barrie, and Nils Asther. Paramount, 1943.

Submarine Base. Dir. Albert Kelley. Perf. John Litel, Fifi D'Orsay, and Alan Baxter. PRC, 1943.

Submarine Raider. Dir. Lew Landers. Perf. John Howard, Marguerite Chapman, Forrest Tucker, and Philip Ahn. Columbia, 1942.

The Sullivans, a.k.a. *The Fighting Sullivans.* Dir. Lloyd Bacon. Perf. Thomas Mitchell, Anne Baxter, Selena Royle, Ward Bond, and Edward Ryan. Twentieth Century–Fox, 1944.

Sunday Dinner for a Soldier. Dir. Lloyd Bacon. Perf. Anne Baxter, John Hodiak, Charles Winninger, Chill Wills, and Anne Revere. Twentieth Century–Fox, 1944.

Sundown. Dir. Henry Hathaway. Perf. Gene Tierney, Bruce Cabot, and George Sanders. United Artists, 1941.

Tanks a Million. Dir. Fred Guiol. Perf. William Tracy, James Gleason, and Joe Sawyer. United Artists, 1941.

Television Spy. Dir. Edward Dmytryk. Perf. Richard Denning, Dorothy Tree, Anthony Quinn, and Minor Watson. Paramount, 1939.

Tender Comrade. Dir. Edward Dmytryk. Perf. Ginger Rogers, Robert Ryan, Ruth Hussey, Patricia Collinge, Mady Christians, and Kim Hunter. RKO, 1943.

That Nazty Nuisance. Dir. Glenn Tryon. Perf. Bobby Watson, Joe Devlin, Johnny Arthur, Frank Faylen, and Ian Keith. United Artists, 1943.

They Gave Him a Gun. Dir. W. S. Van Dyke. Perf. Spencer Tracy, Gladys George, and Franchot Tone. MGM, 1937.

They Made Her a Spy. Dir. Jack Hively. Perf. Sally Eilers, Allan Lane, and Fritz Leiber. RKO, 1939.

They Met in Bombay. Dir. Clarence Brown. Perf. Clark Gable, Rosalind Russell, Peter Lorre, and Jessie Ralph. MGM, 1941.

They Raid by Night. Dir. Spencer G. Bennet. Perf. Lyle Talbot, June Duprez, Victor Varconi, and Charles Rogers. PRC, 1942.

They Were Expendable. Dir. John Ford. Perf. Robert Montgomery, John Wayne, Donna Reed, Jack Holt, and Ward Bond. MGM, 1945.

The Thin Man Goes Home. Dir. Richard Thorpe. Perf. William Powell, Myrna Loy, Lucile Watson, and Gloria De Haven. MGM, 1944.

13 Rue Madeleine. Dir. Henry Hathaway. Perf. James Cagney, Annabella, and Richard Conte. Twentieth Century–Fox, 1947.

Thirty Seconds over Tokyo. Dir. Mervyn LeRoy. Perf. Spencer Tracy, Van Johnson, Robert Walker, Robert Mitchum, and Don DeFore. MGM, 1944.

This above All. Dir. Anatole Litvak. Perf. Tyrone Power, Joan Fontaine, and Thomas Mitchell. Twentieth Century–Fox, 1942.

This Is the Army. Dir. Michael Curtiz. Perf. George Murphy, Joan Leslie, Ronald Reagan, and Joe Louis. Warner Bros., 1943.

This Land Is Mine. Dir. Jean Renoir. Perf. Charles Laughton, Maureen O'Hara, George Sanders, and Walter Slezak. RKO, 1943.

Three Faces East. Dir. Rupert Julian. Perf. Jetta Goudal, Clive Brook, Henry B. Walthall, and Robert Ames. Warner Bros., 1926.

Three Faces East. Dir. Roy Del Ruth. Perf. Constance Bennett, Erich von Stroheim, and William Courtenay. Warner Bros., 1930.

Three Is a Family. Dir. Edward Ludwig. Perf. Marjorie Reynolds, Charles Ruggles, Fay Bainter, and Hattie McDaniel. United Artists, 1944.

Tish. Dir. S. Sylvan Simon. Perf. Marjorie Main, Zasu Pitts, Aline MacMahon, and Lee Bowman. MGM, 1942.

To Be or Not to Be. Dir. Ernst Lubitsch. Perf. Jack Benny, Carole Lombard, Robert Stack, and Felix Bressart. United Artists, 1942.

To Have and Have Not. Dir. Howard Hawks. Perf. Humphrey Bogart, Lauren Bacall, Walter Brennan, and Hoagy Carmichael. Warner Bros., 1944.

Tom Brown of Culver. Dir. William Wyler. Perf. Tom Brown, H. B. Warner, Richard Cromwell, and Slim Summerville. Universal, 1932.

Tomorrow We Live. Dir. Edgar G. Ulmer. Perf. Ricardo Cortez, Jean Parker, and Emmett Lynn. Atlantis, 1942.

Tonight and Every Night. Dir. Victor Saville. Perf. Rita Hayworth, Janet Blair, and Lee Bowman. Columbia, 1945.

Tonight We Raid Calais. Dir. John Brahm. Perf. Annabella, John Sutton, Lee J. Cobb, and Howard Da Silva. Twentieth Century–Fox, 1943.

Twelve O'Clock High. Dir. Henry King. Perf. Gregory Peck, Hugh Marlowe, Gary Merrill, Millard Mitchell, and Dean Jagger. Twentieth Century–Fox, 1949.

20,000 Men a Year. Dir. Alfred E. Green. Perf. Randolph Scott, Preston Foster, Margaret Lindsay, and Robert Shaw. Twentieth Century–Fox, 1939.

Two-Man Submarine. Dir. Lew Landers. Perf. Tom Neal, Ann Savage, and J. Carrol Naish. Columbia, 1944.

U-571. Dir. Jonathan Mostow. Perf. Matthew McConaughey, Bill Paxton, and Harvey Keitel. Universal, 2000.

Uncertain Glory. Dir. Raoul Walsh. Perf. Errol Flynn, Jean Sullivan, Paul Lukas, and Sheldon Leonard. Warner Bros., 1944.

Underground. Dir. Vincent Sherman. Perf. Philip Dorn, Jeffrey Lynn, Kaaren Verne, and Martin Kosleck. Warner Bros., 1941.

Wake Island. Dir. John Farrow. Perf. Brian Donlevy, Robert Preston, William Bendix, and Macdonald Carey. Paramount, 1942.

A Walk in the Sun. Dir. Lewis Milestone. Perf. Dana Andrews, Richard Conte, and Sterling Holloway. United Artists, 1945.

War Comes to America. Dir. Frank Capra. Why We Fight series #7. War Department, 1945.

War Dogs, a.k.a. *Pride of the Army.* Dir. S. Roy Luby. Perf. Billy Lee, Addison Richards, Bradley Page, and Kay Linaker. Monogram, 1942.

Washington Melodrama. Dir. S. Sylvan Simon. Perf. Frank Morgan, Ann Rutherford, Kent Taylor, and Dan Dailey. MGM, 1941.

What a Blonde. Dir. Leslie Goodwins. Perf. Leon Errol, Veda Ann Borg, Clarence Kolb, and Ann Shoemaker. RKO, 1945.

What Price Glory? Dir. Raoul Walsh. Perf. Victor McLaglen, Edmund Lowe, and Dolores Del Rio. Fox, 1926.

When the Lights Go on Again. Dir. William K. Howard. Perf. James Lyndon, Regis Toomey, Barbara Belden, and George Cleveland. PRC, 1944.

The White Cliffs of Dover. Dir. Clarence Brown. Perf. Irene Dunne, Alan Marshal, Van Johnson, Frank Morgan, C. Aubrey Smith, Roddy McDowall, and Peter Lawford. MGM, 1944.

The Wife Takes a Flyer. Dir. Richard Wallace. Perf. Joan Bennett, Allyn Joslyn, and Franchot Tone. Columbia, 1942.

Wing and a Prayer. Dir. Henry Hathaway. Perf. Don Ameche, Dana Andrews, William Eythe, and Charles Bickford. Twentieth Century–Fox, 1944.

Wings over the Pacific. Dir. Phil Rosen. Perf. Edward Norris, Inez Cooper, Montagu Love, and Robert Armstrong. Monogram, 1943.

Without Love. Dir. Harold S. Bucquet. Perf. Katharine Hepburn, Spencer Tracy, Lucille Ball, and Keenan Wynn. MGM, 1945.

Woman of the Year. Dir. George Stevens. Perf. Katharine Hepburn, Spencer Tracy, Fay Bainter, and Dan Tobin. MGM, 1942.

Women in War. Dir. John H. Auer. Perf. Wendy Barrie, Patric Knowles, and Elsie Janis. Republic, 1940.

World Premiere. Dir. Ted Tezlaff. Perf. John Barrymore, Frances Farmer, Eugene Pallette, Sig Ruman, Luis Alberni, Ricardo Cortez, and Fritz Feld. Paramount, 1941.

A Yank in the RAF. Dir. Henry King. Perf. Tyrone Power, Betty Grable, John Sutton, and Reginald Gardiner. Twentieth Century–Fox, 1941.

The Yoke's on Me. Dir. Jules White. Perf. The Three Stooges. Columbia, 1944.

You're in the Army Now. Dir. Lewis Seiler. Perf. Jimmy Durante, Phil Silvers, Jane Wyman, and Regis Toomey. Warner Bros., 1941.

Youth on Parade. Dir. Albert S. Rogell. Perf. John Hubbard, Martha O'Driscoll, Ruth Terry, and Tom Brown. Republic, 1942.

Youth Runs Wild. Dir. Mark Robson. Perf. Bonita Granville, Kent Smith, and Vanessa Brown. RKO, 1944.

INDEX